**Stephen Karcher Ph.D.** writes, translates and lectures on myth, divination, depth psychology and religious experience. An internationally known scholar, he has worked with *I Ching* and other divination systems for over thirty years and has produced definitive translations and commentaries as well as many scholarly articles. As co-director of the *I Ching Project* at the Eranos Foundation, he collaborated with Rudolf Ritsema to translate and produce the Eranos edition of *I Ching: The Classic Oracle of Change*. He is the author of *I Ching Plain and Simple*, *The Illustrated Encyclopedia of Divination*, *Ta Chuan: The Great Treatise* and *The Kuan Yin Oracle: Goddess of Compassion*, the first complete translation of a popular eastern temple oracle.

Also by Stephen Karcher

*The Kuan Yin Oracle*
*Symbols of Love*
*Essential Shiatsu* (with Yuichi Kawada)

# TOTAL
# I CHING
## *Myths for Change*

## Stephen Karcher

piatkus

PIATKUS

First published in Great Britain in 2003 by Time Warner Books
First published in 2004 by Time Warner Paperbacks
This paperback edition published in 2009 by Piatkus
Reprinted 2011, 2012

A CIP catalogue record for this book
is available from the British Library.

ISBN 978-0-7499-3980-9

Typeset in Goudy by M Rules
Printed and bound in Great Britain by
Clays Ltd, St Ives plc

Papers used by Piatkus are from well-managed forests
and other responsible sources.

MIX
Paper from
responsible sources
FSC
www.fsc.org    FSC® C104740

Piatkus
An imprint of
Little, Brown Book Group
100 Victoria Embankment
London EC4Y 0DY

An Hachette Company
www.hachette.co.uk

www.piatkus.co.uk

# Acknowledgements

Deepest thanks to Dorte Koch, who gave me place, time and understanding; to Ian Fenton and Diana Grace-Jones, my long-standing and long-suffering friends; to Steve Moore for friendship, inspiration and painstaking help; to Enrique Pardo for the master's theatre eye; to three great sinologists and mythographers living and dead, Arthur Waley, Marcel Granet and Willard Peterson; to Rudolf Ritsema, Charles Boer and Jay Livernois, for inspirations that go a long way back; to Andreas Schoter for help with the Tools for Change; to Scott Davis for his magnificent insights into the deep structure of change; to LiSe for her beautiful work on the ancient characters; to Steven Poster ASC and his magic house; special thanks to Steve Marshall and his pioneering work on the Mandate of Heaven that informs my translation of several key hexagrams (7, 18, 44, 55) and contributed greatly to my sense of the hidden history in the Classic of Change; and to Michele O'Brien Daniel, without whose editorial skill, knowledge of the I Ching and psychological insight, this book would have been impossible.

# Contents

# Introduction

Like it or not, we live in a whirlpool of change. Our lives are a long dialogue with change, for 'a creature not busy being born is busy dying'. Our dreams, too, are a series of changes through which we seek transformation or try to hold off the inroads of ageing and sudden grief. The world we live in is changing and we are involved in a deep shift in the ground of our being. We search for hidden significance in events, seeking the meaning of the crossroads we confront. We want to know the 'right' thing to do.

Some of these changes are predictable and dependable; some unpredictable and surprising. Some bring joy, some bring sorrow. In fact, our very being is a continual dialogue between what is stable and what is shifting, and our individual actions in this time of change can have far-reaching effects, on ourselves and on others. When we experience ourselves as the passive victims of change we feel cut off, isolated, frightened and angry. When we are a part of the dialogue, we feel connected to the basic creative energy that shapes the world we live in.

We in the modern West tend to see change as objective and predictable or totally random. We use statistics, norms, the law of averages and mass numbers to describe it. We assume that it is the same for all people at all times. This is scientific law; an experience must be repeatable, independent of the subject, in order to be recognized as a valid experience. The sages and diviners who put together *Yijing*, the Classic of Change, saw things differently. They recognized change and what we call chance as the work of the spirit, an individual encounter with reality. They called the basic flow of energy that shapes experience *Dao* or Way, and realised that this Way expresses itself as symbols (*xiang*) that articulate a 'moment' of time (*shi*). They realised that we can use these symbols or images to be in harmony with the time. Through them our actions resonate with the spirit and connect with its hidden transforming power. Using *Yijing* is the art of finding and using these images. This symbolic approach to change helps us to live our lives fully and freely by keeping us in touch with the Way, what the old sages called the ongoing process of the real.

*Yijing* or Classic of Change is the world's oldest and most sophisticated system of wisdom divination, a powerful tool and spiritual vehicle that can help people to navigate the voyage of life. It is designed to help us understand and work with the unconscious forces shaping the situations we confront and to keep us connected with the creative process of life. It brings out the helping spirit (*shen*), the inner voice that helps us on our Way. It does not *describe* Change; it *participates in* and *articulates* Change. It shows how Change happens because it is a part of the process it models. Philosophically, this is a gift to humans that gives us access to the primordial transformations that initiate the process of generation and return of the *Wanwu*, the Myriad Beings or Ten Thousand Things. It shows the symbols (*xiang*) and the spirits (*shen*) through which all transformation occur. By using Change, we actively participate in this creative process rather than being its passive and unwilling victim. This can have a profound effect on our lives. It is a transformation of the way we experience and affect the world we live in. Through it we become a part of what was called the Great Enterprise.

The world of ancient China was peopled with gods and goddesses, spirits and ghosts, heroes and helpers and demons. The landscape was dotted with shrines, altars and places of close encounter with these figures. The rhythm of life and the shape of the year were articulated through a series of festivals and rites and most human activities and important events had their presiding fate or spirit. This was an animate or living world and humans were in regular imaginative contact with all its powers. This mythic world was woven into the divinatory tradition called Change or *Yijing*. It is more than a vanished and foreign past, for it shows us the basic ways we imagine things, how our imagination, our soul, works. By leading our experience back to this mythic ground, we can talk with the spirits, the imaginative powers that are creating the realities we experience. From the perspective of Change, this is a fundamental healing act. From it flow 'blessings' (*fu*).

This tradition of Change evolved in late antiquity as an instrument to open the world of the Way. It focuses on the ideal of a person who is committed to realising themselves as a true individual as the only way to effect Change in the world. Change helps this person by giving practical advice and making the power and virtue of the spirits (*de*) available. This lets us penetrate the transformations and connect with the Way. As we embrace this ideal, we become a Realising Person (*junzi*), one who seeks to realise their destiny and, through that connection with fate and the Way, acquires the real ability to aid others.

*Yijing* has been a spiritual and practical guide and a very real help in times of danger for many people over the 3000 years it has existed. It has certainly changed my life, and I feel a deep gratitude for its presence as it guides me and those I love and care for. I sincerely hope something of this spirit comes through in this book and that you, too, may experience *shen ming*, the friendship of this clear and loving spirit.

## On this Translation

Though based on extensive scholarly work, this is a poetic rather than a historical translation. In the process of making it, I have learned the limitations as well as the advantages of a historical approach, just as I have learned the equal limitations of the received interpretive tradition. To present the voice of Change as a living voice, I have had to break with both the current scholarly approach, which sees the book as limited to a particular period in time and culture, and with the fixed set of meanings and associations that characterize both traditional Confucian and latter-day Daoist perspectives.

To do this I employed several techniques. I have translated directly from Chinese originals, not from other translations. I have used the received classical text (Harvard *Yenching* edition of *Zhouyi zhezhong*), Kunst's reconstruction of the 'original Yijing', and the commentaries of Gao Heng (*Zhouyi gujing jinzhu*) and Wen Yiduo (*Wen Yidou quanji*), amplified by many sources on Chinese myth and ritual and the vast archaeological discoveries that have revealed so much of the Three Dynasties period and its Neolithic predecessors. Most important, I have considered each Chinese character or phrase as a part of an on-going and developing stream of divinatory language, with all its meanings simultaneously present, including loan-words, protographs and cognates. I have developed the translation out of this field, allowing alternate meanings to be simultaneously present in the text.

Further, I have seen the Name (or 'tag') of each figure as not only important, but as implicitly repeated in each line statement, following old models of parallel construction. I have moved back and forth at will between archaic and classical meanings, considering them as simultaneously present in the text. This is equally true of the polyvalent syntax of Chinese, in which most terms can potentially exist as nouns, verbs in any person or tense and modifiers. I have often used old meanings and alternate syntax to deconstruct the fixed interpretation and mood of the later received tradition and reverse its demythologizing tendency. This is particularly relevant to classical China's official attitude to women and the feminine, which reflects a Han and Song Dynasty categorization of the yin as morally inferior to the yang and directly related to gender. This was not true of the earlier tradition. The Tools, the interpretive strategies developed for this translation, are a further attempt to break the stranglehold of the Han Dynasty system of yin-yang line analysis that served to inscribe and enshrine their philosophy and morality in the text.

Conversely, I have let the later tradition's sense of the importance of a specific term counteract the historicist tendency towards 'ruthless literal-mindedness' that sees pre-Imperial China as simply 'primitive' or 'semi-savage'. I have explored the myth and ritual clusters that lurk behind the figures of Change in an equally eclectic and iconoclastic manner, fusing archaic, classical and philosophical meanings in an attempt to tell the story of the time each figure implies. The section on Casting the Vessel brings all this together. It is an attempt to reconstruct the oldest and most imaginatively sophisticated way of reading the omens, a way that has been effectively lost for two thousand years.

All this is put at the service of bringing out the real transformative power of the images by activating what we might call archetypal levels, those places that speak directly to deep layers of our imagination. If I have a metaphor for this endeavour, it is the work of reconstituting the vessel, the process of melting and recasting found in figures 49 Ge and 50 Ding. This Pair images a deep paradigm shift in a 'time of troubles' that contains an injunction to 'change Heaven's Mandates'. It is a shift that enables the past not only speak to us but help us to navigate our own great change and, together, imagine a future. It is my profound hope that this step in the Great Enterprise, the task of living with and through Change with compassion for the Wanwu, the Myriad Beings or Ten Thousand Things, and with the skilful means to help them, might be of service to us all. Through this entrance we might find our own way to those rituals that once linked Heaven and Earth, fed the Great Ancestors and let their blessings flow. For in the words of Change, spoken as I write this, 'The Way to the Source is open'.

# The World of Change

This version of *Yijing*, the classic Eastern system of wisdom divination, gives you the old myths, rituals and images that accompany the received tradition, a World of Change that was lost or hidden in the later development of the book. It does this in an attempt to release the transformative potential of the great symbols at the heart of Change and the practice associated with it. When they are grounded in the world of the psyche and the great archetypes from which they grew, these symbols open a dialogue with the inner powers that has a profound transformative effect. They have the power to change our awareness moment to moment and re-connect us with what the old sages understood as the Way, the on-going process of the real. The depth psychologist C.G. Jung saw this spirit of the East as a mirror of our own deep imaginative processes, the Myths for Change.

*Yijing* or *Change* (*yi*), as it is usually called, is a text, a divination system and a 'Way', a spiritual and imaginative discipline. We know it first of all as a book that was treasured as the key to the mysteries of transformation, elaborated and interpreted throughout the 3000 years of its use. This book consists of sixty-four figures or symbols (*xiang*), often referred to as 'hexagrams' and 'trigrams' (*gua*). These symbols are combinations of linear diagrams, short vivid pronouncements and chains of associations. You do not so much read Change, however, as talk with it. The figures only truly come alive in response to an individual question. The book then 'speaks to your situation', giving you a mirror that 'reaches the depths, grasps the seeds and penetrates the wills of all beings under Heaven'. It teaches you about the fate (*ming*) that Heaven bestowed upon you and helps you follow your innate nature (*jing*).

## The Name of the Book

The most important word in the book is its name, *yi* (pronounced 'yee'), usually translated as Change or changes. Philosophically, *yi* is primordial change, the mutations or transformations that initiate the process of generation and transformation in all the Myriad Beings, the *Wanwu*. It is inscribed in the actual order of things, the on-going process of the real, and offers the symbols according to which change occurs in all phenomena, the changes through which life and spirit transmit and extend themselves. Its meanings include making a gift, healing a sickness, calming and tranquillizing the spirit, pulling up weeds and cultivating a field. It is the sun appearing after clouds, and is seen as a model of the renewal of the Mandate of Heaven through the Zhou rulers King Wen and King Wu. It is the name of a frontier region and suggests borderline and liminal states. The character in its various forms contains the graphs for sun and moon and for a lizard or chameleon.

However, though it contains models of orderly change, such as the round of the seasons and the stages of life, and models of transformation like ice becoming water or life turning into death, *yi* or Change is usually perceived as *destabilizing* change, the precursor of a paradigm shift. It is a challenge to the fixed, overdeveloped, oppressive or outmoded. It indicates sudden storms, times when the stable becomes fluid and structures fail. It is also the response: versatility and imaginative mobility, openness, fluid and light, not difficult and heavy. It suggests a fluid personal identity with a variety of imaginative stances, an imaginative mobility that reconnects you to the deep flow of the *Dao* or Way. The Warring States sages who developed this as an inner Way felt *yi* as a companion or helper, a warm and knowing presence. Through *yi* you can seize the moment (*shi*), changing and moving as fluidly as the creative force behind it. Change and its symbols were made to connect the *yi* of the universe and the Way to your own *yi*, your creative imagination, if you choose to use it.

# Springs, Sources and the Changes of the Moon

Perhaps the best way to imagine Change is as a stream, a living stream of images, words, emblems and myths that marks the Way of Water, the fundamental image of the *Dao*. It is a flow of symbols like the images in dreaming. This flow is described as *wang lai*, going and coming. It is a river of time on which the seeds and symbols of things flow toward us. 'Going' represents what is leaving the field of awareness. It is the stream as it flows away from us, carrying away what is finished. It suggests the past, the dead and the waters of the dead. It means leave, flee, as well as go in the direction of, reflected in the *wang*-sacrifice, an exorcism of noxious influences. 'Coming' is the stream as it flows towards us, carrying the symbols that will unfold into events. It means what is arriving from the future, attracting good influences, what comes from Heaven and the High Lord. It is the Tree on the Earth Altar. It gives us the seeds, the spirits (*shen*) and the symbols (*xiang*) which they unfold into events.

This Way of Water has its source in prehistory, in the myth-time of the Paleolithic hunting groups and Neolithic farming communities. It is associated with the activities of the *wu*, the spirit-mediums and Intermediaries, and with the early moon cults, the women who read the Changes at the time of the Moon Almost Full (*yue ji wang*) to determine the precise point where Change was entering the world (*ji*). It collects phrases and omens from peasant calendars that describe the change of the seasons in terms of animal metamorphoses and from the dances and chants of the spring and autumn River-Mountain festivals. It is full of stories of mythic beings and 'ominous' events, events that were turned into emblems of Change. It is connected with the cult of jade and jade objects like the moon-shaped *bi*-discs and pig-figures buried with the dead, and the first tomb burials, where the 'returning soul' was surrounded by gifts designed to help him or her on the way to the other shore. This Way of Water began in a kind of divinatory practice known all over the world that links water, plants and words. It uses plant substances, like the sacred yarrow stalks or the palm nuts of *Ifa* divination, to produce numbers that key emblematic words and phrases. The words act as the centre of a complex series of associations held in the mind of the diviner, who chants or dances them when a divination is made. These 'magic words' are capable of almost infinite expansion, adding new images and reshaping events.

There is a particular set of words, a 'magical incantation', associated with these old sources of the Way of Water: *yuan heng li zhen*. It is repeated in various forms through the texts. It is a formula that evokes the flow of time through the four seasons and links it with the acts of sacrifice and divination, acts that connect us with the spirits and assure the flow of their 'joyous blessings' (*fu*). We can see this phrase as a fantasy of the history of Change itself. The first term, *yuan*, describes the ancient sources.

*Yuan* is 'source and spring', the origin or beginning of all. Philosophically, it initiates the movement that determines the appearance and development of any individual being, considered by Daoists as the original mystery, the absolute origin of the universe. It is the power of spring and the east, part of the rhythm of all vital movement. It means head, chief, first, eldest, the source of thoughts in the heart and growth in the being. It signifies a good man, connected to the fundamental truths and is a synonym of *xuan*, profound, mysterious, subtle, hidden. Its root is *ren*, people, with the graph for the One Above, the reflection of Heaven in the individual. It is the name of Lady Yuan of Chiang, First Ancestress who mated with the spirit. It is the image of a spring bursting forth on a mountain and the waters in the heart-mind (*xin*) that give birth to the sprouts of virtue (*de*). The term *yuan* intensifies any word with which it is linked, connecting it with the source. It occurs many times with words involving sacrifice as fundamental rituals, originating sacrifice, the great, the inaugurating, the founding act. It is the source of *de*, the power to be an individual connected with the flow of the Way, the pre-classical way of the ancient sages.

## The Bronze Vessels

The next term in the magical incantation, *heng*, takes us into the Bronze Age and the world of the Kings. Fairly early, as the Bronze Age began, the divinatory stream of Change crossed over and picked up a range of images and practices from the other major divinatory stream, what we call fire and bone divination. This stream is based on animal sacrifice, using fire to produce cracks in bone or shell, cracks whose patterns are 'read' by the King or power-person. In China it was directly associated with the rise of the Bronze Age Kings and the royal cycle of ancestral rituals and sacrifices. The tradition of Change is full of references to these rituals. Even more, it took over the image of the beautiful cast-bronze sacrificial vessels covered with dragon and animal images, particularly the tripod vessel known as *ding*, used to make the sacrifices and hold the ritual meal shared with the spirits, and the water-mirror or *jian*, used to reflect one's fate and helping spirit. Both image the act of divining and offering sacrifice in order to connect with the spirit. They became an image of Change itself. This era is reflected in the word *heng*.

*Heng* is 'success through a sacrifice'. It means to penetrate, exercise a profound influence, ripen the fruits. Philosophically, it is the influence of Heaven that penetrates all things, brings them to maturity and makes them prosper, the foundation of the sense of duty and reward for duties performed. It is the power of summer and the south, deployment, expansion and the ripening crops. *Heng* is interchangeable with several other old words: *xiang*, to make a sacrifice; *peng*, to cook or boil meat, melt and work metals; *chun*, pure, loyal, faithful; and *kuo*, to cut off the ears of an enemy and offer him in sacrifice to the ancestor. It also suggests towers to view the omens and hidden temples and ancestral altars where sacrifice was offered and the sacred meal celebrated. It is the presentation and acceptance of a cooked sacrifice and the banquet through which humans experience the pleasure, profit and joy that flow from the ancestors. It suggests joy, blessing and happiness that comes when the two worlds are connected and in harmony.

## The Books of Change and the Mandate of Heaven

By about 1000–800 BCE this divinatory stream of images had become a written tradition known as *yi* or Change, also called 'the yarrow', after the yarrow stalks used in the process. There were at least three yi-books in existence and a class of diviners who used them called book-people, literally bamboo-shamans, after the bamboo strips used to make early books.

Only one of these books of Change has survived, the Zhouyi or Changes of Zhou. Through this text, probably first transcribed about 1000 BCE, re-edited about 800 BCE, the tradition was associated with a series of historical events of mythic proportions, the change in the Mandate of Heaven (Tian ming) that brought the Zhou Kings to power, enabling them to overthrow their corrupt overlords, the Shang. These events, inscribed throughout the text, are what make the Zhouyi unique.

The story of the Mandate of Heaven revolves around the idea that Heaven (Tian) confers a Mandate (ming) on a ruling family, a mandate that can be revoked for immoral or evil behaviour that flaunts the ancestors or harms the people. According to this story, the last Shang Kings were tyrants who ignored the ancestors, oppressed the people and indulged in murderous drunken debauchery. Their overthrow by the rising Zhou line is the story of the establishment of an order that renews the time, an order under which communication with the spirits is re-established and the blessings once again flow for all in a golden age. The story centres on King Wen, the spiritual father of the Zhou who brought them to prominence, and his sons King Wu and the Duke of Zhou, the ruler and war leader who received the Mandate and launched the armies. The key events begin with the marriage of the daughters of Di Yi, a Shang ruler, to King Wen, spiritual father of the Zhou. From this marriage came King Wu and the Duke of Zhou. King Wu received the Mandate for Change when he was in mourning for his father at Feng. Empowered by clear omens from Heaven, he left the Mourning Hut and ordered his war leader, the Duke of Zhou, to launch the armies. They crossed the 'Great Stream' into Shang and fought a critical battle at Muye, the Mu wilderness, which ended in a complete rout of the Shang armies, many of whom deserted and fought with the Zhou. After the battle, King Wu and his entourage entered the Shang capital and executed the Shang tyrant and his concubines.

The result of this, in Chinese thought, was the re-establishment of the ritual connection with Heaven and a re-ordering of the world through which 'blessings' (fu) could flow once more. The story of the Mandate of Heaven, inscribed in the tradition of Change, became an enduring myth in the culture, a story of the good King who, with Heaven's blessing, overthrows a corrupt tyrant, renews the time and helps the people, restoring a golden age of ancient virtue to the land. Even today, using the Change is called 'talking to King Wu'. This development is reflected in the term *li*.

> *Li*, 'to take advantage of the time', means propitious, opportune, a good realization that nourishes and provides what is necessary. With the root 'knife' it is cutting, insightful and trenchant and recalls the knife used to inscribe the oracle bones as well as weapons and edges. *Li* is the power of autumn, harvest, the west and metal. It is the season in which the armies set forth and the opening to the powers of death. It means to utilize, possess, take efficacious action (*shi*), something that can be counted on. It is also an officiant at the rites for the dead.

## The Flowering of a Hundred Schools

By the end of the Zhou period, about 500 BCE, Change or yarrow divination was widespread and its images and omens had become proverbial. It carried an entire world of efficacious myth and ritual with it, omens, magic signs and emblematic histories from the ancient Wu and the Bronze Age Kings to a rising class of Iron Age nobles, merchants and spiritual seekers. It was used in noble courts by a wandering class of specialist diviners (*fang-shi*) to determine the potentials inherent in an action and the 'correct' stance or attitude, spiritual and strategic, to adopt in a given situation.

By about 500 BCE, the last of the Zhou influence had fallen apart and the culture entered what is called the Warring States period, a period of disintegration and civil wars that was, paradoxically, a cultural flowering that saw the development of all the major ideas in later culture. A hundred schools of thought flourished, all discussing and debating over the definition of the Way, how it was lost and how the world might be restored to order. These developments found a place in the Way of Water, Change incorporated the thought of Confucius and the development of the

Confucian school; Laŏzi, Zhuangzi and the development of the Daoist inner way; and Mozi's universal love and logic. Much of this assimilation was facilitated by the 'cosmologists' and their way of describing the actions of the ghosts and spirits (*guishen*) through the symbols of the yin and the yang and the Five Processes (*wuxing*). These formed a kind of shorthand that enabled the development of a new view of nature and the actions of Heaven and Earth that could be directly associated with the linear figures, the *gua*, of Change. All of these developments might be seen in the history of the last term in the magic formula, *zhen*.

> *Zhen*, 'trial', describes the act of divination and the results of a divination, something that is true, real, sincere, reflecting what the Daoists called original authenticity. Philosophically it is the evolution of a life that consciously accomplishes its destiny, adapting to circumstances without losing its true nature. It has the root 'eye/sight', and suggests an expression of the heart as a reflection of the spirits. A *zhenren* is an authentic person, an immortal, founded in the absolute. *Zhen* is the power of winter and of water, reflecting *Kan*, the rushing waters of the Ghost River that underlies all things. It is finding the seed that will germinate in spring. It signifies resolution of doubt and an inner determination, a commitment through which the divinatory sign given by the spirits enters human life. *Zhen* is interchangeable with at least two other characters, *ding*, the vessel used to offer sacrifice and cook the sacred meal, and *cheng*, correcting, a central term in meditative practices which means to test and make true, to establish the foundation and find the right course. It is connected to *xin*, fidelity, and sincerity, a word used by Buddhists to describe the faith that destroys illusions, and to *shan*, the expression of efficacious virtue or *de*. It is *ting*, listen to and acknowledge, verifying what is correct and acting on that knowledge.

## The Great Enterprise

The Warring States (c. 500–220 BCE) saw an evolution of the ritual practices associated with the ancient sages and magicians possessed by the spirits who followed the Way of Heaven. The religious feeling in these words and practices centres on a union between personal and ritual acts, shaping one's imagination to the cycle of ceremonies and the sacrifices marking the critical moments, the Gates of Change. The ancient rituals engendered a profound feeling of the interconnection between the spirit, the world and the human community and produced a significant transformation in the awareness and state of being of those who participated in them, an inner change that could in turn have a profound effect on the world around us. This is the foundation of the Great Enterprise described in *Dazhuan*, the Warring States text on Change as a vehicle of transformation.

This perspective, the culmination of the evolution of the myth-world of Change, responds to the innate human need for contact with and experience of the transpersonal world of the Way. It turned Change and the mythology that it carries into a kind of portable altar, a personal link to the great river of time and space on which the symbols that unfold the Way flow toward us.

One day the Master said:

*Qian* and *Kun* – are they not the two-leafed gate of Change?
Dark yin and light yang join virtues to give the strong and
    the supple a form.
The fates given by Heaven and Earth take shape through
    these forms.
This is how we can penetrate to the bright spirits.
The names are different, but they cover the way of all
    things.
What is upstream from the moment we call the Way.
What is downstream from the moment we call the vessel or
    tool.
The moment of transformation we call Change.
Raising *Change* and setting it forth for the people to use,
That we call the Great Enterprise.

## Classic of Change

In the Han Dynasty (202 BCE–220 CE), the dynasty that emerged after the short-lived universal empire of Chin ended the Warring States period, Change became a Classic or *Jing*, a book recognized as carrying ancient wisdom. The literal image in the word is the warp threads of a loom, so the *Yijing* that was assembled in the Han Dynasty can be called the Classic, Scripture or Loom of Change. Han Dynasty scholars codified and organized the written language around a set of 'radicals' or 'roots'. They assembled and transcribed the old divinatory texts in this new modernized form of writing, a system that was used for the next 2000 years. A range of oral interpretive traditions were also collected, transcribed and added to the basic text as the *Ten Wings*. Three of these Wings, the two parts of the *Dazhuan*, the Great Treatise or Commentary on the Attached Words, and the *Shuogua*, or Explanation of the Diagrams, were founding documents in the later evolution of philosophical, medical and scientific thought.

This period also saw the development of Confucianism as the official Imperial philosophy. Confucians enshrined a dichotomy of interpretation in the tradition of Change, an official set of meanings that were later made a part of the great civil service examinations. This split off another version of Change, a popular Daoist under-layer associated with the imaginative use of the old vocabulary of the ghosts and spirits. By the end of the Han period the text and the various circles of association around it were a fundamental part of the new Imperial world on many, sometimes contradictory, levels. *Yijing* and the divinatory stream that flows through it became the most revered source book in the culture, sponsoring ever-growing circles of commentary and criticism. It reflected and assimilated many of the influences that entered Chinese culture over the centuries, most notably the development of Buddhist practice that culminated in the Tang period. It provided the basis for poetry, magic and philosophical speculation, particularly the Song dynasty revisioning of Confucianism by philosophers such as Zhuxi.

## Change in the West

The stream of Change spread into Japan, Korea and Tibet and was carried by the Chinese diaspora throughout the East. But the twentieth century saw one of the most dramatic moments in its evolution, its globalization and the rediscovery of its mythic roots, primarily through translations into Western languages. Archaeological discoveries and historical scholarship, both Eastern and Western, have revealed the layers of myth and ritual practices hidden in the old word meanings of the World of Change. Archetypal psychology and chaos theory, coupled with an enormous dissatisfaction with formal religious systems, opened a window for this thought in the West. A series of usable translations beginning with the landmark Wilhelm-Baynes version of 1950 and the encounter with the depth psychologist C.G. Jung has made some version of the text available worldwide. Change became a part, albeit often an underground part, of Western imagination and spirituality. It is to this bend in the river, this entrance of the World of Change into Western spirit and culture, that this translation is particularly addressed.

## On Time

Divination is about questions, so let us ask a simple question and imagine the kind of answer we might get. The question is: What time is it?

In ordinary life we look at the clock for an answer to this question. The clock shows us a particular kind of time. To quote Webster's dictionary, it is a 'non-spatial continuum in which events occur and a system by which such intervals are measured'. The units of this time are identical and interchangeable. So we would get an answer like 13:34 GMT 11 April 2001. If two people ask the same question at the same time, they will get the same answer.

However, when we use a divination system, we learn about another kind of time. The answer to the question might be: the right time, the moment of truth, time out, behind the times, making time, bedtime, doing time, keeping time. As divinatory phrases, all these expressions give an individual quality to time that depends on the individual who asks the question. If two different people ask the question at the same time they will get different answers. Now, we all experience both of these kinds of time, but we see them as incommensurate. One goes on inside us, one goes on outside us. This difference marks the point where myth, imagination and spirit are split off from what post-Enlightenment Western thought has called scientific reality.

Divination, however, puts the time back together again. It tells you into a story of the time that connects outer and inner experience. It does not so much answer the question 'What time is it?' as

'Which time is it? What is the quality of this time and how does it affect me? What kind of change is at work in this moment?' It does this by providing a symbol (*xiang*). The word *xiang*, 'symbol/symbolize', means an image, to imagine, to represent as a psychic image. It refers specifically to images that mediate between visible beings and the invisible world, models to which qualities and behaviour of phenomena are attached. It is an imaginative display of innate nature, a figure, form, shape or language that can be imitated, taken as a model or mask, a character to be 'put on'. It means a ritual vessel used to question the spirits and the celestial signs and omens they give that attract good fortune. As the Great Symbol (*daxiang*) it refers to the Way or *Dao*. The symbol articulates and connects you with the basic energy configuration or efficacy of the moment, the *shi*.

> *Shi*, 'moment, right time, efficacy' refers to the internal energy or intensity of a situation, a configuration, gesture, stance or attitude that guides the vital movements of beings. It is the potential, the right time or right season to discern and seize the favourable by regarding the signs of Change, signs from Heaven that describe the activity of the *shen* or spirits who notify and instruct us.

In this view, reality is perceived as a particular deployment of things in a moment of time, an arrangement that can be relied on and worked with. Wisdom lies in yielding to and working with the propensity that emanates from this particular configuration of the Way. The symbol allows you to perceive and seize this moment. By informing and reforming your imagination, it leads you back to the ground in the myth-world and the on-going process of the real. Working with Change 'provides symbols that comprehend the light of the spirits (*shen ming*)'. It adjusts the balance between the inquirer and the moment, activating the spirit of the time and triggering a flow of transformative energy.

## 'The Highest Good is like Water'

Change is articulated through words. These words keyed a stream of memories in the old diviners, setting off a chain of interconnecting associations. They carry the myths and act as centres for their on-going development. They articulate the Way of Water or *Dao*.

> *Dao* or Way is probably the single most important term in Eastern thought. It is made of the graphs for head and walk, the first motion. It is the on-going process of the real, the elusive movement of life, a universal experience or principle not available to rational or dialectical awareness. It is water, a river, the power of a diviner, words that instruct and inspire, a ray of light, the ways that open at death. It offers a way or path to each thing in the world and gives it potential identity. To connect with or be 'in' the Way is to experience meaning, joy, connection, freedom, compassion and creativity. It is a term of highest value.

The Way unfolds through the Two Powers, as described in a famous passage from the Great Treatise:

> The Way gives birth to the One; the One gives birth to the Two; the Two gives birth to the Three; the Three [the interaction between the One and the Two] gives birth to the Myriad Beings.

The earliest images of the Two are the Sun Tree and the Moon Tree, interconnected by the underworld Ghost River. They articulate the year into the two seasons, open and closed, summer and winter, marked by a series of animal transformations. The Two Powers are further seen in the dark waters and the bright sky; in the division of the sexes and their ritualized meetings; and in the Protectors, the great couple who image the union of Heaven and Earth in every village. In the later evolution of philosophical thought, these became the well-known pair, *yin* and *yang*.

> *Yin,* 'shade, secret, cloudy sky', is north, the shady side of things, winter and the power of the female. It is obscure, dark, cold, negative, passive; it signifies shadow and the world of shadows, the dead, the underworld river, the Mourning Hut, cold and ice. It is also the season of marriages and armies who wield the power of death, relations between men and women,

13

sacrifices to the Earth God and the gods of soil and cereals and the Earth Altar. It is what is interior and means to cover, protect, calm, stabilize and secure, support. It is what is below, descending, and all things that flow down to the centre.

*Yang*, 'bright, open, vital, clear', is south, the sunny side of things, summer. It is the dragon, solitary and migratory birds, and the power of the male, brilliant, strong, positive, hot, active, light, aggressive. It is what is exterior and means to inspire, motivate and drive on and the ritual of killing a sacrifice with arrows. It is what is above, ascending and all things that rise, as well as the fertilizing rains.

These two powers are reflected in two old words that represent stances or qualities of the will, being Great (*da*) and being Small (*xiao*).

*Da*, 'great', calls upon you to be great and strong, to protect others. It means to collect your strength, organize yourself around a central idea or purpose, impose your will and act. The Great Person is someone who has done this, acquiring the power to help and support others. The Great People are ancestor spirits and those through whom they manifest blessings: great rulers, sages, ritual experts and diviners, people in contact with the Bright Spirit that offers great insight and a great power of manifestation.

*Xiao*, 'small', calls upon you to be flexible and supple, to adapt to whatever crosses your path. It means letting go of your sense of self-importance and yielding in a spontaneous and flexible way. The Small Person is flexible, a person who follows what crosses his path, an important step in finding the Way. The Small People were nobles without lands who had to take service with a lord and were subject to his whims and commands. They could hope to influence their situation only through adaptation and inner work. The Small Person also became a Daoist byword for those who could see the small beginnings of change, unencumbered by pride and complication.

Using Change to accord with the time, either great or small, and stay in contact with the Way allows you to accumulate *de*, the power to realise yourself, to become who you are meant to be, thus fulfilling your innate destiny. This power and virtue have a profound yet indirect effect on everything around you.

*De*, 'power and virtue', is the strength, power and inner virtue coming from the ancestors that is active in the heart. It means will, intention, to act well, have a straight heart. It is the efficacy of the Way, its revelation through a sage. It gives the power to act, to actualize identity, to rise to higher levels. It is the power that permits individual realization, a mysterious action of the Way that maintains individual existence. It is energy, an influx of spirit that makes one happy and prosperous.

The person who uses Change to act in accord with the Way and accumulate power and virtue is a *junzi*, a Noble One or Realising Person. Originally the son of a sovereign or a clan lord, this term came to indicate a sage or seeker striving for power and virtue (*de*), a person on the way to being realised or accomplished through contact with the spirit of Change. Since oldest times, this Way of Water has been a way of the heart, the *xin* or 'heart-mind'. Divination takes effect in the heart, straightening and correcting the passions and emptying the inner space.

*Xin*, 'heart', the inner space, is the seat of intelligence and affections, spirit, conscience and temperament. The effective centre of being, it is inspired by the spirits (*shen*), guiding the individual on the voyage of life, mediating between innate nature and individual destiny. It is a synonym of the Way or *Dao*, the spirit of the world. An ancient bronze vessel, the *jian* mirror, provides an image of the heart. It is a water-mirror, an open vessel filled with water used in religious ceremonies and placed in the tomb to guide the soul. The heart is filled with water, the water of the Way. The sprouts of virtue or *de* grow in the heart, as plants germinate from water.

*Xin*, heart, connects with the words used to describe the trigrams of Change and with the term *yao*, or crossing, used to describe the transforming (*bian*) lines. As *zhen*, the inner trigram, it is the base or foundation that straightens and empties the inner being, opening it to the spirits. As *hui*, the outer trigram, a word connected with the dark of the moon that means 'distress', it is the place where human drives are corrected through the encounter with trouble and change. As *yao*, the 'crossings', it is the place where Heaven and Earth join, announcing the spirit and guiding humans. Change (*yi*) is a change of heart.

## The World of Change

This process unfolds in and through a particular imaginative landscape, a dynamic yet timeless world that grew out of, but is not limited to, the landscape of northern China and its frontier regions. We can imagine this landscape and its points of encounter with the spirit, reflected throughout the texts of Change, as an archetypal landscape of the soul. This is a world of wide plains (we can see it in figures 26 and 34) bounded and divided by mountains (51, 33), with arching skies where the weather comes suddenly and violently (51, 30, 9). It is a land of extreme contrasts, cut by great rivers (29), dense brush and fertile marshes (58) that drain into the Nine Rivers. There are farms and fields, village clusters (37), fortified cities (45), great palaces, tombs and towers (19, 20). These areas of culture are surrounded and divided by dense brush, wild rivers and rugged mountains inhabited by wild animals, barbarians, nomads, bandits and outlaws, tribal groups apart from the civilizing movement of the plains peoples. This world was a civilized island in a sea of barbarians, with permeable boundaries that allowed a constant fertile interchange with the worlds outside the borders (56, 38). The entire landscape, literal and metaphorical, is dotted with sites of close encounter with the spirit world: ancestral temples (18), tombs (19), grave mounds, Earth Altars (2), hidden mountain shrines (10, 33) and River-Mountain festival sites (31) that were an image of paradise. This is a place where a great variety of people go about their lives. We see peasants, nomads, merchants, wandering sages, nobles and kings, shamans, officials and magicians, husbands and wives, slaves and prisoners, children, craftsmen, soldiers and officers, courtesans, and wide range of spirits and heroes as they eat and drink, carry out a variety of ritual actions and feasts, love and hate, work, hope and scheme, make war and find peace, despair or are enlightened, face death and disaster or sudden joy.

## The Shape of the Turtle

The sacred shape of this world was the form of *Ling gui*, the Numinous Turtle that provided one of its main oracles.

The *Fu Sang* or Sun Tree from which the Ten Suns rise (35) lies to the east; in the far west the *Ruo* or Moon Tree on which they set (36). Each tree has a pool at its base in which the mothers bathe the suns and the moons. Beneath the Earth are the underground Ghost River (29) and the Yellow Springs that connect the two trees and make them one, the World Tree or Bushy Mulberry (3, 12). Above is sky, Heaven (1) and the Great Bear or Dipper (55), the court of Shang Di, the Lord Above who gives the fates, and his court of Royal Ancestors. The flat, square Earth (2), spread between the round sky and the underworld waters, extends to the Four Sides or Directions (*si fang*), home of mysterious bird-headed wind spirits who are objects of high sacrifice. The *fang* are lands from which spirits enter the human world, lands of imagination, home of the winds with power over rain, weather and harvest in which humans cannot survive.

The Great Sacrifice (11) performed to the Directions was also performed to the Mountain or Peak (*Yue*) and the River (*He*). These sites go back to Neolithic times as cult centres. The Mountain was also known as the capital of Yu the Great (8, 39, 50) who tamed the waters, brought forth the land and forged the first bronze vessels, the Nine *Ding*. It is reflected in the sacred mountains throughout the landscape (11, 33, 52). The Four Hidden Lands and the square Earth (2) revolve around an axis that connects Heaven, Earth and the rushing Ghost River beneath (29). This ceremonial axis is a World Tree (3) or *axis mundi*, a zone of absolute reality where there is perfect access to the spirit world. It can be established or invoked at any site where the high ritual or divination is performed, particularly through the use of the bronze sacrificial vessels (50) or at the monumental royal tombs, gates to the ancestors and the High Lord. This centre of the world is where the dead rest in peace and receive the great offerings, the place from which their blessings flow. This sacred cosmos also reflects the shape of the human heart (*xin*).

## Guishen: the Souls and Spirits

This world is not only populated by humans, but also by the souls, the ghosts and spirits. 'Between Heaven and Earth there is no place the *guishen* do not exist.' All the mythical and spirit beings of this cosmos were once souls and partake of the soul's numinous quality, *ling*. These spirits of Heaven and Earth are of many kinds and their identities are constantly changing like the shifting figures in dreams, a direct expression of the Way. There were the Sun Mother and Moon Mother, the bird-headed *fang* or Directions, Mountain and River, Directors of Destinies, Lords of the Hearth, First Ancestors, heroes such as Yu the Great, Yi the Archer and Tang the Completer, the Horse Ancestor and a series of other 'totem' or omen animals, a variety of demons and angry souls, the High Lord and his court in the Dipper, the Earth Lord at the Earth Altar, the Royal Ancestors and the Moon Goddesses. The boundaries between these spirits are permeable, as is the boundary between spirit and human. One thing was common to all: their numinous energy and sacred character (*ling*).

These spirits are loosely divided into two types or appearances. The *shen* are Bright Spirits, spirits that vivify and inspire and are centred in the heart, the spirits of Heaven that draw out and animate the Myriad Beings. They are stars, mountains and rivers. They make things appear and unfold. They inspire awe and wonder, for they cut across boundaries, combine categories and 'cannot be comprehended by the yin and the yang'. The *shen* change things; their main characteristic is transformation. The *gui*, the souls or ghosts, are darker spirits who live in the tomb and the Earth. They are protectors, but can be angered or offended by mistreatment, turning into furies, plagues, haunting spirits of vengeance and hungry ghosts and demons (*li*) who have been offered no sustenance in the other world. Though they represent the whole world of the dead, angry *gui* usually manifest as specific individuals who are trapped by their passions between the world of the living and the world of the dead (38).

Zong or *ancestors* partake of both categories, living in the tomb and, at the same time, sitting at the court of the High Lord. They have the power to bestow blessings and act as intermediaries to Heaven and the powerful *shen*. The creation and enshrining of an ancestor spirit (19 and 20) is an extremely important ritual that involves fixing and feeding the ghost in the tomb and a mourning ceremony that enshrines the bright spirit in an image or tablet on the ancestral altar. The ancestor is fed with the 'essence of beings' through sacrifice and ritual attention (27) that culminates in the sacred meal in which humans and spirits share (21, 50). The ancestors assure a continuous flow of blessing from the invisible world. They are animating spirits. This process of releasing and enshrining the spirit is one of the most important manifestations of Change and its Way of transformation (*bianhua*). It is a paradigm of sacrifice and blessing seen throughout the texts (23 and 24, 31 and 32, 39 and 40, 41 and 42, 59 and 60). Of particular importance is the act of *heng* (32) or 'fixing an omen', giving it an enduring place in human life.

Each noble family had its protectors, ancestor spirits made from the two kinds of soul that join together at birth to form the human being. The *hun* or spirit-soul ascends to the realms of the High Lord and has to be guided on its way, the job of the *wu*-Intermediaries: 'She signs to you, the skilful *wu*, going backwards she walks before you.' The *po* or body-soul has to be escorted to and made comfortable in the tomb and a connection made through the spirit tablet. This soul lives on offerings made at the time of the burial and afterwards and can turn into a *gui* or *li*, an angry ghost or a demon if neglected, wandering to inflict suffering on the living. The ancestors were created and empowered (19, 20, 23, 24). One had to know how to establish them in order to make them into protectors. After this process, the shared meal could be held, at which time a *shi* or 'embodier' (literally, a 'corpse') would be possessed by the ancestor spirit. Through this, the spirit would be present, sharing the meal and extending its blessings (*fu*). The worship of ancestors – the dead, gods, spirits and ghosts – and the recognition of the attention they need in order to exercise their power to channel blessings to the living, is an image of what we call a creative relation to the figures of the psyche and the complexes that people our imagination, figures that come before us and will outlive us.

# Technicians of the Sacred

Communication with the ghosts and spirits was handled through several kinds of intermediaries. They basically fell into three classes: experts on ritual (*shi*) who knew the formulae and procedures involved in important ceremonies; 'Intermediaries' (*wu*) and exorcists who handled spirits directly; and diviners (*shi*) who read the signs and kept the 'ancient virtue' (*de*) inherent in the oracle books. These spirit helpers are personified in the *bagua* or 'eight trigrams' and their hexagram figures: 1 and 2, 29 and 30, 51 and 52, 57 and 58.

The *wu* are without doubt the oldest and the most enduring of the technicians of the sacred, originating far back in the mists of prehistory. The power of the *wu*, the Intermediaries, was used to see, feel and know the spirits. The *wu* could call the spirits down to be present at a ceremony or a healing and dissipate malign influences. They were involved with the cult of the Moon Almost Full (*yue ji wang*) and the masked animal-transformation dances, early forms of Change divination. Three times a year the exorcists or *fang-xiang*, a particular type of *wu*, would perform the great exorcism, driving the outmoded and baneful spirits from palace, house and countryside. As time went by, the *wu* were allowed a smaller and smaller part in official cult, but continued to play a considerable role in the life of the people. Widespread on the personal level, their vivid spirituality was an antidote for an increasingly arid official worship. Though often suppressed and edited out of the classic texts, the *wu* were indispensable intermediaries in personal worship and spiritual practices.

The *shi* were diviners, historians and scribes, 'men of the book' or 'bamboo-*wu*', imaged as a 'hand that holds the centre'. They were painters of word pictures and their work with the oracle books was described as 'eating ancient virtue' (*de*). They became the wandering *fang-shi* of the Warring States period, 'book-*wu* of the Hidden Lands'. The word that describes them is cognate with the character pronounced *shi*, 'signs from Heaven that reveal the activity of the shen and instruct humans'.

The King (*wang*) shared certain basic functions with both kinds of intermediaries. The King was the single great ritual channel through which communication and blessing flowed from the High Ancestors and the High Lord. There are certain ceremonies only he could perform. He was responsible before the High Lord or

Heaven, who had given him the Mandate to rule for the welfare of his people and the proper functioning of the cosmic order. The King's court was the centre of literacy and the oracle books used by the *shi*-diviners. The King, through his person and his actions, could put the messages from the spirits into effect, fixing the omens and spreading the blessings to all.

## Places of Close Encounter

These technicians of the sacred exercised their powers and functions at a series of sacred sites. There were the Earth Altar and Pit for the Earth powers (2, 29); the Heaven Altar for the sun and the High Lord; the Outskirts Altars for major ceremonies that gathered the people, welcomed incoming spirits and invoked the rain (9, 10, 13); the Hidden Temple and Mountain Shrines to connect directly with sky and the ancestors as revealers of fate (10, 33, 51); the sacred River-Mountain places for the spring and autumn festivals (31, 44); the Ancestral Temples in every palace and noble dwelling place (37, 45); and the Altar of the Protectors in each hamlet. Almost all of these were temporary sites, erected for an occasion or recreated for each ceremony. The ancient worship created few great monuments aside from the ancestral hall of the high nobles and the royal tombs. Sacrifice and the meal shared with the spirits were common to all levels of culture. If anything, the temple of traditional worship is a ritual and a divination book.

The rites centred on a few common practices and places. *Shang Di*, the High Lord or *Tian*, Heaven, ruled from his palace in the Great Bear, where he established the fates and conferred the mandates. The ancestors lived in his court as well as in their images or spirit tablets. The altar for the Earth Spirit for each 'land', from the protectors of the hamlet to the Great Lord (*Dashe*) who protected the King, was originally a tree planted on a mound in the middle of a sacred grove (2, 53), with an unpolished stone set up to the north of the tree to represent the god. All great initiatives – war, hunting, marriage, opening and closing the fields, the great festivals – had to be announced at this Earth Altar (7, 55). The Earth Spirit was Lord and Protector; drums were smeared with blood at his altar when the armies marched and he would accompany the troops in a spirit tablet.

21

Souls of the dead ancestors required funerary temples, altars, tombs and indoor shrines; all others were served in the open air. Each had a preference for position and shape. Sky gods had round altars and mounds, on which fires were lit. Earth spirits had square altars and sacrificial victims were buried or drowned in the pit beside the altar. The god of the Soil had a mound in the palace grounds facing the Ancestral Temple. The High Lord had a circular mound at the southern Outskirts Altar. First Husbandman had an altar in the royal fields; the sun had a mound at the eastern Outskirts Altar and the moon had a pit called Night Brightness (*Yeh ming*) at the western Outskirts Altar.

Ancestral worship was held in a temple on the east side of the dwelling, with a large court and a *pei*, a standing stone (3, 37). There were rooms in which the celebrants, the embodiers, dressed. The interior was divided into two rows of small chapels for the two alternating lines of the ancestors, *chao* and *mu*, with a central room dedicated to the First Ancestor. Beyond that were the *tiao*, the rooms for the remoter ancestors where Kings Wen and Wu had their perpetual homes. Each ancestor was present in his spirit tablet, an inscribed wooden tablet enclosed in a stone casket. There were two for each ancestor, one that remained always in the temple and one that travelled with the armies on campaign.

Ceremonies consisted of offerings, prayers and masked dances or ritual combat which had two aims, to feed the spirits, thus securing their blessings and their participation in the course of human life, and to effect an alteration of consciousness in the participants, 'to experience something and be set right'. Offerings included bull, ram and pig for Royal Ancestors (26), foal or horses to River and Mountain, a dog to the god of roads. Blue jade was offered to the High Lord, yellow to Earth and the underworld spirits. Various wines were important as offerings and were consumed in quantity during the ritual meals and the great festivals. Human sacrifices, usually criminals or prisoners of war, were offered to the ancestors and the Earth God. Offerings to the High Lord were burned, to the Earth Lord buried or drowned. For ancestors a complete banquet was served and shared – the great ritual meal served in the bronze vessels.

Each ceremony had its own prayers or chants, formulae for calling spirits. The great dances enacted founding moments in myth and assured that the blessings of the event that occurred in myth-time would continue to flow to the descendants. At ancestral ceremonies the spirit would inhabit the body of one of his descendants chosen for the task by divination. This was the corpse or embodier, who was possessed by the spirit (*shen*) of the ancestor. Through the corpse, the ancestor ate, drank and spoke, sharing the meal and blessing the people. At the end of a ceremony he would proclaim 'the spirits are drunk', indicating they were satisfied and looked favourably on their descendants.

## The Two Powers and the River-Mountain Festivals

The base of this culture developed in the great north-eastern plain of China between the sea and the craggy wall bounding the central plateau, spreading into the beautiful river valleys of the Wei and the Fen and over the passes into the Yangzi Valley. This is a harsh climate, torrid in summer and glacial in winter, when the rivers and earth are frozen solid. The spring thaw is rapid, turning the rivers into torrents full of floating ice. The low lying areas become marshes during the spring and summer, full of a profusion of plants, nesting geese and cranes and swarming fish. They are surrounded by clumps of tall grass and scrub, thickets full of great wild beasts hunted by setting fire to the brush. The fertile border areas of these great marshes were developed into mulberry groves and deep green pastures for horses. The best land was drained and cultivated to produce millet, sorghum and rice, wheat and hemp, beans and gourds. The fields were cultivated on the well-field model (48), eight fields surrounding a central well. Nearby were houses of pounded earth, the hamlets where the people lived in winter. The twenty-five families of a hamlet made up a group centred on an Earth Altar with a cult of the Divine Couple, the Protectors. The manors of the nobles, surrounded by a high pounded-earth wall and ditch, were interspersed among the hamlets.

For the people who formed the bedrock of the culture, the religious year was tied to the two unequal seasons, the time of nature's great labour and the time of repose when work ended, thanks were given and all people joined in the seclusion and closing of the Earth. These archaic rituals, with roots far back into the Neolithic, were considered necessary to the order of things. They participated in the changes of the world, assuring all people's place in it. These two seasons and their rural base are the oldest images of the sacred order.

23

The basis of this ritual year was the peasant calendar and the lunar cycle. Throughout the elaboration of a more sophisticated culture they formed a kind of retreat, a social and religious base that reflected humanity's common needs and common strengths (47, 48, 12).

The year began in spring with a series of ceremonies that lifted the winter restrictions, opened the fields and drove off the spirit of cold (13, 14). The first was the great *jiao* sacrifice at the Outskirts Altar to the High Lord, announcing the movement of the people. The *wu* notified the Four Distant Lands, the King notified the First Ancestor, and the Red Bull was offered in an elaborate ceremony, first to the High Lord and then to *Hou Ji*, the Millet Lord, who would act as intermediary to the High Lord's court in the Big Dipper. A ritual meal was prepared of which all the people partook. The ceremony ended with a great dance and celebration in which even the King participated. This ceremony was repeated in every hamlet throughout the kingdom.

Then came the great exorcism. The *fang-xiang*, male *wu* covered with bearskins with four golden eyes and holding battle axes, drove the old spirits and their pestilence out of the city. The fire was renewed and taken out of the houses, lit with a burning mirror on the great open hearths of the *jing*, the well-fields where the peasants would live and work throughout the summer.

Finally came the great spring festival, the River-Mountain ceremonies, the paradise time. At the time of the thaw, the thunder, the rains and the great purification expelled the dead past and new life began. The people crossed the river to the great dance and feast where young men and women, awakened by the great peals of thunder, gathered, danced and sang the ritual songs. Young women called the souls and spirits from the rivers and mountains. Lines of young women and men danced to the sound of the earth drums, waving feather fans and egret plumes, exchanging ritual insults in verse in a time-honoured manner. Couples formed to sing the love songs transmitted through generations. They came together in the sacred groves and lush meadows, giving the gift of the *orchis*, a magical and aphrodisiac flower, on parting.

The summer was dedicated to the freedom of the open air and work in the fields, work that aided nature's bounty. The next great ceremony occurred in autumn, mirroring the spring sacrifice. It marked the harvest and the end of fieldwork, notification of the

Earth God and the solemn return to the village houses. The great sacrifice was carried out at the Hidden Temple (10, 33) inside the palace walls, the ancient site of the sacred Kings. Sacrifice was offered to the High Lord and to King Wen, the founder of the dynasty who had first received the Mandate of Heaven. Then the King went to meet winter at the northern Outskirts Altar and Earth Pit and proclaimed: 'The breath of Heaven rises, the breath of Earth sinks down, no longer in touch. Shut and barred the passage, winter is established.' The peasants returned to the villages. The fire was extinguished and brought into the houses. By the first month of winter the move was completed and all activities ceased. The Earth God and the ancestors were notified.

The King, dressed in white, offered a black bull to the Earth God and reviewed the armies, for this was the beginning of the military season and the time of death. Celebrants offered sacrifice to all who made the harvest abundant. Then came the Harvest Festival, a great masked celebration, with cat and tiger maskers, men dressing as women, and people giving away their possessions. Everyone changed into rural costume and offerings of meat and wine were distributed among the people. An immense orgy began during which all was eaten and, as at the spring festival, the men and women paired and mated. These ceremonies were carried out in every region and canton. This marked the end of the year; from this point on all work on the Earth was forbidden, the palace gates were closed, the people's doors sealed with earth and the souls of the dead returned to the houses. Life was suspended until, in the last month of the year, seed grain and tools were prepared, the doors re-opened and the *fang-xiang* drove away the spirits who had dwelt with the people during the dead time. The new season was begun.

## The Four Seasons and the Rituals of the Ancestors

Another cycle of four seasons regulated the offerings made to the ancestors. These were noble or patrician ceremonies, connected with the High Lord, the powerful Earth Lord and the Four Sides, the Four Hidden Lands that were sources of weather, blessing and pestilence. The King 'went out to meet' these spirits at the Outskirts Altars, as he did the sun at the equinoxes and solstices: 'Sun, who illuminates above and below, who spreads blessing (*fu*) through the Four Hidden Lands, who displays majesty in all places, here am I, the Solitary Man. I go out to meet you at the Outskirts.'

Noble ritual was above all ancestor ritual. Every meal began with a libation, every gift was first shared with the ancestors and every crop was first offered to them. Each of the seasons brought a festival at the Ancestral Temple, when sacrifice was offered to all. There were also two great celebrations, the *xia* and the *ti* connected with the five-year cycle that installed an ancestor. Xia was held when the mourning period finished, to reunite the ancestor with the whole line of the predecessors. The *ti*, held the following spring, set a departed one among the ranks to 'the right and left of the High Lord'.

The form of the ancestor ceremony was basically the same wherever and whenever it was held. At the beginning of the sacrifice, the priest escorted the spirit tablets to the chamber of the First Ancestor where they would be fed. On the day of a royal ceremony the King and Queen in dragon robe and peasant dress proceeded separately to the temple to receive the Seven 'Corpses', the specially chosen embodiers (*shi*) who would be possessed by the spirit of the ancestors during the ceremony. The spirits were then invited to come down and the libations poured, the first of nine libations that made up the ceremony, and the corpses drank. Then they went to their places on white mao-grass mats facing their spirit tablets.

The King went down into the court and faced the first victim, the Red Bull for *Hou Ji*, First Ancestor, tied to a stone pillar set in the middle of the court. The King cut some head hairs and took blood with the belled knife, offering them in the temple. Then he killed the victim with arrows, as he did the victims for the other ancestors. The ministers took fat from the first victim and gave it to the corpses, who burned it so the ancestors could smell the ritual purity of the offering. Then they called the souls throughout the temple and at the gate, the Distant Ones.

The cooks meanwhile prepared the sacrifices and the King himself set out the dishes, a great variety that allowed the spirits to choose what pleased them. The corpses took the lungs of the victim cooked with millet and offered it to the spirit they each represented. At this point, the spirit who had been summoned entered their bodies and was present. When they then sat to eat and drink, the spirits were present in their bodies and were offered several courses. The King and Queen offered pure water, then a variety of wines. The corpses would rise, pour out several drops for the souls in the Earth and drink, offering the cup in turn to the King and Queen. At the fifth round it was passed to the ministers, at the seventh to the great officers, at the ninth to the lesser officers. Then six of the corpses passed among the people offering wine. When the feast ended, the corpses expressed the satisfaction of their spirits with the sacrifice, the food and wine, and extended their blessings (fu): 'blessings a hundred fold . . . forevermore they grant you highest favours, tens of thousands, hundreds of thousands'. The bells and drums sounded and the priest proclaimed: 'The spirits are completely drunk!' The corpses then retired to stately music.

The final part of the sacrifice was a grand banquet for all, ending in a set of dances that enacted the events of the story of the Mandate of Heaven: the departure from the military capital at Feng, when King Wu received the sign from Heaven, came out of the Mourning Hut and set the armies marching; the great battle in the Wilds of Mu and the defeat and execution of the Shang tyrant and his two concubines; the victorious return to Zhou; King Wu 'fixing the southern frontier'; and the final dance of peace attributed to Yu the Great, the hero and mythical founder who drained the flood and opened the ways of all civilized people. This pattern was followed, in great or in small, in all ancestral ceremonies, whether in the royal temple or in the rooms set off in the house of every noble family.

# Tools for Change

The sixty-four figures or symbols (*xiang*) of Change are composed of words, lines and diagrams (*gua*) that organize and display the divinatory phrases, giving access to them and building complex structures of meaning. The diagrams have meanings of their own, but they act primarily as a matrix that displays and relates the words and phrases that are the centres of associative fields. The figures thus combine two kinds of thought, one that works with words and their associations, another that works with the relation of lines and diagrams. We will see more of these in the section called 'Casting the Vessel'. The different figures and their relations provide a series of important interpretive tools that expand the basic reading, resolve confusion and point out important themes or perspectives. They also provide our entrance to the World of Change. Perhaps the best way to think of these tools is to see them as 'operators'. Each is a style of seeing into the spirit of the words, with a certain similarity to the work of the old magicians and sages.

## The Two Kinds of Lines

There are two basic kinds of lines used to build the diagrams of Change. They are quite old and are felt to participate in the nature of the Two Fundamental Powers that join to articulate the Way.

| | |
|---|---|
| **The Strong** | **The Supple** |
| *Action*: firm, unyielding, moving, persisting, enduring, whole | *Structuring*: flexible, adaptable, still, yielding, pliant, opened |

These lines are referred to as 'whole and opened' and 'strong and supple'. In their oldest version these lines were probably used as a yes–no oracle. The basic answer would describe what kind of stance to take toward a problem: take action, be aggressive and impose your will; or yield, stay where you are and adapt to whatever comes. This perspective sees things through the Two Primal Powers (1 and 2).

## The Four Symbols

The Two Powers represented by these lines are continually in motion, waxing and waning, transforming into each other. They build potential gradually through a slow accumulation then suddenly transform into the opposite state through the constellation of the seed of the opposite at the precise moment of fullness (*bian-hua*). Doubling the two basic lines gives four symbols (*si xiang*) that are an image of transformation that uses the Time Cycle and the Four Seasons to describe the process of qualitative change in the All-Under-Heaven.

| | | | |
|---|---|---|---|
| Old or *transforming* yang energy | Young or *stable* yin energy | Old or *transforming* yin energy | Young or *stable* yang energy |

As in all the diagrams, incoming lines enter from the bottom of the figures and leave at the top. Thus a 'stable' situation is actually a mixture of energies, not truly static but gradually accumulating the energy for change. A situation where one power completely dominates marks a sudden change into the opposite. These four symbols were used to describe the four seasons, the Four Directions or the four stages of life. In Change, they became the four lines, two stable and two transforming. As the transforming lines (*bian*) or the *yaoci* (the 'crossings' or 'calling lines') they

29

indicate the precise points of psychic change and key particular oracular phrases.

| **old yang** | **young yin** | **old yin** | **young yang** |
| *transforms into >* | | *transforms into >* | |

## The Six-line Diagrams

The six-line diagrams (*gua*), usually called 'hexagrams', are the basic units of the matrix. They are all the possible combinations of six whole/strong and opened/supple lines. Because each line can transform itself into its opposite, all of the diagrams flow into each other in a continuous interconnected flow of change. Because each line is determined by a chance method of consultation, it was felt that the spirit (*shen*) of the time (*shi*) could directly choose which diagram was an adequate representation. Together, the sixty-four diagrams and the divination method that keyed them provided the basis for a language through which the spirits could talk to humans.

## The Primary Figure

Each of these diagrams can be thought of as an archetypal moment. Each was thought of as having six empty places, numbered from the bottom up. Energy flows through these places, leaving a trace or track represented by the lines. Each diagram has a name and displays a set of related divinatory phrases. This is the shape of the Primary Figure you receive when you pose a question to the oracle.

```
6 [          ]
5 [          ]
4 [          ]

3 [          ]
2 [          ]
1 [          ]
```

Number: _____
Name: _____

# The Pair

The figures or diagrams were not thought of as being alone. Each had a pair or double associated with it, that was either its inverse or its converse. The sequence of the figures in Change is built of these pairs. A pair is a subtle interpretive tool, for the two figures interact as inspiration and manifestation, agonist and antagonist, light and shadow. They are woven together by the interconnection of the pairs of transforming lines (1 and 6, 2 and 5, 3 and 4, 4 and 3, 5 and 2, 6 and 1) and the thematic relation of the names of the figures. This is explored in detail in 'Casting the Vessel'. The matrix of the Pair, the crossline omens and Nodes it generates and the Shadow site open the Mirror World of a reading, as seen in the layout on page 48.

# The Relating Figure

The oldest form of reading centred on the Primary Figure and one or more of its transforming lines. Diviners soon realised that when these lines changed, they would produce a second figure, called the *ji gua* or Relating Figure. First used to identify the moving lines, the Relating Figure soon became an interpretive tool in its own right. The Relating Figure represents how the inquirer is *related* to the matter presented by the Primary Figure. It can represent future potential, overriding concerns, a warning, a goal, a desired outcome or a past situation that brought you to the present situation. It is anything that *relates* you to the basic situation, the sea or ground feeling in which the Primary Figure swims. Finding the function of the Relating Figure in a specific situation involves an intuitive exploration of the feelings around

**Primary Figure**
Name: *40 Loosening*

*transforms to:*

**Relating Figure**
Name: *8 Grouping*

31

the matter at hand. Here is an example, 40 *Loosening*, with three transforming lines, leading to 8 *Grouping*, or 40, 9/2, 9/4, 6/5 > 8, that we will follow through this section on interpretive tools.

## *Bagua*: The Eight Diagrams or Spirit Helpers

With the *Bagua*, we enter the world of the Shamans and Intermediaries. The six line diagrams (*gua*) were also divided into eight three-line diagrams (also *gua*), the *Bagua* or Eight Trigrams. These are the eight possible combinations of three whole and opened or strong and supple lines. They, too, became fundamental units of Chinese thought, the Eight Helping Spirits. They were felt to embody basic energies, processes or spirits activating the world we live in and they were used to organize a wide range of cycles and associations. The *Bagua* figure in the development of all Chinese medicine and magic. They are used as a powerful talisman to ward off evil and attract beneficent influences. They are seen in two basic arrangements, the symmetrical Order According to *Fuxi* and the cyclic Order According to King Wen. One of the Ten Wings, the *Shuogua*, describes the associations and myths invoked by these powerful figures. This perspective sees any situation in terms of the interaction of two of these fundamental spirits, one active in the outer world, and one active in the inner world. Here are some of their basic associations, given in the King Wen Order.

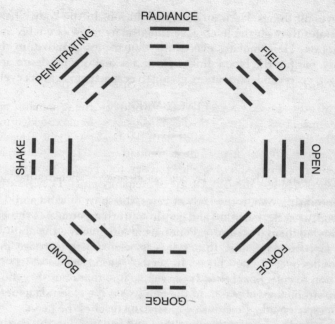

The order according to *King Wen* or Later Heaven arrangement

SHAKE

'Spirit manifests in quake and thunder;'                    **Shake**, *Zhen*

**Shake**, *Zhen*, is the Rouser, the thunder spirit who bursts forth from the Earth below to arouse, excite and disturb. This spirit stirs things up and brings them out of hiding. It can arouse your dormant energy and give you the strength to undertake difficult things. Its symbol is *thunder* and its action is to *rouse and excite*. It is made of a stirring strong line beneath two dormant supple lines. In the family it is the first son. As a spirit guide, Shake is the arouser and exorcist, driving out the old, rousing and opening the field of the new. He is flamboyant and sexual, luxuriating, frightening and inspiriting, green and full of juice. He is motion and

33

moves all things. He is an emerging dragon. In the body, Shake operates through the liver, governing the free flow of energy and emotion. He stimulates everything that moves or moves in the body, purifies the blood, links eyes and sexual organs, desire and anger, vision and motivation, giving the capacity to act decisively.

### PENETRATING

'Spirit works in those who lay out the offerings;'     **Penetrating**, *Sun*

**Penetrating**, *Sun*, is the Lady of Fates, the spirit of wind and wood, a subtle, beautiful and gentle spirit that permeates things, bringing them to maturity. Penetrating can give you the ability to support and nourish things. It is associated with marriage and presides over the new house. Its symbol is *wind and wood*, its action to *enter from below*. It is a supple line that nourishes the two strong lines above it. In the family it is the eldest daughter. As a spirit guide, Penetrating enters and reaches the heart, elegant and powerful, moving like wind and wood in the Earth. She is a healer, matches and couples the beings, lays out the offerings, brings each thing to its fate. In the body, Subtle Penetration operates through the liver with Shake, governing the free flow of energy and emotion. It stimulates everything that moves or moves in the body, purifies the blood, links eyes and sexual organs, desire and anger, vision and motivation, giving the capacity to act decisively.

### RADIANCE

'Spirit reveals itself in the bright omens;'     **Radiance**, *Li*

**Radiance**, *Li*, is the Bright Omens, the spirit of fire, light, warmth and the magical power of awareness, a shape-changing bird with brilliant plumage that comes to rest on things. Radiance clings together with what it illuminates. It can give you the power to see and understand, and to articulate ideas and goals. Its symbols are *brightness and fire*, its action to *hold or cling together*. It is the single supple line in the middle that holds two strong lines together. In the family it is the middle daughter. As a spirit guide, Radiance is the bright presence of things. She leads through her warm clear light, through beauty and elegance, the radiance of living beings holding together. She is the bird dancer with brilliant plumes and brings strange encounters and lucky meetings. She is nets and soft things with shells. She is a bright pheasant, bird of omen. In the body, Radiance acts through the heart, master of the organs and home of the spirits that brings inspiration and joy. It commands the pathways and the blood, brings the spark of life and offers a quiet centre in which the spirits find a voice.

FIELD

'Spirit is offered service at the Earth Altar;' **Field**, *Kun*

**Field**, *Kun*, is the Dark Animal Goddess, the womb that gives birth to all things. This spirit nourishes everything; without it nothing could exist and take shape. It can give you the power to shape things, to make thoughts and images visible. Its symbol is *earth*, its action is to *yield, serve and bring forth*. It is made up of only supple lines. In the family, it is the mother. As a spirit guide, Field opens, yields and closes all things into her. She is the flow, the provider, welcome everywhere, the opening that receives the seed of sky. Her hands give blessings. She receives the dead. She is the mare roaming the Earth tirelessly. In the body, Field acts through the spleen and stomach, stabilizing and transforming nourishment. It rots and ripens, governs the free flow of ideas, controls and protects central energy.

OPEN

'Spirit speaks and spreads joy through the *wu*;' **Open**, *Dui*

**Open**, *Dui*, is the Joyous Dancer, the spirit of open water, the vapours that rise from lakes, ponds and marshes that fertilize and enrich. Friendliest and most joyous of spirits, Open brings stimulating words, profitable exchange, cheerful interaction, freedom from constraint and sexual encounters. It can give you persuasive and inspiring speech, the ability to rouse things to action and create good feeling. Its symbol is the *mists and the lake*, its action to *stimulate*. It is the single supple line that leads two strong lines forward. In the family it is the youngest daughter. As a spirit guide, Open leads through joy and cheering words, magic and pleasure. She dances with the *shen* and feels the spirit in her body and gives it words. She is rising mists and open water. She gladdens all things that welcome her. She is a dancing goat and a sheep. In the body, Open acts through the lungs, skin and nervous system, regulating the rhythm of life, making energy descend and dispersing it. It connects the surface with the central nervous system, and is involved in sexual stimulation and the power of inner images.

FORCE

'Spirit awes and wars in the Heavens;'          **Force**, *Qian*

**Force**, *Qian*, is the Dragon, a creative spirit that lives in the waters and in the heavens. It is a dynamic shape-changer and can give you creative power, inspiration and enduring strength. Its symbol is *Heaven*, its action to *persist*. It is made of only strong lines. In the family it is the father. As a spirit guide, Force is tireless creative energy, shape-changing, relentless, riding a dragon, inspiring and creating dynamic harmony. He is dangerous. He is a tiger. He brings deep abiding joy. In the body, Force acts through the lungs, skin and nervous system, regulating the rhythm of life, making energy descend and dispersing it. It connects the surface with the centre, and is involved in sexual stimulation and the power of inner images.

## GORGE

‘Spirit rewards those suffering in the Pit;’　　　　　**Pit**, *Kan*

**Pit**, *Kan*, is the Ghost River or Ghost Dancer, the spirit of rushing water. It takes risks, like falling water, filling the holes in its path and flowing on. It dissolves things, carries them forward and cannot be stopped. It can give you the energy to take risks, to focus your courage at a critical point, to confront and overcome obstacles. Its symbol is *streaming*, water flowing rapidly between two rocky banks, its action to *risk and fall*. It is the single strong line between two supple lines. In the family it is the middle son. As a spirit guide, Pit leads through danger. He dances with ghosts, risks all and always comes through. He exults in work, he dissolves all things. He is a black pig, hidden riches. In the body, Pit acts through the kidneys, conserving life and pushing the organism to actualize its potential. This is the site of the essence (*jing*) or individual fate and transforms the essence into available energy. It controls the flow of emotion, particularly courage and fear.

## BOUND

‘Spirit’s words bind us, accomplishing fate.’　　　　**Bound**, *Gen*

**Bound**, *Gen*, is the Sacrificer, the mountain spirit who limits and brings things to a close. It suggests the palace of the immortals, the eternal images that begin and end all things. It can give you the power to articulate what you have gone through and make your accomplishments clear. Its symbol is the *mountain*, its action to *still or stop things*. It is the single strong line that stops two supple lines beneath. In the family it is the youngest son. As a spirit guide, Bound leads through perceiving and fixing limits. He is nemesis. He articulates fate. He is the still point in all turning, the refuge of distant mountains. He is a dog, guarding, watching and finding. In the body, Bound acts through the spleen and stomach, stabilizing and transforming nourishment. It rots and ripens, governs the free flow of ideas, controls and protects central energy.

## *Wuxing*: The Five Processes or Moments

The system of Eight Trigrams was meshed with another system that described all phenomena as a cycle of Five Processes (*wuxing*) associated with the 'elements' wood, fire, earth, metal and water. These Processes came in two interconnected cycles or orders, a cycle in which one process generated another, and a cycle in which one process mastered or controlled another. They, too, became a system of energy analysis that permeated the culture. The action of these two systems, the Eight Diagrams (*Bagua*) and the Five Processes or Moments, is described in the section of the hexagrams called *The Shaman Speaks*. This section reflects the configuration of the trigrams into a proper stance to be adopted by the Noble One or Realising Person. Here are the Five Processes:

Wood, *Mu*, describes organic growth, budding, outward movement and expansion, springing up and opening out. It refers to origins, beginnings, the initial burst of energy, rising sap – impulsive, vital, activating, enlivening and free flowing, keen and fresh. It is associated with the east, sunrise and day's beginning, spring and young yang. Its colour is vivid green. Its action is to push through, the germinating thrust of plants bending and straightening as they push up into the light. Wood begins the yang cycle. It includes the powerful and invisible penetration of wind. It expresses itself in the body as the liver/gall bladder orbits, governing the free flow of energy, the capacity to respond and adapt, stimulating mind and emotion – everything that is moving. It links sexuality, will, desire and motivation, and the capacity for action. Wood grows from water, generates fire and is controlled by metal. Wood links with the trigrams Penetrating/*Sun* and Shake/*Zhen*.

Fire, *Huo*, describes burning and combustion, warmth and light, joy and luxuriant growth. It refers to fire, flame, heat; blaze, glow; climax, zenith; maturity and ripening, ease and accomplishment; joy, happiness, expansive feeling, upward movement and excitement. It is associated with summer, the south, midday, blood and body heat. Its colour is red. Its actions are following or depending on and transforming. Fire brings the yang cycle to a close. It expresses itself in the body as the heart, seat of the spirit that commands the blood and energy channels, nourishing, invigorating and bringing the spark of life to full growth. Fire grows from wood, generates earth and is controlled by water. Fire links with the trigram Radiance/*Li*.

**Earth**, *Di*, describes soil, ground, dust, clay and ashes, the wide surface of Earth on which everything rests and from which everything grows. It maintains and preserves, promotes exchange and interchange, the central hub or pivot and place of transformation. Its colour is yellow and its climate is damp and humid. It is the point around which the seasons and directions and the alternation of day and night, yin and yang, revolve, transforming into each other. Its action is yielding and bringing forth, like sowing and hoarding a crop. Earth is the moment of transition between the yin and yang cycles. It expresses itself in the body as the spleen and stomach, assimilating, transforming and distributing nourishment, centring movement and assuring a free flow of thought. Earth grows from fire, generates metal and is controlled by wood. In ancient myth, it emerged from the underworld waters. Earth links with the trigrams Field/*Kun* and Bound/*Gen*.

**Metal**, *Jin*, describes all forms of metal, ores in the Earth, gemstones and the melting, casting and working of metals, particularly gold and bronze. It refers to concentration, coagulation, crystallization; contraction and condensation, casting into form; to insight, conceptual, concentrated thought; to harvesting a crop and gathering the seeds. It moves inward, withdrawing, introverting and moving toward centre. It is associated with autumn, the west, sunset, melancholy and sadness. Its colour is white, colour of death and purity and its climate is drying. Metal is young yin. It begins the yin cycle. Its action is to restrain things into forms, like casting molten metal and then stripping away the mould. It expresses itself in the body as the lungs, mouth and skin, an interface with the outside, draws energy in and distributes it downward, regulating the rhythms of life. Metal grows from earth, generates water and is controlled by fire. Metal links with Force/*Qian* and Open/*Dui*.

**Water**, *Shui*, describes fluids, flowing and streaming. It refers to streams, floods, rivers and all moving water; dissolving structures and liquefying things; the flow of feeling and emotion; the hidden source of life and the underworld River of Ghosts, secret, dark, mysterious; the womb that sustains, cleans and renews; falling, downward motion, hidden depths and sources. It is associated with winter, the north, midnight, fear, cold and lonely toiling. It is old yin and brings the yin cycle to a close. Its action is levelling, dissolving, flooding and spreading out below. It expresses itself in the body as the kidneys and bones, preserver and root of life that pushes the being to actualize its potential, holds individual fate, stores and maintains the blood and regulates body fluids. Water grows from metal, generates wood and is controlled by earth. In ancient myth it is the underworld river from which all things rise. Water links with Rushing Water/*Kan* and the Ghost River.

## Outer and Inner

According to this tradition, each hexagram in Change is seen as being made up of two of the Eight Trigrams, which also connect it to the Five Processes. Between them, the two trigrams involved in a hexagram express the relation and tension between outer and inner worlds. The upper trigram, called the figure of distress or trouble (*hui*), represents the outer world. The lower trigram, called the figure of trial or support (*zhen*), represents the inner world. These two terms reflect an old lunar way of thinking, suggesting the full moon and the dark moon. It was further elaborated to suggest specific meanings for the line positions based on their place in the inner or outer worlds. The first and sixth lines were seen as entrance and culmination; the second and fifth as inner and outer centres; the third and fourth as the threshold of manifestation between the worlds.

| | | | |
|---|---|---|---|
| exit | 6 [ | ] | **Outer** |
| outer centre | 5 [ | ] | **World** |
| transition | 4 [ | ] | **Trigram** |

*threshold of manifestation*

| | | | |
|---|---|---|---|
| transition | 3 [ | ] | **Inner** |
| inner centre | 2 [ | ] | **World** |
| entrance | 1 [ | ] | **Trigram** |

## The Kernel or Hidden Possibility

It was also discovered that there was another figure 'hidden' within each hexagram that could be seen as the kernel or seed (*ho gua*), a Hidden Possibility. This perspective sees things as a constant interplay between cause and *telos* or goal. The Nuclear Figure is constructed by seeing the four inner lines of the hexagram (lines 2, 3, 4 and 5) as two overlapping trigrams and then unpacking them. The new lower trigram is made from lines 2, 3 and 4; the new outer trigram from lines 3, 4 and 5.

| | | | | | |
|---|---|---|---|---|---|
| | | 6 [ | ] | | |
| | | 5 [ | ] | 6 | **Outer** |
| **Inner** | 3 | 4 [ | ] | 5 | **Nuclear** |
| **Nuclear** | 2 | 3 [ | ] | 4 | **Trigram** |
| **Trigram** | 1 | 2 [ | ] | | |
| | | 1 [ | ] | | |

For example, the kernel or Hidden Possibility of *40 Loosening* is *63 Already Crossing*. This shows that the liberation is already underway, a matter of co-operating with an on-going process.

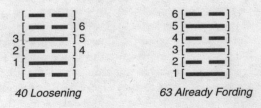

*40 Loosening*          *63 Already Fording*

The Kernel or hidden Nuclear Figure reveals something very interesting about the deep structure of the matrix of Change. The sixty-four hexagrams group into sixteen families of four hexagrams that share a common kernel. Thus there are only sixteen possible first generation kernel figures, indicated in the texts as Seed Figures. If these in turn are reduced to their Nuclear Figures, we find four second-generation figures: the first two and the last two figures of the book, *1 Force* and *2 Field*, *63 Already Crossing* and *64 Not Yet Crossing*. These are indicated in the text as Primal Seed Figures. These four are unique. The first two are their own kernel figures; the last two are each other's kernel figures. This arrangement can be used to trace any situation back to one of four Gates of Change. The following diagram shows each Seed or Nuclear Figure, representing the Hidden Possibilities of the situation, with a short divinatory phrase that is a key to its action.

*1 Force*: You are connected
to a creative force.

*2 Field*: Provide what is needed.

*1 Force*: You are
connected to a
creative force.

*28 Great
Exceeding*: Do
not be afraid to
act alone.

*2 Field*: Provide
what is needed.

*23 Stripping*:
Strip away
old ideas.

*43 Deciding*:
Be resolute!

*44 Coupling*:
Welcome
what comes.

*24 Returning*:
Go back to
the source

*27 Jaws*: Take
the situation in.

*38 Diverging*:
Turn conflict
into creative
tension.

*40 Loosening*:
Release bound
energy.

*37 Dwelling
People*: Find
a supportive
group.

*39 Difficulties*:
Reimagine
the situation.

*54 Converting the
Maiden*: Realize
your hidden
potential.

*63 Already
Fording*: The
situation is
already changing.

*53 Gradual
Advance*: Proceed
step by step.

*64 Not Yet
Fording*: Gather
energy for a
decisive move.

*63 Already Fording*: The situation
is already changing.

*64 Not Yet Fording*: Gather energy
for a decisive move.

The Groups of Nuclear Figures or Hidden Possibilities

## Steps of Change

Another way of seeing the transformation inherent in a reading comes directly from the transforming lines. This perspective sees any change as proceeding through a series of stages or steps. It is of particular help when more than one line is transforming and a series of actions are displayed in what appears to be a confusing or conflicted reading. Each time a single line transforms, it generates a particular Relating Figure. This means each hexagram has six other hexagrams attached to it through the change of each of its separate lines, indicating the steps or stages the change may pass through. If we are working with figure 40 *Loosening*, and three transforming lines in the second, fourth and fifth places that change the figure to 8 *Grouping*, the steps would look like this:

The Step Figures for *40 Loosening* in this situation would be:

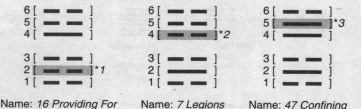

Name: *16 Providing For*    Name: *7 Legions*    Name: *47 Confining*

These three step figures suggest that the change from *Loosening* to *Grouping*, dissolving present connections and finding a new group more spiritually akin to you, will have a tendency to pass through three stages: storing up energy to meet the new situation (*16 Providing for*); organizing your strength and setting out in a determined manner (*7 Legions*); and passing through and out of a confining or oppressive situation (*47 Confining*). The steps result from the change of one single line, with all others remaining the same. They are not cumulative.

# The Change Operators

The Change Operators are a very powerful modern technique for determining the transformative action of the Two Powers in a given situation. This can give you a real sense of inner and outer strategies and a much clearer understanding of the movement of Change as a whole. The Change Operators are independent of the particular figure in question. They work only from the *positions* of the transforming lines in a reading, whether yin or yang. Thus any figure with changing lines in, say, the second, fourth and fifth places, like our example, will have the same Operators.

The Yin, Inner or Context Operator, describes the *place* where Change occurs and its *inner* transformative aspects. It offers an *inner stance* or strategy towards the inner world. To find the Yin or Context Operator, you place a yin or supple line *in each place where change is occurring* in the Primary Figure, and a yang or strong line *in each stable place*. This is independent of the particular quality of the changing and stable lines in the Primary Figure.

The Yang or Energy Operator describes the *actions* through which Change occurs and its *outer* transformative aspects. It offers an *outer stance* or strategy towards the outer world. To find the Yang or Energy Operator, you place a yang or strong line *in each place where change is occurring* in the Primary Figure, and a yin or supple line *in each stable place*. This is independent of the quality of the changing and stable lines in the Primary Figure. For example, 40 *Loosening* with changes in the second, fourth and fifth places would produce 22 *Adorning* as an Inner or Yin Operator and 47 *Confining* as an Outer or Yang Operator.

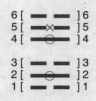

**Primary Figure**
Name: *40 Loosening*

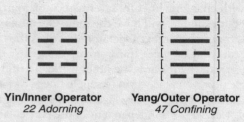

**Yin/Inner Operator**          **Yang/Outer Operator**
*22 Adorning*                   *47 Confining*

This might indicate that while the outer situation feels and is oppressive, an inner sense of beautifying and adorning might lead out of the confinement.

## The Reading and the Layout

The tools explored here give you a basis for understanding something of the matrix through which the tradition of Change organizes and displays its symbols. They provide the means to construct an interpretive web around a basic reading that can extend and clarify the oracle's response. We can lay out these possibilities in a plan for a complete reading that shows the subtle relations in an answer, reflected in the Primary World and the Mirror World. These are tools, however, and you use them when and how you need them. Not all will be equally helpful in each situation. They are perspectives that will become more and more familiar as you become acquainted with the figures of Change.

Here is a form for recording your basic answer.

```
6 [          ]                        [          ]
5 [          ]                        [          ]
4 [          ]                        [          ]

3 [          ]                        [          ]
2 [          ]                        [          ]
1 [          ]                        [          ]
```

**Primary Figure**        *transforms to:*        **Relating Figure**

Number: _____                        Number: _____
Name: _____                        Name: _____

Here is a detailed diagram of the entire layout for a reading in depth, using our example 40, 9/2, 9/4, 6/5 > 8.

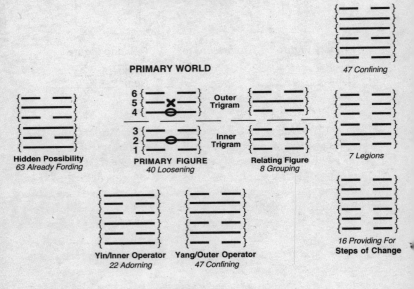

## WORLDS OF CHANGE

### Matrix for a Reading

47 Confining

**PRIMARY WORLD**

6
5
4
Outer Trigram

3
2
1
Inner Trigram

**Hidden Possibility**
*63 Already Fording*

**PRIMARY FIGURE**
*40 Loosening*

**Relating Figure**
*8 Grouping*

*7 Legions*

**Yin/Inner Operator**
*22 Adorning*

**Yang/Outer Operator**
*47 Confining*

*16 Providing For*
**Steps of Change**

### MIRROR WORLD

**Inspiring**
*39 Difficulties*

**Manifesting**
*40 Loosening/Release*

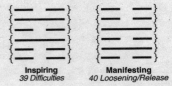

| 16 | 39.5 | > | 40.5 | 15 |
| 8 | 39.3 | > | 40.4 | 7 |
| 48 | 39.5 | > | 40.2 | 47 |

**Crossline Omens and Mediating Pairs**

7:8   15:16   31:32   47:48   53:54 63:64
**Nodes**

**25 : 26**
**Shadow Site**

# Casting the Vessel: Shaping Change

We tend to underestimate, indeed can hardly understand, the immense creative shaping power of the mythological imagination of early cultures and its holographic capacity to produce dynamic models of complex realities. Levi-Strauss described this modeling capacity through the figure of the *bricoleur*, one who 'picks among the rubble' of traditional images and symbols, re-arranging them until a quantum change occurs. This quantum change is what the ancient smiths described as the melting of the metals and their re-casting into a dynamic new form, por-trayed in Figures 49 and 50.

Yu the Great is such a *bricoleur*. He is the culture founder par excellence, at once shaman and Noble Son, the 'child of the chief' or *junzi*. A *wu*, a warrior and the Divine Smith, he created the *Ding* Vessels and gave people writing and metal casting. An orphaned son born by a miracle from his father's belly, Yu carried on and redeemed the work of his disgraced and executed father, Kun, by saving the world from a flood. He opened the waterways and, as a later king remarked, 'Without Yu we would all be fishes!'

In the past, when the Hsia were first distinguished by Sky for their Power and Virtue, the Distant Regions gave their Symbols (*xiang*) and the Nine Shepherds sent the Metals of their Provinces. Yu the Great cast the *Ding*-vessels with these symbols and gave instructions on how to use them, so the

49

people would know the Helping and the Harming spirits. Thus when the people went on rivers, entered marshes, or travelled in mountain and forest they were never attacked by malign beings, for no demon could come near them. Thus a harmony was made between the Above and the Below and all enjoyed the Blessing of Sky. The Ghost River flowed peacefully. People had images of the monsters and no longer suffered from the stormy waves.

This figure haunts the *Classic of Change*, along with the great *Ding* Vessel he created. He is the Intermediary and the hero who connects us to the Golden Age of good rulers and lets us discriminate among the ghosts and spirits. In the texts of Change, he is the 'man in the middle' who walks through the texts of the hexagrams, one foot in each world, a noble and a peasant, a shaman and a sage, a spirit and a human, suffering in his person the change of the time. With Yu the Great we enter the archaic process of shaping the vessel of change.

## Yijing: the Loom of Change

The character for 'classic' (*jing*) is the picture of a loom. It means weave, the weaving of the watercourse way, common to all, immutable. The character shows the warp threads in the loom, the fundamental principles. They are the lines traced from north to south in the cosmos and the energy channels of the body, the paths of the energy that forms all things. These warp threads carry the timeless world of the waterway and the 'comings and goings' of the soul. They are a prayer of the heart, a magical spell woven of words, available to all.

> One day the Master said:
> Was not Change assembled in middle antiquity?
> Did not those who did this have to deal with great
> cares and sorrows?
> They showed us a way to accumulate power and virtue,
> To deal with the transformations of life.
> This is their way to develop our innate power and virtue.

In the creation of the *Classic of Change*, this stream of images, the warp threads of Change, intersects with another stream – the weft, as it were, of history. This is the history of the Change of the Mandate of Heaven, a dynamic thread that challenges the warp of the timeless mythic world. Specifically, it describes the revolution that occurred between the Shang and the Zhou dynasties. Symbolically, it describes the great revolution of the Neolithic and the emergence of the Bronze Age Kings, the smiths and metal workers, and the creation of a written language. It is a paradigm for any great revolution in human culture that changes the basic way we see and understand the world. After such a paradigm shift the world is different. We cannot go back. What we can do, however, is to seek to re-connect the new world we live in with the timeless world out of which it grew. This is the task that faced the magicians, shamans and sages who gave us the *Classic of Change*.

> Sages made Change in ancient times.
> Inspired by spirits they invented yarrow divination.
> They took three from Sky and two from Earth,
> then all the other numbers.
> They observed dark and bright transforming
> and set out the *gua*.
> They developed strong and supple to empower
> the calling lines
> In accord with the power of the Way.
> They understood right action.
> Fully encompassing the nature of things (*jing*),
> They came to understand their fate (*ming*).

The makers of Change were faced with explaining the most momentous thing that could happen to human beings: a change in the Mandate, the *ming*, of Heaven. This change echoed through the fate and affected the essence of every human being. It was, in their eyes, a true renewal of the time and it was their job to give it a voice, to create a vessel through which the change could be carried forward, 'completing the ceaseless activity of heaven'.

The word *ming* connects individual fate with the orders of heaven. It is an edict from heaven that affects the life of each person, setting the length and quality of life, individual destiny, the limits and crossroads that are written in the stream of time. It is an oracular pronouncement that must be 'fixed' (*heng*) through the *de*, the power and virtue of the individual. This covenant with Heaven can lead to brightness, brilliance and true awareness. It is the splendid shining of the ancestors and a perception of the *shen ming*, the light of the gods and their bright symbols. It unites the insight of the Sun and the clairvoyance of the Moon, a true union of the primal powers.

The makers of Change sought to inscribe the history of the change in the Mandate of Heaven in the timeless world of the Way. They sought to create a locus whereby this great change could be eternally experienced and re-enacted, a legacy of the Great Enterprise involved in renewing the time that would make the blessings of the new spirit available to all. In doing so they created what I call a 'bardo explorer', a vehicle capable of investigating and clarifying the states of liminal reality that negotiate all profound change in form.

## New King and Old King: The Ideal of Sacrifice

No idea is more foreign to modern sensibilities than the mythic idea of sacrifice; no idea is more important to understanding the function of Change. The mythic world revolves around the magic or *numen* of the sacrifice and the access to the threshold between the world of the living and the dead that it represents. We see this in all the world's mythologies, from the self-sacrifice of the hero or the death of Christ to the simple pouring out of libations and offerings of the first fruits. It is at the core of all ceremonies of initiation, where the old identity is offered to the spirit and taken apart, to be put back together in a new way. Sacrifice establishes an interchange between the world of life and action and the 'other side', the seed and source of all. An inner attitude of offering is the way that we know and attune ourselves to the change of the times and the change in the will of heaven. In ancient China, this offering revolved around the idea of the New and the Old King: the time that is coming and the time that must pass away. We see this clearly in Figures 11:12 and 41:42. The transformation is effectuated by two 'operators' or technicians of the sacred seen throughout Change: the Rouser and Exorcist (*Zhen*) who calls up the new and drives out the ghosts of the old, and the Sacrificer (*Gen*) who cuts apart and offers up what has become fixed and outmoded.

Kingship in Change is central to this myth: the proper behaviour of the King insures a connection with Heaven and the continual flow of its blessings and benefits to both the human and the natural world. However, the King has a double, a minister or sage who connects his bright virtue with the darker side of life. These two are portrayed in Figures 55:56. This 'Other', the minister, sage or Alter Ego, represents the king's connection to death, his responsibility when called on by Heaven to offer himself for the good of the people. Through this sacrificial act the King becomes a guardian of the frontier of life and death, an archaic ancestor who stands guard at the edges of the world.

This sacrificial interplay between the worlds of the living and the dead is at the centre of all rituals of changing the times. It is enacted at all points of critical transition, regulating the balance between our striving for individual identity and achievement and the necessity of returning to the common source. These are times when we are called on to sacrifice our old identity in order to participate in the advent of the new. The diviners who created Change sought to describe the precise points when such sacrifice was called for and could be efficacious, placing them in an overall model of the 'comings and goings' in the All-Under-Heaven, the world in which we live and change. To do this they sculpted a matrix, a sequence of the 64 six-line figures available to them. They used this matrix to organize and display the vast oral and written omen tradition, inscribing the history of the Mandate into the arrangement. It not only described the fundamental changes that occurred in the world of Heaven and Earth; it magically *participated* in that process.

## The College of Diviners

Let us imagine a convocation of the *Wu* and the *Shi*, shamans and scribes gathered together by a King to revise the sacred traditions at a critical point in history. Such a meeting could have occurred at various times in ancient China: in the Tower where King Wen waited for a sign from Heaven; in the court of King Wu and his immediate successors after the victory over the Shang; in the court of King Yuan when the Zhou kingship was failing; in numerous monasteries or centres throughout the civil wars of the Warring States period; and, perhaps, in the court of King Huai Nan before his imprisonment and execution ended free thought in Han China. The purpose of the meetings was to create an instrument that could renew the time, connecting the fallen world we live in with the sources of ancient virtue.

## The Mirror World: The Dynamics of the Pair

The first problem confronting this College of Diviners would be the arrangement of the matrix, and their basic material would be the sets of related six-line figures called Pairs. The Pairs are the prima materia used in the construction of the matrix of Change. Each locates and describes a transformation, an 'operation' with specific thematic concerns.

The Pairs reflect the basic theme in Eastern thought at what we might call a fractal level: the interconnection of the Sun Tree and the Moon Tree, the interchange between light and dark, life and death, action and interiorization. Nothing stands alone here; each thing is only possible when held in tension with its opposite. A basic way of imagining the interaction within these pairs is as a set of spindles on which an unbroken thread is wound back and forth. The thread is the thread of life itself, as it passes back and forth between the Two Powers at every level of our lives. In Change, these powers are seen as the Dragon and the Dark Animal Goddess, Figures 1 and 2. They represent the 'inspiring' and the 'manifesting' phases of any action or process, the Dragon power that inspires new action and the Dark Animal Goddess that brings it to manifestation, giving it form as a vessel or tool. The matrix creates a space that opens with these powers at a maximum distance from each other (1:2) and closes with them in maximum integration (63:64). The space between shows how time and space swing open and shut, like a gate 'opening and closing'.

Here we need to look at a basic difference among the 64 six-line diagrams or *gua* that were available to the assembled group. This difference would have been immediately apparent to those who contemplated the *gua* and would have had a deep significance for them. This distinction is reflected in the two Chinese words for 'change': *bian* and *hua*.

*Hua* or 'change' describes a gradual change within a being, the slow changes over time inherent in all things that permit their manifestation and evolution. It is a gradual passage from one stage to another, a normal change that occurs in the natural course of life. It is digestion and assimilation, the growth of an embryo in the womb; to instruct, educate or reform the character; to spread the word and change the way people think. It is the slow *growth and maturation* of the yin and the yang.

*Bian*, with the root 'name or command', describes a quantum change, a sudden and radical shift of state. It is a spiritual transformation, a conversion, as well as a sudden unexpected death or accident. *Bian* is not normal; it is extraordinary, a marvellous happening. It is the *conversion* of yin and yang.

The 64 *gua* or six-line diagrams constitute 32 pairs. Of these, 23 pairs or 56 diagrams are related to each other by a process called *inversion* or *rotation*: one figure in a pair becomes the other when it is inverted or rotated on its central axis. This reflects the process called *hua*: gradual, normal change. It is the norm in the matrix.

**Rotational Pair**

*37 Dwelling People*        *38 Diverging/<br>The Shadow Lands*

The other, smaller group represents the 'symmetrical pairs'. They do *not* change when rotated or inverted. To effectuate the change here, each individual line must be *transformed* or *converted* into its opposite (*bian*).

**Symmetrical Pair**

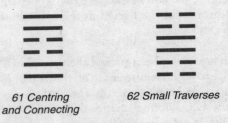

*61 Centring*
*and Connecting*

*62 Small Traverses*

In the mind of the *bricoleur*, these symmetrical pairs represent zones of radical discontinuity where the stream of time is disconnected, turned, and re-connected in a different way. They are negentropic; they reverse entropy, re-charging a situation by connecting it to primal sources of energy. We can describe these pairs in mythic terms: 1:2 is The Gates of Change, The Dragon and the Dark Animal Goddess; 27:28 is The Tiger's Mouth and the Great Transition; 29:30 is The Ghost River and the Bright Omens; 61:62 is The Opened Heart and the Flying Bird who carries a message across the threshold of life and death. They are distributed at key points in the matrix – the beginning, middle and end – acting as the engines of transformation.

## Interconnections and Transformations

The spaces between these great landmarks are modelled out of what we call normal or rotational pairs. As we saw in the section on Tools, the line positions in a *gua* or diagram describe the relation of inner and outer worlds by showing connections at *limits* (lines 1 and 6), *centres* (lines 2 and 5) and *thresholds* (lines 3 and 4). A normal or rotational pair generates a regular set of other paired figures through the change of these interconnected lines (1:6, 2:5, 3:4, 4:3, 5:2, 6:1). This describes the basic pattern of interchange (*hua*) between the limits, centres and thresholds of the two figures involved. Here is an example, using the pair 37:38 (The Dwelling and the Ghosts that Haunt it).

|  | 63 | 54 |  |
|---|---|---|---|
|  | 22 | 10 |  |
| **Dwelling People** | 13 | 41 | **Diverging** |
| **means being on** | | | **means being on** |
| **the inside.** | _threshold_ | | **the outside.** |
|  | 42 | 14 |  |
|  | 9 | 21 |  |
|  | 53 | 64 |  |

These generated figures (53:54, 9:10, 42:41, 13:14, 22:21 and 63:64) accomplish two things. First, they describe the interchange between the interconnected lines. This establishes a basic site where the omens can be displayed in their complexity across the spindles of 'inspiration' and 'manifestation'. We read the words or omen across the interconnected lines of this site. Thus, if you received the line 38.4 in a consultation, you might read:

_Inspiration_
37.3 Dwelling people, scolding, scolding.
Repent past sorrow and adversity, hungry souls and angry ghosts.
Wise Words! The Way opens.
If wife and son are giggling, going on will bring distress.

### Mediated through
### 42:41 (The Blessing and the Offering)

_Manifestation_
38.4 Diverging alone. The Orphan and the Fox.
You meet the Primal Father, mingle and
connect to the spirits.
Adversity, hungry souls and angry ghosts.
This is not a mistake.

This is an example of mythic thinking that connects us with the figure of the _Wu Gui_, the 'shaman of the shadows'. It explains the situation, the sense of isolation and feeling 'outside', as the 'manifestation' part of an attempt to clear up troubles within the family or dwelling, to encounter and deal with the excluded 'hungry souls and angry ghosts' that haunt it. The enquirer's sense of being hurt or diminished is actually an 'offering', for in the lonely journey in the shadow lands he or she will connect with a primal source that can, in turn, bring blessings to the family. Enshrined as an ancestor, this 'hidden father' renovates the exercise of authority within the dwelling.

Second, these interconnections provide a set of nodes, places where a given pair is connected with other pairs in the matrix, echoing backwards and forwards in the stream of time. This projection includes: an *exchange* with another pair in the series, seen as the figures generated by the bottom line of the first figure and the top line of the second; a charge that *motivates* the interchange between the two figures, seen as the figures generated by the top line of the first figure and the bottom line of the second; and *interconnections* between the transforming lines that show how the omens develop, seen as the interchange between the centre and threshold lines. Together, they explain the working of the spindles. A description of these functions is provided with each Pair in this translation.

## The Decades and the Symbolic Life

Here we encounter another major shaping principle used in sculpting the local logics of Change. The matrix seems to incorporate an ancient 'age-grade' system that describes the ideal shape of a life and the formation of character (*de*) in terms of Decades, with the number assigned to each hexagram corresponding to the age of an individual in an ideal lifetime trajectory. This system is based on the number ten, which has a special place in ancient thought.

> **Ten**, *xun*, shows the shape of a life and the shape of the completed periods within it. It describes the 'ten-day week' and the ten Heavenly Stems, the oldest mythic method of describing time. It means loyal, faithful, universal, everywhere, distributed equally, and describes a time when the king 'made a tour of the boundaries' and the diviners looked into the spirit world to see the ghosts and spirits that would influence the next period.

Scholars have shown that the Decades are used throughout ancient texts to describe the shape of a human life, indicating its major events, initiations and passages from one state of being to another. They give shape and meaning to an individual experience by locating it in relation to ritual progression, connecting the different stages we pass through. In Change this works in two ways. The numbers of a pair locate it in a specific Decade, while the figures generated by its lines connect it to other Decades and passages, acting as a sort of 'karmic analysis' of the key events underlying and influencing a given moment. We can look at the ages and events these figures suggest to explore deep personal connections. Here is an example, from 37:38:

**Dwelling People means being on the inside.**
**Diverging means being on the outside.**

### Nodes

9:10 (11:12) 13:14: First River-Mountain festival, puberty; passage into second decade.
21:22: Beginning of initiation (men); marriage (women).
41:42: Beginning of full cultural maturity; empowered to give ancestral sacrifices.
53:54: The Great Marriages; involvement in cultural events on a high level; paradigm of the old and the new and involvement in cultural transformation.
63:64: Crossings: End and Beginning of life, the Great Stream of the generations.

The nodes show that the difficult attempt to found a family dwelling and confront the ghosts of the past is connected with a major transition at puberty and with the ordeal of initiation or becoming a noble. It looks forward to key times when the individual emerges into full stature as an elder and is significantly involved with the crossing between life and death and the generations to come.

We can add the Nuclear Figures or *Hidden Possibilities* to this portrait, along with another sort of numbering, the Shadow Sequence that runs backwards from 64 to 1. This reverse flowing of time evokes the mystic process of death and rebirth. It also establishes the Shadow site, the event or experience that is acting as the entangler and antagonist in the given situation. Together these 'magical numbers' give us a rich and very evocative picture of the time and process symbolized by a Pair. All of the following information would have been in the mind of an old diviner when he or she looked at a set of two related six-line figures called up in response to a specific situation.

<u>37 & 38: The Paradigm</u>
### The Dwelling and the Ghosts that Haunt it
This Pair involves you in an overall model of thought and action elaborated in the interconnected lines of the two figures: the safety of the hearth and the dangers of the wilderness, the spirit world that opens through the dangerous journey of the outcast. It evokes the attempt of a Zhou noble to found a house on the borders of the established world, surrounded by the ghosts of the past and the excluded. Carefully consider your place in and relation to this model.

*Hidden Possibilities*: 64:63, prepare and make the crossing.

The Pair exchanges information with 53:54 (The Great Marriages). It is motivated by 63:64 (The Crossings). The centre and threshold lines relate the process to 9:10 and 13:14 (Ceremonies at the Outskirts Altar), 21:22 (Sacred Meal and Bringing Home the Bride) and 41:42 (Offering and Blessing).

Look at the ages and events these figures suggest for personal connections.

9:10 (11:12)13:14          21:22          41:42          53:54          63:64

*Shadow site*: 27:28, Tiger's Mouth and Great Transition

**Dwelling People means being on the inside. Diverging means being on the outside.**

## Paradigms of Creative Transformation

The final link in the matrix weaves the transformative potential of the symmetrical sites of transformation (*bian*) into the structure of the Decades. When we look at the symmetrical pairs we notice that the zones of radical discontinuity they represent are reproduced *within* certain other figures. These 'gates' are seen as *discontinuities* within the field of gradual change or *hua* described by the normal pair. Such a creative discontinuity can be structurally described as an *irregularity* in the production of figures generated by the interconnected lines of a normal pair, an irregularity that pulls the material in question back through a primary site of transformation. It is a significant irregularity in the normal process of change, a place where radical transformation (*bian*) is possible. These creative discontinuities tell us when a radical change of state is possible at various stages of our lives. An example is the Pair 43:44 (Announcing the Omen and The Lady of Fates). Notice the place of the symmetrical figures 1 and 28, which is doubled in the Nuclear Figure for this pair, 1 Dragon/Force.

| | | | |
|---|---|---|---|
| 6 | **1** | | **28** |
| 5 | | 34 | 50 |
| 4 | | 5 | 57 |
| nuclear | | | **[1]** |
| 3 | | 58 | 6 |
| 2 | | 49 | 33 |
| 1 | **28** | | **1** |

Creative discontinuity at limits:
1 Dragon and 28 Great Transition

Here is an example of an omen displayed across the discontinuity:

*Inspiration*
43.6 Not announcing the oracle.
Trap! Completing this closes the Way.

**Potential for transformation**
**1 Dragon, Primal Force**

*Manifestation*
44.1 Attach it to the bronze spindles.
Wise Words! Trial: The Way opens.
Have a direction to go. See the trap!
A bound pig, balking at the sacrifice.
There is a connection to the spirits
that will carry you through.

The mythic thinking here would say that in this situation you have been charged with the announcement of an oracle, something that destabilizes old structures with the power of the Dragon and announces the advent of the new, the entrance of the Lady of Fate. You must accept the sacrifice involved, attaching it to the spindles of change, and not simply impose your own will. This will result in a profound cultural transformation, a royal marriage and a new heir:

> 44.5 Coupling. The Royal Bride.
> Willow wrapping the melons, jade talisman in the mouth.
> Held in this containing beauty,
> 'It tumbles down from Heaven.'

So make the 'pig sacrifice' to the underworld processes and the Ghost River. Welcome the change. Let go of your need to control things. A connection to spirit, to the primal Dragon or Force, will carry you through this Great Transition.

Secondary sites of transformation like this are distributed at pivotal points throughout the matrix, showing the potential for radical change within a given situation. This is expressed as a discontinuity and exchange at the *limits* (1:6), the *centres* (2:5) or the *thresholds* (3:4). All these show places where we can effect a real transformation by sacrificing our old ways and participating in the new way of Change. They are spread throughout the Decades or stages of our lives.

### Thresholds (Initiation)

9:10 (Gathering the Ghosts and Mating with the Spirit) changes
at threshold lines 3 and 4 to connect us to **1** and **61** (The
Dragon entering through the Opened Heart).

15:16 (Activating Liminal Powers) changes at threshold lines 3
and 4 to connect us to **2** and **62** (The Earth Altar and the Flying
Bird that passes through death).

21:22 (The Sacred Meal and Bringing Home the Bride) changes
at threshold lines 3 and 4 to connect us to **27** and **30** (The
Bright Omens emerging from The Tiger's Mouth).

47:48 (Oppressed Noble Returns to Common Source) changes at
threshold lines 3 and 4 to connect us to **28** and **29**
(The Great Transition and the Ghost River).

## Centres

7:8 (Armies and the New Group) changes at centre lines 2 and 5 to connect us to **2** and **29** (The Ghost River flowing from the Earth Altar).

13:14 (Gathering at the Outskirts Altar and the Great Being that Emerges) changes at centre lines 2 and 5 to connect us to **1** and **30** (Heaven producing the Bright Omens).

31:32 (The Sacred Site and Fixing the Omen) changes at the centre lines 2 and 5 to connect us to **28** and **61** (The Great Transition and the Opened Heart).

41:42 (The Offering and the Blessing) changes at centre lines 2 and 5 to connect us to **27** and **61** (The Opened Heart and The Tiger's Mouth, the great sacrifices).

## Limits

23:24 (Stripping and Returning) changes at limit lines 1 and 6 to connect us to **2** and **27** (Earth Altar and The Tiger's Mouth).

43:44 (Announcing the Omen and the Lady of Fates) changes at limit lines 1 and 6 to connect us to **28** and **1** (The Dragon who empowers the Great Transition).

55:56 (King and Sage) changes at limit lines 1 and 6 to connect us to **62** and **30** (The Flying Bird that spreads the Bright Omens).

59:60 (Dissolution of Self and Articulating the Times) changes at limit lines 1 and 6 to connect us to **61** and **29** (The Ghost River flowing through the Opened Heart).

## The Offering and the Blessing

We are just beginning to understand the fourth-dimensional way images move through this complex and allusive matrix of change and transformation, but all of the information we have discovered has been integrated directly into this translation and the Mirror World of a reading. The great depth psychologist C.G. Jung felt that this way of Change was our true mirror, describing the way our unconscious continually creates new meaning, challenging us to become the person we were meant to be. It puts us in contact with the mythic significance of a moment or situation, helping us to see deeper into its transformative potential, its power to help us realise ourselves and thus change the world we live in.

If all this has a purpose, I think it might be best expressed in a key word that runs like a thread through the texts of Change:

**Connect**, *Fu*: The old character shows the claws of the bird spirit or ancestor holding its young or its prey. With the root 'person' the term means to capture prisoners, take spoils, sacrifice to the ancestors and suggests the punishment and sacrifice of the Old King. With the root 'one, the One' it describes an accord between inner and outer: sincere, truthful, reliable, verified; have confidence; linked to and carried by the spirits; the sheen of jade; hatch, incubate, a sprout in the womb. A shaman would extend it to other members of the family: With the root 'heart' the term *Fu* means a return to the origin, the incessant return of life, renewal and rebirth. With the root 'celestial omen', *Fu* can also mean blessing: a ritual offering of food and wine and the blessings it calls down from heaven; protection and celestial favour, a hidden safe place.

When we consider Change and the hearts of those who made it, we might not be too far off if we see those old diviners, magicians and sages offering us their blessings, we who are helping to restore the magical world they lived in. The last symmetrical pair in Change, 61:62 The Opened Heart and the Flying Bird, describes a place where the events of life can be seen, moving back across the threshold of life and death to the source of all. This, I would suggest, is the imagined place from which they launched their vehicle of transformation. A final picture emerges here, the figure of Yu the Great, the limping shaman who strides across the gap between life and death, one foot in each world. He walks backwards and forwards through time, a flying bird that spreads the word of the Great Enterprise of transformation.

# Consulting Change

Your entry into the world of Change comes through a question. This begins the creative process of talking with the spirit and experiencing its effects on what the sages call the heart-mind (*xin*). The basic experience in using Change is a feeling of being seen and valued. It reflects what the traditional world called the friendship of the spirits.

## The Helping Spirit

Change constellates and focuses the *shen*, the Bright Spirit that resides in the heart, and dissolves the fixations, the 'angry ghosts' that impede its voice and its action. This spirit can act as an inner voice, a guide and healer. It helps us become aware of our destiny and connect our path to the Way. The symbols of Change give it a way to speak.

The spirit will often manifest as a problem or difficulty that interferes with conscious will. You experience this as a disturbance, an unrest in the heart. Anxiety, confusion, a need to know the hidden sense, a desire for validation, or the feeling you are grappling with something that cannot be dealt with through ordinary means of analysis indicate there is probably an unknown force at work in the situation. This place where your conscious will is 'crossed' points at an opening, an opportunity to deepen contact with the invisible world and transform awareness. The symbols of Change are meant to give this spirit voice. They can move the soul or imagination, freeing it from entanglements and re-establishing the flow of the Way.

## The Question of the Question

The first step in the process is to present the problem as a question. You should take time with this. The clearer the question and the deeper your perception of the issues at stake, the more precise and profound Change's answer can be. Making a question is a three-step process. First determine your place or stance as the inquirer. Are you asking this question as an individual or on behalf of others? Are you the spokesperson for a group? Are you seeking information that gives you the best way to help another person or an organization? Are you acting as a parent, a lover, a counsellor or therapist, or a concerned friend?

Then take time to consider the problem. Search out the feelings, images and experiences involved. Articulate what you feel and think about things, what you know and what you do not know. Look for relevant memories and experiences, hopes and fears, dreams and desires. Simply try to see what is there, no matter how contradictory. This will establish a field of associations.

Finally, formulate the actual question as clearly as possible. Base it on what you want to do. Find the border, the place where your desire melts into uncertainty. An effective formulation is: 'What about doing X?'; 'What would happen if I . . .?' or 'What should my attitude towards X be?' If you are confused about the whole situation, you can ask for an image: 'What is happening here? Please give me an image of the situation.' If you are truly on the horns of a dilemma, you can ask for an image of each alternative. You can also ask for a strategy: 'How can I best achieve X?' Change will offer you a symbol that is meant to make you aware of and help you connect with the hidden forces active in the situation, the spirits of the time. It will work through the material you present, but will often offer a strikingly new perspective. Tradition says that the book will respond clearly to a real need but that it will not allow itself to be used for evil or manipulative ends. There is a real, though quite friendly spirit involved that should be treated with respect. This is a matter of imagination and being open to experiencing something. At this point all you need is sincerity, an open mind and a willingness to entertain possibilities.

The question you ask can also be the starting point in a continuing dialogue with Change, what Jung called a kind of active imagination. It may lead to further questions as you explore the matter you are considering in depth. Give the oracle's response careful consideration: turn and roll it in your heart, as the tradition says. But if further questions arise, do not hesitate to ask them. The Change invites this sort of dialogue. It slowly transforms the way we think about our problems, leading us further and further into the great world of the symbols.

## Chance and Fate: Accessing Change

Divination and omens are a universal part of human culture, used for centuries to help us understand and connect with the living world. These procedures all involve an inquirer, a listener and a symbolic language. Uniting them is what we call chance. Flip a coin, draw the lots, pick a number; the die is cast, it is written in the stars, don't tempt fate, my luck is running – all these expressions and practices point at a much older sense of 'chance' than our idea of 'meaningless coincidence'. Old Chinese, for example, has no word for the modern sense of meaningless chance or random events. *All* coincidence was meaningful. Chance for the old sages was either the ability to act spontaneously or the influence of an unseen force. In divination, this chance or coincidence is the vehicle of the spirit, a chance for your fate to talk with you. Acting through the symbolic language, it connects you with the basic patterns and forces creating what you experience. The depth psychologist C.G. Jung called this 'synchronicity'.

All methods of generating the lines of a hexagram rely on chance or synchronicity as something beyond your conscious control that lets a force other than your ego do the choosing. A magical explanation would say that the instruments used to make the choice participate in the nature of the cosmic process. A more modern idea is that they record synchronous clusters of meaning, clusters that create meaning without rational cause. The entrance of chance into the equation participates in the nature of fate. As such, it can connect you to the world of the symbols.

# Generating the Lines

There are several ways to generate the lines, but the best known are the Coin Oracle and the Yarrow Stalk Oracle. I prefer what I call the 16 Token Method. It is direct, elegant and preserves the mathematical ratios of the oldest ways of consultation. All of these methods produce the six lines you need to create a figure.

The Coin Oracle probably comes from the Tang Dynasty and was popularized in the Sung Dynasty, but this type of tossing oracle is found all over the world. You need three coins with a head and tail. Old Chinese bronze coins with a square hole are often used. Heads are given the value 3, tails the value 2. You toss the three coins six times, adding the values each time. With each throw you will get 6, 7, 8 or 9. As you can see from the diagram 6 = transforming yin; 7 = stable yang; 8 = stable yin; 9 = transforming yang.

| old yang | young yin | old yin | young yang |
|---|---|---|---|
| *transforms into >* | slowly changes into > | *transforms into >* | slowly changes into > |

**The Four Kinds of Line for the Primary Figure**

Write your lines from the bottom up to create a Symbol. If any lines are transforming, make the changes and generate the new figure. Then use the Key to the Hexagrams at the end of the book to find your symbols in the text.

The Yarrow Stalk Method is an older, more ceremonial and more complicated form, with a different mathematical ratio between yin and yang. To use it you need a set of fifty thin sticks, about twelve to fifteen inches long, traditionally taken from the tips of the *achillea millefolium* or yarrow. You divide and count out this bunch of stalks three times to produce one line. Each time you go through this process, you produce a number (6, 7, 8 or 9) and thus a line of your figure.

- Put the bunch of fifty stalks on the table in front of you. Take one stalk and put it aside as the Witness. It will remain unused *throughout the whole process.*
- Divide the remaining bunch into two random piles.

- Take one stalk from the pile on your left. Put it between the fourth and fifth fingers of your left hand.
- Count out the pile on your right into groups of four, laying them out clearly on the table in front of you until you have a remainder of 4,3,2 or 1.
- Put this remainder between the third and fourth fingers of your left hand.
- Count out the left pile in groups of four until you have a remainder of 4,3,2 or 1. Put the remainder between the second and third fingers of your left hand.
- Take all the stalks you have put between your fingers and lay them aside. They are out for this round.
- Make one bunch of the stalks that remain and repeat the entire procedure. Again, put the stalks you have collected between your fingers aside for this round.
- Repeat the process a third time. This time, count the number of groups of four left on the table. It will be 6,7,8 or 9. This indicates the first or bottom line of your figure.
- Repeat the entire process five more times to obtain the complete figure. Enter the lines and make the transformations if there are any. Then use the Key at the end of the book to find the names and numbers.

The 16 Token Method combines the ease of the coins, the mathematical odds of the yarrow and an amazing directness, for you do not use the set of four numbers. To use this method, you need a small bowl and sixteen marbles or identically shaped tokens of four different colours: one of a first colour; three of a second colour; five of a third colour; and seven of a fourth colour. The one marble of the first colour indicates transforming yin; the three marbles of the second colour indicate transforming yang; the five marbles of the third colour indicate stable yang; the seven marbles of a fourth colour indicate stable yin. Put the marbles into the bowl and draw one out. It is your first line. Write the line down, return the marble to the bowl and draw again. This is your second line. Repeat four more times until you have completed the symbol, then make the transformations. Then look it up in the Key to the Hexagrams at the end of the book.

# Finding the Way

## Concise Answers and Readings in Depth

The oracle of Change is traditionally used in two different, though related ways. It is used to give quick, concise answers to pressing problems. It is also used to supply the background and insight that lets you understand a situation in depth, thus generating an effective strategy that can provide for long-range planning. This can engender a real transformation of basic attitudes and thoughts and open you to the creative energy inherent in the situation.

These two aspects are reflected in the texts: certain sections of the hexagram texts, the Paradigm, the 'Name and keywords', the 'Response' and the immediate description of the situation that follows it and the 'Transforming Lines' can be used to provide a quick answer. Other sections of the texts, 'Myths for Change', 'The Scholar speaks and 'The Shaman Speaks', along with the interpretive 'Tools and Layout', provide further interconnections and reflection in depth. Use these when you need, and have the time for, greater understanding. You can also use them to study the figures in depth or to go back over a basic reading as the situation develops. These sections are of great help in sensing the manner in which the Way is unfolding deep in your imagination.

## The Divinatory Signs

Similarly, the symbols in Change act in two different, though related ways. On the one hand they deepen and widen awareness by introducing the mythic or archetypal background, thus activating the powers of the myth-mind. On the other hand, they give specific advice about which things are helpful and which are dangerous in a given situation. They do this through a set of divinatory terms or signs.

The primary signs are 'Wise Words! The Way is open' (*ji*) and 'Trap! The Way is closed' (*xiong*). The first portrays words coming from the mouth of a sage-person that point the way to the experience of meaning and good fortune and release transformative energy. The second term portrays a pit or trap, where you are cut off from the flow of spirit and left open to danger. This is an open mouth ready to eat you! A second important term is *fu*, meaning there is a 'connection to the spirits that will carry you through'. This term assembles a wide range of meanings, from blessing and prosperity through enlisting spirit aid to taking captives. It has the quality of being sincere and trustworthy. The term *jiu*, mistake, often used in the phrases 'no mistake' or 'this is not a mistake', refers to trouble caused by faulty action and faulty awareness. Distress, *lin*, describes the shame and confusion of having lost the right Way and a consequent desire for improvement. 'Cause for sorrow', *hui*, often seen in the phrases 'no cause for sorrow' or 'the cause for sorrow disappears', points at an action or attitude that will bring misfortune and unhappiness. It includes the sense of repenting, or becoming aware of conduct that has led to unhappiness. Adversity, *lin*, means danger and hardship, particularly the danger caused by 'hungry souls and angry ghosts', things that return from the past to haunt you. This danger must usually be faced, endured or exorcised. 'Step into the Great Stream', *she da chuan*, refers to stepping into the Stream of Life with a purpose, to begin a great enterprise or set out on an adventure. The term chastising, *zheng*, refers to enforcing discipline or punishing people and to setting out on a campaign or expedition, usually with the aim of reducing things to order.

Finally, there is the set of four divinatory terms *yuan heng li zhen*, referred to earlier on pages 4–8, that are found throughout the texts in various combinations. When they appear together, they are translated as 'Source of Success: Advantageous Trial' or divination. Source, *yuan*, means great, very much, potent, the head of a river and the source of thoughts, spring, the east and sunrise. It also occurs in the phrase *yuan ji*, the 'Way to the Source is open'. Success, *heng*, also translated as 'Make an offering and you will succeed', refers to achievement through offering a sacrifice, to ripening and maturity, to things that are vigorous and effective, summer, the south and the full light of day. It spreads and increases the effects of the spirit. Advantageous, *li*, refers to autumn and harvesting. It indicates what is beneficial, profitable, what will yield both a good outcome and insight into things, a base for incisive action. It often occurs in a phrase that indicates a given action will be of benefit to everything and everyone concerned, 'nothing not advantageous', *wu wu li*. Trial, *zhen*, refers to the act of divination and putting your ideas to the test. It is connected with winter and finding the hidden seed or kernel, the pearl. It is a term of highest value, the means of submitting your wishes to the judgement of the spirits. It also suggests what is proven, just and true.

## Encountering the Oracle

The answer to a question you pose to Change comes through one or more of the sixty-four figures and the web of interconnections it generates. These are the places you encounter the transformative power of the oracle, the voice of Change. The tradition of Change acts primarily as a help in making decisions. It reformulates your awareness of a situation, opening and deepening it, putting you in touch with the places where creative energy is active and available. Through the consultation process we interact with the hidden forces shaping the moment (*shi*) and discover the most efficacious ways to act. By imagining yourself and your situation through the symbols of the oracle you can redirect the manner in which you are thinking about things. The process creates Bright Spirit or intuitive clarity, called *shen ming*. It is 'finding the mind of the Way'. Remember, the purpose of any divination, with yourself or with others, is an expression of what the East calls compassion and skilful means. It aims at a release from unconscious or needless suffering through a recognition of the real situation and the forces at work in it, and seeks to offer the means, the tools and strategies to effect this.

## Description of a Divinatory Figure

The various sections of a divinatory figure (*xiang* or *gua*) in this version of *Yijing* all have a function. They are drawn from various traditional and modern sources, re-imagined in the light of old divinatory practices. Here is a brief description of the sections and how they might be used.

The Paradigm combines two figures, seeing them as an interconnected whole that expresses a particular theme. They embody the interaction between 'inspiration and manifestation', or seed and fruit, the actions of the two Primal Powers. This thinking in terms of pairs is quite old and suggests that the interconnected lines of the figures (1 and 6, 2 and 5, 3 and 4, 4 and 3, 5 and 2, 6 and 1) should be read together. This matrix generates the Nodes and includes the Shadow site, which acts as a Mirror World for the Primary reading.

Look at the Pair to locate yourself in this dynamic, to get a sense of the overriding themes or model of the time, and to see more deeply into its connection with other periods of your life. The text for the Pair is from the Tenth Wing, *Zagua* or Contrasting Diagrams, a collection of brief mnemonic phrases that relate two figures. It is combined with the first and second generation Nuclear Figures, *Hogua*, the Hidden Possibilities. The graph and character for each figure is placed to the left or right of the page to indicate its place in a pair, as 'inspiration' or 'manifestation'.

The 'Name' is the traditional name or 'tag' of the figure that expresses its overall field of meaning, found in *Zhouyi*, the old divinatory text. It is coupled with the 'keywords', a set of meanings from the contexts of the name that 'key' its action.

The 'Myths for Change: The Story of the Time' are an assembly of many old and new sources on myth, religious practices and rituals (see bibliography). They are meant to provide a reading in depth of the basic situation, linking it to spiritual and ritual practices and a wide range of early word meanings. They invest the situation with an imaginative depth, activating deep layers of the imagination.

Simply let these resonate and gradually affect your perception of your situation and its importance in your inner life.

The 'Charge to the Oracle' given in *italics* comes from what is traditionally called the Sequence, the Ninth Wing, *Xugua*. In keeping with old divinatory practice, this is seen as a 'charge' that activates the oracle's 'search engine', pointing at a situation that has been exhausted and focusing on a particular energy that is necessary to its further development.

'The Response' comes from the oldest layers of the text, the *Zhouyi*. This is the central oracular response, describing a field of actions and perceptions inherent in the nature of the time (*shi*). It includes the fields of meaning for the Name and a paraphrasing commentary. This commentary is a guide to direct practical action.

'The Scholar Speaks' is from the commentary parts of the First and Second Wings, *Tuanzhuan*, a later amplification of the significance of the words of the Response that includes an analysis of the actions of the strong and supple lines. This prose paraphrase also repeats key phrases from the other commentary sections.

'The Shaman Speaks' is based on the Third and Fourth Wings, *Xiangzhuan*, which describe a figure in terms of the interaction of the symbols (*xiang*) of the inner (*zhen*) and outer (*hui*) trigrams. It reflects this symbolic interaction in a stance to be taken by the Noble One, the Realising Person or *junzi*. The *italic* phrase that begins the commentary comes from the old 'sequence of the trigrams' in *Shuogua*, the Eighth Wing. The commentary relates the interaction of the trigrams through material from *Shuogua* and connects them to the *wuxing*, the Five Processes or Moments. Use this to analyze the tension between the inner and outer aspects of your situation and to reflect on what a 'noble person' might effectively do to further the movement of the Way.

'Transforming (*bian*) Lines' are the *yao* or *yaoci*, the 'crossings' of Heaven and Earth from the *Zhouyi*, the old divinatory text. *Italic* sections that begin each commentary are from the later *Xiangzhuan*, the Third and Fourth Wings. The *Direction* is formed from the Relating Figure for a specific line change and the resulting Nuclear Figures, indicating a general tendency or potential associated with the change of the line. The lines show the precise points of change, the potential significance of actions taken at these 'crossings' where Heaven and Earth are generating change. This is meant to give you specific advice on action, non-action and strategy, often by pointing out a myth or ritual point that is the 'ancestor' of the situation. Reflect on the possibilities they suggest, look at the divinatory signs and the line with which they are paired.

## A Guide to Using the Oracle of Change

- Find a quiet place. Gently still your mind. Set out the materials you have chosen to use for the consultation. (Consultation methods are described on pages 66–8.) A traditional image for this is to imagine yourself in a little wooden boat, floating on the calm blue sea. You gently float farther and farther out until no land is in sight.
- Consider your question. (You can find help on making a question on pages 65–6.) Reflect on what is involved, your hopes and fears, anxieties and desires, memories and experiences. Formulate the question as clearly as possible, based on what you need to know. Consider the words carefully. Write it down.
- Using whatever technique you have chosen, create the six lines of your Primary Figure. Record them, from bottom to top. See page 68 for the techniques.
- If there are any transforming lines, generate the Relating Figure. Then find the number of your hexagrams in the Key at the end of the book.
- If you need a quick, concise answer, turn to the texts of your hexagrams and read the sections 'Paradigm', 'Name/Keywords', 'Response' and 'Transforming Lines'. Read only the first sections of the Relating Figure.
- If you want to go further into the situation or want help in understanding a complex answer or insight into a particular aspect, read and meditate on the sections 'Myths for Change', 'The Scholar Speaks' and 'The Shaman Speaks' and create the interpretive layout described in the section on Tools (see page 45–7).
- When you first read the texts, you will probably experience a flash of sudden insight often followed by a sense of confusion. Dwell on this for a moment and let the reading of the texts deepen. Consider the many ways in which they might match your situation (*dang*). Consider the Tools and their possible meanings. Let the images and interconnections turn and roll in your heart, your intuitive and imaginative heart-mind. 'Then suddenly the Way will arise.'

- As the connections become clearer, move towards distilling their meanings into a simple phrase or image from the texts. These images can act as a key to on-going reflection and a guide to action. You can repeat and reflect on them as you proceed into the situation invoked by your question or when you confront a difficult decision or critical interaction. The oracle was created to help you navigate these times, when a change of heart is possible.

# THE DIVINATORY
## FIGURES

# Book I: Foundations

# 1 and 2: The Paradigm

### The Gates of Change: Dragon and Dark Animal Goddess

This Pair involves you in a model of thought and action elaborated in the interconnected lines of the figures: the action of the two Primal Powers, the Two-Leafed Gate of Change, as they shape the key transitions in our lives. Carefully consider your place in and relation to this model.

*Hidden Possibilities*: 1:2, you are connected to the interaction of the primal seeds.

The Pair creates sites of creative transformation at 7:8 (Armies and New Group), 9:10 and 13:14 (Ceremonies at the Outskirts Altar) and 15:16 (Activating Liminal Powers to Prepare the Future). The zone of radical change between the figures moves through 43:44 (Announcing the Omen and the Lady of Fate) and 23:24 (Stripping and Returning).

Look at the ages and events these figures suggest for personal connections.

7:8 9:10 (11:12) 13:14 15:16          23:24          43:44

*Shadow site*: 63:64, The Crossings: 'Burning Water'

**Force means being strong. Field means being supple.**

# 1 Inspiring Force/ Dragon QIAN

**Creative energy; persist, create, endure; power to guide and inspire, dynamic and enduring; daimon, protection of the ancestors; the 'key', the male sexual organ; a Gate of Change and a primal seed.**

Myths for Change: The Story of the Time

**Charge to the Oracle:** *Heaven and Earth exist without beginning or end. This is the primal power of inspiration. Use it as a spirit helper.*

Force is part of a pair that forms two of the 'gates' of Change. Inspiring Force, the Dragon, represents inspiration, a shape-changer at once inner and outer that constantly breaches natural reality. The Dragon's inspiring force rises in the heavens as the constellation Cerulean Dragon, who initiates and presides over the growing season. He connects with the Bin (Dipper), where *Shang Di* resides and dispenses the fates of all creatures. His weaving body surrounds us as lifelines in the landscape through which energy flows and as inner imagery, an inexhaustible source of transformation. He rises within us, a mysterious vital force moving and circulating through the subtle body. Dragon/Force is the actualizing potential between seen and unseen, the inspiration in a work of art, the dynamic language of the myth-world. He is connected with the Great Person, the deep personality in all of us, and with the diviners and sages who can help us realise this force. He promotes seeing or visualizing: becoming aware, connecting with inner images, being struck and moved by Inspiring Force.

The Dragon is the central symbol on the bronze sacrificial vessels that offer food to honour the dead and provide the sacred meal where humans and spirits join. As the Beast Face (*shou mian*), he presides over the language of the spirit world and the six places of Change, the animal masks and ritual dance transformations. His earliest image may be the two Staring Eyes found on sacrificial objects and writing from earliest times, signifying the awesome power of the Other, the Ancestor.

乾 ☰

Dragon is a realising spirit-image, gate to the unseen, mediator and conductor of blessings. He is tireless creative energy, shape-changing, inspiring and creating dynamic harmony. He is dangerous. He is a Tiger. He brings deep abiding joy. In the body, Dragon or Force acts through the lungs, skin and nervous system, regulating the rhythm of life, making energy descend and disperse. He connects the surface with the central nervous system, using sexual stimulation and the power of inner images.

## THE RESPONSE

**Inspiring Force. The Dragon.**

**The Source of Success: an Advantageous Trial. Harvesting.**

**Make an offering and you will succeed.**

**Inspiring Force/Dragon,** QIAN: spirit, creative energy, active transforming power, inspiration; the 'key', the male sexual organ and masculine drive; activate, animate, command and guide; strong, tenacious, untiring, firm, stable; *also*: destroy, dry up, exhaust, clear away, clean out. Dragon is the rainmaker, the yang force awakening life. He suggests the abysmal waters where the sunbirds bathe and the Sun Tree or World Tree from which they fly. He is gate to the unseen world of spirit, the dark bird who is the ancestor of dynasties, and the One, the origin, and principle of fate in all the Myriad Beings. The old character shows the graphs for sun at dawn, a three-leafed sprout and lush vegetation and energy flowing from Sky that disperses and spreads to nourish the All-Under Heaven.

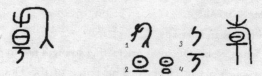

QIAN (1621/5) is composed of 1 YAN[3], hanging vegetation, jungle (1) DAN[4], dawn, the sun just above the horizon (2) and YI[3], vapours or breath (3).

Force/Inspiring describes your situation in terms of the primal power of spirit to create and destroy. Its symbols are the inspiring power of Heaven, the light of the sun that causes everything to grow, the fertilizing rain and the creative energy of the Dragon that breaks through boundaries. You are confronted with many obstacles. The way to deal with them is to persist, for you are in contact with fundamental creative energy. Take action. Be dynamic, strong, untiring, tenacious and enduring. Continue on your path and don't be dismayed. Ride the power of the Dragon and bring the fertilizing rain. Your situation contains great creative potential. It can open up a whole new cycle of time.

## THE SCHOLAR SPEAKS

The hexagram figure shows creative force in action. Heaven moves and persists. This spirit power is available to you. Use it as a source of strength and determination in order to continue on without pause. This great force is the beginning of things. As the clouds spread and the rain falls, all things flow into their shapes. It shows you the end that brings a new beginning, the way energy moves in the world and the proper time to accomplish something. If you become aware of its movement, you can ride this energy in its six different shapes, the six lines of the hexagram, as if they were six dragons. The Way of Force is to change and transform things. It makes the innate spirit within each being manifest. This protects the great harmony of the world. Take advantage of it. Use this creative energy to produce ideas that inspire people and give them models of transformation. Bring together what belongs together. What you create can be the source of a deep and self-renewing peace of mind.

## THE SHAMAN SPEAKS

**Heaven moves and persists.**

**A time when Noble One uses originating strength not to pause.**

*Spirit awes and wars in Heaven.* The Force of the Dragon, the spark of yang born at the centre of the yin. The dynamic tension of this great energy binds opposing forces together. This is the Metal Moment, destroying old forms and creating enduring new relations. The ideal Realising Person reflects this, continually using the power of the origin to revitalize and invigorate his creative efforts.

### INITIAL NINE

**Inspiring Force. Immersed Dragon, don't use it!**

*The spirit power is located below.* Midwinter, dusk. The star-dragon is dormant in the underworld waters. The situation feels confused and uncertain. You would like to take hold and set it right. Don't do it yet. The creative energy is still under water. But have no fear. It will soon emerge.

*Direction:* Have no doubts. You are coupled with a creative force.

### NINE AT SECOND

**Inspiring Force. See the Dragon in the fields!**

**Advantageous to see the Great People. Harvesting.**

*Power and virtue is spreading throughout.* Early spring. The Dragon's horns are visible above the horizon. Creative energy emerges into the lower centre. You have the ability to realise things now. Take the advice of people you know. Seek those who connect you to the great spirits and trust what is great in yourself.

*Direction:* Bring people together. Give them a goal. You are coupled with a creative force.

### NINE AT THIRD

**Noble One completes the day,**

**using the Inspiring Force again and again.**

**At night come alarms and adversity, hungry souls and angry ghosts.**

**This is not a mistake.**

*The Way reverses and returns.* This is a transitional time of incessant activity, plagued by practical and emotional problems. Old ghosts come back to haunt you. Don't worry. This is a very important change and creative energy is available to you. Turn your back on the past and commit yourself to the new. This marks the return of the Way in your life.

*Direction:* Make your way step by step. Find supportive people. Gather energy for a decisive new move.

### NINE AT FOURTH

**Inspiring Force. 'Someone' is playing in the Primal Abyss.**

**This is not a mistake.**

*This means advancing without fault.* Late spring. The Dragon's neck and loops of his body appear above the horizon. Creative energy emerges in the heart centre. Even though you are dealing with big issues, don't lose the playful spirit. Joy is the key to creation in this situation. You are mingling with the Source. Don't get frozen into a single stance.

*Direction:* Accumulate small things to build the great. Gather your ghosts. Turn conflict into creative tension. The situation is already changing.

### NINE AT FIFTH

**Inspiring Force. Flying Dragon in the Heavens.**

**Advantageous to see the Great People. Harvesting.**

*The Great Person is creating.* Midsummer. The Dragon appears, bright against the dark night sky. Spread your wings. Let your creative power emerge. You receive energy and guidance. Now is the time to build something enduring. Seek those who connect you to the Great Spirits and trust what is great in you.

*Direction:* The mandate is changing. This begins a fertile time, rich with warmth and light. Be resolute. You are connected with a creative force.

### NINE ABOVE

**Inspiring Force. Overbearing Dragon, head in the gully.**

**There is cause for sorrow.**

*This means what is overfull cannot last.* Autumn's beginning. The Dragon's head disappears below the horizon. The autumn rains arrive. The creative cycle is ending. Do not keep on pushing. This would be a misuse of creative energy. The time is changing and the Force withdraws into the receptive field. If you try to go on without it, you will certainly have something to be sorry about.

*Direction:* Resolve to do better. Hear the omen. You are connected to a creative force.

# 2 *Field/Yielding*
## *KUN*

**Earth Altar; nourish, provide for; gentle, receptive, welcoming; give all things form; the Dark Animal Goddess and her divinatory tradition; the 'flow', the female sexual organ; Gate of Change and a primal seed.**

MYTHS FOR CHANGE: THE STORY OF THE TIME

**Charge to the Oracle:** *Heaven and Earth exist without beginning or end. This is the primal power of realization. Use it as a spirit helper.*

Field is part of a pair that forms two of the 'gates' of Change. Field/Yielding supplies security and brings things to a good end through the Mare. She is autumn, harvest, the River-Mountain marriage ceremonies, military expeditions and sacrifices at the Earth Altar, home of the spirit that protects, assures fertility and harvest and wards off disaster. From this centre, sacrifice is offered to River and the underworld waters and to Mountain, who connects with Heaven and the Four Directions, the 'four sides' or Hidden Lands of the square field of Earth. An age-old tradition underlies this, the tradition of the Dark Animal Goddess or Valley Spirit that goes back into the Neolithic, often symbolized as jade and jade objects. It suggests *Nu Gua*, the one who made our bodies and the Two, the Couple who protect us. The Way-Power Classic says:

> The Valley Spirit never dies. It is named Dark Animal Goddess. The door of the Dark Animal Goddess is called the Root of Heaven and Earth. Like an endless thread she endures. You can call upon her easily. He who has found this mother understands he is a child. When he understands he is her child and clings to her. He will be without danger when the body dies.

This Goddess carries an ancient heritage of symbols. The Mother of the World (*Tianxia Mu*), so quiet and so empty, acts through these images and seeds to give security and refuge to all creatures. She is the divine, clairvoyant something of the Woman's Way.

*Kun*/Field opens, yields and enfolds all things. She is the flow, the provider, welcome everywhere, the opening that receives the seed of Force. Her hands give blessings. She receives the dead. She is the Mare roaming the earth tirelessly. In the body, Field acts through the spleen and stomach, stabilizing and transforming nourishment. She rots and ripens, governs the free flow of ideas, controls and protects central energy.

## THE RESPONSE

**Field. Source of Success: Advantageous Trial through the Mare.**

**Make an offering and you will succeed.**

**Noble One has a direction to go.**

**'First you lose the Way, then you acquire it.'**

**Advantageous to find a Lord. Harvesting.**

**'Acquire partners in Southwest, lose partners in Northeast.'**

**Trial: You are safe and secure. Wise Words! The Way is open.**

**Field/Yielding, *KUN*:** the earth, the world, space, concrete existence, the power to give things form and existence; moon, mother, wife, belly, servants, ministers; supple, adaptable, receptive, yielding; welcome, consent, respond to, agree, follow; give birth to, bear fruit; nourish, provide for, serve, work. The old character shows the tree at the Earth Altar and two hands making sacrifice to the Ghost River. In its oldest version it is a double spiral, symbol of the primordial waters and rhythm of birth and death.

$KUN^1$ (6477/32) is composed of $TU^3$, earth, an earth altar (1) and $SHEN^1$, spirit, ghost, power of expression (2).

Field describes your situation in terms of the primal power to nourish and give things form. Its symbols are the Earth, the moon, the mother, the devoted servant, and the Mare. You are confronted with many conflicting forces. The way to deal with them is to yield to each thing, nourishing it and providing what it needs to exist. You are in contact with the fundamental power to give things form. This will yield results. It will open up a whole new cycle of time. At first you will be confused by the profusion of things. Keep your sense of purpose. Do whatever presents itself to be done without judging it. This brings profit and insight. You can acquire what you desire and achieve mastery. Join with others in concrete projects, and look to the future, the southwest. Let go of the past, the northeast, but don't shirk your own responsibility in the moment of lonely trial. Put your ideas to the trial. Remain calm and assured. Don't take the lead. This generates meaning and good fortune by releasing transformative energy.

## THE SCHOLAR SPEAKS

The hexagram figure shows an enduring power to yield and serve. The potency of Earth. Let your power to realise things be so generous that it carries everything that approaches you. Field gives birth. It yields and receives. Its power to accept and give things form is unlimited. Reflect this through your generosity. Cherish each thing so its essential quality shines through. Accept it and help it grow. Identify yourself with the Earth. Be fertile and tireless. Move without drawing boundaries. Use the oracle to stay in touch with the Way. At first you will be confused and let go of the Way. Don't be worried by your confusion. Through yielding sincerely to each thing, you will acquire a new set of rules. Joining with people on concrete projects can help you. Letting go of the past as you bring things to completion will bring rewards. Put your ideas to the trial. Remain calm and quiet. Accept hidden processes and energies. Don't define things by setting up boundaries.

## THE SHAMAN SPEAKS

**The potency of Earth. Field.**

**A time when Noble One uses munificent power to carry all the beings.**

*Offer service at the Earth Altar.* The broad Field of Earth yields and brings forth what sustains us, the spark of yin born at the centre of the yang. This is the Earth Moment, common labour that produces concrete results through service. The ideal Realising Person reflects this by yielding to its power and extending its benefits to all.

## TRANSFORMING LINES: CHANGE AT WORK

### INITIAL SIX

**Field. Treading the frost culminates in hardening ice.**

**The marriage time.**

*Yin begins to stabilize. Yield and follow its Way.* The marriage time and the River-Mountain festival. Things solidify and take form out of the watery mass of feelings. Act slowly, carefully and persistently to build a base.

*Direction*: Something important is returning. Provide what is needed.

### SIX AT SECOND

**Field. Straight, to the Four Sides and Great. The Ancestor's Eyes.**

**No need to repeat or rehearse.**

**Nothing not advantageous.**

*Straightening the four sides, the Way of Earth is shining.* Sacrifice at the Earth Altar. The time is ripe for military expeditions and harvests. Everything is correct and the ancestors are with you. Commit yourself fully. Go right to the point. You don't have to plan or rehearse anything. Everything is there. This connection will benefit everything in your life.

*Direction*: Organize your forces. This is the return of something great. Provide what is needed.

### SIX AT THIRD

**Field. Trial: a jade talisman, held in the spirit's mouth.**

**A containing beauty that empowers.**

**If someone follows the King's service,**

**The time of no accomplishment comes to an end.**

*Use this season to shoot forth. You will know the Great shining.* Act through a design that contains and conceals. This is the place of hidden excellence. The spirits hold you. If you don't succumb to the need to accomplish something immediately, you can bring all your plans to a beautiful completion. Think of what is distant. This is a far-reaching time with far-reaching effects.

*Direction*: Keep your words clear and close to the facts. Release bound energy. The situation is already changing.

### SIX AT FOURTH

**Field. Bundled in the bag. The fertile chaos.**

**Without fault, without praise.**

*Careful consideration won't harm you.* Grain in bags, hidden potentials, and Old Mr Hundun, the originating chaos. The situation is pregnant with possibilities. There is nothing to blame or praise, for what you want is already there.

*Direction*: Build reserves of strength for future joy. Re-imagine the situation. Gather energy for a decisive new move.

### SIX AT FIFTH

**Field. Yellow lower garments.**

**Wise Words: The Way to the Source is open.**

*This is the central pattern.* Rites at the Hidden Temple in the presence of the First Ancestor and Great Intermediary. There are processes at work that open the way to enduring connections. Accept them, even though things may look confusing. Have patience and trust. What is happening now will affect you deeply and positively. This will be the source of great good fortune and meaningful events.

*Direction*: Change your group. Strip away your old ideas. Be open and provide what is needed.

### SIX ABOVE

**Field. Dragons grapple in the countryside.**

**Their blood flows down, indigo and yellow.**

*The old way is exhausted.* The dragons struggle and mate at the border of sky and the Earth, and the rains flow down. The new time is coming. Yield, give way, restore the peace. Do not try to dominate the situation.

*Direction*: Strip away your old ideas. Be open and provide what is needed.

# 3 and 4: The Paradigm

### The World Tree: Sprouting and Nurturing the New

This Pair involves you in a model of thought and action elaborated in the interconnected lines of the figures: conception and secret growth in the womb, the 'covered sky'. It prepares the change of the Mandate of Heaven and the emergence of a new guiding figure. Carefully consider your place in and relation to this model.

*Hidden Possibilities*: 23:24 > 2, stripping away the old and the return of the spirit opens the primal power of realization.

The Pair exchanges information with 7:8 (Armies and New Group). It is motivated by 41:42 (The Offering and the Blessing). The centre and threshold lines relate the process to 17:18 (Following the Spirit and Renovating the Ancestral Images), 23:24 (Stripping the Corpse and The Returning Spirit), 59:60 (Dissolution and Articulation) and 63:64 (The Crossings).

Look at the ages and events these figures suggest for personal connections.

7:8      17:18    23:24      41:42      59:60 (61:62) 63:64

*Shadow site*: 61:62, The Opened Heart and The Flying Bird

**Sprouting means it appears, but does not leave its dwelling. Enveloping means this disorder is a conspicuous sign.**

# ♆ ☰☷ 3 *Sprouting/The World Tree* ZHUN

Begin, establish, found; seek a bride; birth pains, massing soldiers; gather your strength to surmount difficulties; the World Tree.

## MYTHS FOR CHANGE: THE STORY OF THE TIME

**Charge to the Oracle:** *First there is Heaven and Earth, then the Myriad Beings truly give birth, overfilling the space between Heaven and Earth. This truly means the Myriad Beings. Accept this and use the energy of Sprouting. Sprouting means that the beginning is truly giving birth.*

Sprouting is the beginning of new being, the renewal of the time. It is the dusk before dawn, and the dusky light is full of the burgeoning grasses. Sprouting suggests the World Tree. It is the Mulberry or Sun Tree (*Fu Sang*) from which the suns rise each day after being bathed by their mother, and its shadow, the Moon Tree, where they rest and begin their underwater journey of return. Each tree has a bathing pool, an abyss, at its root that is connected to the Ghost River. Together they form The Tree, the axis and centre of the world that connects Heaven, Earth and the watery underworld, the Yellow Springs. This *axis mundi* and tree of kings is also imaged as a procession of riders going to fetch brides called 'sprouts' and the massing of soldiers, a gathering force in the Kingdom of Zhou to receive the Mandate of Heaven and establish a new world order. All these things are in their beginnings, the beginning of a new world and a new time.

## THE RESPONSE

Sprouting and Massing.

The Source of Success: an Advantageous Trial.

Make an offering and you will succeed.

Do not use having a direction to go.

Advantageous to install lords as helpers. Harvesting.

**Sprout**, ZHUN: Begin or cause to grow; assemble, accumulate, amass, hoard; establish a base of operations, establish troops at the borders, military camp, garrison, troop; difficult, painful, arduous; to become manifest, the difficulties at the beginning of an endeavour; sacred turtle divination: 'great protection', 'great happiness', the ancestors extend their blessings; riders bunching and gathering, the procession to fetch the bride; *also*: spring, vitality, the internal river of strength, the spark of life, water containing creative force; the murmuring dragon, thunder in the waters, the beginning of spring. The old character shows a deeply rooted sprout that is emerging through the surface of earth.

ZHUN[1] (11813/45) is a picture of a sprouting seedling. (1) shows other forms of the same character that also suggest a child.

Sprouting and Massing describes your situation in terms of beginning growth. The way to deal with it is to assemble things and accumulate energy for a difficult yet exciting task. Like young plants breaking through the covering earth, this will open an entire new cycle of time. It is the tenderness of the sprout, so easy to crush yet capable of pushing through rock-hard ground, the inexorable power of the yielding path that reaches out towards Heaven. Don't try to impose your ideas or direct things. There are many new possibilities emerging. Take advantage of them by installing helpers and delegating responsibilities. Stake out your territory, establish bases of operation, assemble the troops, and collect your possessions. That brings profit and insight.

### THE SCHOLAR SPEAKS

The hexagram figure shows arousing new energy confronting unknown risks. Clouds and thunder. Strip away old ideas. Abundant new possibilities are being born. Stay where you are and let everything come into view. Set up structures and ideas that can weave things together. This is a stirring time. There is heavy work to be done. Things are full to overflowing. The atmosphere is the dusky light before daybreak. Things are coming at you from all sides. Don't try to soothe and pacify them. Install your helpers and give everything a place. This chaotic profusion is in accord with the time. It is the beginning of a new world.

## THE SHAMAN SPEAKS

Clouds and Thunder. Sprouting and Massing.

A time when Noble One uses the clan banners to group the kindred.

*The spirit that manifests in shake and thunder rewards those toiling in the Pit. The Rouser works in the Ghost River. Rushing Water above dissolves direction and shape, while Thunder rouses new potential. This is Water over Wood: a cycle ends in the outer world while new growth sprouts within. The ideal Realising Person reflects this by setting out the standards that give each kind a place in the new world. Work through rousing and inspiring. A cycle is beginning. It will deliver you from past sorrows.*

## TRANSFORMING LINES: CHANGE AT WORK

### INITIAL NINE

Sprouting. A stone pillar.

The riders wheel and turn.

Trial: advantageous for a residence. Harvesting.

Advantageous to install lords as helpers.

*Your purpose is moving correctly. Value what is below. The Great acquires support of the common people.* This is the standing stone in front of an ancestral temple, sprouted from the Earth. Stop and establish your foundations. Connect this experience to your own deep roots. Involve other people. Don't be secretive about your plans. You are on the right track.

*Direction*: Find the new group. Strip away old ideas. Provide what is needed.

### Six at Second

**Sprouting then quitting, bunching and turning,**

**riding the horses in full array.**

**Those you confront are not outlaws, seek a marriage alliance.**

**Trial: the woman will not yet nurse a child.**

**Ten years, then she will nurse one.**

*The hardship of riding a strong line. This will reverse the rules.* You reach out to people, then turn away from them. You are all prepared for an emotional encounter then see your partner as an outlaw. Drop the hostility. Seek a permanent connection. It will be a while before this connection bears fruit, but in the end all will come right.

*Direction:* Articulate your needs and desires. Take in the past. Provide what is needed.

### Six at Third

**Sprouting. 'Chasing the deer' without precaution or guide,**

**You wander alone into the forest centre.**

**Noble One almost fails to realise that going on like this brings distress.**

*Following the wild birds, the young girls. This means distress and exhaustion.* 'Chasing the deer' has definite sexual implications. You are losing yourself, following your impulses and desires without a second thought. You are right on the edge of disaster. Stop now before you lose sight of what is really worthwhile.

*Direction:* The situation is already changing.

### Six at Fourth

**Sprouting. Bunching and turning,**

**Riding the horses in full array.**

**Seek a marriage alliance.**

**Wise Words! Going on opens the Way.**

**Nothing not advantageous. Harvesting.**

*Going and seeking. This is brightening!* The time is right. The difficulties are over. Those you confront are not outlaws. Make the connection. This will be of great benefit to everyone concerned.
*Direction*: Follow this flow of events. Proceed step by step. Gather energy for a decisive new move.

### NINE AT FIFTH

**Sprouting: its juice.**

**Reward of food for the soldiers.**

**Trial for the Small: Wise Words! The Way is open.**

**Trial for the Great: Trap! The Way closes.**

*This is spreading out but not yet shining.* This is the essence of growth, the flowing sap or juice of the World Tree. It brings things to life and spreads the wealth. You have found this source of vital growth but you must be careful. Make no great moves. Adapt to what happens. Make sure everything gets what it needs. Don't impose your will on things.
*Direction*: Something important is returning. Be open to it. Provide what is needed.

### SIX ABOVE

**Sprouting. Turning and bunching.**

**Riding the horses in full array,**

**While weeping blood is coursing down.**

*Why let this last?* This is a disastrous way to proceed. It is a fixation that is doing you real harm, bleeding you in literal and emotional ways. Don't think you can simply fix it. Free yourself from the situation now before it gets worse.
*Direction*: A better time is coming. Strip away your old ideas and be open to new ones. Provide what is needed.

# 4 Enveloping/ Royal Maiden MENG

**Immature, unaware, foolish, the 'foolish youth'; hidden, concealed; a magic plant called Royal Maiden; nurture hidden growth; a foetus in the womb.**

MYTHS FOR CHANGE: THE STORY OF THE TIME

**Charge to the Oracle**: *All being as it gives birth must be enveloped. Accept this and use the energy of enveloping. Enveloping means being immature.*

The basic image of Enveloping is 'covered sky', something veiled and hidden. It is hidden growth protecting a secret gift from the spirit. Enveloping suggests dreaming and the womb, rites of passage and initiations, hidden secrets, oracle consultation, fraud and hidden magic. It points at the entrance of souls into the world, 'fixing' (*heng*) the souls from the Ghost River, and to nurturing a hidden mandate, a command from the spirit. It suggests the growth of a sage or an Intermediary, a *wu*, with great inner power. A major metaphor for this is the parasitic plant known as Royal Maiden (in English, the Dodder) and the process whereby it is gathered and prepared for use. Royal Maiden was thought to appear spontaneously and be a sign of spirit presence. It was gathered and used by the *wu* or spirit dancers in rituals and marriage preparations. Its appearance is also an image of the foetus growing in the womb.

The line 'I do not seek the foolish youth. The foolish youth seeks me' may be a ritual disclaimer against violating the Royal Maiden or an insistence on the respect due to the oracle. It also has a deliberate historical allusion. It is a comment by the Noble Jizi, mentioned in Figure 36 as an image of hidden virtue, lamenting the fall of the Shang. It points at a great hidden secret, the particular moment when the Numinous Turtle informed the Shang that the Mandate of Heaven had been withdrawn and they would no longer receive answers from the spirits through the oracle. Enveloping represents this change. It is a secret event of great import, necessitating hidden process, magic ritual and nurturing through inner awareness. This is represented by the veiled or covered sky. It suggests the preparation of the numinous plant, the hidden messages of the oracle, inner development and the education of the young.

## THE RESPONSE

> Enveloping. The Royal Maiden. Make an offering and you will succeed.
>
> 'I did not seek the foolish youth, the foolish youth sought me.'
>
> At the first consultation, there is a notification: 'the old time is ending'.
>
> You ask two and three times and it is obscured.
>
> When things are obscured, there is no longer a notification,
>
> Advantageous Trial for the 'foolish youth'. Harvesting.

**Envelop,** MENG: cover, hide, conceal, veiled, hidden; lid, covering, womb, hidden growth; dull, unaware, ignorant; uneducated; young, undeveloped, fragile; presence of the unseen; trick, fool, deceive, cheat, fraud, hunters disguised in animal skins; occult, hidden mysteries; guile necessary at the beginnings of things; *also:* a parasitic and magical plant, the Royal Maiden. The old character shows the covered sky as a dwelling. Magical plants sprout from the roof while within is the pig sacrifice to the underworld and the hidden strength of jade. It suggests a hidden temple and nurturing hidden growth.

MÉNG² (7722) shows a pig or jade (3), a cover or roof (2) and plants (1).

Enveloping describes your situation in terms of staying under cover. You are immature and your awareness of the problem is dull and clouded. The way to deal with it is to accept being hidden in order to nurture growing awareness. Pull the covers over. Put the lid on. There is much concealed from you. You don't really know what you are doing. But the beginnings are definitely there, even if you can't yet see them. You didn't ask for this problem. It asked for you and it belongs with you. The first time you consult the oracle about this, it will advise and inform you. If you keep on asking, you muddy the waters. Accept that you are the foolish youth. Your awareness must grow and change. Put your ideas to the trial. That brings profit and insight. Keep working on your problem. It will educate you.

## THE SCHOLAR SPEAKS

The hexagram figure shows an outer obstacle that protects an inner source. Below the mountain a spring emerges. Energy is returning below. Turn back to meet it. The answer is already there, but it is immature and has to be protected. Enveloping means being immature. Don't pretend you know it already. Accept being visibly confused. Work on things gradually, like a plant bearing fruit. Aggressive action is blocked because this is the season for inner growth. The oracle confirms this. Don't keep asking the same question. Use your confusion to envelop your premature desire to act. What you see as an obstacle is there to nourish your awareness and correct your one-sided view of things. When you can really accept and understand this, you will most certainly become wise.

## THE SHAMAN SPEAKS

**Below Mountain, spring water issues forth. Enveloping.**

**A time when Noble One ripens the fruits, nurturing power and virtue.**

*The words of the spirit bind us and accomplish fate.* The Sacrificer works with the Ghost River. Mountain above articulates what is complete to suggest what is beginning, while Rushing Water below dissolves direction and shape. This is Earth over Water: an outer limit hides and shields the inner process. The idea Realising Person reflects this by ripening the hidden fruit that will actualize the Way. Make the sacrifice. A cycle is ending. Let the difficulties dissolve.

## TRANSFORMING LINES: CHANGE AT WORK

### INITIAL SIX

**Enveloping shoots forth.**

**'We dislodge the Royal Maiden.'**

**Advantageous to punish people. Harvesting.**

**Loose the fettered, shackled youth or going on brings distress.**

*This means correcting the laws.* You have to correct a far-reaching error. Be clear and discriminating with the people around you. Free the youthful energy that you are now confining. Simply going on will cover you with distress and confusion.

*Direction:* Decrease passionate involvement. Something important is returning. Be open and provide what is needed.

### NINE AT SECOND

**Enwrapped and Enveloped.**

**'We carry the Royal Maiden.' Wise Words! The Way opens.**

**Let in the wife.**

**This young son can control the dwelling.**

*This means articulating the strong and the supple.* Here being hidden and enveloped turns into caring for and protecting someone. It is time to take a wife and establish a dwelling. You have the ability to do this and the time is right.

*Direction:* Strip away your old ideas and be open to the new. Provide what is needed.

### SIX AT THIRD

**Enveloping. The Royal Maiden. Do not try to grasp this woman!**

**See her armoured husband. Do not try to possess her body!**

**There is no advantageous direction.**

*Do not yield to this impulse!* You are flirting with something that is beyond you. If you become personally involved with this, you will lose your independence and your capacity to express yourself. There is great danger. This is the bride of the King, who will defend her. There is nothing of value here for you. Do not try to grasp and hold on to it.

*Direction:* Renovate a corrupt situation. If you let yourself be led, you can realise hidden potential. The change is already underway.

### Six at Fourth

**Enveloping confined.**

**'We bundle the Royal Maiden.' Distress.**

*This is solitary and distant from the real.* You are locking your youthful spirit in a prison. You don't have to confine your affection and your insights so rigidly. This just leads to distress and confusion. You are cutting yourself off from what is real.

*Direction:* Gather energy for a decisive new move.

### Six at Fifth

**The 'foolish youth' Enveloped. Wise Words!**

**The Way is open.**

*Yielding and using subtle penetration.* King Wu, the great hero, is in hiding, awaiting the right time. This is the perfect way to deal with the situation. You have accepted your immaturity and the fact that there is something hidden in the situation. All will go well. The Way will open and lead to real connection and real understanding. Be patient and have faith.

*Direction:* Disperse obstacles to understanding. Take things in. Be open and provide what is needed.

### Nine Above

**Attacking the Enveloping.**

**'We beat the Royal Maiden!'**

**Not advantageous to act like an outlaw.**

**Advantageous to resist being an outlaw. Harvesting.**

*This means the above and the below must be yielding.* You are fighting against the very processes that, in the long run, will give you what you need. This is a time for inner work. Resist the temptation to act impulsively. The fruit will literally fall into your hand.

*Direction:* Use this time to organize yourself. Return to the source. Be open and provide what is needed.

# 5 and 6: The Paradigm

### In the Temple and the Council: Waiting for 'Visitors'

This Pair involves you in a model of thought and action elaborated in the interconnected lines of the figures: the spirit of the new and the risks involved as it manifests in the ritual and the legal world. Carefully consider your place in and relation to this model.

*Hidden Possibilities:* 38:37 > 64:63, the ghosts that haunt the dwelling. Prepare and make the crossing.

The Pair exchanges information with 47:48 (Oppressed Noble returns to Common Source). It is motivated by 9:10 (Gathering the Ghosts and Mating with the Spirit). The centre and threshold lines relate the process to 11:12 (New and Old King), 43:44 (Announcing the Omen, enter the Lady of Fates), 59:60 (Dissolution and Articulation) and 63:64 (The Crossings).

Look at the ages and events these figures suggest for personal connections.

9:10 11:12          43:44 (45:46) 47:48          59:60 (61:62) 63:64

*Shadow site:* 59:60, Dissolution of the old Self and
Articulating the new Times

**Attending means not advancing yourself.
Arguing means there are no connections.**

# 5 Attending/Service at the Sacrifice Xu

Wait for, wait on, attend to what is needed; wait for the right moment; the rainmakers, waiting for rain; service at a ritual.

## MYTHS FOR CHANGE: THE STORY OF THE TIME

**Charge to the Oracle**: *An immature being must be nourished. Accept this and use the energy of Attending. This means the way of eating and drinking and the sacred meal in the ancestral temple.*

With Attending the enveloped spirit enters the sacrificial and ritual world, the ceremonies that connect us with the spirits. It is the force activated by sacrifice and ritual at work, symbolized by the rites of rainmaking, and being stopped by rain. It is the positive waiting, the change in awareness involved in participating in a great ritual and awaiting the spirit visitors that are coming. The gap in time the ritual opens allows you to step into the Great Stream of existence. The root of the word Attending connects it with jade pendants and tablets and the jade disc *biyu* that represents a hole in Heaven and Earth, an entrance to paradise. It is an ancient jade object of great veneration that assures good harvest or provokes curses, the protector of temples and people, the illustrious long-past ancestors. It evokes a feminine, animating presence and a ritual mask. The water motif that runs through the lines evokes the master of the waters and the ways, the culture hero Yu the Great. It shows the capacity of humans, through attending on the rituals and symbols, to follow the Way of Heaven. Attending also evokes the moment of gathering force and energy before King Wu received the Mandate to set the armies marching into Shang. It means measuring a danger, confident it can be surmounted with the aid of the spirits. Its shadow is timidity, fear or needless striving.

Attending at the sacrifice: a connection to the spirits will carry you through. Shining success.

Make an offering and you will succeed.

Trial: Wise Words! the Way is open.

Advantageous to step into the Great Stream. Harvesting.

Attend, XU: Take care of, look out for, serve; necessary, need, call for; provide what is needed; wait for, hesitate; stopped by rain, wait for rain, confident while the clouds gather; know how to wait, have patience and focus; abundant, fall like rain; the River and Mountain spirits; *also:* a silk garment for the winter sacrifice. The old character shows rain falling from the clouds above and an old man, a sage, whose prayers bring the fertilizing water from Heaven.

XU[1] (4673/173) shows YU[3], rain, above and ER[2], a beard, below. Two older characters (1 and 2) suggest a man standing below rain and the rain falling.

Attending describes your situation in terms of waiting for and serving something. The way to deal with it is to find out what is needed and carefully wait for the right moment to act. You aren't in control of things, but in time you can provide what is needed. Act this way with confidence. You are connected to the spirits and they will carry you through. One day you will bring the rain. Look after things. Think about what is necessary. Illuminate the situation through repeated efforts. This is pleasing to the spirits. Through it they will give you success, effective power and the capacity to bring the situation to maturity. Put your ideas to the trial. That generates meaning and good fortune by releasing transformative energy. This is the right time to enter the stream of life with a goal or embark on a significant enterprise. That brings profit and insight.

## THE SCHOLAR SPEAKS

The hexagram figure shows an inner force confronting outer danger. Clouds mounting above Heaven. Turn potential conflict into creative tension. Attend wholeheartedly to the needs at hand. There is something immature in your situation that must be nourished. Eating and drinking together are in harmony with the Way. They serve to nourish the spirits. This is not a time to advance yourself, to champion a cause or climb a mountain. Spread repose and delight. Help leisure, peace of mind, pleasure and harmony permeate the situation like a banquet or feast. Have patience. Carefully yield to precedence and persist in your efforts. Don't think of your waiting and care as an exhausting burden. It is how you can act justly and righteously in this situation and connect what you are doing with the spirit above. It will bring you accomplishment and praise.

## THE SHAMAN SPEAKS

**Clouds above Heaven. Attending.**

**A time when Noble One feasts with friends to repose and delight in the spirits.**

*The spirit that wars in Heaven rewards those toiling in the Pit.* This is the Dragon and the Ghost River. Rushing Water above dissolves direction and shape, while Heaven toils below, a spark of yang born at the centre of the yin. It is Water over Metal: inner concentration that confronts outer danger through careful and joyous attending on events. The ideal Realising Person reflects this by joining with others to share in the sacred feast. Work through joyous words to bring spirit to expression.

## TRANSFORMING LINES: CHANGE AT WORK

### INITIAL NINE

**Attending at the Outskirts Altar.**

**Advantageous to fix the omen. Harvesting.**

**This is not a mistake.**

*Heavy going. Do not oppose it. This means not letting go of the ritual.* It feels like the spirit is far away, but underneath the connection is certain. Persevere! Don't lose patience. This is the great sacrifice used to call the dragon who brings the fertilizing rain. You are not making a mistake. Create a clear image of your goal.

*Direction*: Stay connected to the source of your values. Turn conflict into creative tension. The situation is already changing.

### NINE AT SECOND

**Attending on the sands as the waters recede.**

**There is the Small, talking.**

**Complete this. Wise Words! The Way opens.**

*The centre overflows. This means completing the ritual opens the Way.* Yu the Great is at work, creating the channels. The waters and the ghosts recede, revealing the sands beneath. You are closer to your goal, but the situation keeps shifting and all around you small voices chatter. They can't hurt you. Keep your eye on what is important and go through this. The way to the centre is opening.

*Direction*: The situation is already changing.

### NINE AT THIRD

**Attending in the bogs and swamps.**

**Danger. This will attract outlaws in the end.**

*This means calamity from without. Respectful consideration will not hurt anything now.* On the riverbank, ready to cross, you have gotten bogged down in negative feelings. You have lost the sense of attending or waiting on something precious. This leaves you vulnerable to attack and loss of what you care for. There is still time, so think it over. What did you do to create this unfortunate situation?

*Direction*: Set limits and articulate things. Take things in. Be open and provide what is needed.

### SIX AT FOURTH

**Attending in blood.**

**Get out of the cave where this begins!**

*Yield and hearken to this!* You are in immediate danger, about to become the victim of this sacrifice. Whatever you are doing, stop! Get out of the place where you are trapped. You can save things now if you will only listen.

*Direction*: Be resolute. Take action. You are connected to a creative force.

### Nine at Fifth

**Attending, drinking liquor and eating. The sacred meal.**

**Trial: Wise Words! The Way opens.**

*This is using the centre correctly.* You make the connection. This is the meal shared with the spirits, the ancestors and noble people. Let pleasure, harmony, peace and joy open the Way. Share what you have. Gather with others. This cheer brings you out of your isolation.

*Direction*: A fertile time is approaching. If you let yourself be led, you can realise hidden potential. The situation is already changing.

### Six Above

**Attending. Enter the cave. The 'visitors' come without urging.**

**There are three coming towards you now.**

**Respect them and bring this to completion. Wise Words! The Way opens.**

*This means that though the situation is not appropriate, you do not let go of the Great.* Though you are trying your best to work with the situation, you do not really know what to do. Don't worry. The spirits will arrive unexpectedly to help you. Go into the hidden centre of energy. There are three unannounced visitors coming who will show you the way. Respect them and the way to happiness will suddenly open.

*Direction*: Accumulate the small to achieve the great. Turn conflict into creative tension. The situation is already changing.

# 6 Dispute/Pleading/ Council SONG

Conflict, quarrels, arguments; plead your case before an authority, express what you feel; retreat from conflict, affirm loyalty; a lover's complaint.

## MYTHS FOR CHANGE: THE STORY OF THE TIME

**Charge to the Oracle:** *Eating and drinking at the shared meal necessarily brings out disputes. Resolve them. Accept this and use the energy of Arguing.*

With Dispute we enter the legal world of duties and laws designed to prevent personal conflict from becoming destructive of society, to establish loyalties and to create the union that enables people to use force collectively. Its root is words, a ritual announcement, a response from the oracle. It means to express, speak, swear, give and take orders. It is language charged with meaning that also suggests the pipes or flute used to set armies marching and send signals. Arguing is all forms of accusation and complaint, making a complaint against someone and contesting it before authority. It means to seek justice, plead a case, a lover's complaint, quarrels between the lords that are judged by the prince. It revolves around questions of loyalty and duty, bonds and struggles, oaths taken, fulfilled or neglected. It involves praise, persuasive speaking, and the necessity to submit personal matters to the authority of King and Heaven. Arguing also represents a council of war, and the ability to make war depends on the inner loyalties of the powers involved in the preparation. Connection to the spirits is necessary to any great endeavour and dissention, conflict or disloyalty blocks it. So the arguing words suggest both pleading a case and taking an oath. This may be the council in which the conflict between the Zhou and their overlords first emerged, leading King Wu to retreat and gather his vassals and allies preparatory to raising the armies to invade Shang.

## THE RESPONSE

Dispute. The connection to the spirits is blocked. Be wary.

Wise Words! Staying in the centre opens the Way.

Completing the conflict closes the Way. Trap!

Advantageous to see the Great People. Harvesting.

Not advantageous to step into the Great Stream.

Dispute/Pleading, SONG: quarrels, wrangles, controversy, disagreement that could develop into violence, struggle for power; dispute, plead your case, state your position; accuse, regret, blame; lodge a complaint, litigate, reprimand, contend in front of a judge, arrive at a judgement, resolve a conflict, encounter opposition and choose to use diplomacy; oaths and duties, loyalties; council of war; oppression. The old character shows a person's face with open mouth, meaning words, and sign for a high feudal lord.

SONG[4] (10136/149) is composed of a mouth (2) KOU[3] making a sound YAN[2] (1), and GONG[1], a high feudal lord, made up of BA[1] (3), divide, and private, SI[1] (4). It indicates the power to divide property and rights, also represented by a phallus (5).

Dispute describes your situation in terms of an argument. The way to deal with it is to clarify and actively express your viewpoint without trying to escalate the conflict. Act this way with confidence. You are linked to the spirits and they will carry you through. Present your case. Plead in court. Demand justice. Don't be afraid or intimidated. Be wary. Restrain your fear of authority. Don't give in, but don't exaggerate or get involved in petty wrangles. Staying in the centre will generate meaning and good fortune by releasing transformative energy. It is advantageous to see Great People. Visit those who are important and can give you advice. Try to become aware of the real purpose behind your desire. This will bring profit and insight. Don't try to bring your plans to completion. You would be cut off from the spirits and left open to danger. It is not the right time to embark on a significant enterprise or enter the stream of life with a purpose.

## The Scholar Speaks

The hexagram figure shows a struggle that lacks a solid base for action. Heaven combined with stream contradicts movement. Something new is being prepared. Stay inside your group. When many people eat and drink together, arguing will break out. This is not a harmonious time. It is full of people and ideas contradicting each other. Don't try to overcome all these things. Use the contradictions to stimulate and stir things up in order to plan the beginning of new activities. Go on arguing and see what it reveals. You are connected to the spirits and they will carry you through. Don't be afraid. By staying in the centre you will encounter what is strong and solid. Don't try to bring your plans to completion. The time is against it. Seeing Great People will help you clarify your own idea, but embarking on a significant enterprise now would be like jumping into an abyss. The great Stream of Life would become a whirlpool that drowns you.

## The Shaman Speaks

Heaven associates with Stream, contradictory movements. Dispute.

A time when Noble One arouses the desire to serve, planning new beginnings.

*Spirit inspires those toiling in the Pit as it awes and wars in Heaven.* This is the Dragon and the Ghost River. Heaven above struggles on, a spark of yang born at the centre of the yin, while Rushing Water below dissolves direction and shape. It is Metal over Water: with no solid inner base for action, struggle expresses itself through arguing words. The ideal Realising Person reflects this by arousing people's desire to aid and serve. Work through subtle penetration. This involves fate.

## Transforming Lines: Change at Work

### Initial Six

Dispute. This is not a place to prolong your service.

Use small words. Bring it to completion.

Wise Words! The Way opens.

*Arguing is not allowed to last. This means brightening your discrimination.* This is not the place for you to be of service. You will always be in conflict, discussing trivial affairs. Be done with it. Bow out gracefully and leave. The Way is open to you.
*Direction:* Proceed step by step. Find supportive friends. Gather energy for a decisive new move.

### NINE AT SECOND

**You cannot master this Dispute through pleading.**

**Change and escape to your capital,**

**To your people's three hundred doors.**

**This is not an error.**

*Change and escape, even sneak away. You reap the benefits when the distress is over.* You cannot win this fight, so change your plans. Go back to your own people, where the doors are open to you. Use any means necessary to effect your escape. This is not a mistake. When the distress comes to an end, your friends will seek you out.
*Direction:* Communication is blocked. Proceed step by step. Gather energy for a decisive new move.

### SIX AT THIRD

**Dispute. Eat the ancient power and virtue.**

**Trial: Wise Words! Complete the adversity, hungry souls and angry ghosts. The Way is open.**

**If someone follows a king's service, it will not be accomplished now.**

*Adhering to what is above opens the Way.* This is the scribe or diviner, eating his way through the ancestor's words to find the omen, the real call to action. To deal with this situation you need the power and the insight of the ancient sages. You are facing a horde of angry ghosts, things from the past that haunt you. Take heart and fight your way through, even though your social and business duties may suffer. This is the way to real union and accomplishment.
*Direction:* This is a fated encounter. It connects you with a creative force.

### NINE AT FOURTH

**Do not try to control this Dispute through pleading.**

**Return to the source, the Mandate is approaching.**

**'There will be changes.'**

**Trial: Wise Words! You are safe and secure. The Way is open.**

*This means not letting go of the return.* You cannot win this fight, so change your plans. Return to the source, disengage from the conflict. A great change of fate, a mandate, is approaching. The situation will deteriorate at first, but have no fear. You are secure. Stay quiet, accepting and peaceful. This is a crucial moment. Don't let go of this chance.

*Direction:* Clear up obstacles to understanding. Take things in. Be open to the new and provide what is needed.

### NINE AT FIFTH

**Dispute. Wise Words! Plead your case.**

**The Way to the Source is open.**

*This is using the centre and correcting.* Now is the time to convince people. State your case with clarity and confidence and expect positive results. This will resolve the situation and open the way to a much better time. The bonding that occurs now leads to great things.

*Direction:* Gather energy for a decisive new move.

### NINE ABOVE

**Dispute. You plead your case.**

**'Someone' bestows a leather belt.**

**Complete dawn three times and you will be deprived of it.**

*Arguing into acceptance and submission. This is not a respectable stance.* The vagaries of a feudal court and an ambitious lord. You are contesting for mastery, trying to conquer in this matter. Due to the situation, you simply cannot win. Anything you gain will soon vanish. It will bring you no respect at all.

*Direction:* Break out of isolation. Find supportive friends. Gather energy for a decisive new move.

# 7 and 8: The Paradigm

### Launching the Armies and the New Group that Results

This Pair involves you in a model of thought and action elaborated in the interconnected lines of the figures: the focused and proper use of force that leads to the emergence of a new group and a new dispensation. It embodies a site of radical transformation at the centres, where the Ghost River emerges from the Earth Altar to change the face of the world. Carefully consider your place in and relation to this model.

*Hidden Possibilities*: 24:23 > 2, the return of the spirit allows the stripping away of the old, connecting you with the primal power of realization.

The Pair exchanges information with 19:20 (Releasing the Spirit and Watching the Omens). It is motivated by 3:4 (Sprouting and Nurturing the New). The centre and threshold lines connect 2 and 29 (the zone of transformation) with 39:40 (Difficulties and Release) and 45:46 (Assembly and Sacred Mountain).

Look at the ages and events these figures suggest for personal connections.

<u>2</u>  3:4     19:20    <u>29</u>     39:40    45:46

*Shadow site*: 57:58, The Intermediaries

**Legions mean grieving. Grouping means delight.**

# 師 ☰☰ 7 *Legions/Leader*
## SHI

**Organize, mobilize, lead; armies and soldiers; master craftsman, martial arts master; discipline, power; appearance of King Wu and his War Leader, the Duke of Zhou; site of creative transformation.**

MYTHS FOR CHANGE: THE STORY OF THE TIME

**Charge to the Oracle:** *When there are disputes, the crowds rise up. Offer service. Accept this and use the energy of Legions. Legions and Leaders mean the crowds rise up.*

Legions is war and battle through which unity arises. It is the power of the world of the dead focused as a weapon, and the unity of spirit necessary to make war, imaged in the experienced people who, by offering themselves to death, can effectively wield and direct this power. The root of the term shows a banner, a central symbol and sign of hidden power that suggests the banners of plain white, sign of mourning and purity, used by King Wu in the Battle of the Mu wilderness. War was fought 'in the spirit'. It was used not only to gain territory, but to redress wrongs and carry out Heaven's Mandate. Captives taken in battle were sacrificed to the Ancestor, feeding him and assuring a continuing flow of blessing to the people.

This figure also suggests a particular campaign central to the founding of the Zhou state. When King Wu was in the Mourning Hut in the military capital of Feng, beginning three years of pre-scribed isolation for the death of his noble parent, he was given a great omen, a solar eclipse, indicating that he had indeed received the Mandate to overthrow the Shang. But he was bound by the rit-uals of mourning and desperately needed to know if this was truly the right moment (*shi*) to begin. He asked the turtle oracle about continuing the three years of prescribed mourning for his royal father, or immediately stepping into the Great Stream, launching his armies across the Fords of Meng. The Numinous Turtle gave a clear answer: 'Perhaps stay in mourning? Trap! The Way closes.' King Wu came out of the hut, performed a ritual announcement of war at the

115

Earth Altar and empowered his War Leader, the Duke of Zhou, to set the armies marching. They carried the corpse of King Wen, the spiritual father of the Zhou nation 'withered and drained in the service of the spirit', into battle in a litter, tossing him about to invoke the tremendous power of Heaven. All of these actions – making war against one's legal lord, breaking out of prescribed mourning and literally carrying a corpse, rather than the ancestor's spirit tablet, into battle – were profoundly shocking. They only could have been performed with the absolute assurance, founded in oracular response, that Heaven had indeed conferred the Mandate to renew the time and that the power of the spirits would 'carry us through'.

## THE RESPONSE

**Legions. Trial: Wise Words! Using experienced people opens the Way.**

**This is not a mistake.**

**Legions/leading,** SHI: troops, part of an army composed of three wings or SHI, right, middle, and left; master, leader, general; Master of the Four Winds, master of martial arts, skilled artisan, sage, 'experienced person'; organize, make functional, mobilize, raise the troops; educate, order, discipline, attack; announce the opening of a campaign at the Earth Altar, invoke the dead; imitate, take as a model. The old character shows a pivot or banner and the sign for circling or going around, joining paths on the way from the Outskirts Altar.

SHI[1] (9741/50): The left part (1) is rolling, waving, circling; the part at right (2) is a banner, ZA[1,] an ox tail attached to a standard, used to give signals to the army. 3–6 are alternate forms of the character.

Legions/Leading describes your situation in terms of organizing a confused heap of things into functional units so you can take effective action. The way to deal with it is to organize yourself and put yourself in order. Develop the capacity to lead. Look at the people you respect, and use them as models. Find who and what you need. This generates meaning and good fortune by releasing transformative energy. The ideal of this army is not just to fight. It brings order, and protects people who cannot protect themselves. It founds cities and defends what is necessary for people to live their lives. It is not a mistake to use force in this way.

## THE SCHOLAR SPEAKS

The hexagram figure shows serving through an inner willingness to take risks. In the middle of the Earth there is the stream. Something significant is returning. Be open to it. A confused crowd of things, all arguing with each other, surrounds you. This is not a pleasant situation. It will take concern and care to correct it. Try to give each thing its proper place. Support and sustain what is beneath or outside your normal value structure. It contains a great undeveloped potential you can accumulate and nourish. Don't simply impose your will. Find what you need by taking risks and confronting obstacles through a desire to serve. This activates a central ruling principle that people will spontaneously adhere to. It generates meaning and good fortune by releasing transformative energy. It is exactly what is needed in the present situation. How could it be a mistake?

## THE SHAMAN SPEAKS

> In the centre of Earth, the Stream. Legions.

> A time when Noble One supports the commoners to accumulate the crowds.

*Spirit rewards those toiling in the Pit. Offer service at the Earth Altar.* This is the Earth Altar and the Ghost River. Field above carries and sustains, while Rushing Water below dissolves direction and shape. It is Earth over Water: an inner willingness to confront danger that supports true service on the wide fields of earth. The ideal Realising Person reflects this by accumulating support through toiling for the common good, carried by the Bright Omens.

## Transforming Lines: Change at Work

### Initial Six

**Legions issue forth using pan pipes and orders.**

**Obstructing their power: Trap! The Way closes.**

*Letting go of real order closes the Way.* Everything needs rules and regulations. Without them, energy and enthusiasm will disintegrate and you will accomplish nothing. But be sure the rules you set and the signals you give are not obstructing your real power. By being too regular, you lose spontaneity and the enemy can read your moves. Your power is blocked and you fall into the trap.
*Direction:* A stimulating influence approaches. Something important returns. Be open and provide what is needed.

### Nine at Second

**Located in the centre of the Legions.**

**Wise Words! The Way is open. This is not a mistake.**

**The King bestows a mandate three times.**

*This is receiving Heaven's favour and cherishing the many regions.* This is the line of the great War Leader, the Duke of Zhou. You are in the leader's position, at the centre of a well-organized force. The Way is open to you. You have corrected your faults. Now you receive a mandate to act and you are in a position to carry out your plans and desires. This is an honour, not a mistake. Carrying this through will change your life.
*Direction:* Be open. Provide what is needed.

### Six at Third

**The Legions are carting the corpse.**

**'Perhaps stay in mourning?' Trap! The Way closes.**

*This means the Great is without achievement.* Dead bodies, old memories, useless ideas and false images, the isolation of mourning the past will defeat you. Step out of the Mourning Hut. This is the moment to emerge. Carry your inspiration with you and trust in the spirit. Set your forces in order. Do it now.

*Direction*: Make the effort. If you let yourself be led, you can realise hidden potential. The situation is already changing.

## Six at Fourth

**Legions retreat. Rest on the left.**

**This is not a mistake.**

*This is not letting go of order.* A tactical move into non-action. Your conflict may be ending or you may be preparing for a new offensive. In any case, value this time of rest and reorganization. It is not a mistake.

*Direction*: Release bound energy. The situation is already changing.

## Six at Fifth

**Legions. The birds of prey take to the fields.**

**Advantageous to seize them and put them to the question. Harvesting.**

**This is not a mistake.**

**Elder Son conducts the Legions, Younger Son carts the corpse.**

**'Perhaps stay in mourning?' Trap! The Way closes.**

*Use moving to the centre. Commissioning others is not appropriate.* King Wu and the Duke of Zhou emerge from the Mourning Hut and enter the decisive battle. Conflict has broken out and you must engage whether you like it or not. Seize the enemy to be questioned and offered in sacrifice. Be aggressive. Do not leave the dirty work to others. Take responsibility yourself. Get rid of old ideas, irrelevant images and bad memories. Carry your inspiration with you and trust in the spirit. Do it now.

*Direction*: Take decisive action. Take risks. Be open and provide what is needed.

## Six Above

**Legions. The Great Leader receives the Mandate:**

**'Lay out the city and receive the dwellers.'**

**Do not use Small People.**

*Correcting and achieving necessarily disturbs the old order of things.* The great War Leader receives a Mandate to found a new capital after the successful battle. You have succeeded in more ways than one. You have turned yourself into a leader and you have been empowered to found the new order. Use all your powers to create a beautiful place. Don't simply adapt. Though you must disturb things, have no fear. Simply carry out the Mandate.

*Direction*: The situation contains hidden possibilities. Something important is returning. Be open and provide what is needed.

# 8 Grouping/Calling and Gathering the Spirits Bi

**Mutual support, spirit kinship; change how you think and who you are grouped with; appearance of Yu the Great, site of creative transformation.**

## MYTHS FOR CHANGE: THE STORY OF THE TIME

**Charge to the Oracle:** *Crowds rising up must have a place to form groups. Accept this and use the energy of Grouping. Grouping means forming new groups.*

Grouping shows the new gathering of forces after the armies had conquered Shang, also imaged as Yu the Great bringing the spirits together after taming the flood. It is the moment when the spirits and lords gather around a new chief, a new time after the flood or chaos of war. It is a ritual gathering of energies, a masked dance with all the animal powers on the sacred mountain that combines instruction, incantation, and the investing of the powers. It also represents a *pi*-sacrifice to the female ancestors and alludes to men and women joining at the River-Mountain festival, a great ritual dance, feast and celebration that affirms the community of humans and spirits and invites the souls to return.

When Yu tamed the waters and established the Way, he called an assembly of the *shen*, the lords and spirits, on Mao Shan, the sacred mountain, to assign the fiefs and help the people. But Feng-fang, demon of the past season, held back and was late. Yu killed him and beheaded his corpse, sending him to the limits of the world to stand guard. Gong Gong was the one who had stirred the waters to crash in waves against the Hollow Mulberry, threatening the world. Yu curbed him and exiled him to stand guard at the edge of the world. Xianlu was Gong Gong's minister, a nine-headed serpent who turned anything he touched to marshes and swamps. Yu killed him. His blood stank so much Yu had to empty the marsh three times. He stabilized this bloody swamp by making it into a great terrace for the spirits from the north and east, bringing them into the group. Then, finally, the Ghost River flowed peacefully in

121

the Way. People made images of the monsters and no longer suffered from the waves. The waters became an ever-flowing source, like the oracles, Earth's springs that nourish all.

The sacrifice of Feng-fang on Mao Shan marks the time when 'the power and virtue (*de*) of Yu and the Xia grew to plenitude'. After a ritual combat and death, the Two Royal Dragons, symbol of the lineage, descended on Yu. He received the homage and loyalty oaths of the Myriad *shen* (River and Mountain spirits) and lords (gods of soil and grains, the Earth Altars) who form the sacred places. Yu became the First Ancestor through the sacrifice of Feng-fang, the Monster at the End of the World. There are temples to both figures on the sacred mountains, victor and victim, Thunder Dragon and Wind Bull. They are *zhen* and *sun*, thunder and wind, and the sacrifice that institutes the Royal Marriage and the River-Mountain festivals.

## THE RESPONSE

**Grouping. Gather the spirits. Wise Words! The Way opens.**

**Trace the oracle to its wellspring. Trial: an ever-flowing Source.**

**This is not a mistake.**

**This is not soothing, they are coming from the Four Hidden Lands.**

**For the 'Late Man', Trap! The Way closes.**

**Group,** Bɪ: join together, ally; spiritual connections; find a new centre, join a new group; find what you belong with; order things in classes, compare and select; harmonize, unite, equal, identical; coordinate, approach, accord with what is good; classified correctly, a fundamental group of five households; gather, group with, align, range, rank; work together, work towards, neighbours; gathering the lords. The old character shows two people standing or walking close together. The figures look backward in order to know the future.

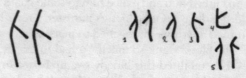

$BI^3$ (8794/81): The character represents two people standing or walking behind each other. A person turned to the left, $REN^2$, (2) is man, a person turned to the right, $BI^3$, (3 and 4: deceased mother) is a symbol for female. North, $BEI^3$, (5) is two people standing back to back or a man and a woman.

Grouping describes your situation in terms of the people and things with which your spirit connects you. The way to deal with it is to look at who you group yourself with, and how you use ideas to categorize things. The way you put things and people together is changing. Stop and take a look around. Try to perceive essential qualities in order to get to the heart of the matter. Compare things and sort them out. Find what you belong with. You can ask your question in many different ways. The oracle will help you. This is not a mistake. It generates meaning and good fortune by releasing transformative energy. This is not a soothing time. Things are coming at you from all sides, demanding that you consider them. Do it now. If you put it off and try to manage it later, you will be cut off from the spirits and left open to danger.

## THE SCHOLAR SPEAKS

The hexagram figure shows relationships dissolving. The stream is above the Earth. Strip away your old ideas. You are confronted with crowds of things and must find new ways to group them. This doesn't have to be painful. You can take delight in this activity. Let harmony, pleasure and elegance be a key. The early Kings used this time to establish cities that connect and define the different peoples. Give each thing a place where it can actively and joyously join with others of its kind. Pay attention to what supports you from below. Try to connect your ideals and goals with an underlying support. Do not put it off! Take advantage of the profusion of things coming at you and change now.

## THE SHAMAN SPEAKS

Above Earth, the Stream. Grouping.

A time when Early Kings ennobled vassals to connect the myriad cities.

*Spirit offered service at the Earth Altar rewards those toiling in the Pit.* This is the Ghost River and the Earth Altar. Rushing Water above dissolves direction and shape, while Earth below yields and sustains. It is Water over Earth: the outer world dissolves and changes, while a new grouping appears on the inner field. The ideal Realising Person reflects this by emulating the early Kings who bestowed responsibility on others and bound them with ties of affection. Hold your heart fast and take the risk.

## TRANSFORMING LINES: CHANGE AT WORK

### INITIAL SIX

**Group them!**

**There is a connection to the spirits that will carry you through.**

**This is not a mistake.**

**This connection fills the earthen vessels to overflowing.**

**The completion is coming. Even more! Wise Words! The Way is open.**

*The beginning will have more. The Way is open.* Becoming part of this group will connect you with the flow of the spirit. Your bodies are the vessels. This connection is certain. There is no mistake here. This group overflows with love and care. As you become part of it, you will find there is more on the way.
*Direction:* Give everything a place to grow. Strip away old ideas and be open to new ones.

### SIX AT SECOND

**Calling and grouping the spirits.**

**Group them from the origin inside.**

**Trial: Wise Words! The Way is open.**

*Do not let go of the origin.* Your connection puts you at the centre of this group, a part of its origin. The Way is open to you. Gather people around this. Don't let the connection slip through your fingers.
*Direction:* Commit yourself. Take risks. Be open to the new and provide what is needed.

### Six at Third

**Grouped with the unpeople, the victims!**

**Trap! The Way closes.**

*Won't this truly injure you?* The people you are involved with now will do you no good. Danger. This is not where you belong. Leave now before you are sacrificed along with the others.

*Direction*: Re-imagine the situation. Gather energy for a decisive new move.

### Six at Fourth

**Outside the Group.**

**Trial: Wise Words! the Way is open.**

*This means adhering to what is above.* You feel outside this group, but you are in this position because of your moral and intellectual worth. Stick to your work and your values and you will influence them. The Way is open.

*Direction*: Assemble things for a great new project. Proceed through gentle penetration. Gather energy for a decisive new move.

### Nine at Fifth

**Illustrious Grouping!**

**The King uses beaters on three sides of the hunt.**

**He lets the game go that runs before him.**

**Thus the capital's people are not frightened away.**

**Wise Words! The Way is open.**

*This situation is centred and correct. Lose the rebellious and grasp the yielding. Employ the centre above.* This is the royal hunt after a battle. You are looking for people to be with and a social identity in which you can find a place. Don't try to coerce or impress people. Let your virtue shine. This creates a true and willing bond in which the people you contact are there because they want to be. Deep affinities have a chance to work. Acting like this opens the way to real connections.

*Direction*: Be open. Provide what is needed.

## SIX ABOVE

**Grouping them without a head.**

**Trap! The Way closes.**

*This is no place to complete things!* This is not the group for you. It has no goal and no purpose. It is going nowhere fast. Leave now or face disaster.

*Direction:* Take a deeper look. Strip away old ideas and be open to new ones.

# 9 and 10: The Paradigm

### Gathering the Ghosts and Mating with the Spirit

This Pair involves you in an overall model of thought and action elaborated in the interconnected lines of the figures: gathering and nurturing the small, what is ignored or ready to emerge, to prepare for a shift of place and fate. It creates a site of radical change at the thresholds of the human world, a Tiger Transformation where the Dragon power emerges into the Opened Heart to begin a new life. Carefully consider your place in and relation to this model.

*Hidden Possibilities*: 38:37 > 64:63, conflict and isolation transformed to creative tension. Prepare and make the crossing.

The Pair exchanges information with 57:58 (The Intermediaries). It is motivated by 5:6 (Temple and Council: Waiting for Visitors). The centre and threshold lines connect 1 and 61 (the zone of transformation) with 25:26 (Disentangling from the Past and Accumulating Spirit) and 37:38 (Dwelling and Ghosts that Haunt it).

Look at the ages and events these figures suggest for personal connections.

<u>1</u> (3:4) 5:6    25:26    37:38    57:58 (59:60) <u>61</u>

*Shadow site*: 55:56, New King Receives the Mandate and the
Wandering Sage Begins his Journey

**Small Accumulates means at first they are few. Treading
means not abiding where you are.**

# 9 Small Accumulates/ Gathering the Ghosts
## Xiao Chu

**Accumulate small to do the great; nurture, raise, support; breed animals; dealings with the ghost world, autumn sacrifice, going to the River-Mountain festival.**

## Myths for Change: The Story of the Time

**Charge to the Oracle:** *The new group must have a place to accumulate and gather the souls. Accept this and use the energy of Accumulating the Small.*

Small Accumulates suggests the mating and pasturing of animals and the deep green pastures and wide plains bounded by mountains that set the scene for the autumn procession of the *wu* to the Outskirts Altar to meet the incoming spirits. It is the ceremonies to bring the autumn rains that signal the end of labour and the harvest, held at the Moon Pit, Night Brightness (*ye ming*), on the western outskirts. This marks preparation for the River-Mountain Time, the dances of men and women and their marriages that affirm human community with the spirits and bring the souls into the world. It marks the coming in of a soul from the Ghost River and the time of the Moon Almost Full, when the Changes were consulted. This time is like a shell or womb, a protective covering that will be broken through in spring. Philosophically, this is the nurturing of the 'smallest possible thing' (*ji*), the emergent point that heralds change. It is a quality of the Way that, though now barely visible, will lead on to illumination.

## The Response

Small Accumulates. Make an offering and you will succeed.

Shrouding clouds bring no rain yet.

'We meet them at our Western Outskirts Altar.'

Small, Xiao: little, flexible, adaptable; humility, what is common to all; adapt to whatever happens; make things smaller, lessen; yin energy; the Ghost World; secondary ancestors, families of common people who till the soil. The old character shows a river dividing two banks, the undifferentiated flow of life between the worlds. **Accumulate**, CHU: take care of, support, tolerate, encourage; help one another, overcome obstacles; tame, train; domesticate, raise, bring up; gather, collect, hoard, retain; seed, shell, carapace, protection of a germ broken through in spring, protection in the womb. The old character shows a field and two bundles of silk or grass, harvested and stored.

XIAO[3,] the character above, shows three grains of rice or sand or a river between two banks. The character below, CHU[4] or XÜ[4] (2538/102), is composed of silk bundles SI[1] (2) and field with plants TIAN[2] (3): the harvest of silk and crops, also read as XUAN[2], profound or dark, mystic, mysterious.

Small Accumulates describes your situation in terms of confronting a great variety of things that don't seem to be related. The way to deal with it is to adapt to each thing that crosses your path in order to accumulate something great. Take the long view. Gather, herd together, retain and hoard all the little things that might seem unimportant. Think of yourself as raising animals, growing crops or bringing up children. Be flexible and adaptable. Tolerate and nourish things. The rain hasn't come yet, but the dense clouds that bring it are rolling in from the western frontier. The successful completion of your efforts is not far away.

### THE SCHOLAR SPEAKS

The hexagram figure shows an enduring force accumulated through gentle penetration. Wind moves above Heaven. Turn potential conflicts into creative tension. You need a place to accumulate things, because right now you only have a few. Focus on the inherent beauty of each thing in order to realise its potency. Persist in your efforts through gentle penetration and you will acquire a solid centre from which to move. The rain has not yet come. Praise and let go of what you have now, so the process can go on. The clouds are still spreading. It is not yet time to act.

Wind moves above Heaven. Small Accumulates.

A time when Noble One brings out the pattern to nurture power and virtue.

*Spirit works in those who lay out the offerings while it wars in Heaven above.* The Intermediaries are working with the Force. Wind and Wood above enter subtly, penetrating, pervading and coupling the fates, while Heaven below struggles on, persistent and unwearied. This is Wood over Metal: an enduring force accumulates within, penetrating and coupling with the small. The ideal Realising Person reflects this by elucidating the innate pattern in each thing that reveals its power and destiny. Persist and work through inner inspiration. This couples you with a new fate.

## TRANSFORMING LINES: CHANGE AT WORK

### INITIAL NINE

Small Accumulates. The procession to the altar.

Returning to the birth of the Way.

How could this be a mistake?

Wise Words! The Way opens.

*Your heart will open the Way.* The procession to the altar to meet the spirit. You have been lost in a cloud of details, but now you see the Way once more. Don't hesitate to return. How could this be a mistake? The Way is open.
*Direction:* Subtly penetrate to the core. Turn conflict into creative tension. The situation is already changing.

### NINE AT SECOND

Small Accumulates. The procession to the altar.

Returning like an animal led to sacrifice on a leash.

Wise Words! The Way opens.

*Located in the centre, this does not let go of the origin.* The procession to the altar to meet the spirit. You have been lost and confused. Now you are simply hauled back to the Way like an animal dragged on a leash. Consider yourself blessed. The Way is open to you.

*Direction*: Stay within your family and dwelling. Gather energy for a decisive new move.

### NINE AT THIRD

**Small Accumulates. The procession to the altar.**

**The spokes of the cartwheel loosen.**

**Husband and consort turn their eyes to one another.**

*This means you cannot correct it by staying at home*. The procession halts. Men and women come together at the spring festival. Turning to each other, they open the Way for new life to enter.
*Direction*: Find the heart's empty centre. Take things in. Be open and provide what is needed.

### SIX AT FOURTH

**Small Accumulates. The procession to the altar.**

**There is a connection to the spirits that will carry you through.**

**Bad blood leaves and apprehension departs.**

**This is not a mistake.**

*This means uniting purpose with what is above*. You make the connection to the spirits. You can act with confidence now. The spirits are with you. Forget about old quarrels and resentments. Announce yourself and your new identity. This is not a mistake. Your purpose is united with those above.
*Direction*: Take action. You are connected to a creative force.

### NINE AT FIFTH

**Small Accumulates. The procession arrives at the altar.**

**There is a connection to the spirits through which you are bound to others.**

**Use your neighbour's affluence.**

*This is not solitary affluence*. Here the spirits bring us together. You are not alone. There is a spiritual connection that binds you to the people around you. Don't be afraid to make use of this connection. Take hold of things and use them for the good of all.
*Direction*: Be active. Find an idea that brings you together. Turn conflict into creative tension. The situation is already changing.

NINE ABOVE

**Small Accumulates. 'We will plant the crop.'**

**The rain has already come.**

**You already abide in honour, power and virtue. Carry on!**

**The Moon Almost Full: 'There will be Changes.'**

**Trial: from the wife's people there will be adversity, hungry souls and angry ghosts.**

**If the Noble One seeks to chastise others,**

**Trap! The Way closes.**

*This means power and virtue are massing and carrying. If Noble One chastises, he will have a place to doubt.* You have achieved your goal. The rain has fallen to bless you and you live in honour and virtue. Don't worry, carry on. Plant the crop. From the wife's side, you will face danger with its roots in the past. The masked dancers are reading the Changes. Don't try to put everything in order. Don't discipline people. Don't set out on an expedition. The Changes are coming. The happiness you know can endure.

*Direction:* Wait for the right moment to act. Turn conflict into creative tension. The situation is already changing.

# 10 Treading/Mating with the Tiger LU

**Step, path; make your way; conduct, support, sustain; good cheer, good luck; meeting the spirit, acquiring a destiny and identity; site of creative transformation.**

MYTHS FOR CHANGE: THE STORY OF THE TIME

**Charge to the Oracle**: *When beings accumulate, they enshrine the fates given by the Hidden Lord. The Joyous Dancer mates with the spirit. Accept this and use the energy of Treading.*

The accumulated power of the Small sets out to find a new fate. Treading is centre of a complex series of myths and rituals linking sexual intercourse, fertility, intercourse with spirits and the *wu* who facilitate it, the Hidden Temple and the Earth Altar. It includes the spring and autumn River-Mountain festivals, exorcisms, the birth of medicine and the miraculous birth of First Ancestor. The character also suggests grass, thus life, birth and sprouts. It implies the corpse-embodier and those who work with the dead and the spirits who control the 'winds'. It is the dangerous process of directing a ritual invocation. It is waking the Earth to open the fields in spring, and the *ge*-vine sandals of marriage. It is the birth of the Founding Ancestor described in the Odes:

> . . . the birth of our people from Lady Yuan of Jiang.
> How did it happen? She made sacrifice at the Hidden Temple
> to exorcize the childless demon. She trod on the big toe of
> Di's footprint. She conceived in awe.
> Good birth, she bore Prince Ji
> She bore Hou Ji, Ancestor Millet.

The site of this occurrence, the Mountain Shrine, is the hidden hollow of a high mountain, the 'lower hidden' (*xia mi*) below the summit where the Tiger Spirit dwells. Since antiquity this land of hidden shrines and retreats has had the power to enlighten and inseminate. Altars were founded there to make the *jiao*-sacrifice to the High Lord, sites of conception in the spirit. The ones who did this were the 'Wu who Tread in the Footprints', walking in the steps of the god. Such a ritual opens the fields in the month of Hibernating Insects, when the King sacrifices the red bull and treads the fields, ploughing the first furrows. It is the birth of great souls with special destinies, 'bringing in the fates'.

Treading is the figure of the Joyous Dancer, the Young Ancestress Wu who goes out to the Mountain Shrine to mate with the Tiger Spirit and Sky. She calls the spirit down. She is an Intermediary, a person who can make the invisible visible, who dances to call down the bright spirits into her body, a skilled technician of the sacred. She exorcises demons and prays for blessings: long life, wealth, health, fertility and the power and virtue that ennobles a life lived according to *ming*, the Mandate from Heaven that she carries.

## THE RESPONSE

**Treading on the Tiger's tail.**

**It does not maul you. Make an offering and you will succeed.**

Tread, LU: walk, step; path, track, way; find your way, develop, cultivation; act, practice, accomplish; social cultivation; in the steps of, the Ancestor's footprints; opening the fields, marriage procession; accomplish a rite or ritual, a dangerous step; salary, position, means of subsistence; happiness, prosperity, luck; virtue, rite, hold an office or domain; *also*: dignity, durable happiness; the paths of the stars and planets. The old character shows a person walking a path that moves back and forth, possibly the 'impersonator' of a deceased ancestor. It includes the body, three footsteps, a shoe and the graph for walk.

LÜ³ (7485/44): The character represents a corpse or sitting man (1) impersonating the ancestor at a sacred meal; a foot on a road (2), a shoe or boat (3), and another foot (4).

Treading describes your situation in terms of how you find and make your way. The way to deal with it is to proceed step by step. The path is there. Practise. Think about the right way to act and how to gain

134

your livelihood. You are walking in the tracks of a tiger, a powerful and dangerous being. If you are careful, this being will give you what you need to exist and frighten off what is trying to harm you. Speak with it and partake of its power and intelligence. Don't do anything to make it bite you. You can't afford to sneer and scold. This is pleasing to the spirits. Through it they will give you success, effective power and the capacity to bring the situation to maturity.

## THE SCHOLAR SPEAKS

The hexagram figure shows an outer struggle met by cheerful self-expression. Heaven is above, the mists are below. Find supportive people. Everyone must amass enough to live on. You must find the right way to do this. Don't stay where you are. Treading and finding your way is the foundation of your ability to realise the Way. It harmonizes and develops your capacity to move in accord with the Way. Carefully differentiate what is above you and what is below you. Set your purpose right. Clarify your relation to the desires that everyone holds in common. The inner stimulation to movement that you feel now can connect you with a powerful creative force. It is like treading on a tiger's tail. You don't want the tiger to bite you. The centre of your desire is solid and correct. You are walking with the highest power. Don't be disheartened. Continuing your efforts to illuminate the situation will bring a real change in awareness.

## THE SHAMAN SPEAKS

Heaven above, mists below. Treading.

A time when Noble One differentiates above and below,

setting right the common purpose.

*Spirit speaks and spreads joy through the Intermediaries as it wars in Heaven above.* The Intermediaries are working with the Force. Heaven struggles above, persistent and unwearied, while Mists rising from below stimulate and fertilize it, joyous words that cheer and inspire. This is the Metal Moment: inner stimulation feeds outer struggle, articulating the path step by step. The ideal Realising Person reflects this by articulating the place of above and below, using their connection to set right our commons needs. Work through the receptive and the power of Earth. Announce the omen and part from the past.

## Transforming Lines: Change at Work

### Initial Nine

**Treading. Going simply in white silk shoes.**

**This is not a mistake.**

*Solitary and moving with your desire.* Go your own way. Be simple and pure about your efforts. Move with your real desire. How could this be a mistake?
*Direction:* Retire from conflicts. Stay in the family and the dwelling. Gather energy for a decisive new move.

### Nine at Second

**Treading the Way, smoothing it, smoothing it.**

**Trial: Wise Words!**

**The Way is open to the Mountain People, hidden in the shadow.**

*This is centred and does not originate in disorder.* You are treading the Way, so be calm about everything. Your work and your life are fine. This is not the time to come out of hiding. Stay in the shade for now, hidden away. You are moving toward the spirit that will reveal your destiny. Your time will come.
*Direction:* Disentangle yourself. Re-imagine the problem. Gather energy for a decisive new move.

### Six at Third

**Treading. Someone squints and thinks they can see.**

**Someone limps and thinks they can Tread.**

**Someone treads on the Tiger's tail and it mauls them.**

**Trap! The Way closes.**

**This is a soldier acting as a Great Leader.**

*Not the place to use brightness, not the time to move with the group. Not an appropriate situation unless you are a Great Chief with a strong purpose.* This is not the way to act. You are presuming on inadequate powers. Go on like this and the tiger will maul you. You are not the leader, so don't presume to be one. It would be a useless sacrifice.
*Direction:* You are confronting a powerful and dangerous force.

### NINE AT FOURTH

**Treading on the Tiger's tail. Joyous Dancer mates with the spirit.**

**Carefully, carefully present your petition.**

**Bring this to completion. Wise Words! The Way opens.**

*Your purpose is moving.* You meet the Great Person, the hidden spirit, the source of power. Present your case clearly and persuasively. Don't be intimidated. The Way is open. Your purpose is moving. Here you acquire your destiny.

*Direction:* Connect your inner and outer life. Take things in. Be open to the new and provide what is needed.

### NINE AT FIFTH

**Treading and parting. Be decisive.**

**Trial: adversity, hungry souls and angry ghosts.**

*It is right to correct this situation.* This next step takes courage. You must decisively separate yourselves from the dangerous past influence that brought you here. Have no fear. Announce the oracle and your new destiny. Correcting the situation is definitely the right thing to do.

*Direction:* Turn conflict into creative tension. The situation is already changing.

### NINE ABOVE

**Treading. Look at your steps and watch the omens.**

**The predecessors are blessing you.**

**Wise Words! Their eternal return opens the Way.**

*The source above opens the Way. There is a great reward.* If you look at the things you have been doing, you will see that they connect with something larger than your personal desires. Keep to this path, for the ancestors bless you. Learn to respect them, for it is their presence that opens the Way.

*Direction:* Express yourself joyously. Find supportive friends. Gather energy for a decisive new move.

# 11 and 12: The Paradigm

### The Great Sacrifice/New King and Old King

This Pair involves you in an overall model of thought and action elaborated in the interconnected lines of the figures: the great symbols of what is coming and going, the New King and Old King, the one who sacrifices on the Great Mountain and the one who is offered to the Ancestor. Carefully consider your place in and relation to this model.

*Hidden Possibilities:* 54:53 > 64:63, the Great Marriages. Prepare and make the crossing.

The Pair exchanges information with 45:46 (Assembly and the Sacred Mountain). It is motivated by 25:26 (Disentangling from the Past and Accumulating the Spirit). The centre and threshold lines relate the process to 5:6 (Temple and Council), 19:20 (Releasing the Spirit and Watching the Omens), 33:34 (Retreat and Advance) and 35:36 (Rising and Setting Sun).

Look at the ages and events these figures suggest for personal connections.

    5:6       19:20   25:26      33:34 35:36     45:46

*Shadow site:* 53:54, The Great Marriages

**Pervading and Obstruction mean reversing the way you sort things.**

# 11 Pervading/Great Rituals TAI

**Expand, communicate; harmony, abundance, flowering, connection; the great spring sacrifice on Mount Tai; the first royal ritual, the New King.**

## MYTHS FOR CHANGE: THE STORY OF THE TIME

**Charge to the Oracle:** *There is Treading and the flowing out of the spirit. It must be stilled and fixed. Accept this and use the energy of Pervading. Pervading definitely means connecting and flowing out.*

*Tai*, Pervading, a form of the character *Da*, great, represents the great sacrifices (*da xeng*) that connect Heaven and Earth and ensure harmony and blessing for all that were made through the spirit of the first of the sacred mountains, *Tai-shan*. Only the King could make these sacrifices, for they involved direct communication between the Royal Ancestors and *Di* or Heaven. These sacrifices made sure that communication between Heaven and Earth was open and flowing. They recall a time when the spirits walked among us bringing ease, joy and prospering for all. *Tai* is phonetically connected to the six stars of the Great Bear or Dipper, home of High Lord of Heaven who sends the fates. Its root is water, crossing the rivers, and its old form is *Kan*, the Underworld River. It means fishes, hidden wealth and the fertile womb. Pervading is the fluid metabolism of things, the flow, the streaming of the Way and the rising juices of sexual attraction, joy and ecstasy. It dissolves the spirit and puts it into circulation. The Great Spirit connects with the world, the joyous flow, revivifying spring.

## THE RESPONSE

**Pervading. Small goes, Great comes.**

**Wise Words! The Way is open. Make an offering and you will succeed.**

**Pervade,** *TAI*: the great; peace, abundance, harmony, communion, love, prosperity, fertility; connection between Heaven and Earth, the opposites unite, things burgeon; permeate, diffuse, smooth, slippery; extreme, prodigious, extravagant; wine cup of the Emperor

Shun. Mount Tai (*Tai-shan*) was where the great sacrifices were made that connected Heaven and Earth. The old character shows the Great Person, his power to protect and shelter, and two hands offering sacrifice at the Ghost River.

TAI⁴ (10306/85): The ideogram has the shape of the great mountain *Tai-shan*, the Zhou people's most direct connection with the divine. At the top is DA⁴ (1) the character 'great', like the great peak of a mountain. Two hands, GONG³ (2), like the woods embracing its flanks, offer sacrifice to the 'water' SHUI³ (3), the brooks and rivers running down its slopes, bringing life and prosperity, symbolised by the Ghost River and the Earth Altar.

Pervading describes your situation in terms of an influx of spirit that brings flowering and prosperity. The way to deal with it is to spread the prosperity and good feeling by communicating it. You are connected to the flow of energy. Be great, abounding and fertile. What is unimportant is departing, along with the necessity to be small and adapt to whatever crosses your path. The time that is coming offers you the chance to develop your fundamental ideas. It generates meaning and good fortune by releasing transformative energy. This is pleasing to the spirits. Through it they will give you success, effective power and the capacity to bring the situation to maturity.

## THE SCHOLAR SPEAKS

The hexagram figure shows a creative force pervading the Earth. Heaven and Earth come together. This is a time of abundance. If you let yourself be led you can realise your hidden potential. Later you can be quiet and settled. Reach out and penetrate things. Sense their interconnections. Radically change your sense of yourself and whom you associate with. Put your possessions at the service of the spirit of the time. Support and encourage people. Use peace and abundance to set life in order. This is a time when the fundamental powers mingle with humans and all the beings connect with one another. What is above and what is below come together. Your purpose is in accord with them. Be firm and focused inside and adaptable in your dealings with the world. Stay connected with the Way through using the oracle. The way of people who are continually adapting to whatever brings them advantage is now dissolving. The great Way will endure.

## THE SHAMAN SPEAKS

**Heaven and Earth mingle. Pervading. The Great Sacrifice.**

**A time when the New King uses his property to accomplish the Way of Heaven and Earth,**

**to brace and mutualize the rituals of Heaven and Earth.**

**He uses the left to right the common good.**

*The Spirit that wars in Heaven is offered service at the Earth Altar.* This is a conjunction of the Primal Powers. Earth above yields and sustains, while Heaven below struggles on, persistent and unwearied. It is Earth over Metal: an enduring inspiration from within that pervades the field of Earth. The ideal Realising Person reflects this by emulating the ancient nobles, who offered their property and service to further the Way of Heaven and aid the common good. Persist and work through inner inspiration.

## TRANSFORMING LINES: CHANGE AT WORK

### INITIAL NINE

**Pervading. The Great Ritual.**

**Pull up and weave the twisted thatch grass, each with its kind.**

**Wise Words! Chastising opens the Way.**

*Locate your purpose outside yourself.* Weaving the sacrificial mat. It is time this great endeavour got off the ground. Take vigorous action to get out of this lowly place and find the people you really belong with. Be firm. Put things in order and set out. The Way is open.

*Direction:* Make the effort. Turn conflict into creative tension. The situation is already changing.

**Pervading. The Great Ritual.**
**Put on the hollow gourds and cross the River.**
**Don't put off leaving. Your partners disappear.**
**You acquire honour by moving to the centre.**

*This is moving toward the centre, using the shining Great.* Alone, you are surrounded by a wasteland. Get out of this situation. Cross the river to the magic landscape of the spring festival. Move toward that vibrant centre. The people you now identify with will disappear, but there is no other choice. Your integrity will be honoured and your desire fulfilled.
*Direction:* Accept the hardship. In the end your light will shine. Release bound energy. The situation is already changing.

Nine at Third

**Pervading. The Great Ritual.**
**'No level that does not slope. No going without a return.'**
**Trial: this hardship and drudgery is not a mistake.**
**Have no cares. You are connected to the spirits.**
**You will share the great meal and find Heaven's blessing.**

*This is the border of Heaven and Earth.* You are facing a difficult time. Remember, after a level road there is always a difficult climb. But if you don't let go of where you are now and your present connections, the spirit cannot return. This difficulty is not a mistake. It is a transition. Don't worry, it has a real spiritual and emotional meaning. Going through the hardship will lead to the meal shared with spirits. It draws the blessing down. You will join with others in this new and loving spirit.
*Direction:* An important connection approaches. Something significant returns. Be open. Provide what is needed.

Six at Fourth

**Pervading. The Great Ritual.**
**'Fluttering, fluttering, like a young bird leaving the nest.'**
**If you are not affluent, use your neighbour.**
**This is not a warning.**
**Use your connection to the spirits. It will carry you through.**

*Let go of possessions and centre the heart's desire.* You are afraid to leave the nest. Don't worry, come out and live in the great world. If you need help, then ask for it. It will be there. There is nothing to feel badly about. Use your basic connection to people who are your spiritual kin. Act on your heart's desire. You have something important to give.

*Direction:* Fill yourself with invigorating strength. Be resolute. You are connected to a creative force.

### Six at Fifth

**Pervading. The Great Ritual.**

**The Great Ancestor offers the maidens in marriage.**

**Use this happiness and satisfaction. It is the footstep of the spirit.**

**Wise Words! The Way to the Source is open.**

*The centre moves by using desire.* Di Yi, the Great Shang King, gave his daughters in marriage to King Wen, ennobling the Zhou people. This is a great ritual union that will have repercussions through the generations. It is an omen of future happiness that, in time, will gratify your desires and realise all your aims. Take joy in this connection. The footsteps of the spirits are here. The Way is fundamentally open.

*Direction:* Wait for the right moment to act. Turn conflict into creative tension. The situation is already changing.

### Six Above

**Pervading. The Great Ritual.**

**The city walls dissolve and return to the moat.**

**Don't use the legions now.**

**This oracle originates from the capital.**

**Trial: distress.**

*Your fate is in disarray.* The structure of things is collapsing. Don't try to force a change by acting aggressively. This dissolution has fate behind it. You may feel confused, but you are in the right position to change your thinking. Take your time. Be of good cheer. Collect the energy and insight to try again.

*Direction:* Find a new central idea. Turn conflict into creative tension. The situation is already changing.

# 12 Stop! Obstruction

## PI

**Stop!; obstacles, blocked communication; cut off, closed, failure; people of no use or worth to you; punishment, execution, the sacrificial victim.**

## MYTHS FOR CHANGE: THE STORY OF THE TIME

**Charge to the Oracle**: *Beings must not only interpenetrate and connect. The Victims. Accept this and use the energy of Obstruction.*

Obstruction is the dark half of the great sacrifices. It means bad words, a bad omen, and a negative pronouncement from the oracle, showing what is opposed to the current will of Heaven, the old that must be sacrificed, literally the *fei-ren*, the non-persons or victims, captives and prisoners who will be given to the Ancestor. It is the enclosure of winter: 'Heaven's breath rises, Earth's breath sinks down; shut and barred the passages, winter established.' It is the victim, the shadow, the Old King, the demon, the thing that blocks and obstructs and must be offered up. In the narrative of the Mandate, these are the Shang prisoners after the victory who will be beheaded and given to the Ancestral Spirit who brought the victory. This is what must die to make way for the new. As an oracular response it means No! Not so! Request denied! Stop! Things are closed in now, obstructed, and the expansion and development of Pervading is reversed. For the Noble One, the action befitting this time is withdrawal, silence, personal offering and atonement, waiting for the re-opening in spring.

## THE RESPONSE

**Stop! Obstruction. The victim people.**

**Trial: not advantageous for Noble One.**

**Great going, Small coming.**

**Obstruction**, PI: No! Stop! Bad words, bad omens; closed, stopped, blocked, bar the way; unable to advance, failure, isolated, alienated; deny, refuse, disapprove; evil, wicked, perverse, unhappy, unfortunate; punishment, chastisement, executions; sacrifice of the Old King; the old dispensation no longer supported by Heaven; opposite of the affirmation *shi*, it is! The old character shows a mouth and growth cut off or an omen bird that flies on without landing.

*PI*[3] (3555/30): a sprout or seedling, *BU*[4], cut off at the surface of the earth, or a flying bird, (1) and a mouth *KOU*[3] (2).

Obstruction describes your situation in terms of being blocked or interfered with. The way to deal with it is to stop what you are doing and accept the obstruction. Do not become the victim of the sacrifice. Communication is cut off. You are connected with the wrong people. If you try to act, you will encounter misfortune. Your proposals will be rejected. You will be personally disapproved of. There is no way for someone who wants to stay in touch with the Way to take advantage of this situation. What is important is departing, along with your ability to realise your plans. The time that is coming is small and mean. You will have to adapt to it. Don't seek to impose your ideas. Retreat and be patient.

## THE SCHOLAR SPEAKS

The hexagram figure shows a struggle in the outer world that blocks expression. Heaven and Earth do not come together. Proceed step by step. You can't always be part of a group. Change your sense of yourself and those you normally associate with. Don't mingle. Be careful about what you become involved with. Avoid heavy work or responsibility. If you avoid honours and don't display yourself, you can continue to draw benefits from the situation. What is happening is not your fault. Deal with it impersonally. It is a time of disconnection and isolation in which you do not have a real field of activity. Be humble and flexible inside yourself, but erect firm barriers outside. What is worthy is being excluded from centres of power, which are currently controlled by people who seek their own advantage. Their way will endure for now. The way of those who use the oracle to stay in touch with the Way is dissolving. Use this advice and diminish your involvement in the world. It can bring you no advantage now.

## THE SHAMAN SPEAKS

Heaven and Earth do not mingle. Obstruction. Stop!

A time when Noble One uses power and virtue carefully to cast out the hardship. Not allowing splendour, he benefits from the sacrifice.

*The spirit that wars in heaven must be offered sacrifice at the Earth Altar.* This is a disconnection of the Primal Powers. Heaven above moves away, while Earth below folds into itself. It is Metal over Earth: outer struggle demands inner service, a time of sacrifice. The ideal Realising Person reflects this by using power and virtue carefully to eliminate ostentation and thus benefit from the great sacrifice. Work through the receptive and the power of Earth.

## TRANSFORMING LINES: CHANGE AT WORK

### INITIAL SIX

Obstruction. Don't be the victim.

Pull up and weave the intertwisted thatch grass, each with its kind.

Trial: Wise Words! The Way opens.

Make an offering and you will succeed.

*Locate your purpose in a leader.* Weaving the mat of sacrifice. It is time to pull back. Take vigorous action together with others to get out of this place and find the people you really belong with. Be firm. Put things in order and set out. The Way will open to you. You are assured of success.

*Direction*: Disentangle yourself. Proceed step by step. Gather energy for a decisive new move.

### SIX AT SECOND

Obstruction. Lay out the wrapped offerings.

Wise Words! For Small People the Way is open.

Great People are Obstructed.

Make an offering and you will succeed.

*Do not disturb the flock.* Accept that you are isolated. Make a hidden offering to the retreating spirit. Adapt to what crosses

your path. Your great idea is obstructed. Do not worry. Stay true to yourself, like a foetus in the womb, and the Way will soon open.
*Direction*: Retreat from conflict. Find supportive friends. Gather energy for a decisive new move.

### SIX AT THIRD

**Obstruction. Don't be the victim.**

**Lay out the wrapped meat offerings.**

*This is not an appropriate situation.* Do nothing. Simply wait. Stop and examine yourself. Think of your situation as an offering to the spirit. Make inner preparations. The time is not right for action. Be like the foetus in the womb.
*Direction*: Retire and be coupled with a creative force.

### NINE AT FOURTH

**In Obstruction there is a Mandate.**

**This is not a mistake.**

**'An oriole in a ploughed field.' Cultivate this in radiant satisfaction.**

*Your purpose is moving.* In the middle of this terrible time, you experience a real connection. This is a lovely fate, an omen offered by Heaven, and it is your job to cultivate it in your withdrawal. Whatever happens, it is not a mistake. Work at it. In the end it can bring joy and satisfaction, spreading light to all.
*Direction*: Let everything come into view. Strip away old ideas. Be open and provide what is needed.

### NINE AT FIFTH

**Relinquishing the Obstruction.**

**Wise Words! For the Great Person the Way opens.**

**It disappears! It disappears!**

**Attach it to the thick-leafed Mulberry Tree.**

*Correcting the situation is appropriate.* If you are fighting the Obstruction, it is time to let go. When you truly feel the connection, the Way will open. The obstacles and troubles are disappearing. Imagine that you are in a quiet rural retreat. That is the place for you. This is the Sun Altar, the place where princes are given their mandate. It is where the World Tree grows. It will correct the whole situation.

*Direction*: You emerge into the light. Re-imagine the situation. Gather energy for a decisive new move.

### NINE ABOVE

**Subverting Obstruction.**

**First bad! then rejoicing.**

*Obstruction is completed. Why let this last?* You see an obstruction and think you are cut off, but the very thing causing you pain is suddenly turned on its head. What used to be an obstruction becomes a cause to rejoice. Thank Heaven the bad time is over! Let it all go.

*Direction*: Gather people and resources for a great new project. Proceed step by step. Gather energy for a decisive new move.

# 13 and 14: The Paradigm

### The Bright Omens Emerge from the Gathering of the People

This Pair involves you in an overall model of thought and action elaborated in the interconnected lines of the figures: the great festivals that bring people together and the great being that emerges, through whom blessings flow. It embodies a site of radical transformation, where the Dragon manifests through the Bright Omens to orient people's lives. Carefully consider your place in and relation to this model.

*Hidden Possibilities:* 44:43 > 1, the Lady of Fate carries the message. Be resolute, you are coupled with a creative force.

The Pair exchanges information with 33:34 (Retreat and Advance, Mountain Shrine and War God). It is motivated by 49:50 (Revolution and Casting the New Vessel). The centre and threshold lines connect 1 and 30 (the zone of transformation) with 25:26 (Disentangling from the Past and Accumulating the New Spirit) and 37:38 (Dwelling and Ghosts that Haunt it).

Look at the ages and events these figures suggest for personal connections.

<u>1</u>        25:26 (27:28) <u>30</u>  (31:32) 33:34 (35:36) 37:38      49:50

*Shadow site:* 51:52, The Rouser and the Sacrificer

**Harmonizing People means making the connections. The Great Being gathers the crowds.**

# 13 Harmonizing People TONG REN

Bring people together, concord, harmony; share an idea or goal; welcome others, co-operate; great sacrifice to welcome the season and open the fields; emergence of a common purpose; making love, making war; site of creative transformation.

## MYTHS FOR CHANGE: THE STORY OF THE TIME

**Charge to the Oracle**: *The gathering beings cannot be forever obstructed. Procession to the Outskirts Altar. Accept this and use the energy of Harmonizing People.*

The basis of Harmonizing People is words: oracular pronouncements on the time, ritual announcements at the Earth Altar informing the ancestors of the opening of the fields, of war, or the spring festival, and the joyous songs of the *wu* who lead out to the Altar at the edge of the fields. Common people and nobles gathered at the Outskirts Altar for these great ceremonies, first among them the spring festivals and sacrifices that united all after the winter isolation through joy, music, wine and sexual contact. This may portray the first spring festival after the conquest of the Shang. The great sacrifices on *Tai-shan* established the axis; now the people move together and the blessings flow. All step into the Great Stream, an image of the primitive and original great unity of humans and spirits, what the Daoists call a return to the original harmony, the original chaos, in the festival or paradise time. As people join together in great number, the rituals establish fellow feeling and common intent. The people come together in harmony and joy, united through the bright presence of the spirits. From this place the united armies were gathered to fight the great battle of Muye through which King Wu renewed the time.

## THE RESPONSE

Harmonizing People moving toward the countryside.
Make an offering and you will succeed.

**Advantageous to step into the Great Stream. Harvesting.**

**Trial: advantageous for the Noble One. A leader emerges.**

**Harmonize,** TONG: unite, share, agree, bring together; concord, recognize common identity; compassion, union, joy, excitement; equalize, assemble, share; things held in common, the same time and place; flow together, gathering and audience of feudatory lords every 12 years, the female musical tones. The old character shows a door, the sign for one and a mouth, speaking with one voice.

**People,** REN: human beings, an individual and humanity as a whole, the original unity. The old character suggests a person kneeling in prayer or submission.

TONG² (11856/30) is composed of a door, gate or box (1) and mouth or opening KOU³ (2), perhaps an opening and a cover, to fit together. REN² (3) is person or people, here probably a woman.

Harmonizing People describes your situation in terms of sharing something with others. The way to deal with it is to find ways to unite the people involved. This is the kind of task that can best be done together and brings mutual advantage in the end. Find places of agreement where goals can be shared. Develop group spirit and a bond of common understanding. This is pleasing to the spirits. Through it they will give you success, effective power and the ability to bring the situation to maturity. This is the right time to embark on a significant enterprise or enter the Stream of Life with a goal. Use the oracle and put your ideas to the trial.

### THE SCHOLAR SPEAKS

The hexagram figure shows warmth and understanding that help people in their struggles. Heaven united with fire. You are connected to a creative force. People should not remain isolated from one another. Think about the ways to connect them. Sort people out by giving them rallying points and finding common ancestors. You can succeed in this situation by being flexible and adaptable.

This leads you to the centre and puts you in contact with the creative force moving there. Say it like this: Bring people together, for creative force is moving in the situation. Persist in your efforts to illuminate the inherent beauty of things. Put central emphasis on not going to one extreme or the other. This enables you to connect with the deep purposes that influence and move the human world.

## THE SHAMAN SPEAKS

**Heaven associates with Fire. Harmonizing People.**

**A time when Noble One sorts the clans to differentiate and brighten the beings.**

*Spirit reveals itself in the Bright Omens as it wars above in Heaven.* This is an omen site, the Bright Presence among the people. Heaven above struggles on, persistent and unwearied, while Fire and brightness below radiate light and warmth. It is Metal over Fire: A Bright Presence lights up the inner world, born through people's struggle to harmonize with the great spirits. The ideal Realising Person reflects this by helping us realise how we are different and how we unite. Hold the heart fast and take the risk.

## TRANSFORMING LINES: CHANGE AT WORK

### INITIAL NINE

**Harmonizing people gathering at the gates.**

**This is not a mistake.**

*How could this be a fault?* You are poised on the threshold. Join with others and take the first step. This is certainly not a mistake. *Direction:* Retire from other engagements. You are coupled with a creative force.

### SIX AT SECOND

**Harmonizing people in the Ancestral Hall.**

**Distress.**

*Distress is the Way.* Announcing the new. A source of anxiety. You stand before the ancestor images in the temple. You are exposed to their power and are distressed. This is exactly the right feeling to have. As you think about it you will see the right way to act. It will reorganize your connection to the Way. *Direction*: Take action. You are coupled to a creative force.

### NINE AT THIRD

**Harmonizing People hide arms in the thickets**

**Ascend your high grave mound.**

**For three years' time you won't rise up.**

*This is a strong enemy that quiets your movements.* The people at war; a time to retreat and prepare a counter movement. Be careful of resentment. This may keep you isolated for quite a while, though in the end you will succeed.
*Direction*: Disentangle yourself. Proceed step by step. Gather energy for a decisive new move.

### NINE AT FOURTH

**Harmonizing People. Riding your city ramparts.**

**Nothing can control or attack you.**

**Wise Words! The Way is open.**

*Nothing limits your uprightness, so confinement is then reversed.* You stand in your own city, on the harmony of its people, deeply engaged and fully committed. Have no doubts. Trust your purpose. Let it give you the courage to go on. Nothing can stop you. This will reverse what feels like an oppressive situation.
*Direction*: Stay in your family and dwelling. Gather energy for a decisive new move.

### NINE AT FIFTH

**Harmonizing People first cry and sob and then they laugh.**

**Great leaders meet and mutualize their power.**

*Straighten the centre. Use words to mutualize your purposes.* This portrays crossing to the spring festival, a real connection between men and women. There is often loneliness and separation involved, but when you work your way through the tears, the joy will soon be there. Everything you encounter will conspire to help you. 'Sweet as the fragrance of orchids, it shatters the strength of iron.' This is the time when great leaders come together in friendship and pool their powers for the good of all.

*Direction*: Spread warmth and awareness. Don't be afraid to act alone. You are connected to a creative force.

## Nine Above

**Harmonizing People at the Outskirts Altar.**

**Without a cause for sorrow.**

*The purpose is not yet acquired.* The sorrow of winter is past. The people reach the altar to welcome the spirit and open the fields. This is a culmination that points at the emergence of a new leader and freedom from past sorrow. The sun rises in the sky. It presages a great victory. Commit yourself to this. Enjoy it with others. You won't have any cause to regret.

*Direction*: Take off the dead skin and take action. You are coupled to a creative force.

# 14 Great Being/Great Possessions DA YOU

A great idea; great power to realise; concentration, wealth, abundance; great results, great achievements; share your wealth; the Bright Presence revealed, the moon cult; site of creative transformation.

## MYTHS FOR CHANGE: THE STORY OF THE TIME

**Charge to the Oracle**: *Associating with the Harmonizing People means you truly return to the origin. Accept this and use the energy of the Great Being.*

The people's union results in the emergence of a significant power. Great Being shows a great sacrifice and the Bright Presence that comes from it. As an omen it would say Good Moon! Beneficial Changes! It describes the Great Beings and Noble Persons filled with spirit and ancient virtue and the abundance, prosperity and protection that flow through them, symbolized by the full moon and the moon cult of the Changes. These are powerful nobles, sages, diviners, war leaders and *wu*. They are the venerable ones who connect with and will be ancestors, founding people who can protect others from whom benefits flow. The Great Being embraces all, expressing the quality of the real. This is the sign for an individual being full of power and virtue, the power to become a fully realised person. It is a hand offering meat or flesh, both in sacrifice and as the shared meal with humans and spirits. It is a hand holding the moon, a master of Change.

## THE RESPONSE

**Great Being, Great Possessions.**

**Make an offering and you will succeed.**

**Great**, DA: big, noble, important; able to protect others; orient your will to a self-imposed goal; venerable, powerful, ancestor; yang energy. The old character shows the Great Person and suggests his power to protect and shelter.

**Possess**, YOU: to be, individual being, to exist in its own right; being as opposed to non-being; have, own, possessions, goods; enjoy, dispose of, arise, occur; present in sacrifice, witness at a ceremony, enjoy, have, hold. The old character shows a hand offering a meat sacrifice to the moon and the moon cult of the Changes.

DA⁴ (10210/37) shows the Great Person; the lower character (2) is CHI⁴, a hand, to offer, which was replaced by YOU³ (12936/74) and another sign added (3) ROU⁴, meat or YUE⁴, the moon.

Great Being describes your situation in terms of acquiring great abundance and prosperity through the development of a central idea. The way to deal with it is to concentrate your energies in one place and share the fruits of your efforts. Focus on a single idea and impose a direction on things. Be noble and magnanimous with the results. This can be a continuing source of fertility and excellence. It is pleasing to the spirits. Through it they will give you success, effective power and the capacity to bring the situation to maturity. Make a great offering and share with others.

## THE SCHOLAR SPEAKS

The hexagram shows a concentrated inner force that spreads brightness and warmth. Fire above Heaven. This is a time of creative abundance. Be resolute. You can associate with people and convert them to your ideas. You can gather crowds around you. Firmly check hatred in order to bring out what is virtuous and usable. Yield and work with the spirit above and let go of your personal limits. What is flexible and adaptable has acquired the ability to give honour to things. This will bring your idea to the centre of attention. What is above and what is below respond to it. This is what is called Great Being. You can realise the Way through firm persistence. Make the inherent beauty of things brighter and brighter. This connects you with Heaven above and with the right time to do things. It is pleasing to the spirits. Through it they will give you success, effective power and the capacity to bring the situation to maturity.

## THE SHAMAN SPEAKS

Fire located above Heaven. Great Being.

A time when Noble One checks hate to display improvements.

By yielding to the Great, he releases the Mandate.

*The spirit that wars in Heaven reveals itself in the Bright Omens.* This is an omen site, the Bright Presence in the Great Person. Fire and brightness above radiate light and warmth, while Heaven below struggles on, persistent and unwearied. It is Fire over Metal: Great inspiration from within spreads brightness, warmth and beauty. The ideal Realising Person reflects this by checking negative emotion to support positive change. By yielding to the force of the spirit he makes conscious Heaven's will, carried by the Bright Omens.

## TRANSFORMING LINES: CHANGE AT WORK

### INITIAL NINE

Great Being. Great Possessions.

Crosswise omens. Without harm, mingle with this spirit.

This is not a mistake.

The hardship involved is also not a mistake.

*In this beginning there is no harm.* The crosswise movement now is a good omen at the beginning. There is nothing harmful in your aims and desires. You are not making a mistake in feeling the way you do. There is hard work involved, but this isn't a mistake either. Success is assured.

*Direction:* You can connect to the spirits and found something enduring. Be resolute. You are connected to a creative force.

### NINE AT SECOND

Great Being. Great Possessions.

Use the Great Chariot to carry this.

Have a direction to go. This is not a mistake.

*Massing at the centre, this is not a defeat.* You have to have a vehicle, an inspiring idea that can carry your feelings and desires. Make a plan. Dedicate yourself. Feel the spirit of Heaven. You will not be making a mistake.

GREAT BEING

*Direction*: Spread warmth and awareness. Don't be afraid to act alone. You are coupled with a creative force.

### NINE AT THIRD

**Great Being. Great Possessions.**

**A prince makes this sacrifice to the Son of Heaven.**

**Small People cannot control it.**

*Small People are harmful now.* This is the moment of truth. Concentrate everything you have and offer it to the highest principle you know. Do not simply adapt. Do not let others control your ideas. This can create a firm and lasting connection.
*Direction*: Turn conflict into creative tension. The situation is already changing.

### NINE AT FOURTH

**Great Being. Great Possessions.**

**Do not seek dominance!**

**This is not the war dance or the fixing ritual at the ancestral gate.**

**This is not a mistake.**

*Brighten understanding and differentiate clearly.* Don't try to dominate or polarize the issues. This is not the time for aggression or insistence on your ideas. Let your Great Spirit shine through others. Bring out their qualities. Be very clear about this. You will not be making a mistake.
*Direction*: Gather energy for a great undertaking. You can realise hidden potential. The situation is already changing.

### SIX AT FIFTH

**Great Being. Great Possessions.**

**You truly have a connection to the spirits. It will carry through to others.**

**Mingle and you will impress them! An awesome presence!**

**Wise Words! The Way is open.**

*Trust the purpose to shoot forth. Be versatile and do not prepare things.* You have made a connection to the spirits and everyone will be the beneficiary. Act with complete confidence. Stay true to your purpose. With spirit like this you can deal with anything.

*Direction:* You are in contact with a creative force.

### NINE ABOVE

**Great Being. Great Possessions.**

**Heaven shields its birth. Blessings.**

**Wise Words! The Way is open.**

**Nothing not advantageous. Harvesting.**

*Great possesses the above and opens the Way. This truly originates from Heaven's shielding.* Heaven protects you, your loved ones and the birth of this new destiny. The Way is open to you. In the long run, this will benefit everything you touch. This is Heaven's Mandate.

*Direction:* Invigorate your sense of purpose. Be resolute. You are connected to a creative force.

# 15 and 16: The Paradigm

### Activating Liminal Powers and Preparing the Future:
### The Grey Rat and the Elephant

This Pair involves you in an overall model of thought and action elaborated in the interconnected lines of the figures: the flow of energy into the unconscious world and the emergence of a spirited strength that allows a joyous response to any situation. It embodies a site of radical transformation at the threshold of the human world, a Tiger Transformation where the power of Earth expresses itself in the Opened Heart to move and change us. Carefully consider your place in and relation to this model.

*Hidden Possibilities*: 40:39 > 63:64, Release bound energy to re-imagine the situation. Make the crossing and prepare the new.

The Pair exchanges information with 35:36 (Retreat and Advance, Mountain Shrine and War God). It is motivated by 51:52 (Rouser and Sacrificer). The centre and threshold lines connect 2 and 62 (the zone of transformation) with 39:40 (Difficulties and Release) and 45:46 (Assembly and Sacred Mountain).

Look at the ages and events these figures suggest for personal connections.

<u>2</u>        35:36 (37:38) 39:40     45:46      51:52      <u>62</u>

*Shadow site:* 49:50, Revolution and Casting the Vessel

**Humbling means becoming agile. Providing for means the joyous response.**

# 15 Humbling/The Grey One QIAN

Balance, adjust, cut through pride and complications; stay close to fundamentals; think and act in a modest way; omen animal showing liminal unconscious processes are activated.

## MYTHS FOR CHANGE: THE STORY OF THE TIME

**Charge to the Oracle**: *Being Great means you do not overfill things. The Grey One appears. Accept this and use the energy of Humbling.*

This figure presents a 'dream-animal' or omen animal, sign of the activation of liminal, numinous powers. The literal animal is the great grey rat-headed hamster (*Cricetelus triton nestor Thomas*). It is a large, silver-grey animal, solitary and untameable, with a human stance. It lives in an extensive system of burrows that suggest the underworld, where it hides a great store of stolen grain. It will attack and eat other rodents and can appear suddenly and ominously, standing on its hind legs with forepaws folded. The figure links this omen animal to the quality of humbling or equalizing, the moment when a lack is filled through activation of unconscious powers moving in underworld ways. As a stance in the world, this 'humbling' cuts through the pride and complication of an over-developed ego. It breeds an agile, extremely effective personal power connected with the Noble One or ideal of the Realising Person. This quality is considered to be the 'handle' of the power and virtue (*de*) that allows you to become an effective person. The souls and spirits extend blessing through it and the people love it. Heaven augments it and Earth diffuses it. The appearance of this omen animal indicates that your situation has constellated the unconscious powers and that you can trust in the outcome.

## THE RESPONSE

Humbling. The Grey One. Make an offering and you will succeed.

Noble One brings things to completion.

**Humble**, QIAN: think and speak of yourself in a modest way; polite, modest, simple, respectful; cut through pride and complication; balance and adjust, harmonize; yielding, compliant, reverent; omen animal indicating that unconscious powers are at work. The old character shows a man's face with an open mouth, suggesting words, and a hand offering two bundles of grain, balancing the powers.

QIAN[1] (1676/149) shows words (1) YAN[2] (12705), to speak in such a way that speaker and listener come together, and JIAN[1] (1508), made up of a hand YOU[2] or CHI[4] (3) holding many stalks of grain HE[2] (2) or arrows SHI[3]. With the radical 'rodent' (at right) it is the character QIAN, the Great Grey Rat.

Humbling describes your situation in terms of cutting through pride and complication. The way to deal with it is to keep your words and thoughts simple and connected to fundamental things. Think and speak of yourself in a modest way. Take the lower position. By yielding you acquire the power to realise the Way. This is pleasing to the spirits. Through it they will give you success, effective power and the capacity to bring the situation to maturity. If you use the oracle to keep in touch with the Way, you can complete what you want to do. Your acts will not bring things to an end, but will open new possibilities. Cutting through pride and the need to dominate brings a great power of realization. Be clear about this, then act directly.

## THE SCHOLAR SPEAKS

The hexagram figure shows an inner limit that connects you to the power of the Earth. In the middle of the Earth there is a mountain. This will release you from constraint and bring creative balance. Don't go to extremes. Be agile and alert. Humbling gives you a handle on the power to realise who you are meant to be. It dignifies and clarifies things, cutting away formality by keeping rules simple and clear. Reduce the many to augment the few. Carefully appraise the value of things to equalize the flow of energy. This is a time of connection between the spirit powers. Heaven moves below to bring brightness and clarity. Earth's modesty moves in the above. Heaven's way is to lessen what is overfull and augment what is humble. Earth's way is to transform what is overfull and spread what is humble. The souls and spirits that govern the world harm what is overfull and bless what is humble. The people's way is to hate what is overfull and love what is humble. Humbling brings dignity and makes things shine. It is modest and does not try to go beyond what is there. Through it you can accomplish and complete things.

## THE SHAMAN SPEAKS

> In the Earth centre, Mountain. Humbling. The Grey One appears.

> A time when Noble One reduces the many to augment the few, evaluating, evening and spreading out the beings.

*Offered service at the Earth Altar, the spirit's words bind us and accomplish fate.* The Sacrificer is working in the Field. Earth above yields and sustains while Mountain below articulates what is complete to suggest what is beginning. This is the Earth Moment: articulating the treasure hidden in the field of life. The ideal Realising Person reflects this by balancing the opposites to correctly spread the blessings that flow from the spirit world. Work through the receptive and the power of Earth. Strip the corpse.

## TRANSFORMING LINES: CHANGE AT WORK

### INITIAL SIX

> The Grey One biting through. Humbling, humbling.

> Noble One uses this to step into the Great Stream.

> Wise Words! The Way is open.

*This means lowly birth as a herdsman.* Work hard at making this work. Keep your pride out of the way. Think everything through twice, then take the big step. The Way is open to you. Unconscious powers are at work.

*Direction:* Accept difficulties. Release bound energy. The situation is already changing.

### Six at Second

**The Grey One calling.**

**Humbling signals to others.**

**Trial: Wise Words! The Way is open.**

*This means centring and acquiring the heart.* The inner work you are doing calls out to others like the cry animals use to recognize each other. Unconscious powers are at work. Don't hesitate. The Way is open.

*Direction:* Make the effort. Let yourself be led. You can realise hidden potential. The situation is already changing.

### Nine at Third

**The Grey One at work.**

**Noble One, toiling, toiling through Humbling,**

**Brings what he desires to completion.**

**Wise Words! The Way is open.**

*The myriad common people submit to this.* Humbly work at this idea, following its connection to the Way. Carry on. Unconscious powers are at work. You don't need to advertise. Whatever you desire will simply appear.

*Direction:* Be open. Provide what is needed.

### Six at Fourth

**The Grey One tearing through.**

**Demonstrating Humbling. Seize the moment.**

**There is nothing for which this will not be advantageous.**

**Harvesting.**

*There is no contradiction.* Let your actions show what Humbling really is. Cut through pride and complication. If you can do this, everything will benefit. Unconscious powers are at work. Don't be attached to your ideas and do not get involved in arguments. Everything will fall into your hands.

*Direction:* Pay careful attention to the Small. Don't be afraid to act alone. You are connected to a creative force.

## SIX AT FIFTH

**The Grey One. Humble them.**

**If you are not affluent, use your neighbour's wealth.**

**Advantageous to attack and subjugate. Harvesting.**

**There is nothing for which this will not be advantageous.**

*Chastise and do not submit!* It is time to expand. Take what you need, for people will offer. You have a real purpose. Work together. Do not be timid. Attack your problems aggressively. Everything will benefit from this behaviour. Unconscious powers are at work. *Direction*: Re-imagine the situation. Gather energy for a decisive new move.

## SIX ABOVE

**The Grey One calling.**

**Humbling signals to others.**

**Advantageous to move the legions and chastise the capital city. Harvesting.**

*Purpose is not acquired yet, but you are allowed to capture the capital.* The inner power of your purpose calls out to others. Unconscious powers are at work. Focus your energies on a major plan, marshal your forces and attack. You can set right your place in the social world, eliminate negativity and help others.
*Direction*: Articulate past experiences. Release bound energy. The situation is already changing.

# 16 Providing for/ Riding the Elephant YU

**Spontaneous, direct response; enjoy, take pleasure; collect what you need to meet the future; omen animal indicating great available reserves of grace and power; site of creative transformation.**

## MYTHS FOR CHANGE: THE STORY OF THE TIME

**Charge to the Oracle:** *A Great Being who can be humble responds to the commands of Heaven. Ride the Elephant. Accept this and use the energy of Providing for.*

Activating unconscious creative powers builds the strength for spontaneous response. The name of this figure, which evokes Yu the Great, centres around building up the ability to respond directly, joyously, spontaneously and effectively to any situation, a quality highly valued in the ancient world. It depicts gathering reserves of energy and grace into a store of power and virtue (*de*) from which you can respond without thought. This is the sort of training involved in the martial arts and many performing arts, a kind of sub-cortical patterning whereby a corrected or straightened response becomes almost simultaneous with stimulus, bypassing cerebral systems of rational choice. This ability to respond directly and correctly allows you to enjoy the moment, to take pleasure in life. The process is imaged by a child riding on an elephant, combining spontaneity with great power and grace in an emblem of a paradise state prior to the restrictions of culture. The elephant was an omen animal widespread in ancient China, used in war and sacrifice. It was also used to mean 'symbol' (*xiang*), the term that describes the divinatory figures of Change and their power of storing and discharging spirit that enables you to move effectively with the stream of experience. Joyous Response is a response to life. It indicates smooth moving, moving with the flow or current, the moment when a spirit power spontaneously triggers other forces into action.

## THE RESPONSE

Providing for a Joyous Response. Ride the Elephant.

Advantageous to install the lords to move the legions.

Harvesting.

**Provide for**, YU: take precautions, arrange for, make ready; happy, content, prepared for; joyous, pleasure, delight; spontaneous response, enthusiasm, carried away; one of the nine provinces established by Yu the Great. The old character shows a hand holding the shuttle of a loom and an elephant, sign of grace, strength and the hidden power of the great symbols.

$YU^4$ (13190/152) shows an elephant, $XIANG^4$, (1) and a shuttle, $YU^4$, (2): weaving big images. In later characters this becomes two hands, passing something on or handing over power (3).

Providing for describes your situation in terms of gathering what is needed to meet and enjoy the future. You can deal with it by accumulating strength and resources so you can respond spontaneously and fully when the time comes. Prepare things. Take precautions. Think things through so you can move smoothly with the flow of events. It is like riding an elephant that you have previously tamed, a creature of great grace and power. Establish and empower helpers, so your forces can be easily mobilized to respond to any situation. That brings profit and insight.

## THE SCHOLAR SPEAKS

The hexagram figure shows accumulated energy bounding forth at a sudden call to action. Thunder comes from Earth impetuously. Re-imagine the situation. Humbly amass a great store of things to provide for what comes. Then you don't have to worry. Double the gates and establish the watch so you are ready for violent visitors. That way you understand what the situation means. When thunder came bursting forth from the Earth, the rulers of earlier times were ready. They aroused delight, made music and thus honoured the power to realise the Way. They exalted the highest spirit and thus became very wise. Have a firm purpose and act on it. Yield and build up the capacity to spontaneously respond to a stimulus. This is why the old world worked so well. This is why you should establish helpers to mobilize your forces. This is the way Heaven and Earth work together, how they create time and order the seasons. The old wise people acted like this. They could respond immediately from their store of power to punish what was clearly wrong and thus the people accepted them. The time of providing for a spontaneous response is both righteous and great.

## THE SHAMAN SPEAKS

> **Thunder comes out of Earth impetuously, providing a Joyous Response.**
>
> **Early Kings used this to arouse people's delight and honour power and virtue.**
>
> **They exalted the worship of the Lord on High to equal the Ancient Fathers.**

*The spirit that manifests in quake and thunder is offered service at the Earth Altar.* The Rouser is working with the Field. Thunder above rouses and germinates new potential, while Earth below yields and sustains. This is Wood over Earth: the inner gathering of energy allows immediate response to an outer call to action. The ideal Realising Person reflects this by emulating the practices of the Early Kings, delighting in actualizing power and connecting his personal desires with the High Lord and the Great Ancestors. Persist and work through inner inspiration. The Spirit is returning.

## TRANSFORMING LINES: CHANGE AT WORK

### INITIAL SIX

**Trumpeting Elephant.**

**Calling out for a response.**

**Trap! The Way closes.**

*Purpose exhausted, this is a real trap.* You are trying to get others to take care of you. You have to provide for yourself now. If you keep calling for help you will exhaust all your strength.

*Direction*: A fertile shock! Re-imagine the situation. Gather energy for a decisive new move.

### SIX AT SECOND

**Bound Elephant. Provide for it.**

**The limits are turning to stone. Don't even complete the day.**

**Trial: Wise Words! The Way opens.**

*Use centring and correcting.* The limits have become so rigid they are turning you to stone. Don't wait. Let go of them now. The Way is open to you. Correct yourself.
*Direction*: Release bound energy. The situation is already changing.

### SIX AT THIRD

**Elephant watching and staring. Provide for it.**

**Skeptical response brings cause for sorrow.**

**Holding back brings cause for sorrow.**

*This is not an appropriate situation.* Don't be skeptical about this connection and don't hold back. This is real. Doubting and equivocating will only bring you sorrow. Provide what is needed, simply and directly. You won't be sorry about that.
*Direction*: Be very careful of details. Don't be afraid to act alone. You are connected to a creative force.

### NINE AT FOURTH

**Hesitating Elephant. Provide for it.**

**Do not doubt! This source provides for a joyous response.**

**Great acquisitions.**

**'You join friends together like a string of cowries, as a hair clasp gathers the hair.'**

A *great purpose is moving here*. This undertaking is sent from Heaven. It gives you everything you need. Have no doubts. Partners join together in this, gathered in by your accumulated power and virtue. Together your purpose can move mountains.
*Direction*: Be open and provide what is needed.

### Six at Fifth

**Troubled Elephant. Provide for it.**

**Trial: affliction.**

**Fix the omen and he will not die.**

*Riding a strong line, the centre is not exhausted.* This is a hard time – sickness, hostility, isolation, disorder – but don't give up. It and you will certainly survive. Give things an image. The wisdom you gather will provide for you.

*Direction*: Gather resources for a great new project. Proceed step by step. Gather energy for a decisive new move.

### Six Above

**Elephant in the shadow world. The waning moon.**

**Provide for new accomplishments. 'There will be Changes.'**

**This is not a mistake.**

*Why let this last?* You are working in the dark to provide for the future. Though the situation will deteriorate, this is not a mistake. Deny the past. Find what you need and climb out of the cave. Everything will be better in the end.

*Direction*: Emerge into the light. Re-imagine the situation. Gather energy for a decisive new move.

# 17 and 18: The Paradigm

### Follow the spirit and Renovate the Ancestral Images

This Pair involves you in an overall model of thought and action elaborated in the interconnected lines of the figures: following the flow of inspiring energy to a source of corruption and renovating the ancestral images. Through this process a child becomes an adult and participates in the great events of the world. Carefully consider your place in and relation to this model.

*Hidden Possibilities:* 53:54 > 63:64, the great marriages. Make the crossing and prepare the new.

The Pair exchanges information with 45:46 (Assembly and the Sacred Mountain). It is motivated by 25:26 (Disentangling from the Past and Accumulating the Spirit). The centre and threshold lines relate the process to 3:4 (Sprouting and Nurturing the New), 49:50 (Revolution and the New Vessel), 51:52 (Rouser and Sacrificer) and 57:58 (The Intermediaries).

Look at the ages and events these figures suggest for personal connections.

   3:4     25:26     45:46 (47:48) 49:50 51:52        57:58

*Shadow site:* 47:48, The Oppressed Noble returns to the Common Source

**Following means leaving old grounds for dissension behind.**
**Finding Corruption means there will be stability.**

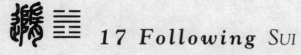 *17 Following* SUI

Move with the flow, strong, natural attraction; inevitable,
natural and correct; influence, guidance; hunter and prey; the
spirit joyously moves in the world.

MYTHS FOR CHANGE: THE STORY OF THE TIME

**Charge to the Oracle:** *Provide for responding to the commands of
Heaven and you will soon have followers. Accept this and use the energy
of Following.*

Through Following, your accumulated power and virtue (*de*) connects with the flow of events in such a way that the spirit moves
into the world through you. The earliest images of this come from
the mysterious identity between hunter and prey, reflected in the
relation between celebrant and sacrificial victim. Through
Following, a very basic and much-prized quality, you are in direct
touch with the flow of the Way. You insert yourself into the universal flow of events, the river of time, and are thus able to
conform effectively and spontaneously to the unfolding of the
moment (*shi*). You are drawn into an ancestral line and the power
of its unfolding. The root of the word shows a hill or grave mound
and great abundance, growing riches, a spreading multitude. It suggests accepting the spirit's influence gladly, letting yourself be
moved and drawn, being connected to the Way, one foot in the
world of light, one foot in the darkness. The term also refers to following a way, a school of thought, tradition or spiritual practice
and the paradoxical freedom that occurs when you submit to its
discipline.

THE RESPONSE

> **Following. The Source of Success: Advantageous Trial.
> Harvesting.**
>
> **This is not a mistake.**
>
> **Follow,** SUI: yield to a strong attraction; influence, guidance; con-
> form to, follow a way, school or religion; move in the same
> direction; natural, correct, inevitable; Following the Way, in har-
> mony with the time; the moment when you connect with the

flow of the universe. The old character shows a foot and a cross-roads, curving and winding path, a banner or grave mound with three pennants, and a warrior with a raised weapon who offers a sacrifice.

 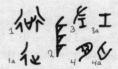

SUÌ (10101/170) centres on (1) a foot and a crossroads, abbreviated to 1a. The left part of the character (2) is a banner or a grave mound and the right part is a hand with a weapon or metal tool (3/3a) and meat (4). It suggests sacrificial meat, willingly offered at a crossing or crossroads.

Following describes your situation in terms of been drawn forward. The way to deal with it is to follow the inevitable course of events. Yield to the path set out in front of you. Be guided by the way things are moving. You are involved in a series of events that are firmly connected. Don't fight it, move with it. It opens a whole new cycle of time. This is not a mistake. The situation cannot harm you. This is pleasing to the spirits. Through it they will give you success, effective power and the capacity to bring the situation to maturity.

## THE SCHOLAR SPEAKS

The hexagram figure shows an outer stimulus rousing inner energy. In the middle of the mists there is thunder. Proceed step by step. When you have provided for the call, it comes. Let go of what is past, all the old quarrels and sorrows that led up to this situation. Dim your discriminating power so old mental habits can dissolve. A firm new focus is emerging, called up by an outer stimulus. This great new idea is pleasing to the spirits. Through it they will give you success, effective power and the ability to bring the situation to maturity. This is not a mistake. Put it to the trial. The whole human world must follow the times and the seasons. What you are actually following is a righteous idea inherent in the time.

## THE SHAMAN SPEAKS

Thunder in the centre of Mists. Following.

A time when Noble One turns towards inner darkness to enter a reposing pause.

*Spirit that manifests in quake and thunder speaks and spreads joy through the Intermediaries.* These are the Operators, the ones who work with the spirits. Rising Mists above stimulate and fertilize, while Thunder rouses new potential, sprouting energies that thrust up from below. It is Metal over Wood: stimulating words from without that stir up a deep inner impulse to follow. The ideal Realising Person reflects this by turning to his own fertile inner darkness, allowing the old to dissolve so he can follow the new. Work through subtle penetration. This involves fate. If you let yourself be led, you can realise hidden potential.

## TRANSFORMING LINES: CHANGE AT WORK

### INITIAL NINE

Following. If you have an office, deny it.

'There will be Changes.' Trial: Wise Words! The Way is open.

Issue forth from the gate and mingle with others.

There will be achievements.

*This means adhere to correcting things. Don't let go of the Way.* Leave your old life behind. Let following this influence transform you. Walk out of your old thoughts and mix with new people. This will definitely produce new achievements. The Way has opened to you. *Direction:* Gather resources for a great new project. Re-imagine the situation. Gather energy for a decisive new move.

### SIX AT SECOND

Following. Tied to the Small Son,

Letting go the Experienced Husbandman.

*This means having nowhere to join helpful companions.* This is a mistake. You have picked the wrong influence to follow. You will end up alone, without anyone to trust. All you can do then is adapt to whatever crosses your path.

*Direction*: Be cheerful. Express yourself. Find supportive friends. Gather energy for a decisive new move.

### SIX AT THIRD

**Tied to the Experienced Husbandman,**

**Letting the Small Son go.**

**Through Following, you seek and acquire what you desire.**

**Trial: advantageous for a residence. Harvesting.**

*This means what is below realises its purpose.* You have made the right choice. You are following the right influence. You will get everything you desire from this connection. Staying right where you are brings you profit and insight.

*Direction*: Change the way you present yourself. It will couple you with a creative force.

### NINE AT FOURTH

**Following to hunt and to catch.**

**Trial: Trap! The Way closes.**

**Connect to the spirits and locate yourself in the Way,**

**Make a covenant. Use the Mandate given you.**

**Your understanding will then be brightened.**

**How could this be a mistake?**

*Your righteousness is a trap. Brightening your understanding brings achievement.* You have turned Following and influence into a kind of hunt. This will trap you and cut you off from the spirit. However, you can change things easily if you want to. Connect with the flow of events rather than your will and put yourself in harmony with the Way. Use what you have been given by Heaven. Then things will come of themselves. You will understand what it is to follow rather than pursue.

*Direction*: This is an important new beginning. Strip away old ideas. Be open to the new. Provide what is needed.

### Nine at Fifth

**Following. A triumph.**

**A connection to the spirits that leads to excellence.**

**Wise Words! The Way opens.**

*The situation is centred and correct.* You have made the connection. This works. It will lead you on to real achievements. Have no doubts. Follow it. The Way is open to you.

*Direction:* Stir things up and act. Gather energy for a decisive new move.

### Six Above

**Following. Grappled and tied, they are held fast.**

**The King sacrifices and receives blessings on the Western Mountain.**

*Here the above is exhausted.* You are firmly attached to the person you follow. Others are held fast through your devotion. The King makes the great sacrifice. Offer up what you know and let go of the old. You will be enshrined in the hall of ancestors. You help in the flow of blessings. You can go no farther than this.

*Direction:* Disentangle yourself from the past and re-imagine the situation. Gather energy for a decisive new move.

# 18 Corruption and Pestilence/ Renovating Gu

**Perversion, corruption, decay; plague, pestilence, death of a parent, negative effects of parents on children; parental images, inner family; sexual infatuation; renew, renovate, new beginning.**

## Myths for Change: The Story of the Time

**Charge to the Oracle:** *Having a joyous Following means you must render service to the ancestral images. Accept this and use the energy of Corruption. Corruption means offering service to the ancestors.*

This figure probably refers to a turtle divination done to determine the most auspicious time for King Wu's army to cross the Fords of Meng on the Yellow River ('The River') and move on to battle with the Shang in the Wilds of Mu. One of its traditional images is a vase containing the five poisonous insects – snake, scorpion, centipede, gecko and toad – that were put into a jar and left until one had killed and eaten the others. This became the *Gu* – a spirit venom capable of not only crazing and killing a victim but also securing his possessions and wealth for the perpetrator of the magic. It suggests hallucination, loss of reality, sexual debauch, the insects that appear in rotting or fermenting grain, miasma, sorcery and, most of all, the curse of the ancestors, the pestilence they send when they are neglected or offended. *Gu* is first of all poisonous acts done by or to fathers and mothers that become manifest in the children. It extends to straightening, handling, managing these affairs in an individual's life, work with the inner family or parental images we all carry with us. This is the time when the new seed sprouts, a 'stem-day', and must be carefully watched. It is the moment when we pass into action, cross the river, to deal with these things.

Ancestral *Gu* played a great part in the fall of the Shang. Zhou Xin, the last tyrant, deeply angered the ancestors by disregarding the sacrifices. It was said they had not eaten in sixty years! The search for the offended ancestor causing trouble is alluded to in the lines of this figure, which have the shape and rhythm of oracle bone consultation pairs. These might have been made just before the conquest in a desperate attempt to find which ancestors were cursing the state. The Zhou preserved them in the yarrow stalk oracle as an example of the kind of corruption to be remedied.

## THE RESPONSE

**Corruption and Pestilence. The Source of Success.**

**Advantageous to step into the Great Stream. Harvesting.**

**Before 'seedburst' three days, after 'seedburst' three days.**

**Corruption/Pestilence,** GU: rotten, poisonous, defiled; intestinal worms, venomous insects; perversion, evil effects of parents and the past; black magic, hallucinations; seduce, pervert, flatter, put under a spell; disorder, error; engage in business; the first Celestial Stem, the first day of the ten-day week when decay is removed to support new growth. The old character shows worms in the meat contained in a sacrificial vessel, the shared meal spoiled.

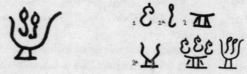

GU³ (6159/142) shows a sacrificial vessel MIN³ (2/2a) with insects or worms CHONG² (1/1a) in the meat.

Corruption/Renovating describes your situation in terms of poison, putrefaction, black magic and the evil deeds done by parents that are manifested in their children. The way to deal with it is to help things rot away so that a new beginning can be found. You are facing something that has turned to poison. Search out the source so new growth can begin. This is pleasing to the spirits. Through it they will give you success, effective power and the capacity to bring the situation to maturity. This is the right time to enter the Stream of Life with a goal, or to embark on a significant enterprise. That brings profit and insight. Prepare the moment when the new time arrives and carefully watch over its first growth. It will take three days, a whole period of activity, before the seed of the new energy bursts open, and a similar period afterwards to stabilize it.

## THE SCHOLAR SPEAKS

The hexagram figure shows an obstacle in the outer world that turns inner growth back on itself. Below the mountain there is wind. If you let yourself be led, you can realise a hidden potential. Being engaged in the world of affairs and the service of kings always implies corruption. If you find its source, you can stabilize the situation. Rouse up the undeveloped potential outside your normal set of values in order to nurture the power to realise what you must do. A solid limit above is stopping the nourishment of new growth. This means corruption. This rotting away can be the beginning of a new spring. Make the effort. This is pleasing to the spirits. Through it they will give you success, effective power and the capacity to bring the situation to maturity. You can regulate the world anew. Set out with a firm purpose. You will soon have enough to keep you busy. Watch carefully before and after the opening. You can bring things to a conclusion that results in a new beginning. The spirit above is moving in this situation.

## THE SHAMAN SPEAKS

**Wind below Mountain. Corruption and Pestilence.**

**A time when Noble One joins and rouses the commoners**

**to nurture power and virtue.**

*Spirit works in those who lay out the offerings. Its words bind us and accomplish fate.* These are the Operators, the ones who work with the spirits. Mountain above limits and articulates what is complete to suggest what is beginning, while Wind and Wood enter subtly from below, penetrating, pervading and coupling with the new. It is Earth over Wood: an outer limit that turns the focus on inner corruption. The ideal Realising Person reflects this by rousing a sense of our common needs, strengthening the power to renew the Ancestral images. You are journeying into the world of the great symbols.

### Initial Six

**Corruption. Managing and straightening the Father's Pestilence.**

**The offspring correct the faults of the predecessors.**

**Adversity, hungry souls and angry ghosts.**

**Wise Words! Completing this opens the Way.**

*This means taking predecessor's intention in hand.* You must deal with the corruption of authority. This means danger with roots in the past. If you can manage this, the Way will open. Take on the responsibility like a son or daughter who redeems the ancestors and go through it to the end. This is the place of Yu the Great, the hero who redeemed his father's work and of King Wu, who launched the armies and redeemed the time.

*Direction:* Concentrate. Focus. Be active. If you let yourself be led, you can realise hidden potential. The situation is already changing.

### Nine at Second

**Corruption. Managing and straightening the Mother's Pestilence.**

**This is not an Enabling Trial.**

*This means acquiring the centre and the Way.* You must deal with the corruption of nourishment and care. Get to the source of the trouble before you put things into motion. You cannot simply take action. Put yourself in the middle of the situation and try to find the Way. Then you can see and change the obstruction.

*Direction:* Find and articulate the obstacles. Release bound energy. The situation is already changing.

### Nine at Third

**Corruption. Managing and straightening the Father's Pestilence.**

**Small has cause for sorrow.**

**Without the Great, a mistake.**

*Completing this is not a mistake.* You must deal with the corruption of authority. There will be regrets that you co-operated with it in the past. You must have a strong central purpose to come through.

*Direction*: There is something hidden that will unfold in this situation. Be open and provide what is needed.

### Six at Fourth

**Abundant Corruption. Enriching the 'bathing' Father.**

**Going on like this you will see distress.**

*This means going and not acquiring it.* You are colluding with the corruption of authority. This figure is in the process of changing, so don't simply follow the old ways. If you do, you will end up both lonely and confused, cut off from the Way.
*Direction*: Transform your awareness. Be resolute. You are connected with a creative force.

### Six at Fifth

**Corruption. Managing and straightening the Father's Pestilence.**

**Use praise to accomplish the task.**

*This means receiving and using power and virtue.* You must deal with the corruption of authority. Don't attack directly. Use praise to accomplish the task. You will disarm your opponent and reclaim your own power. In the process you will find out what your purpose really is.
*Direction*: Subtly penetrate to the core of the problem. Turn conflict into creative tension. The situation is already changing.

### Nine Above

**Corruption. Don't involve yourself in the Pestilence affecting the kings and the lords.**

**Honouring what is highest is your affair.**

*This allows you to find your purpose.* You should keep clear of the current corruption of business and politics. You have another job, finding and honouring what is truly noble in the human spirit. You will be rewarded for this. These are the people who work on in a dark time to prepare the new dawn.
*Direction*: Make the effort. If you let yourself be led, you can realise hidden potential. The situation is already changing.

# 19 and 20: The Paradigm

## Releasing the Spirit and Watching the Omens

This Pair involves you in an overall model of thought and action elaborated in the interconnected lines of the figures: releasing a spirit force and reading the omens of its emergence as a basis for action and change. This begins the ordeal of initiation. Carefully consider your place in and relation to this model.

*Hidden Possibilities*: 24:23 > 2, the return of the spirit allows stripping away the old, connecting you to the primal power of realization.

The Pair exchanges information with 7:8 (Armies and the New Group). It is motivated by 41:42 (The Offering and the Blessing). The centre and threshold lines relate the process to 23:24 (Stripping the Corpse and The Returning Spirit), 11:12 (New and Old King), 53:54 (The Great Marriages) and 59:60 (Dissolution and Articulation).

Look at the ages and events these figures suggest for personal connections.

7:8    11:12    23:24    41:42    53:54    59:60

*Shadow site*: 45:46, Gather the People and Ascend the Sacred Mountain

**Nearing and Viewing are righteous. 'Someone' helps you; 'Someone' will trace the pattern.**

# 🁢 ☷☳ *19 Nearing/Releasing the Spirit* LIN

Arrival of the new; approach of something powerful and meaningful; welcome, draw nearer and closer; funeral celebrations, ritual mourning.

MYTHS FOR CHANGE: THE STORY OF THE TIME

**Charge to the Oracle:** *When you serve the ancestors you can become Great. Accept this and use the energy of Nearing. Release the spirit. This means becoming Great.*

Nearing or Approaching describes the ceremonies through which a newly dead noble is turned into an ancestor. The soul or ghost is escorted into the tomb through elaborate funeral ceremonies and ritual mourning that feed it, while the spirit is enshrined in a spirit image or tablet in the Ancestral Temple that serves as a connection or doorway to the power above. The ancestor that mounts from the tablet acts as an intermediary. It calls down Heaven's protection, protection from above that showers blessings on the people. The root of the word 'Nearing' also shows a dignitary, an official in royal service, who directly carries out orders from above and suggests signs and oracles, divination books, oracle books in temples.

The creation of this power, symbolized as the Ancestor's Eyes watching from above on the bronze ritual vessels, is surrounded by the formal lamentations of a funeral procession and the activities of the *wugui*, Intermediaries concerned with the unquiet dead. Mourners exhaust themselves in the ceremony, offering sacrifice of rare goods and vessels. The Crane Dancers literally followed the dead into the tomb, accompanied by lamentations and cries of triumph. All these rituals are part of an investment in darkness, a ceremony that turns the experience of death into an ancestor through whom blessings can flow. They make the ghost comfortable in the tomb, releasing it from the desire to re-enact earthly passions, so that it will eventually merge once again with the Ghost River. It suggests that any great accomplishment, any great blessing or approach, must be founded on a sacrifice, an acknowledgement of the dark powers without whom nothing can grow or flourish.

The *xia* and *di* ceremonies complete the creation of the ancestor spirit. In the *xia* sacrifice and feast, the newly dead ancestor is re-united with and installed in the line of ancestors after the end of the mourning period. The *di* ceremony sets the royal ancestors among the ranks that sit at the right and left of the High Lord in his court in the Great Bear. This marks the 'Nearing', the beginning of the ancestor's power to bestow blessings and act as intermediary, moving between the spirit tablet in the Ancestral Temple and the court of the High Lord.

## The Response

**Nearing. The Source of Success: Advantageous Trial. Harvesting.**

**Ending this in the eighth moon: Trap! The Way closes.**

**Nearing,** *LIN*: a beneficent spirit or an honoured person approaches to confer favour and blessing; look at with love, care and sympathy; arrive, make contact, point of arrival; be honoured with a visit, be commanded to come nearer; moment when positive force comes to the fore; mount in power, watch over, shower blessings, the ancestor's eyes; ceremonies at a funeral to ensure the repose of the dead; bring boats together, facing; lamentations, public mourning; 'descending to the valley', approaching a critical point, nearing death, mourning and sickness. The old character shows a spirit-person bending down to pour out blessings from a vessel, blessings that pass through his descendant to three open mouths that receive it.

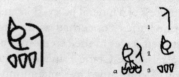

*LIN²* (7135/131) is composed of a man, *REN²* (1), bending over, a vertical eye *MU²* (2), a vassal or descendant *CHEN²* and three mouths *PIN³* (3), indicating a number of people one cares for. Another old form (a) shows connecting lines between the eye and the mouths.

Nearing describes your situation in terms of something approaching, particularly something great approaching something smaller. It is the first arrival and point of new contact. The way to deal with it is to move towards what is approaching without expecting to get what you want immediately. Look at things with care and sympathy. Welcome the approach of others. Keep your expectations modest. This contact opens a whole new cycle of time. It is particularly favourable for what is growing. So beware. Trying to rush to completion and an early harvest will cut you off from the spirits and leave you open to danger.

## THE SCHOLAR SPEAKS

The hexagram figure shows desire for contact expressed through a willingness to work and serve. Above the mists there is Earth. This is the return of the great. Invite it to come nearer. The proper thing to do is to bring things together. When you teach, use your teaching to continually ponder the heart's concerns. Tolerate and protect things and people outside your normal set of values without setting limits on them. There is an undeveloped potential that you rely on without knowing it. What is strong and firm in this situation increases gradually. Work to express it. Keep yourself centred and connected to things. If you want something great to come of this, you must continually correct yourself. That is Heaven's Way. Stay on an even path. Rushing to finish things will leave you open to harm. The whole situation will dissolve.

## THE SHAMAN SPEAKS

Earth above Mists. Nearing. Releasing the Spirit.

A time when Noble One teaches and ponders without exhaustion,

tolerating and protecting the commoners without limit.

*Spirit speaks and spreads joy through the Intermediaries. Offer service at the Earth Altar.* The Intermediaries are working in the Earth. Field above yields and sustains, while Mists rising from below stimulate and fertilize, joyous words that cheer and inspire. This is Earth over Metal: stimulation within the Earth that prepares the approach of great power. The ideal Realising Person reflects this, meditating on the Way, spreading the teachings to inspire the lives of all. Work through joyous words to bring spirit to expression. Gather the resources for a great project.

## Transforming Lines: Change at Work

### Initial Nine

**Chanting, keening, salty tears.**

**Conjunction Nearing. Release the spirit.**

**Trial: Wise Words! The Way is open.**

*This means your purpose is moving correctly.* Lamenting at the funeral. The spirit liberated now belongs with you like parts of a previously separated whole. This is a connection made in Heaven. It will stimulate and inspire you. Have no doubts. The Way is open.

*Direction:* Organize your forces. This is the return of something important. Be open. Provide what is needed.

### Nine at Second

**Chanting, keening, salty tears.**

**Conjunction Nearing. Release the spirit.**

**Wise Words! The Way is open.**

**Nothing not advantageous.**

*Not yielding to fate.* Lamenting at the funeral. The spirit liberated now belongs with you like parts of a previously separated whole. This is a connection made in Heaven, at the centre of the inner world. It will stimulate and inspire you. There is nothing that will not benefit from this connection. The good consequences have hardly begun.

*Direction:* This is the return of something important. Be open. Provide what is needed.

### Six at Third

**Enough lamenting!**

**Sweetly Nearing, there is no advantageous direction.**

**If you are already grieving, there will be no mistake.**

*Not an appropriate situation, but the fault does not last.* Leave off! The approaching spirit may look sweet, but no good can come of it. This is simply not right for you. Painful though it may be, if you have already realised it you won't make mistakes. Let go of the influence or the opportunity.

*Direction:* This change begins a flourishing new time. Turn conflict into creative tension. The situation is already changing.

## SIX AT FOURTH

**Wailing and crying.**
**Climax Nearing. Release the spirit.**
**This is not a mistake.**

*This is an appropriate situation.* The climax approaches. Don't hold back. Give yourself fully. This is not a mistake. It releases the spirit.
*Direction:* Turn conflict into creative tension. The situation is already changing.

## SIX AT FIFTH

**Overseeing the sacrifice.**
**Knowledge Nearing. Release the spirit.**
**The Great Leader sacrifices at the Earth Altar.**
**Wise Words! The Way is open.**

*This is called moving the centre.* This is the Great War Leader announcing the launch of the armies that will conquer Shang. It is the knowledge a great leader uses to help and change the people. It is time to take action. The spirit will be with you. This can change the way you see yourself and your life.
*Direction:* Articulate this. Find your voice. Take things in. Provide what is needed.

## SIX ABOVE

**Chanting and keening without restraint.**
**Generosity and wealth are Nearing. Release the spirit.**
**Wise Words! The Way opens.**
**This is not a mistake.**

*Locate your purpose within.* The ancestor spirit responds fully. Generosity, wealth and the power of enjoyment enter your life through this connection. Be generous with what you acquire. Hold on to your sense of inner purpose. Your desires will be fulfilled.
*Direction:* Decrease present involvement to make new energy available. Make the sacrifice. Something important returns. Provide what is needed.

# 20 *Viewing* GUAN

**Reading the signs; let everything come into view, examine, contemplate, divine the meaning; the invisible manifests in the visible world; the Tower, initiation begins.**

## MYTHS FOR CHANGE: THE STORY OF THE TIME

**Charge to the Oracle**: *Being Great lets you see the hidden things. The ancestor's eyes. Accept this and use the energy of Viewing.*

Viewing represents the perception of the invisible influences that spread from the spirit released through the ceremonies in Nearing. It is the moment when you read the omens of the ancestor spirit as and where they appear in the world and you are thus able to seize the influx of hidden energies. In ritual terms, this is 'fixing the spirit' (*heng*), making its influence endure. It is a certain mood and moment in a ceremony, just before the wine libation that calls the spirit presence, and the place where its omens are observed, a tomb, tumulus, grave mound, temple or observatory tower. The root of the term suggests visualizing in all its aspects: watching, appearance, clairvoyance and the intelligence that makes things clear. It is the word used to translate 'yoga'. King Wen, spiritual father of the Zhou, built such a magic tower at Feng, watching the skies and consulting the Intermediaries from a ritual platform raised high above the ground. He was searching for the appearance of the *ming xing*, the 'Mandated Star', waiting for the command of Heaven and the Great Ancestor to be implemented below.

## THE RESPONSE

> Viewing. The ablution, then the libation.
>
> The connection to spirit will come like a presence.

**View, GUAN**: contemplate, look at from a distance, examine, judge, conjecture; let everything emerge into view; divine the meaning; instruct, inform, make known; a tower on the outskirts where initiation begins; observatory, observing bird signs and celestial omens; grave mound, high tower, high terrace for worship, moment in a ceremony between ablutions and libation, the pouring out of the dark wine that calls the spirits. The old character shows a bird face with bright eyes and a standing person whose head has filled with spirit.

GUAN[1] (6294/147) represents a bird with big eyes and a crest, GUAN[2], the 'old gatekeeper', and a man with a big eye, JIAN[2].

Viewing describes your situation in terms of the need to look without acting in order to find the right perspective. The way to deal with it is to let everything emerge and divine the central meaning. Particularly, look at what you usually don't want to see or think about. This figure describes a particular moment in a religious ceremony, when the purification has been made and the libation is about to be poured out. Have confidence. Examining things will bring you the insight you need. When you have made the preparations, the spirit will arrive and carry you through.

## THE SCHOLAR SPEAKS

The hexagram figure shows images appearing on the inner field. The wind moves above the Earth. Strip away your old ideas. There is something of great importance here and you can seek it out. The early rulers used this time to inspect the borders. They contemplated the needs of the people and set up ways to instruct them. Take a high view of the matter at hand. Yield to things and give them space on the inner ground. Stay correctly centred and you can let the whole world come into view. Prepare things well and the spirit will answer, the things you are trying to influence will change spontaneously. By viewing the way that Heaven moves through the spirits, you can see the proper times for things. When the sages used the Way of the spirits to establish and teach, the whole human world would listen.

## THE SHAMAN SPEAKS

Wind moves above Earth. Viewing.

A time when the Early Kings watched the Four Hidden Lands
to view the common good and set up teachings.

*Spirit works in those who lay out the offerings. Offer service at the
Earth Altar.* The Intermediaries are working with Earth. Wind and
Wood above enter subtly, penetrating, pervading and coupling,
while Earth below yields and sustains. This is Wood over Earth:
images of spirit come into view as they emerge on inner field. The
ideal Realising Person reflects this by emulating the Early Kings
who acted as guides and protectors for all. Work through subtle
penetration. This involves fate. Ascend the Sacred Mountain.

## TRANSFORMING LINES: CHANGE AT WORK

### INITIAL SIX

Viewing the children's omens.

For Small People this is not a mistake.

Noble One: distress.

*This is Small People's Way.* Watching the children play. You may
read things that can disturb the entire state. These are beginnings
of danger. The Small People see nothing in this. The Noble One
perceives the distress. Don't see things like a child. Be aware of the
first stirrings of disturbance.
*Direction:* Increase your efforts. Strip away old ideas. Be open and
provide what is needed.

### SIX AT SECOND

Viewing through a patterned screen.

Advantageous if the women divine. Harvesting.

*This can be shameful.* Watching furtively to catch a sign of the new.
Work through. If you ask the oracle you will see how the spirit is
moving here. The woman and the Yin. Don't fall into negative
emotions.
*Direction:* Clear away obstacles to understanding. Take things in.
Be open and provide what is needed.

### SIX AT THIRD

**Viewing our birth, advance or withdraw?**

*Not letting go of the Way.* Watching the spirit manifest in the clan. This is a transition. You have to decide whether to go on with this connection or to pull back. Look at the things you have done in this context, what they give birth to, what they create in you. Use that to answer your question.

*Direction*: Proceed step by step. Gather energy for a decisive new move.

### SIX AT FOURTH

**Viewing the city shining.**

**Advantageous to be a guest when the King hosts the ancestors. Harvesting.**

*An honoured guest.* You witness the great ceremony when the King hosts the ancestor spirit. This connection can bring you power and wealth. The city is spread out before you. Remember, however, you are only a guest. Be careful and polite. This is a long-term experience.

*Direction*: Communication may be obstructed. Don't be the victim. Proceed step by step. Gather energy for a decisive new move.

### NINE AT FIFTH

**Watching the sacrifices. Viewing our birth.**

**Noble One makes no mistake.**

*This is viewing the common people.* The new ancestor spirit manifests in the world. Look deeply at this connection and your relation to it. Observe what you have in common with those around you. Look at the things you have done in this context, what they give birth to, then commit yourself. If you measure your desires against the ideal of the Noble One, you won't make any mistakes.

*Direction*: Strip away old ideas. Provide what is needed.

### NINE ABOVE

**Watching the sacrifices. Viewing its birth.**

**Noble One makes no mistake.**

*Your purpose is not calm yet.* The new ancestor spirit manifests in the world. Look deeply at this connection. Look at where and how it started and the effect it has had on your life and the lives of others. Measure it against the ideal of Noble One, then commit yourself. You won't be making a mistake.

*Direction:* Change who you associate with. Strip away old ideas. Be open and provide what is needed.

# 21 and 22: The Paradigm

### 'Eating Ancient Virtue' and Bringing Home the Bride

This Pair involves you in an overall model of thought and action elaborated in the interconnected lines of the figures: biting through obstacles at the sacred meal and a wedding procession that brings a new bride to the ancestral home. It embodies a site of radical transformation at the threshold of the human world, a Tiger Transformation where the Bright Omens arise from the Tiger's Mouth as images of a new life: initiation for a man and a woman's journey to a new home and status as a bride. Carefully consider your place in and relation to this model.

*Hidden Possibilities*: 39:40 > 63:64, re-imagine the situation to release bound energy. Make the crossing and prepare the new.

The Pair exchanges information with 35:36 (Rising and Setting Sun). It is motivated by 51:52 (The Rouser and the Sacrificer). The centre and threshold lines connect 27 and 30 (the zone of transformation) with 25:26 (Disentangling from the Past and Accumulating the New Spirit) and 37:38 (Dwelling and the Ghosts that Haunt it).

Look at the ages and events these figures suggest for personal connections.

25:26 <u>27 30</u>    35:36 37:38        51:52

*Shadow site*: 43:44, Announce the Omen: Enter the Lady of Fates

**Biting Through means joining in the sacred meal.
Adorning means you begin without a face.**

# 21 Biting Through/ The Sacred Meal
## SHI HE

**Confront the problem, bite through the obstacle; tenacious, determined, enduring; a time for action and punishment; shared meal in the Tower, 'eating ancient virtue'; site of creative transformation; beginning of initiation ordeal.**

MYTHS FOR CHANGE: THE STORY OF THE TIME

**Charge to the Oracle:** *When you view the omens you have a place to unite. The sacred meal. Eating ancient virtue. Accept this and use the energy of Biting Through. This means uniting the nobles.*

Biting Through connects eating and biting through an obstacle with words and questions. The root is mouth, speech and language. It suggests posing a question to an oracle and getting a response, the bird dances of the *wu*-Intermediaries and the pulses taken at the wrist in medical diagnosis. It means to Bite Through to something hidden, to invade or annex territory, to eliminate obstacles to harmony and thus to the beauty and union with spirits suggested in the following figure.

Biting Through portrays the shared ritual meal that unites spirits and humans, held in an Ancestral Temple. It was metaphorically, and sometimes literally, eating the ancestor's flesh. It is also the punishment and sacrifice of criminals and prisoners who were 'eaten by the ancestor'. It deals with the act of judging and punishing, imaged as two dogs that stand guard, and portrays three of the significant punishments, foot-cutting, nose-cutting and the cangue, a heavy wooden yoke strapped across the shoulders that immobilized the hands. It further suggests executions, human sacrifice and reading omens in the remains of sacrifices and bodies that had been ritually exposed.

The characters also share a root with *shi,* the book diviners or book-Intermediaries who hold the *te* or virtue of the ancestors in the oracle books and records. It suggests the *shi* or 'corpse', the embodiers who were possessed by ancestor spirits at the shared meals, and the statues and images in the temples that 'held the spirits'. The ritual meal is doubled in the picture of the diviners 'eating the ancient virtue' of the ancestors through the spirit-books, Biting Through the words to the bright omens they hide.

## THE RESPONSE

**Biting Through. Make an offering and you will succeed.**

**Advantageous to judge and punish. Harvesting.**

**Bite**, *SHI*: gnaw, chew, nibble away, bite by bite; arrive at the truth, attain the goal, remove what is extraneous and reveal what is necessary; annex, take in invade, reach, come to; question, ask why. The old character shows an open mouth, the pillar of an ancestral hall with two people facing each other, diviner and inquirer, and the yarrow stalks or spirit plants growing from the roof. It suggests the *WU* or spirit-mediums associated with the Four Hidden Lands **Through/unite**, *HE*: close the jaws, crush; destroy an obstacle; unite, bring together; sound of spirit voices, recipient with cover filled with food; drink, laugh, laughter. The old character shows an open mouth, a sacrificial vessel with a charge to Heaven inside it, and the lid being lowered to seal the vessel for cooking. Both suggest the shared meal and divination as contact with the spirit. Through this ordeal, an inner voice speaks until it is clear.

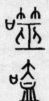 

*SHI*[4] (9723/30) is composed of bamboo *ZHU*[2] (1), shaman or wizard *WU*[1] (3) and mouth *KOU*[3] (4). It indicates oracle consulting with yarrow stalks. The element *WU* is made up of work (2) and two people *REN*[2.] Another character, (8), is a picture of a female shaman or *WU* dancing with long sleeves. These Four *WU* were the assistants of the great ancestor Di, each associated with one of the four Hidden Lands. *KE*[4], (3855/30) or, without the mouth, *HE*[2,5] (3871) is composed of mouth *KOU*[3] (4), a vessel *MIN*[3] (6) and a lid or a 'closer' (5). The lid (10) was originally a drawing of a man with a ball between his legs and suggests an initiation ordeal.

Biting Through describes your situation in terms of confronting a tenacious obstacle. The way to deal with it is to gnaw away what is unnecessary and bite through the core of the problem. Something is keeping the jaws from coming together. Take decisive action. Gnaw away at the obstacles until you reach the hidden centre, then Bite Through what is keeping things apart. This is pleasing to the spirits and they will help you. Take things to court. That brings profit and insight. This is a time for legal action, punishment and a warning against criminal activity.

## The Scholar Speaks

The hexagram figure shows inner determination breaking through obstacles and spreading clarity. Thunder and lightning. Gather your forces. Re-imagine the situation. You have contemplated long enough. Take resolute action. You have the opportunity to bring things together. Provide what is needed. This is a severe time. The early Kings used it to clarify criminal punishments and thus enforce the laws. There is something between the jaws. Say it this way: gnaw and Bite Through! This is pleasing to the spirits. Through it they will give you success, effective power and the capacity to bring the situation to maturity. Decide when to be adaptable and when to be firm. Stir things up and clarify them. Create a structure that unites thunder, the shock that comes from below, and lightning, the sudden clarity that comes from above. Keep your centre flexible and act from above. Even though the situation may not be appropriate, bringing things to judgement brings profit and insight.

## The Shaman Speaks

**Thunder and Lightning. Biting Through. Eating ancient virtue.**

**A time when Early Kings used severe punishments to clarify and enforce the laws.**

*The spirit that manifests in quake and thunder reveals the Bright Omens.* The Rouser is working with the Bright Omens. Fire and brightness above radiate light and warmth, while Thunder rouses and germinates new potential, sprouting energies that thrust up from below. This is Fire over Wood: inner rousing that breaks through obstacles to awareness. The ideal Realising Person reflects this by emulating the ancient Kings and their use of precise and severe punishments to clarify what is right and what is harmful. Hold the heart fast and take the risk. The new King is emerging.

## TRANSFORMING LINES: CHANGE AT WORK

### INITIAL NINE

**Biting Through. His shoes locked in a wooden stock.**

**His feet disappear.**

**This is not a mistake.**

*This means not moving.* You are the prisoner this time. Trying to control the situation, you have been locked up and cannot move. Don't worry. This is for your own good. It is the right thing to do now. It will make you think.

*Direction:* You will emerge into the light and be recognized. Reimagine the situation. Gather your energy for an impressive new move.

### SIX AT SECOND

**Biting Through flesh at the sacred meal, his nose disappears.**

**This is not a mistake.**

*This is riding a strong line.* The ritual meal in the Ancestor Temple. Enthusiastically Biting Through obstacles, you go a little overboard. Don't worry about your enthusiasm. Keep it up. This is not a mistake. You are on the right track.

*Direction:* Turn conflict into creative tension. The situation is already changing.

### SIX AT THIRD

**Biting Through dried meat at the sacred meal, meeting poison.**

**Small is distressed.**

**This is not a mistake.**

*Not an appropriate situation.* The ritual meal in the Ancestor Temple. Biting Through the obstacles, you encounter something old and dangerous. Take it on. Don't try to hide it. If you simply adapt, you will be ashamed and confused. Bring it out into the open. This is not a mistake.

*Direction*: Clarify the situation. Be warm and insightful. Don't be afraid to act alone. You are connected to a creative force.

### NINE AT FOURTH

**Biting Through parched meat with bones at the sacred meal.**

**Acquiring a bronze arrow.**

**Trial: hardship is advantageous. Harvesting.**

**Wise Words! The Way opens.**

*This is not shining yet.* The ritual meal in the Ancestor Temple. Getting through this is a long, arduous task, but you will find something of great value. The drudgery will definitely be worth it in the end. This will open the Way for you and everything you wish for. The effects will be lasting.
*Direction*: Take things in. Be open and provide what is needed.

### SIX AT FIFTH

**Biting Through parched meat at the sacred meal.**

**Acquiring bronze and gold.**

**Trial: going through adversity is advantageous.**

**Hungry souls and angry ghosts.**

**This is not a mistake. Harvesting.**

*You acquire what is appropriate.* The ritual meal in the Ancestor Temple. Getting through this confrontation is a long, arduous task. In the end you acquire something of very great value, wealth and the possibility it gives to establish a line of descent. You are going to have to confront other people's ghosts and shadows in the process. Have no fear, this is not a mistake.
*Direction*: Disentangle yourself. Proceed step by step. Gather energy for a decisive new move.

**Biting Through.**

**Why are you locked in a wooden stock so your ears disappear?**

**Trap! The Way closes.**

*Your understanding is not brightened.* This means serious punishment. This time you have seriously cut yourself off. You can lose important relationships and goals. Why can't you hear this? You certainly won't accomplish anything this way!

*Direction:* A fertilizing shock is coming. Re-imagine your situation. Gather energy for a decisive new move.

# 22 Adorning/Bringing Home the Bride Bi

**Beautify, embellish; display courage and beauty; elegance; make appearance reflect inner worth; wedding procession, bring home the bride; site of creative transformation.**

## MYTHS FOR CHANGE: THE STORY OF THE TIME

**Charge to the Oracle:** *Beings cannot come together without a new way to unite. Bring the bride home. Accept this and use the energy of Adorning. This means beautifying things.*

Adorning, which means to decorate, beautify, ornament in magnificent, resplendent, many-coloured beauty, primarily refers to a marriage procession, when the groom and his horsemen go to fetch the bride and escort her back to the ancestral home. It is a festive procession that crosses the river to the paradise time, surrounded by the Bright Presence. It represents vigorous measures to establish the harmony of above and below, a display of brilliance and courage that reflects inner worth. Medically, this process clears away stagnation of yin energy and opens the yin channels. The root is cowries, shells used as money and presented as ritual offerings, that suggest the vulva. It connects the signs for heart, bamboo strips for writing and the act of revealing and making the omens manifest. The procession itself would have been striking, the horsemen plumed and decked out, the sleek horses plunging through the river, bamboo screens and red leather harness tossing many tassels, all surrounding the beautifully adorned bride. 'You came for me with horses to take me and my dowry away,' she says. 'The River Wen is swollen, the escort a great band. Treading this road is easy: the bride goes to pleasure.'

## THE RESPONSE

Adorning. Wedding Procession. Make an offering and you will succeed.

Work through the Small.

Advantageous to have a place to go. Harvesting.

## 22

**Adorn**, *Bi*: embellish, ornament, beautify; grace and elegance; cosmetics, make-up; inner worth that shines in appearance; energetic, brave, eager, passionate; display of courage. The old character shows a flowering plant growing from a cowry shell, sign of worth and symbol of the female.

*BI*[4] (8841/154) represents a flowering plant, which means brilliant, luminous, ornate, bright, decoration, to honour. This may be *Artemisia Stelleriana*, important in pharmacology as a restorer of energy.

Adorning describes your situation in terms of its outward appearance. You can deal with it by decorating, beautifying and embellishing the way things are presented. This builds up intrinsic value. Be elegant. Be brilliant. Display your valour. Think of this as a festive marriage procession. Let the way you present yourself signal the changes in your life. This is pleasing to the spirits. Through it they will give you success, effective power and the capacity to bring the situation to maturity. Be flexible and adapt to what presents itself to be done. Have a place to go. Impose a direction on things. That brings profit and insight.

## THE SCHOLAR SPEAKS
The hexagram figure shows an outer limit that produces a radiant display. Beneath the mountain there is fire. Release tensions and display energy. People can't come together carelessly. They must be embellished to be seen. At present you lack a face, a means of expression. Brighten and clarify all the different parts of how you present yourself. Don't cut off social and legal processes that are already underway. Adorning things is pleasing to the spirits. Through it they will give you success, effective power and the capacity to bring the situation to maturity. Be adaptable. This reveals the strength of the underlying design and its source. Having a direction now will help reveal Heaven's design. Brightening and clarifying the pattern, and stopping there, reveals it to the people

involved. Contemplate the overall pattern. Look at the transformation the seasons can bring. Contemplate the pattern of the people involved. Use gradual, continuous change to accomplish things in the human world.

## THE SHAMAN SPEAKS

Fire below the Mountain. Adorning. A wedding procession.

This is a time when Noble One brightens the multitude's standards without daring to be severe.

*Spirit words bind us and accomplish fate, revealing its presence in the Bright Omens.* The Sacrificer is working with the Bright Omens. Mountain above limits and articulates what is complete to suggest what is beginning, while Fire below radiates light and warmth and people experience the Bright Presence of things. This is Earth over Fire: an outer limit that articulates inner beauty. The ideal Realising Person reflects this by brightening the goals of the myriad people. Understanding without judging or attempting to control them, he is carried by the Bright Omens. Set out on your journey.

## TRANSFORMING LINES: CHANGE AT WORK

### INITIAL NINE

Adorning his feet.

He leaves the chariot and goes on foot.

The riders set out for the bride.

*Righteous to ride on nothing.* Adorn yourself with courage and independence. Make your own way. Start out alone. Don't take the easy way out.
*Direction:* Stabilize your desires. Things are already changing.

### SIX AT SECOND

Adorning his growing hair and beard.

The horses are sleek. Have patience.

*This is associating with the above and rising.* Be brave and patient. Display yourself and your virtues. It will take time, but a new connection to a really superior person is already there. If you adorn yourself with elegance and patience, it will lift you into a better sphere. This is a boy letting his hair grow in preparation for the ceremony in which he puts on the cap of manhood, becomes a warrior and acquires a ritual presence.

*Direction*: Collect your forces. Prepare for an active time. If you let yourself be led, you can realise hidden potential. The situation is already changing.

### NINE AT THIRD

**Adorned and sleek, impregnated with this.**

**Trial: Wise Words! This is an ever-flowing Way.**

*The result is a great grave mound.* Let the coming connection impregnate you. This is the one. Don't try to bring it to an end. This can open the Way for you and all your descendants.

*Direction*: Take things in. Be open and provide what is needed.

### SIX AT FOURTH

**Adorned and venerable, they ride the soaring white horse.**

**Those you encounter are not at all outlaws. Seek the marriage alliance.**

*A proper place to doubt. Complete this without being excessive.* Attribute great wisdom and worth to this connection. It can carry you like the sacred flying horse. These people are not trying to steal anything from you. This is the time for a marriage, not distrust. This can be an ever-flowing source of inspiration and pleasure.

*Direction*: Spread light, warmth and clarity. Don't be afraid to act alone. You are connected with a creative force.

### SIX AT FIFTH

**Adorning in the hilltop garden. The marriage gifts.**

**The roll of undyed silk is little, little.**

**Distress. Wise Words! Completing this opens the Way.**

*There will be rejoicing.* You are now asked to become a formal member of this group and present a sacrifice at the ancestral graves. You must offer something at the shrine, the marriage gifts, but you have very little to give. Go through with this, even if you are embarrassed, for it will open the Way. Soon you will have great cause to rejoice.

*Direction*: Find supportive friends. Gather energy for a decisive new move.

### NINE ABOVE

**Adorned in white. The riders arrive with the bride.**

**This is not a mistake.**

*This means acquiring a purpose in the above.* The culmination of the procession. White is the colour of death and thus what is plain, clear, pure and releases the spirit. Don't hide things. Bring out the essentials. Adorn yourself with real virtue. It is necessary to know the truth here, no matter what it costs. This is not a mistake.

*Direction*: Accept the difficult task. It releases bound energy and delivers from sorrow. The situation is already changing.

# 23 and 24: The Paradigm

### Stripping the Corpse and the Return of the Spirit

This Pair involves you in an overall model of thought and action elaborated in the interconnected lines of the figures: stripping away the old and a reversal and renewal of the time, the entrance of a new spirit. It embodies a site of radical transformation at the limits of the world, a paradigm of passing through the Tiger's Mouth to the primal power of Earth, an experience of death and re-birth. Carefully consider your place in and relation to this model.

*Hidden Possibilities*: 2, the primal power of realization.

The Pair exchanges with and is motivated by 27 and 2, the Tiger's Mouth and the Earth Altar. The centre and threshold lines connect the zone of transformation with 3:4 (Sprouting and Nurturing the New), 19:20 (Releasing the Spirit and Watching the Omens), 35:36 (Rising and Setting Sun) and 51:52 (Rouser and Sacrificer).

Look at the ages and events these figures suggest for personal connections.

<u>2</u>  3:4    19:20    <u>27</u>    35:36         51:52

*Shadow site*: 41:42, The Offering and the Blessing

**Stripping means something is rotten.**
**Returning means the way is reversing.**

# 𥄗 ䷖ *23 Stripping* Bo

**Strip away old ideas, eliminate what is outmoded or worn out;
first burial, 'stripping the corpse', site of creative
transformation; a seed figure.**

## MYTHS FOR CHANGE: THE STORY OF THE TIME

**Charge to the Oracle**: *When you beautify things, the obligations of the
old come to an end. Strip the corpse. Accept this and use the energy of
Stripping. This means someone who strips away the old.*

The root of Stripping is knife. It represents stripping off skin and
flesh, slicing into the body and revealing the bones, uncovering
the meats offered in sacrifice. There is deprivation and loss of
direction and focus, imaged as a period of time spent in the grave.
The outmoded and decadent spirit is displaced in preparation for
the return of the new. Literally, Stripping represents the first
burial or exposure of the corpse to animals and elements, when
the flesh is rotted and stripped away. During this period the soul
would be fed and guided in the underworld, a job for the *wu*-
Intermediaries that is not to be confused with an exorcism or
driving out a negative influence. The bones were then gathered
or disinterred, rubbed with red ochre and put into a vase or urn
that served as the spirit-home, the equivalent of the spirit tablet
in the Ancestral Temple. At this point, the soul would be ready
to return, to re-enter the human community and, through the
image, the spirit could begin to act as a guide, mediator and bene-
factor. The exposure is prepared by stripping the corpse of its
clothing, changing the bed-mat and laying it out on a 'water-bed'
made of three planks. The ceremony would also include talking
to the newly deceased spirit, persuading it to return to the body
and the tomb rather than exorcising it as a bad influence. The
palace women referred to in the lines may be attendants on the
Queen Mother of the West, Queen of the Dead, and the ripe
fruit at the end an allusion to the achievements of a life truly
lived. The character also suggests the knife used to carve the
oracle bones, which had been stripped of flesh, to record the
words of the spirit.

# THE RESPONSE

**Stripping the corpse. Not advantageous to have a direction to go. Harvesting.**

**Strip,** Bo: flay, peel, skin, scrape away; remove, uncover, take off; reduce to essentials, diminish; prune trees, slaughter animals; deplume, deprive of, uncover, wound; divination through examining entrails or body. The old character shows an inscribed bone and the knife used by diviners to carve the characters that recorded the words of the spirit. It announces an oracle of change.

BO[1,5] (9219/18) is made up of LÙ (1), which combines an inscribed oracle bone and the picture of a windlass or winch drawing water for irrigation. It is found carved in good luck charms and also suggests a wooded mountain slope for privileged hunting and heavenly blessing. It may also be a tree with chopped-off branches or a picture of a hanging sack, pierced by arrows, with drops falling from it. The other element (2) is a knife, which suggests divining by cutting away or cutting through.

Stripping describes your situation in terms of habits and ideas that are outmoded and worn out. The way to deal with it is to strip away what has become unusable. This brings renewal. Remove and uncover things. Cut into the problem and strip away the unessential without thought of immediate gain. If you can do that, then you can impose a direction on things or have a place to go.

# THE SCHOLAR SPEAKS

The hexagram figure shows the end of a cycle and the preparation for the new. The mountain rests on the Earth. Be open to new ideas. Provide what is needed. Re-establish creative balance by stripping away outmoded embellishments. There is something rotten here. Take action. Give generously to what is below to stabilize your position. Stripping away the old implies someone to carry it out. You need a base. What is flexible and adaptable is transforming what is solid and firm, so it is not advantageous to impose a direction on things. Those who adapt to what is coming will endure. Yield to the situation and stop what you have been doing. Concentrate on the symbolic value of things, their power to connect you with the world of the spirits. Use the oracle to stay in touch with the *Dao*. This is a time when old structure dissolves so new action can emerge. Fill the empty, fertile inner space to overflowing. Heaven is moving there.

## THE SHAMAN SPEAKS

**Mountain adjoins Earth. Stripping.**

**This is a time when Noble One acts as the person above, using munificence to quiet the people below.**

*Spirit words bind us and accomplish fate. Offer service at the Earth Altar.* The Sacrificer is working with the Field. Mountain above limits and articulates what is complete to suggest what is beginning, while Earth below yields and sustains. This is the Earth Moment, stripping away the outworn products of the previous cycle. Noble One reflects this, giving care and concern freely to those below him. Offer sacrifice. A cycle is ending.

## TRANSFORMING LINES: CHANGE AT WORK

### INITIAL SIX

**Stripping the corpse.**

**Change the bed, use the stand.**

**Ignoring the Trial: Trap! The Way closes.**

**This is not an exorcism.**

*This means what is below can disappear.* You have to confront basic questions of support and intimacy, the place where you feel at home. It isn't working now. Strip the old away. Take a stand for change. This is important. If you simply ignore the message, the Way will close. Don't turn this into a ghost to be gotten rid of.

*Direction*: Take things in. Be open and provide what is needed.

## Six at Second

**Stripping the corpse.**

**Change the bed, mark things off.**

**Ignoring the Trial: Trap! The Way closes.**

**This is not an exorcism.**

*You do not have associates yet.* You have to confront basic questions of support and intimacy, the place where you feel at home. It isn't working now. Strip away the old. Mark things off. Differentiate yourself from others. This is important. If you simply ignore the message, the Way will close. Don't turn this into a ghost to be gotten rid of.

*Direction:* Don't act out of ignorance. Wait and be sure. Something significant is returning. Be open and provide what is needed.

## Six at Third

**Stripping the corpse. Strip it away!**

**This is not a mistake.**

*This is letting go of both above and below.* The time is now. Do it! Strip away the old. By taking decisive action you can renew yourself and your relations. This is not a mistake. Don't be sidetracked.

*Direction:* Articulate the limits. Release bound energy. The situation is already changing.

## Six at Fourth

**Stripping the corpse.**

**Changing the bed, cutting close to the flesh.**

**Trap! The Way closes.**

*This is slicing close to calamity.* You are getting carried away with the renovation of your life and are about to do serious harm. This is not what the time is about. Pull back, let go for now, or you may see yourself alone.

*Direction:* You will emerge and be recognized. Re-imagine the situation. Gather energy for a decisive new move.

### Six at Fifth

**Stripping the corpse. Thread the fish by the gills.**

**You obtain the favour of the palace women.**

**Nothing not advantageous. Harvesting.**

*Complete this without being excessive.* Pull things together now. A culmination is coming. There is profit and fertility hidden in the stream of events. The palace women confer their grace and favour. Use your connections and trust your imagination. Anything is possible. There is nothing that will not benefit from the connection you are making now.

*Direction:* Let things be seen. Strip away old ideas. Be open and provide what is needed.


### Nine Above

**Stripping the corpse. A ripe fruit not eaten.**

**Noble One acquires a cart.**

**Small People merely strip their visage.**

*A place to carry the commoners. You are not allowed to end this.* You have stripped away the outmoded and found the new. Now take in the fruits of your actions. Move on, carry it all away with you. Don't go back to your old ways. It would be like painting your house to avoid moving.

*Direction:* Be open and provide what is needed.

# *24 Returning* FU

Love and spirit return after a difficult time; renewal, re-birth,
re-establish the relationship; go back to the beginning;
leave the complicated and return to the simple;
death as a return to the Source; site of creative
transformation; new hope; a seed figure.

## MYTHS FOR CHANGE: THE STORY OF THE TIME

**Charge to the Oracle:** *Being cannot be completely exhausted. What is
above is stripped away, what is below reverses and returns. Accept this
and use the energy of Returning.*

Return is one of the fundamental motifs in all the myths and
philosophies of Change, the Return to and of the Way and the
eternal Return of all things. It is the Return of spirit after the first
burial and stripping way the old. It is the emergence from death
and the underworld Ghost River, the incessant Return of life and
spirit. It is the root of power and virtue, the power to become who
you are meant to be. It discriminates the beings and gives birth to
self-knowledge. This root is a footstep, one step on the Way. It is
starting at daybreak to cross the river to the spring festival and a
renewal of spirit, joy and human community in the paradise place.
It suggests the souls that return and the rituals to call them, the
ritual return to an original paradise time, and death through which
we all return to the Source. Return is the 'coming and going' on
the river of time and the flow of symbols that unfold the Way.

## THE RESPONSE

Returning. Make an offering and you will succeed.

'Going and coming' on the stream of time without affliction.

Friends are coming. This is not a mistake.

The Way reverses and returns. Return comes on the seventh
day.

Advantageous to have a direction to go. Harvesting.

**Return,** *FU*: go back, turn back, come back; return to the starting
point; resurgence, renaissance, rebirth; renew, renovate, restore;

again, anew; the beginning of a new time; turn from the city to the countryside; recover, take back, call back spirit of deceased; return of the ancient past and the time of the great sages. The old character shows footsteps leaving the city.

FU (3594/69) shows a foot (2) leaving a town (1). In later characters the element for 'road' was added.

Returning describes your situation in terms of re-emergence and rebirth. The way to deal with it is to go back to meet the Returning energy in order to begin anew. Retrace your path, Return to the Source, re-establish what is important, restore the Way. Find the intensity of the earlier time and the purity of the original feeling. This is pleasing to the spirits. Through it they will give you success, effective power and the capacity to bring the situation to maturity. Let things emerge and come back without pressure or upset. People will suggest mutually profitable projects. It is not a mistake to join them. Turning and moving in the opposite direction from your former path will return you to the Way on the seventh day. Have a place to go. Impose a direction on things. That brings profit and insight.

### THE SCHOLAR SPEAKS
The hexagram figure shows inner energy returning to the field of activity. Thunder in the Earth. Be open to new ideas and provide what is needed. The old situation has been stripped away. Turn in your tracks and go back to meet what is re-emerging. This Return to the Way is the root of your power to realise the Way in action. Be small, adaptable and differentiate yourself from others. Use your own knowledge of the source of things. To nurture this Returning energy, early rulers would close the frontiers and the markets at the time of the solstice. Merchants and sojourners would not move. The prince would not go on tours of inspection. This kind of attention is pleasing to the spirits. Through it they will give you success, effective power and the capacity to bring the situation to maturity.

What is strong and firm is reversing it. Stir things up and work with the movement. Let things emerge and come back without pressure or upset. People will suggest mutually profitable projects. It is not a mistake to join them. Turning and moving in the opposite direction from your former path will Return you to the Way. On the seventh day, after the cycle of the six places of a hexagram, the Return will come from below. Heaven is moving here. Impose a direction, have a place to go, for the strong and firm will endure. By returning, you see the heart of the union of Heaven and Earth.

## THE SHAMAN SPEAKS

> Thunder located in Earth centre. Returning.
>
> A time when Early Kings used the solstice to bar the passages.
>
> At this command, sojourning merchants did not move.
>
> The Crown Prince did not inspect the Four Hidden Lands.

*Spirit manifests in quake and thunder. Offer service at the Earth Altar.* The Rouser is working with the Field. Earth above yields and sustains, while Thunder below rouses and germinates new potential, sprouting energies that thrust up from beneath. This is Earth over Wood: rousing energy returning within that opens a new field of activity. The ideal Realising Person reflects this by emulating the early Kings, who closed the boundaries and the gates to nurture the returning spirit. Work through rousing and inspiring. A cycle is beginning. Prepare the joyous response.

## TRANSFORMING LINES: CHANGE AT WORK

### INITIAL NINE

**Not distancing the Return.**

**No harm or cause for sorrow.**

**The Way to the Source is open.**

*This means adjusting the total personality.* You have been keeping at a distance, probably because of pain or isolation. Now is the time to let it go. Return to the Way. The spirit is emerging. Don't just think about. Do something. The Way is fundamentally open.
*Direction*: Be open and provide what is needed.

### Six at Second

**Released and Returning. Let it go!**

**Wise Words! The Way is open.**

*Using humanity to connect with the below.* Relax your grip. Let things rest. The spirit is emerging. Be unselfish and benevolent. The Way is open to you.
*Direction:* An important connection is approaching. Be open and provide what is needed.

### Six at Third

**Returning from the brink. Pressing and urgent.**

**Adversity, hungry souls and angry ghosts.**

**This is not a mistake.**

*This is righteous and not a mistake.* Pulling back from a crisis, you return to yourself. You confront danger with its roots in the past. Difficult though this may be, it is not a mistake.
*Direction:* Accept the difficult task. Release bound energy. The situation is already changing.

### Six at Fourth

**The centre is moving. Return alone.**

*This means adhering to the Way.* Moving the capital city. The centre of life is shifting. Move with it even if it involves going on alone. This returns you to yourself. You won't be sorry. You are following the Way.
*Direction:* A fertilizing shock is coming. Re-imagine the situation. Gather energy for a decisive new move.

### Six at Fifth

**Generous Return. Returning from a triumph.**

**No cause for sorrow.**

*Centred and originating in the omens.* A victory. Wealth and pleasure return. As the time renews itself, give with open arms. You will meet the same qualities in return. You will have no cause to regret what you do.
*Direction:* Give everything a place to grow. Strip away old ideas. Be open and provide what is needed.

SIX ABOVE

**Delusion Returning.**

**Losing the Way. There will be calamities and errors.**

**If you try to move the legions, it will end in great destruction.**

**Trap! The Way closes for the city and its leader.**

**This will end in ten years of uncontrolled chastisement.**

*Trap! The Way of the leader is reversed.* You are returning to an old delusion, blinded by self-deception and infatuation. If you go on in this way, your hard-won growth will be destroyed. It will take at least ten years to deal with the repercussions of this catastrophe. The Way is closed. Think about where this desire comes from. Whatever you do, don't act this out.

*Direction*: Take things in. Be open and provide what is needed.

# 25 and 26: The Paradigm

### Disentangling from past affliction and
### Accumulating the Spirit

This Pair involves you in an overall model of thought and action elaborated in the interconnected lines of the figures: disentangling from negative emotions and past traumas and nurturing the great within yourself. It suggests the birth of the Great Being and the sage-mind through 'eating ancient virtue'. Carefully consider your place in and relation to this model.

*Hidden Possibilities*: 53:54 > 63:64, the Great Marriages. Make the crossing and prepare the new.

The Pair exchanges information with 11:12 (The New and the Old King). It is motivated by 17:18 (Following the Spirit and Renovating the Ancestral Images). The centre and threshold lines relate the process to 9:10 and 13:14 (Ceremonies at the Outskirts Altar), 21:22 (Sacred Meal and Bringing Home the Bride) and 41:42 (Offering and Blessing).

Look at the ages and events these figures suggest for personal connections.

9:10 11:12 13:14 (15:16) 17:18 (19:20) 21:22    41:42

*Shadow site*: 39:40, 'Comings and Goings' and Deliverance

**Disentangling means disaster has come from outside. Great
Accumulates means you find the right time.**

# 25 Disentangling
## WU WANG

**Disentangle yourself; spontaneous, unplanned, unexpected; free from confusion, pure; exorcism, purification from plague or miasma; waning moon, don't give up hope; demons of the past.**

## MYTHS FOR CHANGE: THE STORY OF THE TIME

**Charge to the Oracle**: *The spirit returning can disentangle you from affliction. Accept this and use the energy of Disentangling.*

Entanglement means letting yourself go, succumbing to perverse influence or disease, being without order or rule, crazy, vain, the compulsive or afflictive emotions, something twisted, perverse, abusive and cruel. Being released from entanglement results in a state of balance and purity, the image of an original and originating connection with Heaven. Disentangling suggests the ways to maintain that purity and freedom from affliction. It enables you to act spontaneously, to deal successfully with what comes on the stream of time, to attract and welcome the unexpected. It suggests the *wang* demon who carries contagious disease, plague, miasma and drought, and the purification, exorcism and rituals used by *wu*-Intermediaries to drive out these diseases and demons. It is particularly concerned with the *nei ye* or inner way and the sage person or sage-mind. The meditative practices of the inner way centre on 'correcting', which calms, tranquillizes, rectifies and frees the body in order to restore a state of neutrality and align with Heaven. This allows energy and breath to circulate freely and transform awareness. It enables a person to collect great energy and move with or be blessed by Heaven, disentangled from the afflictive emotions of greed, anger, desire and ignorance.

## THE RESPONSE

**Disentangling. Source of Success: Advantageous Trial. Harvesting.**

**If you do not correct yourself there will be blunders.**

**Then it will not be advantageous to have a direction to go.**

**Dis-/Without, WU:** not having any, devoid of, become free of. The old character shows a person exerting himself in vain and suggests the demons that haunt old tombs.

**Entangled, WANG:** embroiled, caught up in, succumb to; entangled, trapped, deeply involved; vain, rash, reckless, brutal behaviour; lie, deceive; idle, foolish, futile, without foundation; disordered, insane; plague or disease demons, drought, sickness; forget, lose sight of; waning moon. The old character shows the Wang plague demon that spreads physical and spirit disorders, a barren woman and a hidden place.

WU[2] (12345/71) is a man exerting himself in vain against an obstacle (1). It is a demon of old abandoned tombs. WANG[4] (12091/38) is composed of NÜ[3] (3), a woman, and WANG[2] (2), a broken sickle or entering a hidden place. It suggests a yin disorder or affliction by ghosts, an empty womb, a barren, poisonous woman.

Disentangling describes your situation in terms of acquiring the capacity to act spontaneously and confidently. The way to deal with it is to free yourself from disorder. Disentangle yourself from compulsive ideas, confusion, vanity, anger, lust, hatred and the desire for revenge. By freeing your awareness from these entanglements, you gain the capacity to act directly. This opens up a whole new cycle of time. If you do not correct yourself, you will consistently make mistakes through ignorance and faulty perception. Your sight will be clouded. Imposing a direction on things or having a place to go will bring you no advantage.

## THE SCHOLAR SPEAKS

The hexagram figure shows new actions inspired by the spirit above. Below Heaven, thunder is moving. Proceed step by step. The spirit has really returned. If you return to it, you will not be the source of disaster. Associate with others without getting caught up in disorder. The early rulers, whose virtue was strong, used this flourishing time to nourish the Myriad Beings. Firmness and strength have come from the outside to activate a central principle within you. Respond and persist in this connection. This solid purpose is central and links you with the spirits. By staying in touch with it and continually correcting yourself, you can begin a great period of growth, effective power and enjoyment. Heaven will bestow it as fate. You must continually correct yourself, for if you lose the capacity to act in accord with the spirits, how can you do anything right? Heaven will not protect you. Disentangle yourself. Do it now!

## THE SHAMAN SPEAKS

> Thunder moves below Heaven. Beings associate through Disentangling.

> This is a time when Early Kings used the luxuriance of this season to nurture the Myriad Beings.

*The spirit that wars in Heaven manifests in quake and thunder.* The Rouser is working with the Force. Heaven above struggles on, persistent and unwearied, while Thunder below rouses new potential, sprouting energies that thrust up from beneath. This is Metal over Wood: rousing inner potential that disentangles itself from affliction through its connection to Heaven. The ideal Realising Person reflects this by emulating the early Kings, using the generosity of a time inspired by Heaven to nurture and inspire all things. Persist and work through inner inspiration. It is time to advance.

## TRANSFORMING LINES: CHANGE AT WORK

### INITIAL NINE

> Disentangling. Waning moon. An unexpected encounter.

> Wise Words! Go on, the Way is open.

*Here you acquire the purpose.* Disentangle yourself, then go forward. You can do what you wish to do now, counting on the fact that you will not get tied up in negative emotions. The coast is clear. The Way is open.

*Direction:* Communication may be blocked. Proceed step by step. Gather energy for a decisive new move.

### Six at Second

**Disentangling. Waning moon.**

**'They don't till, but have a harvest. They don't clear the land, but have fields to plant.'**

**Advantageous to have a place to go. Harvesting.**

*This means you are not affluent yet.* Unexpected success, but this is not the time or place to start something. If you realise what this means, your plans will bring you success. Move on. Empty your mind of immediate goals. What you want is around the corner.
*Direction:* Proceed step by step. Go your own way. Find supportive friends. Gather energy for a decisive new move.

### Six at Third

**Disentangling. Waning moon.**

**There is an unexpected disaster.**

**Someone has tethered cattle.**

**If the moving people take them,**

**It is the capital people's disaster.**

*This is the capital people's disaster.* Even though you are without blame, you have lost something you care about. Understand that you can see your loss two ways. If you identify with the capital people, if you stay where you are, it is a disaster. If you identify with the moving people, who are on their way to a new place, you actually acquire new strength. This may rid you of an old affliction.
*Direction:* Unite for a common goal. You are coupled with a creative force.

### Nine at Fourth

**Disentangling. An Enabling Trial.**

**This is not a mistake.**

*You possess it firmly.* Whatever you are contemplating, go through with your plan. This is an enabling divination. You disentangle yourself and are freed of mistakes.
*Direction:* Increase your efforts, pour in more energy. Strip away old ideas. Be open and provide what is needed.

NINE AT FIFTH

**Waning moon. Disentangling from an unexpected affliction.**

**If you don't use medicine, you will soon rejoice.**

*This does not allow testing things.* You are suffering from sickness, anger or negative emotion. Though you may be in pain, don't treat it as a medical or a literal problem. See it imaginatively and spiritually. It will soon clear up and you will have cause to rejoice.
*Direction:* Bite through the obstacles. Re-imagine the situation. Gather energy for a decisive new move.

NINE ABOVE

**Disentangling. Waning moon.**

**It is a blunder to make a move.**

**No advantageous direction.**

*This means disaster and exhaustion if you move.* Even though you are not caught up in negative emotions, there is nothing you can do for now. The time is wrong. Leave things alone. No plan you could make will help you. Empty your mind of immediate goals.
*Direction:* Follow the flow of events. Proceed step by step. Gather energy for a decisive new move.

# 26 Great Accumulates/ Gathering the Spirit DA CHU

**Concentrate, focus on one idea; accumulate energy, support, nourish; bring everything together; great effort and great achievement.**

## MYTHS FOR CHANGE: THE STORY OF THE TIME

**Charge to the Oracle:** *When you are disentangled from affliction, you can Accumulate the Spirit of the new. Accept this and use the energy of Great Accumulates.*

This refers to the offerings made by the King to the High Lord through the First Ancestor. They include offerings to the Four Winds and Directions, to River and Mountain and to the Five Sacrifices of the House. These were great *jiao*-sacrifices that included dances, wine drinking and celebration in which a spirit-meal was shared. These sacrifices included all the clans, bringing them out of their dwellings, and were held in a great assembly at the Outskirts Altar. They opened and closed the seasons and announced the Changes. This power to open and to close was invested in the King. Most important, he could end the isolation and restriction of winter and open the fields. To do this, he had to announce the Change to the ancestors, waking and nurturing the Great.

The King prepared the Change by offering to the Four Distant Ones at the Hidden Temple, using the *wu*-Intermediaries to invoke and call them. The victim for the main ceremony, the Red Bull, was selected and prepared long in advance. On the appointed day, all mourning or funeral practices ceased, for it was a day of rejoicing. The King dressed in the Sun and Moon robe and stepped into the chariot of Heaven, holding the Twelve Flame Standard adorned with dragons and heavenly bodies, and proceeded to the Southern Mound. Peasants lined the way, standing at the edge of the fields with torches. The Blind Musicians played as the King entered the Mound and faced east, calling the spirits down. A large pyre was lit on top of the Mound. The Boundary Men, those who drew the limits of the fields, brought in the flawless Red Bull with a horn-board attached to his horns, leading him to the sound of gongs and singing stones. The Great Minister then invited the King to kill the victim. He shot it with arrows. The blood was collected and presented to Heaven as first offering. Then the body was placed on the pyre together with a long bolt of silk and circular pieces of blue jade, the 'holes to paradise'. The Chief Priest lit the fire with the Burning Mirror – the new fire – and recited the prayer for the good year. The Choir of the Blind sang the *Sheng-min* ode that recalled the founding rite established by *Hou Ji*, Sovereign Millet, the First Ancestor.

> We fill the wooden cups with offering, cups of wood and earthen vases.
> The aroma rises. The High Lord begins to eat.
> How fine the aromas, how perfect the ritual moment.
> Hou Ji founded this. We carry it out without error or omission
> From that first day until now.

When everything on top of the mound had been burned, it was swept and the King ascended, accompanied by the corpse-embodier, the person whose body First Ancestor inhabited, dressed in the same costume as the King. Hou Ji, who 'gave grain to all the people, a marvellous gift without equal', ascended to the court of Shang Di in the Dipper to act as intermediary to the High Lord. The ceremony ended with a great dance and celebration called the Gate of Clouds in which the King himself took part.

## THE RESPONSE

Great Accumulates. Gather the spirit.

Advantageous Trial. Harvesting.

Don't eat in your dwelling or clan. Wise Words! The Way is open.

Advantageous to step into the Great Stream.

Great, *DA*: big, noble, important; able to protect others; orient your will to a self-imposed goal; venerable, powerful, ancestor; yang energy. The old character shows the Great Person and his power to protect and shelter.

223

**Accumulate**, CHU: take care of, support, tolerate, encourage; help one another, overcome obstacles; tame, train; domesticate, raise, bring up; gather, collect, hoard, retain; seed, shell, carapace, protection of a germ broken through in spring, protection in the womb. The old character shows a field and two bundles of silk or grass, harvested and stored.

DA⁴ (10210/37) shows the great person and his ability to support and protect. The character CHU⁴ or XU⁴ (2538/102) is composed of silk bundles SI¹ (2) and a field with plants TIAN² (3): the harvest of silk and crops, also read as XUAN², profound or dark, mystic, mysterious.

Great Accumulates describes your situation in terms of having a central idea that defines what is valuable. The way to deal with it is to focus on a single idea and use that to impose a direction on your life. Concentrate everything on this goal. Gather all the different parts of yourself and all your many encounters. Take the long view. Think of yourself as raising animals, growing crops or bringing up children. Tolerate and nourish things. Develop an atmosphere in which things can grow. Putting your ideas to the trial brings profit and insight. It can culminate in great abundance. Don't stay at home. Be active. Take in what is coming. This generates meaning and good fortune by releasing transformative energy. This is the right time to enter the Stream of Life with a purpose or to embark on a significant enterprise.

## THE SCHOLAR SPEAKS

The hexagram figure shows creative force accumulating within. Heaven in the centre of the mountain. If you let yourself be led, you can realise your hidden potential. Put your purpose in order and use it as an accumulating point. It is the right time to act. Assimilate the records of what your many predecessors have done and go on from there. Accumulate the power to realise things. Be firm, persist. Your efforts to shed light on things will bring you glory and substantial rewards. Renew your power, your virtue and your connection to the Way every day. Have a firm overriding purpose. Honour what has moral and intellectual power. Stabilize what endures and correct your focus. Don't stay at home. Taking in what comes generates meaning and good fortune by releasing transformative energy. It nourishes intellectual and moral power. This is the right moment to make a move. The connections reach to Heaven.

## THE SHAMAN SPEAKS

Heaven located in the centre of Mountain. Great Accumulates.

This is a time when Noble One uses the numerous records of the predecessor's words to move, nurturing power and virtue.

*Spirit wars in Heaven; its words bind us and accomplish fate.* The Sacrificer is working with the Force. Mountain above limits and articulates what is complete to suggest what is beginning, while Heaven below struggles on, persistent and unwearied. This is Earth over Metal: hidden power that accumulates in the inner field. The ideal Realising Person reflects this by 'eating ancient virtue', finding the realising power inherent in the words of the sages. Work through the receptive and the power of Earth. Retreat to the Mountain Shrine.

## TRANSFORMING LINES: CHANGE AT WORK

### INITIAL NINE

Great Accumulates. There is adversity, hungry souls and angry ghosts.

Advantageous to end it.

Offer a sacrifice to Heaven. Harvesting.

*This is not opposing disaster.* This connection is haunted by old angry ghosts. Eliminate the negativity now. Commit yourself to what you truly believe in.
*Direction:* Renovate a corrupt situation. If you let yourself be led, you can realise hidden potential. The situation is already changing.

225

**Great Accumulates.**

**Loosen the cart's axle-straps.**

**Say it this way: Hidden cargo.**

**Draw round the carts and make a barrier each night.**

*Centred without going to extremes.* Forward motion of the great vehicle is stopped. Draw up the wagons and make contact. Think of it this way: you are escorting a covered cart with your secret treasure inside. Join together and nurture things.

*Direction:* Beautify things, be brave. Release bound energy. The situation is already changing.

NINE AT THIRD

**Great Accumulates. Fine horses in pursuit.**

**Trial: hardship is advantageous. Harvesting.**

**Advantageous to have a direction to go.**

*This is uniting purpose with what is above.* You are pursuing your great ideal. Don't lose heart, the drudgery will bring you profit and insight in the end. Stay focused and work together. Be careful day and night. Having a plan will help you.

*Direction:* Present hardship is future gain. Diminish passionate attachments. Make the sacrifice. Something important returns. Be open and provide what is needed.

SIX AT FOURTH

**Great Accumulates. A horn-board for the young bull.**

**Wise Words! The Way to the Source is open.**

*There will be rejoicing.* This is the preparation for the great spring sacrifice, protecting and guiding the growth of the young bull's horns and preserving him from flaw or stain. You can accumulate the force to carry heavy loads and confront difficult situations. Don't give up now, the Way is fundamentally open. In the end you will have cause to rejoice.

*Direction:* Abundance is coming. Be resolute. You are connected to a creative force.

## SIX AT FIFTH

**Great Accumulates. A gelded boar's tusks and a thorn hedge.**

**Wise Words! The Way is open.**

*There will be rewards.* You have managed to confront and disable what could have been a powerful obstacle, accumulating and focusing a significant force. The Way is open. This will bring rewards in the end.

*Direction:* Collect the Small to achieve the Great. Turn conflict into creative tension. The situation is already changing.

## NINE ABOVE

**Great Accumulates. Could this be Heaven's highway?**

**We receive the Blessing.**

**Make an offering and you will succeed.**

*This is moving on the Great Way.* The energy has accumulated. You are walking Heaven's highway. Your sacrifice is accepted and blessing will flow. There is no doubt about your success.

*Direction:* A flourishing and productive time is coming. If you let yourself be led, you can realise hidden potential. The situation is already changing.

# 27 and 28: The Paradigm

### Tiger's Mouth and Great Transition

This Pair involves you in an overall model of thought and action elaborated in the interconnected lines of the figures: an ordeal that transforms the spirit, giving you the power to become an individual, free of collective judgements. It is a site of radical transformation at all levels. Carefully consider your place in and relation to this model.

*Hidden Possibilities*: 2:1, connected to the interaction of the primal powers to realise and inspire.

The Pair connects with sites of creative transformation at 21:22 (Sacred Meal and Bringing Home the Bride), 31:32 (Sacred Site and Fixing the Omen), 41:42 (The Offering and the Blessing) and 47:48 (Oppressed Noble returns to Common Source). The zone of radical change between the figures incorporates 43:44 (Announcing the Omen and the Lady of Fate) and 23:24 (Stripping and Returning).

Look at the ages and events these figures suggest for personal connections.

21:22 (23:24)     31:32     41:42 (43:44)     47:48

*Shadow site*: 37:38, The Dwelling and the Ghosts that Haunt it

**Jaws means correcting the source of nourishment. Great Traverses means shaking things up and pushing them over.**

# 27 Jaws/The Tiger's Mouth YI

Nourishing and being nourished; take things in; the mouth, daily bread; speaking, words; major site of initiation and creative transformation; a seed figure.

## MYTHS FOR CHANGE: THE STORY OF THE TIME

**Charge to the Oracle:** *Accumulating the beings means you can nourish the spirit. Clear the channels. Accept this and use the energy of Jaws. This means truly nourishing it.*

Jaws refers to the ritual meal and sacrifice offered on all important occasions through which we nourish and are nourished by the spirits, the world of the invisible. To nourish the people, it was of first importance to see and seek the invisible presence that supports us and 'fills our mouths'. The essence of the beings offered in sacrifice fed and nourished the ancestor and ennobled his descendants. The word refers literally to the jaws and lower part of the head that allow us to eat and speak, that support or brace the activities that nourish us literally and spiritually. It means to take in and understand what is past in order to nourish the future, 'eating ancient virtue'. It points at the great value of the words of the oracles, the spirit words that nourish us and connect us with Heaven.

## THE RESPONSE

**Jaws. Trial: Wise Words! The Way is open.**

**View the Jaws. Seek the origin of what fills our mouths.**

**Jaws,** YI: Jaws, mouth, what we use to eat and speak; source of nourishment; take in, swallow, digest; eat; feed, sustain, nourish, support, bring up; what goes in and out of the mouth; nourished by the spirit, nourishing the spirits. The old character shows the tiger's open mouth and a person whose head is filled with spirit.

YÍ (5478/181) is composed of a jaw or chin YI² (1) and 'HEAD' ye⁴ (2), a person with a big head, filled with spirit, an influx that illuminates. Pronounced as SHEN³ (9677) it means to raise the eyes to look at something and is cognate with *shen* or Bright Spirit.

Jaws/Nourishing describes your situation in terms of what goes in and out of an open mouth. The way to deal with it is to take things in to provide for yourself and others. Take in what has been said and done and let it nourish the new. Provide what is necessary to feed yourself and those connected with you. Putting your ideas to the trial generates meaning and good fortune by releasing transformative energy. Contemplate what nourishes people and what you are nourishing. Think about what you give and what you ask for. Seek out the source of what goes in and out of your mouth and the mouths of others. The answer to your question lies there.

## THE SCHOLAR SPEAKS

The hexagram figure shows previous accomplishments being swallowed to nourish new growth. Within the mountain, there is thunder. Provide what is needed. After beings are brought together, they must be nourished. Correct the way things are nourished and nourish the ability to correct things. Consider your words carefully when you speak with others. Articulate how you eat, drink and take things in. Putting your ideas to the trial generates meaning and good fortune by releasing transformative energy if you use them to correct how things are nourished. Contemplate the open mouth. Look at where and how things are nourished. Look at the source of your own nourishment.

## THE SHAMAN SPEAKS

Below the Mountain, Thunder. Jaws.

This is a time when Noble One considers his words and articulates the time of the sacred meal that unites us with the spirit.

*Spirit words bind us and accomplish fate, manifesting in quake and thunder*. This is the Rouser and the Sacrificer. Mountain above limits and articulates what is complete to suggest what is beginning, while Thunder below rouses and germinates new potential, sprouting energies that thrust up from beneath. This is Earth over Wood: previous accomplishments that are sacrificed to nourish rousing new growth. The ideal Realising Person reflects this by considering and articulating the nourishing power of words and the sacred quality of the meal shared with spirits and friends, carried by the Bright Omens.

## TRANSFORMING LINES: CHANGE AT WORK

### INITIAL NINE

**Jaws. Nourishing. Take it in!**

**Abandoned by the Numinous Turtle, you say:**

**'View our Jaws hanging down.' Trap! The Way closes.**

*This is truly not a stance to value*. When you confront the problems involved in this matter, you simply give up and fall into self pity. You put your source of nourishment from the magical world and your imagination aside. So, of course, the Way closes. This sort of attitude has no value at all. The Turtle Oracle that reveals the Mandate of Heaven simply abandons you. Through not providing nourishment you will lose the connection. These are the last Shang rulers who displayed their wealth even though the spirit had left them.
*Direction*: Strip away your old ideas. Be open and provide what is needed.

### SIX AT SECOND

**Jaws. Nourishing. Take it in!**

**Shaking the Jaws, clearing the channels, rejecting the rules.**

**Move to the hilltop shrine and make an offering.**

**Chastising closes the Way. Trap!**

*Moving and letting go of your own kind*. The source of nourishment is disturbed. This shakes things up and clears the channels through which spirit and energy flow. Don't follow the rules now. Move to the place where you feel secure and make offering to your ideals.

Even though this is a difficult time, don't try to punish people or set out on expeditions. That would only close the Way.

*Direction*: Diminish passions and involvement. Make the sacrifice. Something important returns. Be open and provide what is needed.

### Six at Third

**Rejecting the Jaws. Trial: Trap! The Way closes.**

**You won't be able to act for ten years. Take it in!**

**No advantageous direction.**

*Rebelling against the Great Way*. You reject the source of nourishment. The Way is definitely closed. If you go on like this, you will be paralyzed for an entire cycle of time. There is nothing that you can do here. Your idea goes against the Way.

*Direction*: Beautify things. Release bound energy. Deliver yourself. The situation is already changing.

### Six at Fourth

**Jaws. Nourishing. Take it in!**

**Shaking the Jaws. Wise Words! The Way is open.**

**A tiger observes, glaring, glaring.**

**Pursuing, pursuing his desires.**

**This is not a mistake.**

*This means spreading out and shining above*. The source of nourishment is disturbed. This action will shake things up and free you. Search out the new with the ferocity and passion of a tiger. Be full of force and concentration. This energy is not a mistake. It brings light and clarity to the situation.

*Direction*: Bite through the obstacles. Re-imagine the situation. Gather energy for a decisive new move.

### Six at Fifth

**Jaws. Nourishing. Take it in!**

**Clearing the channels. Rejecting the rules.**

**Trial: Wise Words! Staying in your residence opens the Way.**

**This does not let you step into the Great Stream.**

*Yield and adhere to the above*. Nourishment is disturbed. This clears the channels through which spirit and energy flow. You are rejecting the rules most people live by. The Way is open if you stay where you are and don't start any big projects for now. What you feel in doing this is entirely correct. It will connect you with a higher ideal.

*Direction*: A fertile new time is coming. Strip away old ideas. Be open and provide what is needed.

NINE ABOVE

**Jaws. Nourished at the source. Take it in!**

**Adversity, hungry souls and angry ghosts.**

**Wise Words! The Way is open.**

**Advantageous to step into the Great Stream. Harvesting.**

*There is a great reward*. You are nourished by what came before you, a legacy of ancient virtue. Go back to the source and correct things. Have no fear, the Way is open. The best way to deal with doubts is launch a brand new enterprise. Your ideas will be rewarded if you do.

*Direction*: Something significant is returning. Be open and provide what is needed.

# 28 Great Traverses
## DA GUO

A crisis; gather all your strength; hold on to your ideals;
breaking the rules, becoming an individual; the great
transition, major site of transformation; a seed figure.

MYTHS FOR CHANGE: THE STORY OF THE TIME

**Charge to the Oracle:** *What is not nourishing cannot be rousing. A
great transition. Accept this and use the energy of Great Traverses.*

This figure marks a dialogue between structure, the house and
the ridgepole as the social structures that support and constrain
us, and the process of becoming a true individual, a Great Being
with an individual identity. This can mark the initiation of a
noble child becoming a warrior and acquiring a ritual presence,
the transition of marriage, the transition to a higher class, or
becoming a high-ranking lord. It marks a transition time in a
ritual or a life, an entry into liminal space where structures dissolve and there is a re-ordering of the fundamental principles. It
is the act of standing for your ideals and stepping across the
threshold, a crisis in life when you must stand by what you
know to be true and find the power to exist independent of
collective norms. Life and death are involved in this step. This
is a letting go of the past and the emergence of the power to
lead your life.

THE RESPONSE

**Great Traverses. The ridgepole twists and sags under the strain.**

**Advantageous to have a direction to go. Harvesting.**

**Make an offering and you will succeed.**

**Great,** DA: big, noble, important; focus on a goal, lead or guide
your life; able to protect others; yang energy. The old character
shows the Great Person and his power to protect and shelter.
**Traverse/Exceed,** GUO: go across, go beyond, surpass, overtake,
overgo; get clear of, get over; cross the threshold, surmount difficulties; transgress the norms, outside the limits; anomaly, unique,

different; an irreversible transition or a serious transgression; surpassing others through inner strength. The old character shows a mountain pass and a crossroads.

 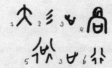

DA[4] (10210/37) shows the Great Person and his ability to support and protect. GUO[4] (6574/162) is a mountain pass and the completion of an action: steps (2), a foot (3) and the crossing (4). It suggests a skeleton or a mountain-ridge (5), a crossroads (6) and a foot (3).

Great Traverses describes your situation in terms of how to act in a time of crisis. The way to deal with it is to push your principles beyond ordinary limits and accept the movement it brings. Have a noble purpose. Find what is truly important and organize yourself accordingly. The ridgepole of your house is warped and sagging. The structure of your life is in danger of collapse. But there is a creative force at work in this breakdown. So impose a direction on things. Have a place to go. This is pleasing to the spirits. Through it they will give you success, effective power and the capacity to bring things to maturity.

## THE SCHOLAR SPEAKS

The hexagram figure shows outer contacts overwhelming inner penetration. The mists submerge the ground. There is a creative force at work in this breakdown. If your situation doesn't nourish you, if it can't stir up new growth, push it over and leave. Don't be afraid to order things by yourself. Don't be sad about retiring from the community. Having a great idea means being excessive. The structure of your life is warped and sagging. The roots and the tips, the places where you make contact and are nourished, are fading. Let the strong force gathering in the centre penetrate and stimulate movement. Impose a direction on things. The spirits will help you. This is a very great time.

## The Shaman Speaks

Mists submerge the trees. Great Traverses.

This is a time when Noble One establishes himself in solitude without fear,

And retires from the age without melancholy.

*Spirit works in those who lay out the fates, speaking and spreading joy through the Intermediaries.* This is the Joyous Dancer and the Lady of Fates. Rising Mists above stimulate and fertilize, joyous words cheer and inspire, while Wind and Wood enter subtly below, penetrating, pervading and coupling. It is Metal over Wood: outer stimulation and inner penetration that take you beyond the norms. The ideal Realising Person reflects this by standing alone without fear or sorrow. Hold the heart fast and take the risk.

## Transforming Lines: Change at Work

### Initial Six

Great Traverses. Offer the sacrifice using a mat of white mao-grass.

This is not a mistake.

*The supple is located below.* Weaving the sacrificial mat, sign of simplicity, humility and purity of motive. Prepare your move very carefully. Think about your motives. Be clear and pure. This is not a mistake. The beginning is humble, but the result will be great. This is the ceremony through which the King installs a lord or prince. In the end you will be recognized. Prepare carefully.
*Direction*: Be resolute. You are connected to a creative force.

### Nine at Second

Great Traverses. A withered willow gives birth to a shoot.

An older husband acquires a younger consort.

Nothing not advantageous. Harvesting.

*Exceeding and mutually associating.* In the midst of the crisis, something happens that gives it a whole new lease on life. A new branch emerges, a new start. This will benefit everything. This is a young woman who becomes consort of an older, high-ranking man. They enjoy one another and there are progeny. Everyone benefits.

*Direction*: This connects what belongs together. It couples you with a creative force.

### NINE AT THIRD

**Great Traverses. The ridgepole warps and buckles.**

**Trap! The Way closes.**

*You are not able to brace this*. The structure of your life buckles and fails, collapsing under the weight of the transition. There is nothing you can do to brace it up. The Way closes. Accept the change. See it as a sacrifice of the old.

*Direction*: Don't let yourself be isolated. Find supportive friends. Gather energy for a decisive new move.

### NINE AT FOURTH

**Great Traverses. The ridgepole is crowned.**

**Wise Words! The Way is open.**

**If you try to add more, there will be distress.**

*This reaches to the below without sagging*. You have come through the great transition. The structure of your life is strengthened and crowned with love and joy. The Way is open. The house is stabilized. You have all you need. If you try for more, you will only see distress and confusion and lose what you have.

*Direction*: Find your relation to common needs and basic order. If you let yourself be led, you can realise hidden potential. The situation is already changing.

### NINE AT FIFTH

**Great Traverses. A withered willow gives birth to flowers.**

**An older wife acquires a young noble as husband.**

**Without mistake, without praise.**

*How can it last?* As the transition passes, something happens to produce a burst of beauty. There is neither blame nor praise involved. Enjoy it. It may soon be over. This is a young man who becomes consort of a high-ranking woman. He learns and she enjoys, but there are no progeny.

*Direction*: Continue on. Be resolute. You are connected to a creative force.

### SIX ABOVE

**Great Traverses. If you exceed stepping into the water, you will be submerged to the top of your head.**

**Trap! The Way closes.**

**Do not make this mistake. The cause for sorrow will disappear.**

*This does not allow a mistake*. These are deep and troubled waters. Be clear about how much you can become involved. If you do more than get your feet wet, chances are you will be swept away. Be careful! It is not a mistake to realise this is not the Way. When you do, the potential cause of sorrow disappears.

*Direction*: Be resolute and part from this. You are connected to a creative force.

# 29 and 30: The Paradigm

### Ghost River and Bright Omens

This Pair involves you in an overall model of thought and action elaborated in the interconnected lines of the figures: the interaction of two fundamental powers as they establish the inner axis of change. This is a site of radical transformation, where the Ghost River releases Bright Omens of Heaven's presence to guide us through the passages in our lives. Carefully consider your place in and relation to this model.

*Hidden Possibilities*: 27:28 > 2:1, passing through the ordeal of initiation connects you with the interaction of the primal powers.

The Pair connects with sites of creative transformation at 7:8 (Armies and New Group), 13:14 (Gathering People and Great Being), 21:22 (Sacred Meal and Bringing Home the Bride) and 47:48 (Oppressed Noble returns to Common Source). The zone of radical change between the figures incorporates 55:56 (The New King and the Wandering Sage) and 59:60 (Dissolving the Self and Articulating the Times).

Look at the ages and events these figures suggest for personal connections.

7:8    13:14    21:22        47:48    (55:56)  (59:60)

*Shadow site*: 35:36, Rising and Setting Sun

**Radiance means what is above. Pit means what is below.**

# 墉 ䷜ 29 Repeating Pit/Ghost River
## XI KAN

Collect your forces, confront your fears, take the plunge; practise, repeat, rehearse; rise to the challenge; the Earth Pit and the ghost world; danger; an axis of change, prima materia.

## MYTHS FOR CHANGE: THE STORY OF THE TIME

**Charge to the Oracle:** *The Great Being cannot simply make the transition. The Ghost River. Use this as a spirit helper. Accept this and use the energy of the Pit. This means sacrificing at the Earth Altar.*

Pit is the sacrificial pit at the Earth Altar and the underworld waters that flow through it, the Ghost River that connects the Sun Tree and the Moon Tree, the axis of the world, and opens the gate of destinies through which souls enter. It alludes to religious rites where the victims were drowned and buried and to the moon goddesses who sponsored the earliest form of the Changes. Its symbols are rushing water, holes, pits and snares, tombs and graves, prisons and the Yellow Springs, the deep centre where the dead live. It evokes the north, midnight, winter and cold, dark waters. In action, it represents a critical moment that requires courage and determination in face of great fear engendered by the presence of the ghost world. It confronts and dissolves obstacles, venturing, falling and moving on.

Kan/Pit, The Ghost River or Ghost Dancer, is part of the Axis of Change, the 'burning water' or prima materia. He leads through danger. He dances with ghosts, risks all and always comes through. He exults in work and dissolves all things. He is a black pig, hidden riches. In the body, Pit works through the kidneys, conserving life and pushing the organism to actualize potential. It is the site of the essence (*jing*) or individual fate and transforms the essence into available energy. It controls the flow of emotions, particularly courage and fear.

Repeating the Pit. Danger. The Ghost River.

There is a connection to the spirits that will carry you through.

Hold your heart fast! An offering brings you success.

Making a move in the face of danger brings honour.

**Repeat, XI:** repeated pyromantic divinations; repeat, recommence; skill, routine, learning by training or exercise, dedication to study, train; repeatedly confront danger; instruct, tame; learning to fly; the sound of the east wind, gentle and continuous. The old character shows wings or feathers and the sun.

**Pit, KAN:** A dangerous place; hole, cavity, pit, hollow; steep precipice; snare, trap, grave; a critical time, a test; take risks; the underworld waters, the river in the pit; human sacrifice; pay taxes; *also:* venture and fall, take a risk without reserve at the key point of danger. The old character shows the Earth Altar and the breath of the Ghost River beneath.

$XI^2$ (4052/124) is composed of $YU^3$ – 'wings' or flying (1), $ZI^4$, a nose, or $RI^4$, the sun, (2). $KAN^3$ (5807/32) is made up of $TU^3$ – earth (3) – and $QIAN^4$ (4) exhale, vapours, breath – suggesting the Ghost River beneath the Earth Altar.

Pit/Ghost River describes your situation in terms of repeatedly confronting something dangerous and difficult. The way to deal with it is to take the risk without holding back. You cannot avoid this obstacle. Conquer your fear and faintheartedness. Jump in, like water that pours into a hole, fills it up and flows on. Practise, train, accustom yourself to danger. This is a critical point. It is a pit that could trap you and become a grave. But there is no way around it. Summon your energy and concentration. Repeatedly confront the challenge. You can act this way with confidence, for you are linked to the spirits and they will carry you forward. Hold fast to your heart and its growth. This is pleasing to the spirits. Through it they will give you success, effective power and the capacity to bring the situation to maturity. Moving, acting, motivating things will bring you honour, so give them first place.

## THE SCHOLAR SPEAKS

The hexagram figure shows water repeatedly flowing into the Pit. Streams continually reach the goal. Take in the situation. Overflowing energy from your central idea moves toward the depths. Act on your principles. When you teach and when you act, repeat things again and again. Redouble your efforts, spread your energies. Don't get caught in one place. Gather your desires and hold on to your heart's growth. Then you will have a solid centre. Moving and acting will bring honour. Push on and achieve things. Pit means danger. Heaven's dangers cannot be ascended. Earth's dangers are its mountains and rivers, its hills and mounds. Kings and their vassals set up dangers to guard their cities. A danger confronted and used is both an accomplishment and a defence. Now is the time to concentrate your forces and take risks.

## THE SHAMAN SPEAKS

> Streams double, culminating. Repeating the Pit.
>
> This is a time when Noble One uses the power of the symbols to move, repeatedly teaching and serving.

*Spirit rewards those toiling in the Pit*. This is the Ghost Dancer. Rushing Water dissolves direction and shape, flowing on through toil and danger. It is the Water Moment: structures dissolve and you must risk, fall, labour and flow on. The ideal Realising Person reflects this by entering the symbolic world, teaching and spreading its values, carried by the Bright Omens.

## TRANSFORMING LINES: CHANGE AT WORK

### INITIAL SIX

**Repeating the Pit.**
**Entering the pitfall.**
**Trap! The Way closes.**

*This means letting go the Way and falling into a trap.* The Pit as a trap. By responding in the same way again and again, you get caught in a dead end. This is the tomb of depression and melancholy. Don't get caught here. It closes the Way.
*Direction:* Set limits. Find your voice. Take things in. Be open and provide what is needed.

### NINE AT SECOND

**A Pit with sheer sides.**

**Seek and acquire through the Small.**

*Do not leave the inner centre.* The Pit as a strategic moment. As you venture into danger, you will get what you need by being flexible and adaptable. Have modest goals, don't impose your will and you will succeed.
*Direction:* Change whom you associate with. Strip away old ideas. Be open and provide what is needed.

### SIX AT THIRD

**They come into the Pit again and again.**

**Steep and deep, the victims are drowning.**

**Don't get trapped in this pitfall!**

*An end without results.* The Pit as a grave. Don't be a victim. Relax and pull back. What is coming is more than you can handle right now. If you push on, you will be trapped in a fatal diversion. Are you sure you know what you want? Think about your values.
*Direction:* If you let yourself be led, you can realise hidden potential. The situation is already changing.

### SIX AT FOURTH

**In the Pit. Wine in a flask, two sacrificial bowls.**

**Use the earthen vessels.**

**Let in the bonds that come through the window.**

**Complete this! This is not a mistake.**

*This is the border between the strong and the supple.* The Pit as a prison. If you are trapped or cut off, don't fight it. Lay out an offering to the hidden spirits. Give of yourself. Open the window and let them in.

Your rescuers are coming. You are right on the border, the liminal place where events emerge. Go through with your plans. This is not a mistake. This is the story of a Queen of Xia, pregnant with the heir, who was imprisoned in a pit when her husband was killed in an insurrection. She escaped 'through the window in the pit' with the aid of allies. Her son restored the royal power.

*Direction:* Move out of isolation. Find supportive friends. Gather energy for a decisive new move.

### NINE AT FIFTH

**The Pit is not full. The Earth Spirit is already appeased.**

**This is not a mistake.**

*This is centred but not yet Great.* The sacrifice to the Earth Spirit is over. The danger passes. The spirits are appeased. Go on with your life and your plans. Be happy with your release.

*Direction:* Organize your forces. Something important is returning. Be open and provide what is needed.

### SIX ABOVE

**In the Pit. Tied with stranded ropes and sent away to the dense thorn hedges.**

**For three years you will get nothing.**

**Trap! The Way closes.**

*This means losing the Way and being trapped for three years.* The Pit as a snare. If you go on like this, you will commit a serious transgression. You will be bound and judged and imprisoned. Change now or be trapped!

*Direction:* Dispel illusions! Take things in. Be open and provide what is needed.

# 30 Radiance/Bright Omens Li

**Light, warmth, awareness; join with, adhere to; articulate and spread the light, see clearly; the Bright Presence of the spirit in the omens; an axis of change, prima materia.**

MYTHS FOR CHANGE: THE STORY OF THE TIME

**Charge to the Oracle:** *Make the sacrifice at the Earth Altar and you will have a place where people congregate. The bright omens. A spirit helper. Accept this and you can use the energy of Radiance. This means congregating.*

Radiance is the Bright Presence of things, a numen that surges from the depths, turning them into omens that reveal the spirits. She is the yellow *lia*-bird whose song makes the silkworms appear and who sponsors lovers. She is associated with birds, nets and victims taken for sacrifice, the rituals of the Bird Dancers who call the spirits down and the openings on the oracle bones through which they can talk. She is the dance of the pheasant drumming the Earth to call to her mate, a dance that wakens the thunder in spring. Radiance makes people go in pairs. She is stringed instruments, a bride's veil and a woman's decorated girdle. She brings extraordinary happenings and separates people from the conventional. She is associated with brightness, fire and the light of the heavenly bodies, midday sun, summer, the south and the beauty and splendour of things.

*Li*/Radiance or Bright Omens is part of the Axis of Change, the burning water or prima materia. She is the bright presence of things. She leads through warm clear light, through beauty and elegance and the radiance of living beings holding together. She is the bird dancer with brilliant plumes and brings strange encounters and lucky meetings. She is a bright pheasant, a bird of omen. In the body, Radiance operates through the heart, master of the organs and home of the spirits that brings inspiration and joy. It commands the pathways and the blood, brings the spark of life and offers a quiet centre in which the spirits find a voice.

Radiance. The Bright Presence.

Advantageous Trial. Harvesting.

Make an offering and you will succeed. Accumulate the cattle.

Wise Words! The Way is open.

**Radiance/Bright Presence**, LI: Spreading light; illuminate, discriminate, articulate, arrange and order; shine, brilliance, fire, warmth; consciousness, awareness; Mandate, omen or sign from heaven; distinguish yourself, distinguished person; leave, separate yourself from, step outside the norms, abandon; two together, encounter by chance, meet with, partners; belong to, adhere to, depend on; fall into, fastened, attached; a bright bird, the oriole, and a bird-net, sign for the holes in the oracle bones. The old character shows a sign for the bright bird and a net through which one reflects and captures this brightness, a pattern of words and symbols.

LÍ: (6939/172) shows a bird (2) or (3) being caught in a net (1).

Radiance describes your situation in terms of awareness and coherence. The way to deal with it is to articulate and spread light and warmth. Illuminate, articulate, discriminate, make things conscious. Bring together what belongs together. This is a time of intelligent effort and accumulating awareness. It includes unexpected and meaningful encounters, separations from the old and experiences outside the ordinary. Put your ideas to the trial. That brings profit and insight. It is pleasing to the spirits. Through it they will give you effective power, enjoyment and the capacity to bring things to maturity. Nurturing the receptive strength that can carry burdens generates meaning and good fortune by releasing transformative energy.

## THE SCHOLAR SPEAKS
The hexagram figure shows awareness enduring and spreading. Brightness doubled arouses Radiance. Concentrate your energy.

You have fallen and found bottom. Now the time calls for bringing things together. Radiance shines above you. Connect your idea with this brightness and use it again and again to spread clarity and care to the Four Corners of the world. Radiance means connecting and illuminating. The sun and moon connect with and illuminate Heaven. The many grains, grasses and trees connect with and illuminate the Earth. Brightening things again and again reinforces correcting. This is how change occurs in the world. Being flexible and adaptable connects you with what is central and correct. It is the source of growth and is pleasing to the spirits. That is why nurturing receptive strength is so important.

### The Shaman Speaks

> **Brightness doubled arouses Radiance.**
>
> **This is a time when the Great Person uses consecutive brightening to illuminate the Four Hidden Lands.**

*Spirit reveals itself in the Bright Presence.* These are the Bright Omens. Fire radiates light and warmth, while people experience the Bright Presence of things. It is the Fire Moment: brightness and warmth spread beauty and changing awareness. The ideal Realising Person acts through the great in himself, allowing this spirit to illuminate all around him. Hold the heart fast and take the risk.

### Transforming Lines: Change at Work

#### Initial Nine

> **Radiance. The Bright Presence. Treading crosswise.**
>
> **Honour the omen! This is not a mistake.**

*This uses casting out faults!* These are good omens, a Bright Presence at the beginning. Be very careful with the first steps. Polish and clarify your motives and feelings. Treat this beginning with real respect. You won't be making a mistake.

*Direction:* A transition. Be small and careful. Search outside the norms. Don't be afraid to act alone. This connects you with a creative force.

### Six at Second

**Yellow Radiance. The Bright Presence.**

**Wise Words! The Way to the Source is open.**

*You acquire the Way and the centre.* The Yellow Lord and the underworld waters. The bright omen bird rises. You have found the connection here. Light and power surge up from below. The Way is fundamentally open.

*Direction:* A creative, blossoming time is approaching. Be resolute. You are connected with a creative force.

### Nine at Third

**Setting sun's Radiance.**

**If you don't beat the clay drum and sing**

**You will lament like a great old person. Alas!**

**Trap! The Way closes.**

*Why let this last?* Instead of spreading the light and warmth of the Bright Presence, you see everything in the light of the setting sun. You don't beat your drum and sing your songs. Instead, you lament all the terrible things that have happened in your life. Why go on like this? This could prove dangerous if someone wants you out of the way. It refers to an archaic practice of killing those too old to care for themselves.

*Direction:* Bite through the obstacles! Proceed step by step. Gather your energy for a decisive new move.

### Nine at Fourth

**Radiance. The Bright Presence. It comes suddenly,**

**Like burning, dying, abandoning.**

*This has no place in your life.* This is an omen of what must be cast out. Leave it behind. It has no place in your life.

*Direction:* Beautify things. Re-imagine the situation. Gather energy for a decisive new move.

SIX AT FIFTH

**Radiance. The Bright Presence. Tears flowing like rivers.**

**This is lamenting like mourners at a funeral.**

**Wise Words! The Way is open.**

*The King and the minister are brightened and shine.* It feels as if you have lost a connection with someone important to you. Let your sadness be seen, like mourners at a funeral rite who earth the ghost and release the spirit. This will open the Way.

*Direction:* Find supportive friends. You are coupled with a creative force.

NINE ABOVE

**Radiance. The Bright Presence. The King sets out on campaign.**

**There will be excellent results.**

**Sever the heads, offer the rebel chiefs in sacrifice.**

**Put them to the question.**

**This is not a mistake.**

*Use this to correct the balance of power.* The King reflects the Bright Presence. The omens cheer him on. This is a time to take aggressive measures. Something harmful has occurred and you must deal with it. Be determined and aggressive. You will have excellent results. Get rid of the leaders. Seize what is truly important. Offer the old in sacrifice. This is not a mistake. Opposition will fall apart.

*Direction:* A time of abundance is coming. Don't be afraid to act alone. You are coupled with a creative force.

# Book II: Foundations

# 31 and 32: The Paradigm

### Influx in the Sacred Place: Fix the Omen

This Pair involves you in an overall model of thought and action elaborated in the interconnected lines of the figures: the process through which spirit enters and influences the human world, giving us omens that help the heart endure on the voyage of life. It embodies a site of radical transformation at the centres, the Tiger's Mouth and the Opened Heart, where the events of life pass through the two great initiation sites. Carefully consider your place in and relation to this model.

*Hidden Possibilities*: 43:44 > 2:1, be resolute, you are coupled with the primal powers.

The Pair exchanges information with 49:50 (Revolution and Casting the New Vessel). It is motivated by 33:34 (Retreat and Advance, Mountain Shrine and War God). The centre and threshold lines connect 28 and 61, the zone of transformation, with 39:40 (Difficulties and Release) and 45:46 (Assembly and Sacred Mountain).

Look at the ages and events these figures suggest for personal connections.

<u>27</u>    33:34    39:40    45:46 (47:48) 49:50    <u>62</u>

*Shadow site*: 33:34, Retreat and Advance: Mountain Shrine and
First Herdsman / War God

**Conjoining means urging them on.
Persevering means lasting.**

# 和 ☶ *31 Conjoining/ Uniting in Spirit* XIAN

**Excite, stimulate, influence; strong attraction; bring together what belongs together; the sacred River-Mountain place where sacrifice is offered; site of creative transformation.**

## MYTHS FOR CHANGE: THE STORY OF THE TIME

**Charge to the Oracle**: *There is Heaven and Earth, then there are the Myriad Beings. There are the Myriad Beings, then there is Man and Woman. There is Man and Woman, then there is Husband and Wife. There is Husband and Wife, then there is Father and Son. There is Father and Son, then there is Leader and Server. There is Leader and Server, then there is Above and Below. There is Above and Below, then there is a place to perfect the rites and nourish the righteous. Uniting in Spirit. Accept this and use the energy of Conjoining.*

Conjoining is an image of the sacred sites, the River-Mountain places, where the spirits dwell. They are places where rituals are offered to influence, attract and connect with the spirit and bring union among people, places where the *wu*-Intermediaries call and contact the *shen*. It is the *xian chi*, the pool at the base of the Sun Tree where the new sun is bathed and set on its journey. The implicit root of the word is heart, the heart moved and moving. The spirit influx fills, moves and transforms the heart. This is the attraction and union of contraries, man and woman, human and spirit. It is an influx, stirring sentiments, desires, ruling ideas and deep wellsprings of feeling.

The term also means 'to influence, to join with, to feel an influx', in the sense of 'I have a feeling in my bones'. It is a physical sensing of spirit moving, an 'ominous' experience in the body that moves us. The lines of the figure trace the path of the influence in the body, relating what happens when spirit appears in the different body parts and how to react. This is allied with the practice of the *wu* or mediums, the ancient sages of later tradition, who experienced the spirits and set out the omens for others. Another variant refers to sacrifice: the cutting or opening of the sacrificial victim that opened the gates to the spirits. Here, the same omens refer to opening parts of the victim's body, whether animal or human, and the implications for action that are found there. Tradition saw this opening as the connection or influence between things that expressed how Heaven and Earth influences the hearts of the Myriad Beings. It was an influx of feeling that brought people together in sexual attraction and courtship.

In all of these, a central injunction is 'embrace the woman and the yin', that is, be open to the influence, submit and be moved. This is a basic idea in the inner Way, *wu-wei* or non-acting, the contrary to heroic efforts.

## THE RESPONSE

**Conjoining. Uniting in Spirit. Make an offering and you will succeed.**

**Advantageous Trial. Harvesting.**

**Embrace the woman. Wise Words! The Way is open.**

**Conjoin**, XIAN: Excite, stimulate, influence, mobilize; strong attraction, connection; bring together what belongs together; touch, move, transform, trigger; all, totally, universal, harmonize; unite, conjunction (as planets); literally: a broken piece of pottery, the two halves of which are used to identify partners. Xian Wu is an important Shang ancestor. The character also suggests Yu the Great who united the Nine Provinces and cast the Nine Vessels. The old character shows an axe, used to cut into a sacrificial animal, and a mouth, the response from the spirits. It suggests the pervading influence of the sacrificial act and the spread of the spirit blessing.

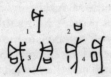

XIAN (4381/30) shows an axe or halberd (1) and a mouth (2); alternate forms (3). It is an exchange for CHENG[2] (4), the personal name of Di Yi, founder of the Shang and the name of the new Zhou capital founded after the victory over Shang.

Conjoining describes your situation in terms of an influence that excites, mobilizes or triggers you into action. The way to deal with it is to find the best way to bring things together. This influence is working to unite the separated parts of something that belongs together. Reach out, join things and allow yourself to be moved. This is pleasing to the spirits. Through it they will give you success, effective power, enjoyment and the capacity to bring the situation to maturity. Put your ideas to the trial. That brings profit and insight. The woman and the yin are the keys to the situation. Understanding, accepting and acting through the woman generates meaning and good fortune by releasing transformative energies.

## THE SCHOLAR SPEAKS

The hexagram figure shows inner strength submitting to outer stimulation. Above the mountain there are the mists. Accept what is coming as the sign of something greater. This reflects the way the world is made. Relations are clarified and individuals have a way to order their hearts. Bring things and people together through emptiness, the empty yet fertile space within you. Make peace, spread satisfaction and agreement. Something is indeed influencing and exciting you. Through it you can move the hearts of others. The flexible and adaptable is above, the firm and persistent is below. They excite and invoke each other, moving through mutual interaction. The man is below, the woman above. Accepting, understanding and submitting to the woman and the yin is pleasing to the spirits. Through it they will give you success, effective power, profit and insight. When Heaven and Earth influence each other this way, the Myriad Beings change and give birth. When the sage influences people's hearts this way, the world is harmonized and made even. Contemplate the place where things can be influenced and touched. By doing so you can see what moves the hearts of Heaven, Earth and the Myriad Beings.

## THE SHAMAN SPEAKS

Mists above Mountain. Conjoining in the Spirit.

This is a time when Noble One uses emptiness to accept the people.

*Spirit words bind us and accomplish fate, speaking and spreading joy through the Intermediaries.* These are the Operators, those who work

咸 ☷

with the Spirit. Rising Mists above stimulate through joyous words that cheer and inspire while Mountain below limits and articulates what is complete to suggest what is beginning. It is Metal over Earth: outer stimulation that articulates the inner field, drawing down the spirit to the sacred place. The ideal Realising Person reflects this by emptying his heart. By exhibiting compassion for each person he encounters, he encourages them to draw near. Make the sacrifice. A cycle is ending.

## TRANSFORMING LINES: CHANGE AT WORK

### INITIAL SIX

**The sacred place. Uniting in Spirit.**

**It conjoins your big toes.**

*The purpose is located outside you.* You feel the first stirrings of creative desire. The influence is just beginning. There is no telling what will happen. This influence could change the way you see your life.
*Direction*: Revolution and renewal. You are coupled with a creative force.

### SIX AT SECOND

**The sacred place. Uniting in Spirit.**

**It conjoins your calves. Trap! The Way closes.**

**Wise Words! Abide in the dwelling and open the Way.**

*Yielding to this advice will not harm you.* Don't get swept off your feet by this powerful infux. A hasty move will lead to nothing but trouble. Stay right where you are and you'll soon have what you want.
*Direction*: Don't be afraid to act alone. You are connected to a creative force.

### NINE AT THIRD

**The sacred place. Uniting in Spirit.**

**It conjoins your thighs. Hold on to your following!**

**Going on brings distress.**

*This means truly not abiding. A place to hold on to what is below!* You are in danger of becoming obsessed by this influence. This will do

you no good. Hold on to yourself and what supports you. If you go on running after this, you will simply be covered in distress.
*Direction*: Gather resources for a great new project. Proceed step by step. Gather energy for a decisive new move.

### NINE AT FOURTH

**The sacred place. Uniting in the Spirit.**

**Trial: Wise Words! the Way is open.**

**The cause of sorrow disappears.**

**You waver back and forth, 'coming and going'.**

**Partners will simply follow your thoughts.**

*This is not a harmful influence, but the Great is not shining in it yet.* Express your aims and desires. This is a very favourable influence. Your sorrow over the past will simply disappear. The Way is open. You go back and forth in your thoughts, trying to understand this new feeling. Have no fears. Your friends will be there for you.
*Direction*: Re-imagine the situation. Gather energy for a decisive new move.

### NINE AT FIFTH

**The sacred place. Uniting in Spirit.**

**It conjoins your neck, moves along the spine.**

**No cause for sorrow.**

*These are the tips of the purpose.* This is a very deep connection that will endure over time. You are feeling the beginnings. This will wipe away past sorrows.
*Direction*: A transition. Be very small. Don't be afraid to act alone. You are connected to a creative force.

### SIX ABOVE

**The sacred place. Uniting in Spirit.**

**It conjoins your jaws, cheeks and tongue.**

*The mouth is loosened and bursts forth.* This influence inspires you and you burst forth in passionate speech. It may not last long, so be ready to retreat when words run out.
*Direction*: Pull back. It will connect you with a creative force.

# 32 Fixing the Omen/ Persevering HENG

**Continue, endure; constant, consistent, durable; self-renewing; a stable married couple.**

## MYTHS FOR CHANGE: THE STORY OF THE TIME

**Charge to the Oracle:** *The Way of the husband and wife must last to the end. Accept this and use the energy of Persevering. Fix the Omen. This means enduring to the end.*

Persevering refers to creating rituals and symbols that fix the spirit influence so that it endures in your life. This symbolic activity is similar to writing down a dream, perceiving its message and making a symbol that recalls the influence and acts as a guide to action. This gives form and enduring influence to the message from the spirits, making their power and virtue (*de*) endure in the heart. It extends to fixity of purpose, constancy and faith in the images as a personal characteristic. This is particularly important for diviners and spirit-workers. It is what makes their power firm. It is what keeps harm away. Confucius said: 'It is said in *Change*: A man without *heng* will not succeed as a *wu*-Intermediary. How true! Not fixing the *de* of an omen leads to failure. Just reading it is not enough.' Such fixings range from literal rituals through meditations that 'fix' the heart to ceremonies of marriage that 'fix' the attraction. The word is related to *keng*, and suggests the moon cult that read the Changes, the oldest form of Yi divination. The character suggests the regular movement of a boat between two shores, the faithful heart, laws and habits, continuity in development. It implies the continued interaction of spirits and humans and delivers a warning: one who does not fix the realising power of the omen given by the spirit faces disaster.

The later tradition saw this as enduring in good conduct or enduring in proper social relations. It expressed the ideal of an organized, integrated being or a self-contained and self-renewing whole. For the later commentators, the previous figure, Conjoining, represents attraction and courtship, while Persevering represents the enduring union, the Way of the husband and wife.

> **Persevering. Fix the Omen. Make an offering and you will succeed.**
>
> **This is not a mistake.**
>
> **Advantageous Trial. Harvesting**
>
> **Advantageous to have a direction to go.**

**Persevere**, HENG: continue on, endure and renew the way; constant, consistent, continue in what is right; continue in the same spirit; stable, regular, enduring, perpetual, self-renewing; ordinary, habitual; extend everywhere, universal; the moon that is almost full; tradition, fixed rule, at ease; most northern of the five sacred mountains; Wang Heng, younger brother of Wang Hai, a worker dedicated to his master, the person to whom the king conveys his orders. The old character shows the two shores of a river, a boat, a heart and an increasing moon.

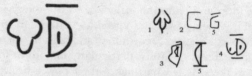

HÉNG (3913/61) shows a heart, XIN[1] (1) and GEN[4] (4), a boat ZHOU[1] (2) between two shores (3) or GENG[4], a moon between two lines (5, bottom), an increasing moon which looks like a spiral (5, top).

Persevering describes your situation in terms of what continues and endures. The way to deal with it is to continue on the way you are going. Be constant, regular and stable. Persist in your normal way of life and what you feel is right. This is pleasing to the spirits. Through it they will give you success, effective power and the capacity to bring things to maturity. Proceeding in this way is not a mistake. Put your ideas to the trial. Impose a direction on things. Have a place to go. These things bring profit and insight.

## THE SCHOLAR SPEAKS
The hexagram figure shows arousing energy coupled with inner penetration. Thunder and wind. This is a time for resolute action. It is the Way of the husband and wife. It implies that things endure over time. Persevering fixes and steadies the power to realise the

Way in action. It mixes things but does not repress them. It focuses on the Way and the power that is common to all. Don't be fluid and versatile. Establish principles and boundaries that endure. Persevering endures over time. The solid is above, the flexible is below. Thunder and wind work together to ground things and stir them up to new growth. What is solid and what is supple are completely in harmony. Putting your ideas to the trial brings profit and insight. Endure in the Way. The Way of Heaven and Earth endures without coming to an end. Imposing a direction or having a place to go brings profit and insight. When you complete something let it become the beginning of the new. The sun and the moon have Heaven, and thus their light endures. The four seasons transform and change, and thus they enable lasting accomplishment. The wise person endures in the Way, and thus the human world changes and perfects itself. Contemplate where you persevere. By doing so you can see the deep purpose of all the Myriad Beings.

## The Shaman Speaks

**Thunder and Wind. Persevering. Fixing the Omen.**

**This is a time when Noble One establishes the borders of the Four Hidden Lands without change.**

*Spirit manifests in quake and thunder, working in those who lay out the offerings.* These are the Operators, those who work with the spirit. Thunder above rouses and germinates new potential, while Wind and Wood enter subtly from below, penetrating, pervading and coupling. It is the Woody Moment: inner penetration and outer stimulation that renew each other, creating enduring structures. The ideal Realising Person reflects this by establishing the omens as firm boundaries on all four sides to receive the blessing.

## Transforming Lines: Change at Work

### Initial Six

**Deepening Persevering.**

**Trying to fix the whirlpools of Jun!**

**Trial: Trap! The Way closes.**

**There is no advantageous direction.**

*This means seeking depth at the beginning.* You are trying to fix this influence too deeply, too soon. This is the wrong way to go about it. The Way is closed. Nothing you come up with can help you.
*Direction:* The strength is there. Let the situation mature. Be resolute. You are connected to a creative force.

### NINE AT SECOND

**Persevering. Fix the Omen.**

**The cause of sorrow disappears.**

*Able to last in the centre.* If you persevere in what you have established, your cares and sorrows will disappear. Commit yourself. The power and the ability are there.
*Direction:* Be very small at the beginning. Don't be afraid to act alone. You are connected to a creative force.

### NINE AT THIRD

**Not Persevering in power and virtue. Not Fixing the Omen.**

**'Someone' gives you a gift, then you are embarrassed.**

**Trial: distress.**

*No place to tolerate this!* You are betraying your own promise. Everything will lead to your embarrassment because you cannot keep your heart steady and realise the gift the spirit has given. Surely you can do better than this!
*Direction:* Release bound energy. The situation is already changing.

### NINE AT FOURTH

**Persevering. Trying to Fix the Omen.**

**The fields without game.**

*No lasting at all in this situation.* There is simply nothing in sight, no possibility of a real connection that can fix the influx of feeling. The best thing to do is to leave quietly. Then you may find what you need.
*Direction:* Make the effort. If you let yourself be led, you can realise hidden potential. The situation is already changing.

## Six at Fifth

**Persevering in power and virtue. Fix the Omen.**

**Wise Words! The Way opens if the wife makes the Trial.**

**Trap! The Way closes if the husband makes the Trial.**

*Adhere to the wife and complete this. The husband must decide.*
Persevere in your own virtue. Decide it and fix it. A favourable situation if you act as a wife. Let the woman make the divination and trial. Then things will open up in this situation. If you force the husband's way, you will be cut off.
*Direction*: A transition. Don't be afraid to act alone. You are connected to a creative force.

## Six Above

**Persevering. Trying to fix the distant horizons.**

**Trap! The Way closes.**

*The Great is without achievement here.* You cannot make anything endure like this. Too much excitement and agitation, trying to drum up support that is not there.
*Direction*: Find a vessel, an image of transformation, and use it. Be resolute about this. It will connect you with a creative force.

# 33 and 34: The Paradigm

### Retreat and Advance: Mountain Shrine and First Herdsman/War God

This Pair involves you in an overall model of thought and action elaborated in the interconnected lines of the figures: retreat and advance and strategies at the borders. It evokes the Mountain Shrine and the powerful First Herdsman and War God, the archaic ancestor Wang Hai. It suggests that a retreat to reflect on the matter at hand is the adequate first step in any action. Carefully consider your place in and relation to this model.

*Hidden Possibilities:* 44:43 > 1, the Lady of Fate emerges. Announce the Omen. Be resolute, you are coupled with a creative force.

The Pair exchanges information with 13:14 (People at the Outskirts Altar and the Great Being that Emerges). It is motivated by 31:32 (the Sacred Site and Fixing the Omens). The centre and threshold lines relate the process to 11:12 (New and Old King), 43:44 (Announce the Omen and the Lady of Fates), 53:54 (The Great Marriages) and 55:56 (King and Wandering Sage).

Look at the ages and events these figures suggest for personal connections.

11:12 13:14     31:32     43:44    53:54 55:56

*Shadow site:* 31:32, Influx in the Sacred Place: Fix the Omen

**Retiring means you withdraw. Great Invigorates means you must first still yourself.**

# 33 Retiring/Young Pig DUN

**Withdraw, conceal yourself, pull back; retreat in order to advance later; the Mountain Shrine.**

## MYTHS FOR CHANGE: THE STORY OF THE TIME

**Charge to the Oracle**: *Beings cannot simply reside in their places. Accept this and use the energy of Retiring. This means withdrawing.*

Retiring is a strategy and a sacrifice, the pig-sacrifice to the hidden powers. It suggests a tactical move, an army retiring or retreating using disguise, deception and guile, a retreat that allows you to conquer in the end. The retreat gathers and focuses positive qualities, connecting you to Heaven-energy, the Dragon Force. It leaves the Small People, those who simply adapt to circumstances, behind. It suggests a sojourn in the Mountain Shrine, talking to the Tiger Spirit, and the Mountain Men, the sages hidden in the mountains and beyond the borders, a retreat to a more primitive state, animal dances and transformation rituals. The pig involved is a sacrifice to the Ghost River and the hidden powers of Earth. It is both the animal used in this sacrifice and the *dun-ding* or pig-vessel. A herd of pigs was also a sign of the autumn rains and the coming retreat into winter, for they were released into the muddy stubble-filled fields to feed. Pig omens in general are sign of wealth and good fortune. Here the wealth comes through retiring.

## THE RESPONSE

**Retiring. Make an offering and you will succeed.**

**Advantageous Trial through the Small. Harvesting.**

**Retire**, *DUN*: withdraw, conceal yourself, retreat; pull back in order to advance later; run away, flee, escape, hide; disappear, withdraw into obscurity; secluded, anti-social; fool or trick someone; the young pig, sacrifice to the Ghost River; the Mountain Shrine. The old character shows three footsteps and the sign for stop, and the signs for meat, a little pig and a hand making an offering. It suggests stopping in order to make the pig sacrifice to the underworld powers.

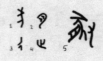

DUN⁴ (11806/162) shows a pig, SHI³ (1), and meat, ROU⁴. It includes CHOU⁴, going or road, and CHI⁴ which equals foot (3 and 4). Another version (5) shows a suckling pig taken by a hand – a pig offered in sacrifice.

Retiring describes your situation in terms of conflict and withdrawal. The way to deal with it is to pull back and seclude yourself in order to prepare for a better time. This is pleasing to the spirits. Through it they will give you success, power and the capacity to bring the situation to maturity. Putting your ideas to the trial brings profit and insight. Don't impose yourself on the world. Be small. Adapt to whatever crosses your path.

### THE SCHOLAR SPEAKS

The hexagram figure shows an inner limit that connects with the spirit above. Below Heaven, the mountain. Retire and be coupled with Heaven. You can't stay where you are. Withdraw, pull back, decline involvement, and refuse connections. Keep people who busily seek their own advantage at a distance, not through hate but through a demanding severity that inspires fear and awe. Retiring is pleasing to the spirits. It is strong, appropriate and corresponds to the movement of the time. Be small, adaptable and flexible. Immerse yourself in the situation and endure. Knowing when to retire is a great and righteous thing!

### THE SHAMAN SPEAKS

**Mountain below Heaven. Retiring.**

**This is a time when Noble One distances Small People, not through hate but through awe.**

*Spirit's words bind us and establish fate while it awes and wars in Heaven.* The Sacrificer is working with the Dragon. Heaven above struggles on, persistent and unwearied, while Mountain below limits and articulates what is complete to suggest what is beginning. This is Metal over Earth: an outer limit that works on the inner field, drawing you nearer to Heaven's inspiring power. The ideal Realising Person reflects this by keeping the Small at a distance through his focus on real integrity. Make the sacrifice. A cycle is ending. Accumulate the spirit of the new.

## TRANSFORMING LINES: CHANGE AT WORK

### INITIAL SIX

**Retiring at the tail. Adversity, hungry souls and angry ghosts.**

**Make the pig sacrifice.**

**Do not act. Have a direction to go.**

*If you do not move, how could there be a disaster?* Pulling back, you get caught in old plans and old promises. You can't cut through this yet. Be ready. Have a plan to use when you get a chance.
*Direction:* Find supportive friends. You are coupled with a creative force.

### SIX AT SECOND

**Retiring. Held in the yellow bull's skin.**

**Absolutely nothing can succeed in loosening this.**

*This means a firm purpose.* You put on the shaman's mask. This is an inner retreat through which you see into things. Do not let go of what you have seen. It is your purpose and belongs with you. Work with these plans and these people.
*Direction:* You are coupled with a creative force.

### NINE AT THIRD

**Tied retiring. Pig bound for sacrifice.**

**There is affliction and adversity, hungry souls and angry ghosts.**

**Accumulate servants and concubines.**

**Wise Words! The Way opens.**

*Afflicting weariness does not allow Great affairs now.* Attempting to retire, you become entangled in a web of difficulties, duties and connections, and you can't get out of this alone. Let others help you. Then you can begin to put it all at a distance.

*Direction*: Proceed step by step. Gather energy for a decisive new move.

### NINE AT FOURTH

**A fine pig.**

**Love and goodness through retiring for the Noble One. Follow the woman.**

**Wise Words! The Way opens.**

**Small People obstructed.**

*Small People can obstruct this.* The sacrifice is accomplished. Goodness and love come through Retiring. Think about what you care for. It will open the Way. Keep greedy people who are eager to serve you at a distance now.

*Direction*: Proceed step by step. Gather energy for a decisive new move.

### NINE AT FIFTH

**Celebration pig! Excellence through Retiring.**

**Trial: Wise Words! The Way is open.**

*This is using the purpose correctly.* The sacrifice is accomplished. Excellence comes through retiring. It will open the Way and give you a lot to do. Have no regrets. The Way is open.

*Direction*: Search on your own. Don't be afraid to stand alone. You are coupled to a creative force.

### NINE ABOVE

**Rich pig! Wealth and fertility through Retiring.**

**There is nothing that is not advantageous. Harvesting.**

*No place to doubt it!* The sacrifice is accomplished. By retiring, you bring wealth and fertility to everything around you. You are doing exactly what is needed and will be very successful at it.

*Direction*: This is a significant influence. It will couple you with a creative force.

# 34 Great Invigorating Strength DA ZHUANG

**Great invigoration, a great idea; advance, focus, drive on; injury, wound, harm; driving animals, the First Herdsman.**

MYTHS FOR CHANGE: THE STORY OF THE TIME

**Charge to the Oracle:** *Beings cannot simply remain in withdrawal. Accept this and use the energy of Great Invigorating and the First Herdsman.*

The retreat is over and great strength takes the field. Invigorating Strength means both great strength and the strength of the Great Ones. It is cognate with a word that means injuring or doing harm and can signify: 'Attack them and injure them!'; causing or being injured. It signifies being adult, full-grown, in full vigour, with the capacity to kill and to offer sacrifice. It is the eighth month when the plants are resplendent and the grain ripens. It combines animal strength, force and treachery in the person of the First Herdsman, the nomad warrior and metal-magician, and tells the story of ultimate success in a battle or raid. This is the story of Wang Hai, the Shang ancestor who combines fertility, sexuality, ritual combat, great animal strength and violence. From him came the line of civilized rulers.

Wang Hai was the Herdsman, a metal-magician and a warrior, an Arouser. When he was guest of the ruler of Yi, Mian Chen, pasturing his flocks, he performed the war dance. He 'took a bird in each hand, ate its head and went into trance'. When he 'danced with metal shield and plumes', Mian Chen's wife was inflamed with desire. They enjoyed each other in secret and she became pregnant. Mian Chen killed him and exposed the corpse. The Lord of the River mourned him. Wang Hai's son used the River Lord's armies to invade Yi and kill Mian Chen, 'leading back the herds and flocks'. He 'used his neighbour's wealth'. This is a story of a cattle raid and change through force that established a new power. Wang Hai became a hero endowed with the strength of the Ram, able to make and wield bronze weapons. He was First

Herdsman, who protected the flocks that fed the people and supplied the sacrifices.

It also tells the story of Chi You who invented metal weapons, head butting and sanctions the use of force. It is an image of the strength that bursts from the mountain retreat and its underworld waters.

Ko-lu Mountain burst open and out came water. Chi You gathered it and made bronze weapons from it. He conquered nine lords that year. Yung-hu Mountain burst open and out came water. Chi You gathered it and made lances and dagger axes. He conquered twelve lords that year. He has a bronze head and iron eyebrows. His ears are like swords and his head has horns. When he fights he butts people with his horns like a ram.

### THE RESPONSE

**Great Invigorating Strength. Drive the herds.**

**Advantageous Trial. Harvesting.**

**Great**, DA: big, noble, important; orient your will towards a self-imposed goal; ability to lead your life; yang energy. The old character shows the Great Person and his power to protect and shelter.

**Invigorate**, ZHUANG: inspire, animate, strengthen; strong, robust, vigorous, mature; a warrior, distinguished or eminent man; flourishing herds; eighth month when vegetation matures and the tenth moon, the moon of harvest; damage, wound, unrestrained strength. The old character shows a wooden or bamboo weapon and a robust man. It suggests Wang Hai, the First Herdsman.

DA[4] (10210/37) shows the Great Person (1). ZHUÀNG (2624/33) (another version at 5) is composed of QIANG, the left half of a tree (2), meaning stiff and strong, and SHI[4] (3), a phallus or a weapon.

Great Invigorating describes your situation in terms of strength, drive and invigorating power. The way to deal with it is to focus your strength through a central creative idea. Putting your ideas to the trial will bring profit and insight. Beware of hurting others through excessive use of force.

## THE SCHOLAR SPEAKS

The hexagram figure shows inner force expressing itself directly and decisively. Thunder located above heaven. This is a time for resolute action. Come out of retirement. It is important to be able to hold on to your strength, for you must judge things for yourself and proceed on your own. A great idea implies strength and power. Something solid and strong is stirring things up. This is the source of your strength. Put your ideas to the trial. Correct one-sidedness in yourself and others. Having a great idea and continually correcting your path lets you look into the heart of Heaven and Earth.

## THE SHAMAN SPEAKS

**Thunder located above Heaven. Great Invigorates.**

**This is a time when Noble One uses the rules nowhere, treading outside them.**

*The spirit that awes and wars in Heaven manifests in quake and thunder.* The Rouser is working with Force. Thunder above rouses and germinates new potential, while Heaven below struggles on, persistent and unwearied, the spark of yang born at the centre of the yin. This is Wood over Metal: great inner force that is directly expressed through rousing action. The ideal Realising Person reflects this by allowing the invigorating force to break through established codes of action. Work through rousing and inspiring. A new cycle is beginning. Disentangle yourself from the past.

## TRANSFORMING LINES: CHANGE AT WORK

### INITIAL NINE

**Great Invigorating Strength in the feet.**

**Trap! Chastising closes the Way.**

**There is a connection to the spirits that will carry you through.**

*Don't exhaust the connection.* You are out to conquer the world. Hold back just a moment. Don't try to tell other people what to do and don't set out on any adventurous expeditions. The spirits are with you, but start slowly.

*Direction*: Continue on. Be resolute. You are connected to a creative force.

### NINE AT SECOND

**Great Invigorating Strength. Drive the animals forward.**

**Wise Words! Trial: The Way is open.**

*This is using the centre.* Drive on. Whatever you want to do will be successful. This begins a flourishing time.

*Direction*: A time of abundance. Don't be afraid to act alone. You are coupled to a creative force.

### NINE AT THIRD

**Small People use Great Strength.**

**Noble One uses the empty spaces of a net.**

**Trial: adversity, hungry souls and angry ghosts.**

**'The ram butts a hedge and entangles his horns.'**

*This means Noble One uses strategy.* You drive on, trying to catch something. Don't force it. Use strategy and an open heart rather than aggression. You are confronting some troublesome past experiences. If you use force, like the ram you will only get yourself entangled.

*Direction*: If you let yourself be led, you can realise hidden potential. The situation is already changing.

### NINE AT FOURTH

**Great Invigorating Strength. Wise Words! Trial: the Way is open.**

**The cause for sorrow disappears.**

**The hedge is broken through, no more entanglement.**

**Invigorate the axles of the great war chariots.**

*This is going towards honour.* The obstacle vanishes and you can do what you want. The past simply disappears. Drive on. There is nothing holding you back. Attack. Put your shoulders to the wheel and do the great things that are in you to do.

*Direction:* A great and flourishing time approaches. If you let yourself be led, you can realise hidden potential. The situation is already changing.

### SIX AT FIFTH

**Great Invigorating Strength.**

**He loses the flock in Yi. We change with ease.**

**Without a cause for sorrow.**

*Not an appropriate situation.* This is Wang Hai who, through his lust and carelessness, loss his flocks. Let go of forward drive. Change your considerable strength into imagination. Don't always charge into obstacles. There are more interesting ways to deal with things. If you realise this, your sorrows will simply disappear. You will soon regain what you have lost.

*Direction:* Be resolute. You are connected to a creative force.

### SIX ABOVE

**Great Invigorating Strength.**

**The ram butts a hedge. 'He can't pull back and he can't push through.'**

**There is no advantageous direction.**

**Wise Words! Accept the hardship and open the Way.**

*Do not worry, the fault will not last.* You are stuck and you are in for a bit of hard work. You can't force your way out of this one. Just sit there and go through the painful analysis of your mistakes. As you do this, the Way will open of itself.

*Direction:* Your hard work begins a better time. Be resolute. You are connected to a creative force.

# 35 and 36: The Paradigm

### Rising and Setting Sun

This Pair involves you in an overall model of thought and action elaborated in the interconnected lines of the figures: being recognized and being outcast, the hardship that leads to new light and release from suffering. It is a paradigm of the action of the Way. Carefully consider your place in and relation to this model.

*Hidden Possibilities*: 39:40 > 63:64, re-imagining difficulties delivers you from tension and obstruction. Make the crossing and prepare the new.

The Pair exchanges information with 21:22 (The Sacred Meal and Bringing Home the Bride). It is motivated by 15:16 (Activating Liminal Powers to Prepare the Future). The centre and threshold lines relate the process to 11:12 (New and Old King), 23:24 (Stripping the Corpse and The Returning Spirit), 55:56 (King and Wandering Sage) and 63:64 (The Crossings).

Look at the ages and events these figures suggest for personal connections.

11:12 (13:14) 15:16     23:24          55:56        63:64

*Shadow site*: 29:30, Ghost River and Bright Omens

**Flourishing means living in the daylight. Brightness Hiding means being an outcast.**

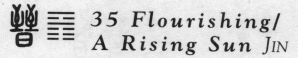

# 35 Flourishing/ A Rising Sun JIN

**Emerge into the light; advance, be noticed; give and receive gifts; dawn of a new day.**

## MYTHS FOR CHANGE: THE STORY OF THE TIME

**Charge to the Oracle**: *You cannot simply invigorate things. A Rising Sun. Accept this and use the energy of prospering. This means advancing.*

'At the rising of the sun, everything on Earth is pushed into sprouting.' The root of Flourishing is the spirit that protects and animates the sun. Suns and kings or powerful figures are synonymous, so this is also a Rising Sun, the emergence of a powerful noble recognized at the centre of power, the Royal Court. Literally, it is Kang Hou, younger brother of King Wu, who was given lands and titles twice after the battle of Muye and the takeover of the Shang. He is the Powerful Prince, possibly a war leader who now turns to peace. Here he is emblem of the good feudal lord, and his flourishing signifies a return of peace and prosperity after the War of the Mandate. It also suggests the Sun Tree and the suns or *jun*-ravens who, bathed by their mother Xihe, fly each day to rest in the Moon Tree and return on the underworld river. These suns were seen as the Royal Ancestors who recognized and were received by their descendants through the *bin*-sacrifice or 'guesting'.

## THE RESPONSE

**Flourishing. A Rising Sun. Joy and delight to the Prince of Kang.**

**Gifts of horses that multiply in multitudes.**

**In one day you are received three times.**

**Flourish, JIN**: Emerge into the light; advance and be recognized; receive gifts; spread prosperity, the dawn of a new day; increase, progress; grow and flourish, as young plants in the sun; go forward, rise, be promoted received in audience; permeate, impregnate; spirit that animates and protects the sun; a rising sun, a new king, royal ancestors. The old character shows the sun, the horizon and two plants flourishing.

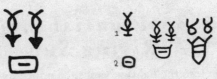

JÌN (1960/72) shows two arrows ZHI⁴ (1) being put into a container (2) which also represents the sun RI⁴, suggesting being brought forward, presented. It also represents Kang Hou mating his horses three times a day. In that case (1) becomes a phallus and (2) a vulva.

Flourishing describes your situation in terms of emerging slowly and surely into the full light of day. The way to deal with it is to give freely in order to help things emerge and flourish. Be calm in your strength and poise. Take delight in things. Give gifts of strength and spirit to enhance those connected with you. You will be received by the higher powers three times in a single day.

## THE SCHOLAR SPEAKS
The hexagram figure shows light emerging from the covering Earth. Brightness issues forth above the Earth. The time has come to re-imagine the situation. Invigorating strength has carried you forward. This implies advancing, exerting yourself, furthering the development of things, stepping into the light. Use the source of this new light to brighten your own power to realise the Way. Prospering is a time to advance. Be yielding and join with others in order to brighten your own great idea. What is flexible and adaptable is advancing and will move you to the position above. Be calm in your strength and poise and give gifts of strength and spirit. You will be recognized by the higher powers.

## THE SHAMAN SPEAKS
**Brightness comes out of Earth. Flourishing.**

**This is a time when Noble One uses originating enlightenment to brighten his power and virtue.**

*Offered service at the Earth Altar, spirit reveals itself in the Bright Omens.* Bright Omens arise from the Field. Fire above radiates light and warmth and people experience the Bright Presence of things, while Earth below yields and sustains. This is Fire over

Earth: brightness, warmth and awareness emerge from the field and are recognized. The ideal Realising Person reflects this by using the light that emanates from the source to enhance his power to actualize the Way. Make the sacrifice. A cycle is ending.

## TRANSFORMING LINES: CHANGE AT WORK

### INITIAL SIX

**Flourishing, advancing with brandished weapons. A Rising Sun.**

**Wise Words! Trial: the Way is open.**

**There is a net of relations that connect to the spirits.**

**You will be enriched. This is not a mistake.**

*Moving alone and correcting it, not a victim of fate.* At the beginning of your rise, you feel held back. Don't worry. You are connected through a net of spiritual relations. Advance vigorously. This situation will enrich you. It is definitely not a mistake.
*Direction*: Bite through the obstacles. Re-imagine the situation. Gather energy for a decisive new move.

### SIX AT SECOND

**Flourishing, then apprehensive. A Rising Sun.**

**Wise Words! Trial: the Way is open.**

**Accept this fine armour and the blessing of the Queen Mother.**

*Using the centre and correcting.* You set out, but feel anxious and sorrowful. Don't worry. The Way is open. Take on this difficult task and receive the Queen Mother's blessing.
*Direction*: Gather energy for a decisive new move.

### SIX AT THIRD

**Flourishing. The crowds are loyal and sincere. A Rising Sun.**

**The omen is fulfilled. The cause for sorrow disappears.**

*This is moving with the above.* Everything is in order. People have confidence in you. Don't hold back. Give of yourself unstintingly. Let your sun shine on all. Your sorrows will vanish.
*Direction*: Begin your travels. Don't be afraid to act alone.

### NINE AT FOURTH

**Flourishing. Advancing like a bushy-tailed mouse.**

**Trial: adversity, hungry souls and angry ghosts.**

*Not an appropriate situation.* Though you have the strength to advance, you are being timid, furtive and scattered. As you prosper, greedy people and bad memories attack you. Make a bold move. Don't give up what you know is right.
*Direction*: Strip away old ideas. Be open and provide what is needed.

### SIX AT FIFTH

**Flourishing. A Rising Sun. The cause for sorrow disappears.**

**'Letting go or acquiring, have no cares.'**

**Wise Words! Go on, the Way is open,**

**There is nothing that is not advantageous. Harvesting.**

*Go on, there will be rewards.* All your sorrows will vanish. Let your sun shine on all. Don't worry about anything; simply give yourself to the work. The Way is open and the time is right. Everything will benefit from this endeavour.
*Direction*: Do not be the victim and identify with the old. Proceed step by step. Gather energy for a decisive new move.

### NINE ABOVE

**Flourishing with lowered horns. A Rising Sun.**

**Adversity, hungry souls and angry ghosts.**

**Hold fast and attack the capital.**

**Wise Words! The Way is open.**

**Trial for distress: this is not a mistake.**

*The Way is not shining yet.* You can control the situation through direct action. Hold fast and deal with your own troubles first. You have to confront the negative images you have of things, based on past experience. This is difficult, but it opens the Way. Though you may feel distressed, this is not a mistake. Attack and take the capital city.
*Direction*: Gather energy in order to respond when the call comes. Re-imagine the situation. Gather energy for a decisive new move.

# 36 Brightness Hiding/ Calling Bird MING YI ☷☲

**Hide your light; protect yourself; accept and begin a difficult task; oppression and hidden influences.**

## MYTHS FOR CHANGE: THE STORY OF THE TIME

**Charge to the Oracle**: *Advancing will lead to a place where you are injured. Accept this and use the energy of Brightness Hiding. This means injury.*

In contrast to the rising sun, *Ming Yi* is the dark sun, the sun in the Earth and the sacrifice to the dark powers at Earth Altar. This is the World of the Dead and mourning, the Demon Country, and travelling among the barbarians – outcast, marginalized, exiled away from the centres of culture and power. A central image is a solar eclipse, the eclipse at Feng that signalled King Wu's receipt of the Mandate of Heaven when he was 'hiding' in the Mourning Hut for his father King Wen. It is also help in hardship and accepting a difficult task. It evokes a series of heroes: Yi the Archer in the Demon Country, shooting the three-legged crow that is eating the sun; Yu the Great taming the demons through enduring hardship; King Wen imprisoned by the Shang tyrant, creating the *Book of Changes* in his cell; King Wu who sets his armies marching to over-throw oppression; Jizi who endured hardship at the court of the tyrant, a voice in the wilderness. Accepting the hardship implied in Brightness Hiding, symbolized by the Calling Bird, will bring about deliverance and the new day.

## THE RESPONSE

**Brightness Hiding.**

**Trial: this hardship is advantageous. Harvesting.**

**Brightness**, MING: light from fire, sun, moon and stars; awareness, intelligence, consciousness; understand, illuminate, distinguish clearly; lucid, clear, evident; dew ritually collected on mirror in moonlight, light ritually collected on or kindled by a mirror turned to the sun; clairvoyance, knowledge of inherent good-ness, inner light which is sign of health; vision, divine action, cleanse; luminous, restore virtue, the divine action of the *shen*; the bright bird, a golden pheasant; *also*: a mandate, fate, command, order or destiny; make a covenant, the Mandate of Heaven. The old character shows the sun and the moon.

**Hide**, Yı: keep out of sight; distant, remote; raze, lower, level; ordinary, plain; cut, wound, destroy, exterminate; barbarians, vulgar uncultured people; prepare the cover for a corpse, close the passes; the spirit bird and wind of the west that blows from the realm of the dead, protector of the soil and its life. The old character shows a great man holding a bow. It suggests the archer hero Yi, who shot down the ten suns that threatened to destroy the world.

MING[2] (7919/72) shows the sun RI[4] (1 and 3) and the moon YUE[2] (2). YI[2] (5297/37) shows a man with an arrow or arrows, perhaps a string-arrow (4).

Brightness Hiding describes your situation in terms of entering the darkness to protect yourself, or to begin a difficult new endeavour. The way to deal with it is to hide your light. Conceal your intelligence by voluntarily entering what is beneath you, like the sun as it sets in the evening. There is a real possibility of injury in the situation. By dimming the light of your awareness and entering the darkness you can avoid being hurt. You have the chance to release yourself from your problems and inaugurate a new time. Putting your ideas to the trial by accepting drudgery and difficulty will bring you profit and insight.

### THE SCHOLAR SPEAKS

The hexagram figure shows inner light hidden in common labour. Brightness enters the Earth's centre. Deliverance from your problems is already being prepared, so accept what is confronting you. Advancing always creates the possibility of injury. Hiding implies injury. You are being proscribed and excluded. Carefully watch the desires that connect you with others so you can consciously choose when to darken or to brighten them. Brighten the pattern within

≡≡ 卿象

yourself while yielding to outer darkness. Use the enveloping obscurity and the difficulties confronting you to clarify worthy ideas. Be like King Wen, who organized the Changes when he was imprisoned by a tyrant. Accept drudgery and difficulty. This brings profit and insight. Darken your light, accept the inner heaviness and let it correct your purpose. Be like Prince Ji, who knew how to distinguish what is right in difficult times and who became a model for others.

## THE SHAMAN SPEAKS

Brightness enters the centre of Earth. Brightness Hiding.

This is a time when Noble One uses supervising the crowds, darkening and brightening.

*The spirit that reveals itself in the Bright Omens is offered service at the Earth Altar.* The Bright Omens are held in the Field. Earth hides and contains the Bright Presence of things. This is Earth over Fire: brightness, awareness and warmth that are hidden within the field of common experience. The ideal Realising Person reflects this by carefully supervising his involvement in the human crowd, working from a concealed position. Work through rousing and inspiring. A cycle is beginning.

## TRANSFORMING LINES: CHANGE AT WORK

### INITIAL NINE

Dark Bird calling. Hiding your Brightness through flight,

Dipping your wings in the waters.

Noble One goes three days without eating.

Have a direction to go.

Master your words to influence others.

*It is right not to take things in now.* You are escaping from an impossible situation, embarked on a dangerous and important mission. Have courage and stamina. Have a plan. You can convince people if you master your words. This is King Wu at the beginning of the campaign to restore the Mandate.
*Direction:* Stay humble and connected to the facts. Trust hidden processes. Release bound energy. The situation is already changing.

**Dark Bird calling. Hiding your Brightness.**

**Hidden, hurt in the left thigh. Use a horse to rescue it.**

**Wise Words! Invigorating strength opens the Way.**

*Yield to this impulse.* This is a serious but not deadly wound. To deal with it, you must mobilize your spirit. Come to the rescue. If you can invigorate your imaginative power, the Way will open and you will free yourself.

*Direction:* A flourishing time is coming. If you let yourself be led, you can realise hidden potential. The situation is already changing.

NINE AT THIRD

**Dark Bird calling. Hiding your Brightness in the Southern Hunt.**

**Hounding them, you acquire their Great Head.**

**Trial: this does not allow affliction.**

*You acquire the Great.* This is the great hunt and a campaign into the Demon Country. In the midst of very considerable difficulties, you find the central illusion that causing this chaos. Though it may act slowly, this will release you from the pain and sadness that afflict you. It lets you open your heart once more.

*Direction:* Something important returns. Be open and provide what is needed.

SIX AT FOURTH

**Dark Bird calling. Enter the left belly.**

**Catch the heart of the Hidden Brightness.**

**Issue forth from their gate and chambers.**

*Be intent on catching the heart.* You find the heart of the darkness obscuring you. Get out of this terrible place. Take aggressive action. Go right to the heart of it and reclaim your lost intelligence. Leave this situation and don't come back.

*Direction:* This begins a time of abundance. Don't be afraid to act alone. You are connected with a creative force.

SIX AT FIFTH

**Dark Bird calling. Jizi Hides his Brightness.**

**Advantageous Trial. Harvesting.**

*Brightness is not allowed to pause.* This is the place of Jizi, the man with integrity who serves a tyrant. You have to pretend to be a part of this situation. Disguise yourself. Don't lose your integrity. You will survive. This will bring you profit and insight in the end. Be clear about what is really happening.
*Direction:* The situation is already changing.

NINE ABOVE

**Dark Bird calling. Brightness Hiding.**

**'A time of brightening, a time of darkening.'**

**First it mounts to Heaven, then it enters the Earth.**

*At first it illuminates the four cities, then it lets things go.* These are the suns, the sons of Xihe, that go out from the Sun Tree then return to the Moon Tree. This cycle is over. The tyrant falls. The darkening ends and you are free. Life once more comes forth from hardship. Think about this set of events and how it started. There is a lesson to be learned.
*Direction:* Renovate a corrupt situation. The situation is already changing.

# 37 and 38: The Paradigm

### The Dwelling and the Ghosts that Haunt it

This Pair involves you in an overall model of thought and action elaborated in the interconnected lines of the two figures: the safety of the hearth and the dangers of the wilderness, the spirit world that opens through the dangerous journey of the outcast. It evokes the attempt of a Zhou noble to found a house on the borders of the established world, surrounded by the ghosts of the past and the excluded. Carefully consider your place in and relation to this model.

*Hidden Possibilities*: 64:63, prepare and make the crossing.

The Pair exchanges information with 53:54 (The Great Marriages). It is motivated by 63:64 (The Crossings). The centre and threshold lines relate the process to 9:10 and 13:14 (Ceremonies at the Outskirts Altar), 21:22 (Sacred Meal and Bringing Home the Bride) and 41:42 (Offering and Blessing).

Look at the ages and events these figures suggest for personal connections.

9:10 (11:12) 13:14    21:22    41:42    53:54    63:64

*Shadow site*: 27:28, Tiger's Mouth and Great Transition

**Dwelling People means being on the inside. Diverging means being on the outside.**

# 37 Dwelling People
## JIA REN

Hold together, family, clan, intimate group; support, nourish, stay in your group; people who live and work together; a seed figure.

## MYTHS FOR CHANGE: THE STORY OF THE TIME

**Charge to the Oracle**: *Injured outside, you must turn back to the dwelling and its people. Accept this and use the energy of Dwelling People.*

Dwelling People is above all the hearth fire and the household altar, the room with the ancestral altar and the spirit tablets. It means 'our ancestral altar, our own'. It is the extended family, the married pair, the inhabitants of a house, the Royal House, and extends to mean a master and a school of thought or 'way' that provides a spiritual dwelling for its followers. Dwelling People is all things inside or *wei*: protection, being among one's own people, concord and safety. It is the fundamental unit of noble life, a family grouped around the ancestors, and emphasizes the *de* or power and virtue of the woman as centre. The progression with the figure suggests founding a dwelling: establishing boundaries, the hearth fire and the woman, settling relations, and the influx of spirit blessings from the ancestors and the mothers.

## THE RESPONSE

**Dwelling People. Advantageous Trial through the woman. Harvesting.**

**Dwell**, *JIA*: home, household, family, relations, clan; room in a dwelling with ancestral altar; family affairs, marry and found a family; business, school of thought; master a skill; have something in common; good, proper; patrimony; the house, the altar, and the inhabitants. The old character shows a pig inside a roof or house, a sign of riches.

**People**, *REN*: an individual person; all human beings, humanity, benevolence. The ideogram shows a person kneeling in submission or prayer. The old character suggests a person kneeling in prayer or submission.

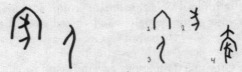

JIA¹ (1114/40) shows a pig SHI³ (2) under a roof or in a house MIAN¹ (1). Another version suggests a man controlling or riding a boar (4). REN² (5546/9) is a person or people (3).

Dwelling People describes your situation in terms of living and working with others, sharing work, spirit and ancestors. The way to deal with it is to care for your relationship with the people who share your space and your activities. Take care of the dwelling and what is within it. Profit and insight come through the woman and through a flexible, nourishing attitude. Dwell in the yin.

### THE SCHOLAR SPEAKS
The hexagram figure shows warmth and clarity spreading within the dwelling. Wind originating from fire issues forth. Gather energy for a decisive new move. When you are injured in the outer world, you naturally turn back towards the dwelling. Dwelling People means what is inside. Use your words to connect with people and make your actions persevering. A woman's yin attitude can correct the situation inside; a man's yang attitude can correct the situation outside. Together they reflect the great righteousness of Heaven and Earth. The dwelling needs a strong head. The roles of father and mother should be clearly designated. Let whoever is the father be a father, the son be a son; let whoever is the elder be the elder, the younger be the younger. Let whoever is the husband be a husband, and whoever is the wife be a wife. This is the correct way of the dwelling. When you correct the dwelling, you set the world right.

Wind originates from Fire and issues forth. Dwelling People.

This is a time when Noble One uses words to connect the beings and movement to persevere on the path.

*Spirit reveals itself in the omens, working through those who lay out the offerings.* The Lady of Fates is working with the Bright Omens. Wind and Wood above enter subtly, penetrating, pervading and coupling, while Fire below radiates light and warmth and people experience the Bright Presence of things. This is Wood over Fire: the Bright Presence within the dwelling that penetrates and brings people together. The ideal Realising Person reflects this by using his words to connect people. Moving their hearts bring to them to the Way, he is carried by the Bright Omens. Seek the vessel of transformation.

## TRANSFORMING LINES: CHANGE AT WORK

### INITIAL NINE

**Dwelling People. Through enclosing there is a Dwelling.**

**The cause for sorrow disappears.**

*Do not change the purpose.* The founding of the house. Stay inside your dwelling. Don't venture out now. Your sorrows will disappear. You are not ready to act yet. Through this enclosure you create the sense of the secure group.
*Direction:* Proceed step by step. Gather energy for a decisive new move.

### SIX AT SECOND

**Dwelling People. Have no concern for achievements or glory.**

**Locate yourself in the centre and feed the people.**

**Wise Words! Trial: the Way is open.**

*This is yielding and using subtle penetration.* The hearth fire. You and your work are the centre of this group. Give open-handedly. Don't impose yourself on anyone. Help and nourish the others in your group. This will open the Way for all of you.
*Direction:* Accumulate small to achieve the great. Turn conflict into creative tension. The situation is already changing.

### Nine at Third

**Dwelling People, scolding, scolding.**

**Repent past sorrow and adversity, hungry souls and angry ghosts.**

**Wise Words! The Way opens.**

**If wife and son are giggling, giggling,**

**Going on will bring distress.**

*Take the past in hand. Do not let go of articulating the dwelling.* Establish family relations by dealing with the past. Make sure your house is in order and that people know their places and roles. The confrontation isn't easy, but facing old habits will open the Way. This calls for honest repentance of past mistakes, cleaning the house, opening the heart. If you simply let things go on, everything will be confused. Take charge! Articulate relations clearly.

*Direction*: Increase your efforts. Pour in more. A fertile time is coming. Strip away old ideas. Be open and provide what is needed.

### Six at Fourth

**Dwelling People. An affluent Dwelling.**

**Wise Words! The Great Way is open.**

*This means yielding is located in the centre.* Wealth and family connections. Goodness, riches and happiness will flow in this dwelling. The Way is open. Make this abundance serve a real purpose. There is your challenge.

*Direction*: Bring people together. Take action. You are coupled to a creative force.

### Nine at Fifth

**The King approaches his Dwelling Altar to receive the Ancestor's blessings.**

**Care for the Myriad Beings.**

**Wise Words! The Way is open.**

*This is mingling in mutual affection.* The indwelling of the spirit. You can create a world around you like a temple or a house of the spirit. Act from your heart. Try to help others. Your care for other people will open the Way.

*Direction*: Adorn the house with beauty. Bring home the bride. Release bound energy. The situation is already changing.

### NINE ABOVE

**Dwelling People. Majestic and resplendent, he has a connection to the spirits that impresses others.**

**Wise Words! Completing this opens the Way.**

*This reverses your name and personality.* The blessings of the Mothers. This is the head of the house, full of the power of the spirits after the sacrifice. Whatever you want to do is possible. You have the spirit and the intelligence to carry all before you. Act on your desires. Do what you need to do. The Way is open.

*Direction*: The situation is already changing.

# 38 Diverging/The Shadow Lands GUI

**Opposition, discord, conflicting purposes; outside the norm, cast out; strange meetings with hidden spirits, the ghost world; change conflict to creative tension through awareness; a seed figure.**

## MYTHS FOR CHANGE: THE STORY OF THE TIME

**Charge to the Oracle:** *When the Way of the dwelling comes to an end, you must turn away. Accept this and use the energy of Diverging. This means turning away.*

Outside the dwelling, exposed to the night, Diverging points at a Bright Presence in the night sky, the star mansions of the Ghost Cart (*Yugui*) that presides over punishments, executions and dire fates. It includes others: the Heavenly Horse, the Heavenly Swine, the Man leading the Ox, the Bow and Arrow, the Orphan or Fox. It suggests autumn, for the rains are here and the gates of winter are closing. This is the sun and moon in opposition and, metaphorically, the minister cut off and exiled from the royal presence. It suggests the *Li sao*, the Nine Songs, an intense and shamanic lament of the virtuous minister betrayed by schemers and cast out by his prince. It is all things outside, *wai*: isolation, danger, foreigners, wilderness, punishments, the Demon Country. It suggests strange visions, alternate realities and chance meetings with important spirit beings: the Primal Father, Yi the Archer and the Dark Lord or Hidden Master. It combines the themes of discord, punishment and exile with the difficult voyage, travelling in alternate realities.

This is the world of the *wugui*, the shamans or Intermediaries who deal with angry ghosts and spirit presence outside the normal and of the border regions, beyond the frontiers. Phonetically and thematically, this links with the cyclic character marking the last day of the ten-day week, a day on which divinations were performed for ghost signs and demons coming from the Four Hidden Lands, angry ancestors and ghosts who could bring misfortune upon the living. A related character portrays waters running from the Four Directions or Hidden Lands into the centre, the Earth Pit and its underworld or Ghost River. It represents the yin aspect of water, linked with the ghost world and the appearance of a certain set of star clusters or mansions.

The lines centre on the terms 'see' (*jian*) and 'meet' (*yu*), carrying through the sense of perceiving the strange suggested by the Name. The figure as a whole is an extended pun on *gui*, ghost, which describes spirits of the newly dead. 'When a spirit returns (*gui*) he first becomes a ghost (*gui*), a human with a demon head; the breath of the *gui* is insidious and harmful.' Daoists call these souls who are continuing rebirth as slaves of passion. The word is a curse, directly linked to the Hidden Lands and to all who are outside and foreign. Dealing with these spirits, transforming the negative power of the ghost world into a creative tension with the living is essential to the continuation of human life and culture. This is the job of the wandering sage, the one who voyages outside the norms, the *wugui*.

## THE RESPONSE

**Diverging. The Shadow Lands.**

**Wise Words! Small's affairs open the Way.**

**Diverge**, GUI: opposition, discord; change conflict into creative tension; separate, oppose, move in opposite directions; distant, remote from each other; animosity, anger; astronomical opposition; ghosts and the ghost world; exile, cast out. The old character shows a sacrificial mat and the eyes of the Ancestor.

KUI$^2$: (6435/109) consists of an offering mat for oblations GUI$^3$ (2) and two eyes MU$^4$ (1) that indicate the presence of the Ancestor. The offering mat is a cyclical character indicating the last day of the ten-day week – (3) shows descriptions of offerings to ancestors. The first shows the ancestor descending, his big eye upon the living, a hand with the offering knife of the sacrificing son and the bundle of grass for the libation. The second shows the ancestor in the sacred niche from whence his influence emanates the temple or a box with gifts and the hand and libation mat.

Diverging describes your situation in terms of opposition and discord, being outcast. The way to deal with it is to change potential conflict into dynamic tension. Separate and clarify what is in conflict while acknowledging the essential connection. Small things are important now. Be flexible and adaptable in all your affairs. That generates meaning and good fortune by releasing transformative energy. Be open to strange occurrences, sudden visions and non-normal ways of seeing things.

## THE SCHOLAR SPEAKS

The hexagram figure shows expression and awareness in conflict with each other. Fire rises, the mists descend. The solution to this conflict is inherent in the situation. When the way of dwelling together is exhausted, you must necessarily turn away. Diverging implies turning away. It is what is outside, what is unfamiliar, foreign and strange. You must be able both to join things together and to separate them. Fire stirs things up and rises. The mists stir things up and descend. They are like two women who agree to live together while their purposes move apart. These two things, individual expression and holding together, can be connected through brightness and awareness. Use what is flexible and adaptable to move to the position above. You can acquire the centre and connect with what is strong and solid. That is why being concerned with small things generates meaning and good fortune by releasing transformative energy. Heaven and Earth are polarized, but in their work they come together. Man and woman are polarized, but their purposes interpenetrate. The Myriad Beings are polarized, but they all are busy with the same things. Examine what separates and what connects people. Diverging is a time when you connect with what is truly great.

## THE SHAMAN SPEAKS

**Fire above, Mists below. Diverging.**

**A time when Noble One uses both concording and dividing.**

*Spirit speaks through the Intermediaries, revealing itself in the Bright Omens.* The Joyous Dancer is working with the Bright Omens. Fire above seeks to rise, while Mists hold joyous words within. This is Fire over Metal: the conflict between inner form and outer radiance that creates a polarizing tension. The ideal Realising Person reflects this by mobilizing his ability both to accept and reject. Hold the heart fast and take the risk. Change the Mandate of Heaven.

## TRANSFORMING LINES: CHANGE AT WORK

### INITIAL NINE

**Diverging. The Shadow Lands.**

**The cause for sorrow disappears.**

**If you lose your horse, do not pursue it.**

**It will return to its origin of itself.**

**You see the Hateful People. This is not a mistake.**

*This means using casting out faults.* Meeting the Heavenly Horse. Don't worry over what seems gone. Harmony, strength and love will return by themselves. The pain and sorrow and disconnection you feel will vanish. You will see the angry ghosts. It is vital that you don't let them poison your mind. Keep your thoughts warm and clear and you will make no mistakes.
*Direction:* Gather energy for a decisive new move.

### NINE AT SECOND

**Diverging. The Shadow Lands.**

**Meeting the Hidden Lord of the Crooked Path.**

**This is not a mistake.**

*This is not letting go of the Way.* In an unexpected way, in an unexpected place, you meet a spirit power of great importance. This is the meaning of being outside the norms. This influence enters your heart and makes everything clear. Don't be afraid. This is not a mistake.
*Direction:* Bite through the obstacles! Gather energy for a decisive new move.

### Six at Third

**Diverging. The Shadow Lands.**

**You see your cart pulled back and your cattle hobbled.**

**The Branded Man with his nose cut off.**

**'What you initiate will not be completed.'**

*Not an appropriate situation. You meet a strong line.* These are punishments and obstacles. A serious setback, the end of your plans. You have tried to force your way through and have met unexpectedly strong opposition. Nothing can come to fruition now. Do not identify yourself with these people and their violent passions.
*Direction*: Clarify and brighten your central idea. Be resolute. You are connected to a creative force.

### Nine at Fourth

**Diverging alone. The Orphan and the Fox.**

**You meet the Primal Father, mingle and connect to the spirits.**

**Adversity, hungry souls and angry ghosts.**

**This is not a mistake.**

*Mingling and connecting without fault. Your purpose is moving indeed.* Alone and isolated, you encounter something or someone inspiring, a primal source. Though there may seem to be danger, don't be afraid. Joining with this force will put you in touch with the spirits. Cut through past pains and sorrows. What you have in your heart will come to pass.
*Direction*: Diminish passion and past involvement. Make the sacrifice. This is the return of something significant. Be open and provide what is needed.

### Six at Fifth

**Diverging. The Shadow Lands.**

**The cause for sorrow disappears.**

**You see the ancestors eating flesh.**

**How could going on like this be a mistake?**

*This means in going there will be rewards.* Lost in the wilderness, you find the ancient virtue and power. You are blessed by your ancestors. They bite their way through and confer their blessings. This is the meal shared with spirits and great ones. Your sorrows will soon vanish. There is no way in which this can be a mistake.

*Direction:* Proceed step by step. Find supportive friends. Gather energy for a decisive new move.

NINE ABOVE

**Diverging alone. The Orphan and the Fox.**

**You see the Heavenly Swine covered with muck,**

**the Chariot Carrying Dead Souls.**

**'First you stretch the bow, then you loosen the bow.'**

**Those you are confronting are definitely not outlaws.**

**Seek a marriage alliance.**

**Going on you meet the rain. Wise Words! The Way will open.**

*The doubt of the flock disappears.* Yi the Archer comes to your aid. Alone and isolated, you see the people around you as dirty pigs or ghosts. At first you are hostile, but then you relax. Where does this hostility come from? These people are not trying to hurt you. Reach out and seek an alliance. As you begin, the falling rain will wash the past away and the Way will open. The time of isolation is over.

*Direction:* If your let yourself be led, you can realise hidden potential. The situation is already changing.

# 39 and 40: The Paradigm

### 'Comings and Goings' and Deliverance

This Pair involves you in an overall model of thought and action elaborated in the interconnected lines of the figures: re-imagining difficulties and a consequent release from tension and suffering. It evokes the culture founder Yu the Great and an interchange across the Ghost River that releases the hidden spirit. Carefully consider your place in and relation to this model.

*Hidden Possibilities*: 64:63, prepare and make the crossing.

The Pair exchanges information with 63:64 (The Crossings). It is motivated by 53:54 (The Great Marriages). The centre and threshold lines relate the process to 7:8 (Armies and New Group), 15:16 (Activating Liminal Powers to Prepare the Future), 31:32 (Sacred Site and Fixing the Omen) and 47:48 (Oppressed Noble returns to Common Source).

Look at the ages and events these figures suggest for personal connections.

7:8    15:16    31:32    47:48    53:54    63:64

*Shadow site*: 25:26, Disentangling from past affliction and Accumulating Spirit

**Limping means hardship. Loosening means relaxing.**

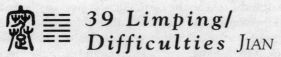

# 39 Limping/ Difficulties JIAN

Obstacles, afflictions, feeling hampered; overcome difficulties
by re-imagining the situation; appearance
of Yu the Great, the limping god; a seed figure.

MYTHS FOR CHANGE: THE STORY OF THE TIME

**Charge to the Oracle**: *When you turn away, there will be heaviness
and trouble. Accept this and use the energy of Limping. This means
heaviness and trouble.*

Limping invokes the hero Yu the Great, the limping god, who
tamed the flood, fixing the omens and opening the channels. It
combines the meanings 'lame, limping, hobbled; difficulties,
poverty, suffering' with the meanings 'straight, honest, frank'. The
advice is: 'progress not possible, stop and change your ideas'. This
is imaged in the person of Yu, who combines unceasing toil and
great adaptability.

Yu channelled the overflowing waters from the underworld Ghost
River, inheriting the task from his father, Gun. He changed the
strategy from heroic, lonely striving to collective effort, building the
dikes, channels and dams that opened the Watercourse Way, the
foundation of culture. He obtained the aid of Responding Dragon
and Numinous Turtle. He called the lords and spirits together. He
established the divinatory vessels, the *Nine Ding*, clearing communication with the spirit world. In doing this he redeemed his father,
the disgraced and executed Gun. Yu limps on through great difficulties, flowing like water. His limping is a sign of selfless toil and an
enduring connection with the underworld.

This is reflected in the phrase that runs through this figure,
*wang lai*, going and coming, the river of time on which the seeds or
symbols of events flow toward us. 'Going' represents what is leaving the field of awareness. It suggests the past, the dead and the
waters of the dead. It means leave, flee, as well as put into practice,
go in the direction of. It is the *wang*-sacrifice, an exorcism of noxious influences. 'Coming' represents arriving from the future,
attracting good influences, grain received in tribute, what comes

from Heaven. It is the tree on the Earth Altar. It gives us the seeds, the spirit and the symbol, *shen* and *xiang*, that unfold into events. This shuffling step, backwards and forwards, is the 'step of Yu' used in many rituals. It is the movement of Limping and of Yu the Great: 'bad influence going, exorcize it!; seeds of good are coming.' This change in the time occurs through a shift in awareness represented by the change from northeast, the past and lonely striving, to the southwest, common effort and future good. It sets the stage for the deliverance to follow.

## THE RESPONSE

**Limping. Difficulties. Southwest advantageous.**

**Advantageous to see this Great Person. Harvesting.**

**Wise Words! Trial: the Way is open.**

**Difficulty,** JIAN: Obstacles, afflictions, blocks; to feel hampered; overcome difficulties by re-imagining the situation; honest, frank, strong, resistant; limp, lame; weak, crooked, unfortunate; the limping god, Yū the Great. The old character shows a house, a person with an injured foot, and graphs that suggest both a grass sleeping mat and hands supplicating aid.

 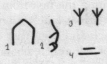

JIAN³: (1600/157). The character represents a man (2) with an injured foot in a hut, MIAN² (1), filled with grass or straw (3), in some versions the sign for hands. He is sealed in by (4), which suggests SAI¹ – plug, wall up, block up a house – and HAN³ – cold, wintry.

Limping describes your situation in terms of confronting obstacles and feeling afflicted by them. The way to deal with it is to see through the situation in a new way and gather energy for a decisive new move. Don't magnify your problems. You are limping along and your circulation is impeded. Retreat and join with others in view of future gains. That brings profit and insight. Attack, lonely efforts and dwelling on the past won't help at all. See Great People.

Contact important people who can help you and think about what your central idea really is. Putting your ideas to the trial generates meaning and good fortune by releasing transformative energy.

## THE SCHOLAR SPEAKS

The hexagram figure shows an inner limit and an outer danger. Above the mountain is the Pit. Gather your energy for a decisive new move. Turning away from something is always arduous and heavy. Limping implies heaviness. But by reversing the direction of what you are doing, you can renovate your power to realise the Way. This is a difficult and heavy time. There is danger in front of you; if you can see it and stop, you will really understand the situation. In a difficult time, retreating and joining with others brings profit and insight. You can acquire the strong, calm centre. Through attack and lonely striving you will only exhaust your Way. See Great People. Consult those who can help you to see what is great in your own ideas. This brings profit and insight. Proceeding in this way leads to achievement. The situation is appropriate. Correct the way you are apportioning power and who you depend on. By re-imagining your situation, you connect with what is truly great.

## THE SHAMAN SPEAKS

> **Stream above Mountain.**
>
> **This is a time when Noble One reverses his personality to renovate his power and virtue.**

*Spirit words bind us and accomplish fate, rewarding those toiling in the Pit.* The Sacrificer is working with the Ghost River. Rushing Water above dissolves direction and shape, flowing on through toil and danger, while Mountain below limits and articulates what is complete to suggest what is beginning. This is Water over Earth: an inner field that blocks and articulates the outer flow. The ideal Realising Person reflects this by turning back on himself to renew his connection to the Way. Hold the heart fast and take the risk. Nurture the new.

## Transforming Lines: Change at Work

### Initial Six

**Limping. Difficulties going, praise and ease coming.**

*It is proper to await this.* Limping on, while feeling cut off and frustrated. Resist the temptation to push your way through. If you wait and open yourself to new thoughts, all these frustrations will disappear. You will be praised for doing this.
*Direction*: The situation is already changing.

### Six at Second

**Limping like Yu. The King's servant: Difficulties, Difficulties!**

**His own person is definitely not the cause.**

*This means completing it without excess.* This is the line of the great hero Yu, through whose ceaseless work the land we live on emerged from the swamps. 'Without Yu, we would all be fishes.' You are pushing on through a sea of troubles and you don't really know why everything is so complicated. Be calm in your heart. The difficulties you are facing are not your fault. Though it doesn't make it any easier, you are truly called on to confront them. Much good will come of this.
*Direction*: Connect with common needs and strengths. Turn conflict into creative tension. The situation is already changing.

### Nine at Third

**Limping. Difficulties going, reverse is coming.**

*What is inside will rejoice in this.* You are limping on, but don't keep chasing what you want. Don't force it. If you just wait calmly, the whole situation will reverse itself. Then you will truly have cause to rejoice.
*Direction*: Change who you associate with. Strip away your old ideas. Be open and provide what is needed.

### Six at Fourth

**Limping. Difficulties going, connection is coming.**

*This is an appropriate and substantial position.* Limping on, you feel lonely and think the world is against you. You are beating your head against a brick wall. Relax. There are people looking for you right now who can see how valuable you are.
*Direction:* Open yourself to this influence. It couples you with a creative force.

### Nine at Fifth

**Limping like Yu. In Great Difficulties, partners come.**

*This means articulating the centre.* Yu calls the spirits and the lords. You are in the middle of great difficulties, about to give up. New spirit and new partners will soon be there to help you. What you are doing is very important. Don't give up now.
*Direction:* Stay humble and connected to the facts. Release bound energy. Dissolve obstacles to understanding. The situation is already changing.

### Six Above

**Limping. Difficulties going, ripeness and abundance coming. The seeds.**

**Wise Words! The Way opens.**

**Advantageous to see this Great Person. Harvesting.**

*The purpose is inside. Adhere to it and value it.* Do not try to impose your will. Let go and the situation will drop into your hand like a ripe plum. Things are full of promise. Talk to someone who can connect you with the great and help you reflect on what is going on. See the spirit at the heart of the situation. A whole new world is appearing from the waters.
*Direction:* Proceed step by step. Gather energy for a decisive new move.

# 40 Loosening/ Deliverance JIE  ䷧ 解

Solve problems, untie knots, release blocked energy;
liberation, freed from suffering; a seed figure.

## MYTHS FOR CHANGE: THE STORY OF THE TIME

**Charge to the Oracle:** *Difficulties must come to an end. Accept this and use the energy of Loosening. This means relaxation.*

Deliverance shows the Arouser who frees us from difficulties, the emergent dragon, released from the river of ghosts. It is a critical moment, an opening in time that combines release and good augury or blessings. The root of the term is horn: the horns of a sacrificial victim, a horned instrument to undo knots, the rhinoceros-horn wine cup used at the River-Mountain festivals, the one-horned beast who attacks evil-doers, the cornucopia. It represents a juncture, a point of insertion or critical point when the sacrifice is accepted and the blessings flow, as well as the shared feast and celebration after the solemn ritual. It is escape, release, the loosening of the trap, released from the knot or noose of a hostile fate. It means dissipating melancholy, an exorcism of the city walls, awakening from illusion, fever breaking, satisfying natural needs, opening communication and sexual climax, when inhibited forces are set free. It was used to describe release from the body, liberation through spiritual practices and becoming an immortal, a sage who perceives through the Bright Spirits and is thus released from compulsion and fear.

## THE RESPONSE

Loosening and Deliverance.

Southwest advantageous. Northeast not advantageous.
Harvesting.

If you have no direction to go, the return is coming.

If you have a direction to go, begin at daybreak.

Wise Words! The Way opens.

**Loosen**, *JIE*: Solve problems, untie knots, release blocked energy; Place of insertion, joint or articulation; liberation, deliverance, free from suffering and constraint, dispel sorrow, solve problems, eliminate bad effects, release blocked energy; divide, detach, untie, scatter, dissolve, dispel; liberate, set free; analyze, explain, understand; sexual climax, discharge water, fever breaking, defecation. The old character shows two hands removing the horn from an ox, so that it can be used to aid people.

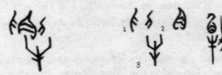

$JIE^3$ (1474/148) shows two hands $JOU^2$ (1) removing the horn $JIAO^3$ (2) of a cow $NIU^2$ (3).

Loosening/Deliverance describes your situation in terms of a release from tension and the new energy that it makes available. The way to deal with it is to untie knots, dispel sorrows, solve problems and understand motivations. Forgive and forget, wipe the slate clean. Join with others to realise plans for future gain. That brings profit and insight. Do not struggle on alone, carrying the burden of the past. If you have no unfinished business to attend to, simply wait for the energy to return. It will generate meaning and good fortune. If you do have directions to impose or places to go, the first light of dawn generates meaning and good fortune by releasing transformative energy. Be up and doing and greet the new day.

### THE SCHOLAR SPEAKS

The hexagram figure shows the fertile shock of a stirring new time. Thunder and rain arousing. The situation is already changing. The time can't always be heavy and arduous. Deliverance implies relaxing and letting things go. Forgive excesses, pardon violations and faults. Act to stir things up. Loosening means arousing things and avoiding danger. Join with others to realise plans for future gain. That brings profit and insight. By going on you will acquire the crowds. The returning energy that is coming towards you will generate meaning and good fortune. Use it to stay in the centre. If you must do something, start at the break of dawn. Proceeding in this way brings achievement. Heaven and Earth loosen and free things through the arousing power of thunder and rain. Thunder and rain arouse the seeds of all the fruits, grasses and trees to burst forth. The time of Loosening and Deliverance is a great time indeed.

## THE SHAMAN SPEAKS

Thunder and Rain arousing. Loosening and Deliverance.

This is a time when Noble One forgives excesses and pardons offences.

*Spirit rewards those suffering in the Pit, manifesting in quake and thunder.* The Rouser is working with the Ghost River. Thunder above rouses and germinates new potential, while Rushing Water below dissolves direction and shape, flowing on through toil and danger. This is Wood over Water: a new time begins outside while the old dissolves within, releasing blocked energy. The ideal Realising Person reflects this through a great upwelling of compassion, washing away old knots of pain and sorrow, carried by the Bright Omens. The new time is being born.

## TRANSFORMING LINES: CHANGE AT WORK

### INITIAL NINE

Loosening and Deliverance. This is not a mistake.

*This is the border of the strong and the supple. Righteous and without fault.* You will be delivered by acting on your plans. Be vigorous. You are in exactly the right position. This is not a mistake.
*Direction:* Let yourself be led. You can realise hidden potential. The situation is already changing.

### NINE AT SECOND

Loosening and Deliverance.

You catch three foxes in the fields and acquire a yellow arrow.

Wise Words! Trial: The Way is open.

*This is acquiring the centre and the Way.* The royal hunt after a victory. Deliverance comes through vigorously pursuing your objectives. There are forces that seem to be threatening you, but you catch them in the act and acquire their power. You have the ability to realise your desires, which are in harmony with the Way. *Direction:* Gather energy in order to respond when the call comes. Re-imagine the situation. Gather energy for a decisive new move.

### Six at Third

**Deliver yourself through Loosening.**

**'He bears a burden yet rides in a carriage.'**

**This attracts outlaws in the end.**

**Trial: distress.**

*Truly shameful. Whose fault is this?* You are tied in a false position, acting above or beneath yourself and either way it invites disaster. Who are you trying to impress? Is it really worth it? If you go on like this, you will be covered in shame. Deliver yourself from the situation.
*Direction:* Endure in what is right. Be resolute. You are connected to a creative force.

### Nine at Fourth

**Deliverance. Loosen your thumbs.**

**Partners will come in the end.**

**Splitting apart brings a connection to the spirits that will carry you through.**

*This not an appropriate situation yet.* Deliver yourself from your current relationships. They are doing you no good. New friends will come after a time of loneliness. The act of splitting away from what you now think necessary will draw the spirits to you. Have no doubt about it. Act now.
*Direction:* Organize your forces. Something significant is returning. Be open and provide what is needed.

### Six at Fifth

**Deliverance. Noble One's tether is Loosened.**

**Wise Words! The Way opens.**

**There is a connection to the spirits that reaches the Small People.**

*Small people are withdrawing him*. If you are truly committed to what you are doing, you will be delivered and loosed from the constriction you feel. Hold fast to what you believe. It opens the Way and connects you to the spirits. Talented people without a leader will feel this and come to your aid.

*Direction*: Look within to find the way out. Find supportive friends. Gather energy for a decisive new move.

### Six Above

**Loosening and Deliverance.**

**The prince used this to shoot a hawk on a high rampart above.**

**He catches it.**

**There is nothing that is not advantageous.**

*This delivers him from the perverse*. You capture the force opposing your plans and desires. Don't worry. Be brave. Attack now and you will most certainly win. This will begin a new cycle of time, released from the old. Everything will benefit.

*Direction*: Gather energy for a decisive new move.

# 41 and 42: The Paradigm

### The Offering and the Blessing

This Pair involves you in an overall model of thought and action elaborated in the interconnected lines of the figures: making a sacrifice and the blessing that results. It embodies a site of radical transformation, the Tiger's Mouth and the Opened Heart, where the events of life pass through the two great initiation sites. Carefully consider your place in and relation to this model.

*Hidden Possibilities:* 24:23 > 1:2, return of the spirit strips away the old, connecting you to the interaction of the primal powers.

The Pair exchanges information with 3:4 (Sprouting and Nurturing the New). It is motivated by 19:20 (Releasing the Spirit and Watching the Omens). The centre and threshold lines connect 27 and 61 (the zone of transformation) with 25:26 (Assembly and Sacred Mountain) and 37:38 (Dwelling and the Ghosts that Haunt it).

Look at the ages and events these figures suggest for personal connections.

3:4     19:20     25:26 <u>27</u>     37:38     <u>61</u>

*Shadow site:* 23:24, Stripping the Corpse and the Return of the Spirit

### Diminishing and Augmenting are the beginning of increase and decrease.

# 41 Diminishing/ The Offering SUN

Decrease, sacrifice, loss; concentrate, diminish your
involvement, decrease your desire; aim at a
higher goal, see the significant pattern of things;
site of creative transformation.

## MYTHS FOR CHANGE: THE STORY OF THE TIME

**Charge to the Oracle:** *Relaxing the bonds we must find a place to let
go of things. Make the Offering. Accept this and use the energy of
Diminishing.*

Diminishing and Augmenting offer a paradigm of sacrifice and its
results. Diminishing is the offering: 'What is below gives to what is
above.' The root is hand and a sacrificial vessel, pouring out the
libation. It is the food and wine, the cooked grains in the vessel,
the objects and victims offered in sacrifice or put into the tomb. It
suggests making a reverence, a full ritual prostration. Others meanings include to lessen, harm, destroy, lose or weaken, for the things
offered are truly destroyed. It includes biting or mordant speech,
criticism and self-reproach. It is a gift that costs much effort.
Philosophically, it is the cultivation of power and virtue, what
keeps harm away. It reduces things to the essential, eliminating the
useless or outmoded, and thus reveals the Way. It is the waning
moon, the victim, the old King, what is offered.

## THE RESPONSE

Diminishing. The Offering.

A connection to the spirits will carry you through.

Wise Words! The Way to the Source is open.

This is not a mistake.

This is an Enabling Trial.

Advantageous to have a direction to go. Harvesting.

You ask how to make use of this?

Two vessels allow you to make the presentation.

**Diminish**, SUN: lessen, take away, make smaller, weaken, damage; minus, a debt; lose, spoil, hurt, blame; criticize, reproach, biting; offer in sacrifice, give up, give away; concentrate, aim at a higher goal; diminish the unnecessary, reduce to the essence. The old character shows an empty vessel and an offering hand.

   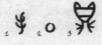

$SUN^3$ (10109/64) shows the palm of a hand, $SHOU^3$ (1) and $YUAN^2$, made up of a cauldron $DING^3$ (3) and a circle $LING^2$ (2), indicating empty, hollow, nothing, zero. The hand is a special form meaning to join the hands and bow reverentially.

Diminishing describes your situation in terms of loss, sacrifice and the need for concentration. The way to deal with it is to decrease your involvements and free yourself from emotional entanglements. This makes energy available for new developments. Act this way with confidence, for you are connected to the spirits and they will carry you through. This is the origin of great good fortune and meaningful events. It is not a mistake. This is an enabling divination. Put your ideas to the trial. Have a place to go. Impose a direction on things. That brings profit and insight. Inquire into motivations; ask yourself why you are doing things. Use two ceremonial vessels to present your results to the spirits.

## THE SCHOLAR SPEAKS

The hexagram figure shows an outer limit that brings inner development to expression. Below the mountain there are the mists. Go back and start over. Something significant is returning. To release blocked energy, you must have a way to let things go. Diminishing is the way, for decreasing is the beginning of increasing. This is the way you adjust and repair your power to realise the Way. Diminishing is heavy and arduous at first, but it lets you be versatile and change with the time. It keeps harm at a distance. Curb your anger and resentment in order to block passions and desires. This changes the flow of energy. Diminish what is below and augment what is above. Your Way is moving in what is above.

Diminish things with confidence, for you are connected to the spirits and they will carry you through. This is the origin of great good fortune and meaningful events. It is not a mistake. This is an enabling divination, so put your ideas to the trial. Inquire into motivations, particularly your own. Two ceremonial vessels correspond to the time. They signify diminishing what is strong and solid and augmenting what is supple and adaptable. This fills what is empty. It connects you to the time. Accompany it as it moves.

## THE SHAMAN SPEAKS

**Mists below Mountain. Diminishing.**

**This is a time when Noble One curbs anger and restrains passions.**

*Spirit speaks and spreads joy through the Intermediaries; its words bind us and accomplish fate.* These are the Operators, those who work with the spirit. Mountain above limits and articulates what is complete to suggest what is beginning, while Mists rising from below stimulate and fertilize, joyous words cheer and inspire. It is Earth over Metal: the outer field that diminishes involvement, stimulating inner growth and giving voice to the spirit. The ideal Realising Person reflects this by freeing himself from compulsive, unreflected emotions. Make the sacrifice. A cycle is ending. Be open to the influx of the spirit.

## TRANSFORMING LINES: CHANGE AT WORK

### INITIAL NINE

**Diminishing. The Offering.**

**Bring it to an end and go swiftly.**

**This is not a mistake. Discussing diminishes it.**

*This is honouring and uniting purposes with the above.* This involvement is a mistake. Leave now, quickly. Talk about how you can get out of the way, but don't let it diminish your resolve.
*Direction:* There are hidden forces at work. This is the return of something significant. Be open and provide what is needed.

NINE AT SECOND

**Diminishing. The Offering.**

**Advantageous Trial. Harvesting.**

**Chastising closes the Way. Trap!**

**This Diminishes nothing, it augments it.**

*This is centring and activating the purpose.* This is a very advantageous connection. Everyone will benefit. It won't help if you try to discipline people and it is not the time to set out on an expedition. This connection won't diminish things, it will augment them.
*Direction*: Take things in and nourish them. Be open and provide what is needed.

SIX AT THIRD

**Diminishing. The Offering.**

**'When there are three people moving, they will be diminished by one.**

**When one person is moving, he will acquire a friend.'**

*This means the three are doubtful.* If you are involved in a triangle, it will soon become a couple. If you are alone, you will soon have a friend. You acquire the Inner Companion.
*Direction*: A time for a great endeavour. Let yourself be led. You can realise hidden potential. The situation is already changing.

SIX AT FOURTH

**Diminishing his affliction. The Offering.**

**Commission someone to carry it swiftly.**

**There will be rejoicing. This is not a mistake.**

*This truly allows rejoicing.* This connection is seriously harming you. Diminish your involvement. Send someone quickly to give the message. Then you will have cause to rejoice. Have no doubts, this is not a mistake.
*Direction*: Turn conflict into creative tension. The situation is already changing.

**Diminishing. The Offering.**

**'Someone' augments him.**

**Ten pairs of tortoise divinations cannot control or contradict this!**

**Wise Words! The Way to the Source is open.**

*This originates in protection from above.* A blessing and a Mandate from Heaven. The Way is fundamentally open. Nothing can get in the way of your plans and your desires. You will be showered with blessings. Enjoy it!

*Direction*: Bring your inner and outer lives together. Take things in. Be open and provide what is needed.

NINE ABOVE

**Diminishing. The Offering.**

**Does not Diminish it, augments it.**

**This is not a mistake. Wise Words! Trial: The Way is open.**

**Advantageous to have a direction to go. Harvesting.**

**You acquire servants, not dwellings.**

*This is acquiring a Great purpose.* You will not be diminished but augmented by this. It will bring good things to everyone involved. The feelings you have now are not a mistake. They actually open the Way. Draw up a plan. Be sure of yourself. You will get considerable help, but this will not be a sedentary affair.

*Direction*: An important connection approaches. Something significant returns. Be open and provide what is needed.

# 42 Augmenting/The Blessing Yi

**Increase, expand, develop, pour in more; fertile and expansive; ancestors send their blessings, rain spirits; site of creative transformation.**

## MYTHS FOR CHANGE: THE STORY OF THE TIME

**Charge to the Oracle:** *Diminishing without end will necessarily augment things and bring blessing. Accept this and use the energy of Augmenting.*

Diminishing and Augmenting offer a paradigm of sacrifice and its results. Augmenting is the blessing: 'What is above gives to what is below.' The root is a recipient for food, the meats eaten at the feast, a vessel overflowing with blessing, the sun that appears through the grace of the ancestor after a dark time, gladdening and enriching everything. This is the feast in which all partake and the blessings (*fu*) showered on us through the ancestors after they have received and accepted the sacrifice and presented our needs to the High Lord. It is a synonym of *yi*, change, as gift or blessing, a transformation affected by a crossing. Like a transforming line in the Change, it is a connection of Heaven and Earth brought about by ritual, sacrifice and inner work. Philosophically, it is what enriches power and virtue, rising and opening from the seeds. It is the waxing moon, the celebrant, the new King, the blessing.

## THE RESPONSE

**Augmenting. The Blessing. Advantageous to have a direction to go.**

**Advantageous to step into the Great Stream. Harvesting.**

**Augment,** *YI*: increase, advance, expand, add to; benefit, strengthen, support; pour in more, overflowing, super abundant; restorative, fertile; useful, profitable, advantageous; grant or blessing. The old character shows a container and the sign for river or water, a stream of blessings.

YÌ (5381/108) shows a vase *MIN*³ overflowing with water *SHUI*³. 1–3 show early versions of the character meaning effectuate the sacrifice – *YI* (1); to give, grant (2); measure for metal and grain, precious commodities (3).

Augmenting describes your situation in terms of increase, advance and development. The way to deal with it is to increase your involvement and pour in more energy. This is a time of gain, profit and expansion. Have a place to go. Impose a direction on things. Enter the stream of life with a purpose or embark on a significant enterprise. These things bring profit and insight.

## THE SCHOLAR SPEAKS

The hexagram figure shows arousing new energy penetrating the outer world. Wind and thunder augmenting. Strip away your old ideas. By continually diminishing things, you have created augmenting, for increase and decrease are each other's beginning. Through augmenting you enrich your power to realise the Way. Augmenting continually enriches things without setting up structures. It uses flourishing and harvesting. When you can imagine improvement, shift the way you do things. When there is excess or error, correct it. Diminish what is above and augment what is below. Stimulate people at their work without limiting them. The Source above has descended, and its Way is shining greatly. Let it stimulate you. Having a place to go or imposing a direction on things brings profit and insight. Make correcting one-sidedness and error the centre of your concerns. It will bring rewards. Step into the Stream of Life. Secure your vehicle, the boat to carry you, then make your move. Augmenting stirs things up and grounds them. Like the sun rising, it has no limits. When Heaven spreads out, Earth gives birth. Together they increase and augment things on all sides. Augment everything. This connects you with the time, so you can accompany it as it moves.

Wind and Thunder. Augmenting.

This is a time when Noble One visualizes improvement and consequently shift his position. If there is excess, he alters it.

*Spirit manifests in quake and thunder, speaking and spreading joy through the Intermediaries.* These are the Operators, those who work with the spirit. Wind and Wood above enter subtly, penetrating, pervading and coupling, while Thunder below rouses and germinates new potential, sprouting energies that thrust up from beneath. This is the Woody Moment: rousing energy within that expands into outer penetration, coupling and augmenting all things. The ideal Realising Person reflects this by perceiving how things can be improved and shifting his stance accordingly. Work through rousing and inspiring. A cycle is beginning. Fix the omen.

## TRANSFORMING LINES: CHANGE AT WORK

### INITIAL NINE

Augmenting. The Blessing.

Advantageous to arouse and activate the Great. Harvesting.

Wise Words! The Way to the Source is open.

This is not a mistake.

*The below is not a question of riches.* You need a purpose, a great idea around which you can organize yourself and your passion. Build the city, cast the vessel. The Way is fundamentally open. It is the right time to act. Go forward. This is definitely not a mistake.
*Direction:* Let everything come into view. Strip away old ideas. Be open and provide what is needed.

### SIX AT SECOND

Augmenting. The Blessing.

'Someone' augments him.

Ten pairs of tortoise divinations cannot control or contradict this!

Wise Words! Trial: an ever-flowing Way.

The King makes presentations to the Supreme Power.

The Way is open.

*Originating outside, this is coming.* A blessing, a Mandate from Heaven. Anything you wish to do will prosper. The Way is open to your ideas, not just now, but in the future. Enjoy it! But remember the spirit in your happiness. Then the Way will truly be open.
*Direction*: Bring your inner and outer life into accord. Take things in. Be open and provide what is needed.

### Six at Third

**Augmenting. The Blessing**

**Augmented through service when the Way is closed.**

**This is not a mistake.**

**There is a connection to the spirits that will carry you through.**

**The centre is moving.**

**Inform the prince. Use the jade baton.**

*This is possessing it firmly.* What seems like an unfortunate happening will turn out to your benefit. Act on your ideas. This is not a mistake. The capital city is about to be moved and you are part of it. Tell your prince and your people what is happening. Insist on your right to speak. You are connected to the spirits and they will carry you through.
*Direction*: Find supportive friends. Gather energy for a decisive new move.

### Six at Fourth

**Augmenting. The Blessing. Moving the centre.**

**Inform the prince and he will follow.**

**Advantageous to participate in shifting the capital city.**
**Harvesting.**

*This means augmenting the purpose.* This is a great change in the centre of power. The centre of life is shifting. Stay loyal to your friends. Act on your ideas. Depend on the fact that everything is changing and you are an important part of it.
*Direction*: Stay out of quarrels and wrangles. Proceed step by step. Gather energy for a decisive new move.

≡≡ 祘

NINE AT FIFTH

**Augmenting. The Blessing.**

**You have a connection to the spirits and a benevolent heart.**

**No question, the Way to the Source is open.**

**A connection to the spirits will carry you through.**

**Wise Words! 'A benevolent heart is my power and virtue.'**

*Do not question it. This is acquiring a Great purpose.* Act through your virtue and kindness. You have a kind, generous heart and a noble spirit. Don't question this. Use it. The Way is fundamentally open. Your kindness and compassion are the way to create something that endures.

*Direction:* Take things in. Be open and provide what is needed.

NINE ABOVE

**No blessing. This absolutely does not augment you.**

**'Someone' will smite you.**

**Tries to order his heart without fixing the omens.**

**Trap! The Way closes.**

*One-sided evidence. This means disaster comes from outside.* You are refusing the blessing, being fickle, wayward and deceitful. Nothing good can come of this. Don't play with people. The Way will close and you will be left open to danger. This is a warning you can heed if you will. Fix and steady your emotions.

*Direction:* Articulate the limits. Strip away old ideas. Be open and provide what is needed.

# 43 and 44: The Paradigm

### Announce the Omen: Enter the Lady of Fates

This Pair involves you in an overall model of thought and action elaborated in the interconnected lines of the figures: the announcement of an oracle at a critical moment and the arrival of the fate thus announced. It embodies a site of radical transformation, a Great Transition that connects you to the Force of the Dragon. Carefully consider your place in and relation to this model.

*Hidden Possibilities:* 1, you are connected to creative force.

The Pair exchanges with and is motivated by 1 and 28, the Dragon and the Great Transition. The centre and threshold lines connect the zone of transformation with 5:6 (Temple and Council), 33:34 (Retreat and Advance), 49:50 (Revolution and the Vessel) and 57:58 (The Intermediaries).

Look at the ages and events these figures suggest for personal connections.

<u>1</u>   (3:4) 5:6   <u>28</u>   33:34   49:50   57:58

*Shadow site:* 21:22, 'Eating Ancient Virtue' and Bringing Home the Bride

**Deciding means breaking through.
The strong breaks through the supple.
Coupling means meetings. The supple meets the strong.**

# 43 Deciding and Parting GUAI

Resolution, act clearly; make a decision and announce it, carry
the message; move quickly; breakthrough; part
from the past, separate; clean it out and bring it to light;
site of creative transformation; a seed figure.

## MYTHS FOR CHANGE: THE STORY OF THE TIME

**Charge to the Oracle:** *Augmenting without end will necessarily break
up the obstacle. Accept this and use the energy of Deciding. This means
breaking up the obstacle.*

Deciding and Parting refers to making known an oracular message or
pronouncement or notifying the ancestor at the Earth Altar of an
important move: war, challenge or the arrival of an important spirit
who carries fate. It includes the idea of parting with the past through
the image of rivers separating, and a decisive moment, a critical
time for a breakthrough. The root shows a thimble worn by archers
who shoot through openings in armour or formations in battle. It
includes a loan word for skipping, running, galloping animals and
suggests moving quickly from one place or state of mind to another.
The figure is centred on signals and words, a messenger announcing
the results of an oracle, raising a banner or war axe. It further suggests
bringing something dangerous to light, opening and cleansing a
wound, a critical announcement in the King's court. This is the
arrival of a message from Heaven, a fate or mandate. It challenges us
to respond fully, quickly and decisively to make the spirit known.

## THE RESPONSE

Deciding and Parting. Bring it to light. Display it in the King's
Chambers.

There is a connection to the spirits that will carry you through.

Cry out even in adversity, the hungry souls and angry ghosts.

This decree comes from the capital city.

Not advantageous to approach them under arms.

Advantageous to have a direction to go. Harvesting.

**Decide**, GUAI: choose; resolute, decisive, act clearly; breakthrough, critical moment; jade objects giving the right to speak; prompt, certain, clear; clean out a wound, bring something to light; separate, divide, cut off, divide in two; parting of two rivers, parting of the ways. The old character shows a hand holding a jade object that gives the right to speak.

GUÀI (6232/37) shows a hand holding up an object, probably a jade baton or jade ring, a token of identity and rank that confers the right to speak.

Deciding/Parting describes your situation in terms of resolutely confronting difficulties. The way to deal with it is to clarify what you must do and act on it, even if you must leave something behind. Move quickly. Display your decision resolutely at the centre of effective power. Have confidence in proclaiming it, for you are connected to the spirits and they will carry you through. You will confront difficulties. There is an angry old ghost in the situation that has returned to take revenge for past mistreatment. Notify those who love, trust and depend on you. Don't resort to arms, attack or build up defences. Have a place to go. Impose a direction on things. That brings profit and insight.

## THE SCHOLAR SPEAKS

The hexagram figure shows inner force coming to expression. The mists rise above Heaven. Act with drive and persistence. By continually augmenting things you break through obstacles. Resolution implies breaking through. What is solid and strong breaks through and breaks up what is supple and adaptable. Spread your wealth so you can depend on what is below you. Concern yourself with realising the Way and keep out of other activities. This is a time to break through. Persist in your efforts to express things. Break through the obstacles to harmony. Display your resolution in the centre of power. Though you may be small, five strong forces are behind you. Have confidence. The spirits will give you the power to express yourself. Although you must confront difficulties, this exposure to danger will make you shine. Notify those who depend on you. Don't resort to arms. If you do you will exhaust all chance of honour and eminence. What is strong and solid endures, so you can bring your plans to completion.

## THE SHAMAN SPEAKS

> Mists above Heaven. Deciding and Parting.
>
> This is a time when Noble One spreads benefits to extend to those below,
>
> By residing in power and virtue, he keeps away harm.

*The spirit that awes and wars in Heaven speaks and spreads joy through the Intermediaries.* The Joyous Dancer is working with the Force. Rising Mists above stimulate and fertilize, joyous words cheer and inspire, while Heaven below struggles on, persistent and unwearied. This is the Metal Moment: an inner struggle breaks through into decisive words, clearing out old problems. The ideal Realising Person reflects this by extending his strength and support to all below. He resides in his power to actualize the Way and thus keeps us from harm. Work through joyous words to bring spirit to expression. You are confronting the Tiger.

## TRANSFORMING LINES: CHANGE AT WORK

### INITIAL NINE

> Deciding and Parting. Invigorating the leading foot.
>
> Going without overcoming them. Acting now is a mistake.

*This is a fault.* If you try to take the lead, you will most certainly fail. You simply aren't prepared for it yet. This is not the way to go about things.
*Direction:* Don't be afraid to be alone. You are coupled to a creative force.

321

**Deciding and Parting. Alarms and outcries. Bring it out.**

**'No rest at night.'**

**Stay under arms. Have no cares.**

*Stay armed and have no cares. You acquire the centre and the Way.* A tense and invigorating situation, with things coming from all sides. Don't worry, but stay alert. Let past sorrows go. Bring out what is hidden. You will obtain what you want. This can renew your creative life.

*Direction*: Revolution and renewal. You will be coupled with a creative force.

**Deciding and Parting. Strong in their cheekbones.**

**This is a Trap! The Way closes for them.**

**Noble One: Parting! Parting!**

**He goes on alone and meets the rain, feeling soiled and indignant.**

**This is not a mistake.**

*Parting, completing this is not a mistake.* You are involved with cruel people intent on their mastery. This Way will close for them. See this clearly and leave now. You will be caught in a flood of unfair insults and abuse that deeply anger you. This is not a mistake. Announce your decision. Be very clear and leave now.

*Direction*: Express your feelings. Find supportive friends. The situation is already changing.

**Deciding and Parting. Buttocks without flesh.**

**Like Yu he moves haltingly,**

**Like an animal led to sacrifice on a leash.**

**The cause for sorrow disappears.**

**'When you hear people's words, do not trust them.'**

*This is not an appropriate situation Words won't brighten you now.* You have been punished or hurt and are isolated. You must move to a new location. Stay adaptable. See this as a gift from fate. Yield to the spirit of Yu the Great. Don't get caught up in negative emotions. Don't believe what people tell you right now, and keep your own speech guarded. Your sorrows will soon disappear.

*Direction:* Wait for the right moment. Turn conflict into creative tension. The situation is already changing.

### NINE AT FIFTH

**Deciding and Parting. Bring it out!**

**The mountain goat runs Quickly! Quickly!**

**down the centre of the road.**

**This is not a mistake.**

*The centre is not shining yet.* You have to choose between two alternatives and decide quickly. Don't be afraid of radical change. There is a creative force at work. Move decisively. Do it now!

*Direction:* Invigorate your ruling idea. Be resolute. You are connected to a creative force.

### SIX ABOVE

**Deciding and Parting. Not announcing the oracle.**

**Trap! Completing this closes the Way.**

*Completing this will not allow lasting.* If you don't communicate your important message, you will be cut off and isolated. Call out. Tell us now. Now.

*Direction:* Take action. You are connected to a creative force.

# 44 Coupling/Royal Bride GOU

**Welcome, encounter, open yourself to; intense contact; all forms of sexual intercourse; the Lady of Fate, act through the yin; site of creative transformation; a seed figure.**

## MYTHS FOR CHANGE: THE STORY OF THE TIME

**Charge to the Oracle:** *Break things up and you will necessarily meet the new fate. Accept this and use the energy of Coupling. This means encountering and meeting.*

Coupling is the appearance of the fate announced by an oracular message. It is the procession of the Royal Bride, her appearance at the borders and her journey to the sacred marriage that will produce an heir and renew the time. She is the strong or invigorating woman: queen, empress, mistress, ruler, anima-figure, the one who 'distributes the fates'. She symbolizes the return of the feminine power, of desire, joy, beauty, the ability to manifest and take pleasure in life. She brings strange encounters with a spirit, an ancestor, a king. She inaugurates the River-Mountain festivals and all forms of coupling and mating, the brief encounters when men and women meet and take joy in each other. She presides over the autumn marriages and the omen of fertility, the *bin*-ritual, 'fish in the wrapping', and suggests the willow-world of sexuality symbolized by melons and creeping vines. This is the Young Ancestress coming back from the mountain after receiving the spirit or the appearance of the Royal Bride and her entourage at the borders. It is the Weaver Girl crossing the river of stars on a bridge of magpies, the lover's bird, to mate with Draught Ox on the Feast of Women, the seventh day of the seventh moon. The great injunction here is not to grasp the woman, not to take this Queen by force, but rather to help her on her journey to the King and the royal marriage. For in that is the inauguration of a new order, a containing beauty that 'tumbles down from Heaven'.

## THE RESPONSE

**Coupling. The Royal Bride. The Strong Woman.**

**Do not try to grasp this woman! She goes to the King.**

**Coupling**, GOU: meet, encounter, pair off, copulate; open yourself to, find someone on your path; happen, occur, entertain, luck, opportunity; meeting of minds, win confidence coupling of yin and yang; all forms of sexual intercourse; mating, magnetism, gravity; gripped, overcome by passion; favourable, fortuitous; *also*: two fish, sign of fertility and happy encounters; the autumn festivals. The old character shows the sign for woman and the sign for queen, the Royal Bride who appears at the borders, carrying fate and announcing the new.

 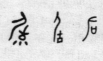

GÒU (6065/38) shows a woman ($NU^3$) and another woman giving birth ($HOU^4$), probably a later addition. Without this second figure the character is HOU (3928), the empress or new queen, who gives birth to the heir through the sacred marriage. The small figures show two examples and include another loan character $HOU^4$, a woman who looks over the people and a mouth that issues orders.

Coupling describes your situation in terms of opening yourself to welcome what comes. You can deal with it by realising that the brief and intense moment of encounter reflects a connection of the primal powers. Don't try to control it. The connection is there, even if it seems accidental. The woman and the yin are full of invigorating strength. Don't try to grasp and hold on to things. What seems a brief contact connects you with creative force.

## THE SCHOLAR SPEAKS

The hexagram figure shows the spirit spreading throughout the world. Below Heaven there is wind. You are coupled with a creative force. Coupling implies unexpected encounters, lucky coincidences and enjoyable happenings. What is supple and what is solid are meeting. Queens and Kings use this time to spread their mandates to the Four Corners of the world. This is a time of meetings. Don't grasp and hold on to things. The time does not permit these contacts to endure. Heaven and Earth meet each other and all the different kinds of beings join together in beautiful display. What is solid and strong meets what is central and correct. The great is moving below Heaven. The time of welcoming and Coupling is truly and righteously great!

## THE SHAMAN SPEAKS

Wind below Heaven. Coupling. The Royal Bride.

This is a time when the Crown Prince spreads the mandate, commanding the Four Hidden Lands.

*Spirit works in those who lay out the offerings while it awes and wars in Heaven.* The Lady of Fates is working with the Force. Heaven above struggles on, persistent and unwearied, while Wind and Wood enter subtly from below, penetrating, pervading and coupling. This is Metal over Wood: primal forces couple in the inner world, creating enduring new beings and forms. The ideal Realising Person reflects this by emulating the nobles of old, spreading the words given by the spirit to command the energies of the Four Hidden Lands. Work through subtle penetration. This involves fate. Gather the ghosts.

## TRANSFORMING LINES: CHANGE AT WORK

### INITIAL SIX

Coupling. The Royal Bride arrives.

Attach it to the bronze spindles.

Wise Words! Trial: The Way is open.

Have a direction to go. See the trap,

a bound pig balking at the sacrifice.

There is a connection to the spirits that will carry you through.

*This means being hauled along the Way of the supple.* The Way is open and you are connected to the spirit if you can hold back. Don't act this impulse out. See the trap inherent in the situation and accept the sacrifice. Give up your immediate plans. If you try to control things, you'll get all tangled up.

*Direction:* You are connected to a creative force.

NINE AT SECOND

**Coupled. Fish in the willow wrapping.**

**This is not a mistake.**

**Hospitality is not advantageous.**

*It is right not to extend hospitality*. Stay quiet and withdrawn. Your ideas have borne fruit and the womb is full. They need quiet and intimacy. It won't help you to be or receive a guest.
*Direction*: Retreat and nourish the growing creative force.

NINE AT THIRD

**Coupling with fate, buttocks without flesh.**

**Like Yu, he moves haltingly.**

**Adversity, hungry souls and angry ghosts.**

**Without the Great, you will make a mistake.**

*This is moving, not being hauled along.* You are isolated, have been punished or hurt, and are moving to a new place. Like Yu the Great, see it as a message from destiny. You will have to confront your past, but don't give in! Find and believe in your central idea and you will gather new friends.
*Direction*: Don't get involved in quarrels and wrangles. Find supportive friends. Gather energy for a decisive new move.

NINE AT FOURTH

**Coupled. No fish in the willow wrapping.**

**Trap! Rising up to action closes the Way.**

*This means keeping what is common at a distance.* There are no creative possibilities in this. A barren womb. Objecting or rebelling won't help.
*Direction*: Subtly penetrate to the core of the problem. Turn conflict into creative tension. The situation is already changing.

### Nine at Fifth

**Coupling. The Royal Bride.**

**Willow wrapping the melons, jade talisman in the mouth.**

**Held in this containing beauty,**

**'It tumbles down from Heaven.'**

*This is a centred, correct purpose, not a victim of fate.* This is a beautiful inspiration, the Coupling of King and Queen, literally made in Heaven. What you do now will add elegance and beauty to life. It inaugurates a wonderful new time.

*Direction:* The founding of a noble line. Be resolute. You are connected to a creative force.

### Nine Above

**Coupling with your horns.**

**Distress. This is not a mistake.**

*This is exhausting the distress above.* You have turned this into a trial of strength or sexual prowess. This is not a serious mistake, in fact it may be necessary, but it does leave you quite confused about what things are all about. Let this confusion return you to the Way.

*Direction:* Don't be afraid to act alone. You are coupled with a creative force.

# 45 and 46: The Paradigm

### Gather the People and Ascend the Sacred Mountain

This Pair involves you in an overall model of thought and action that elaborated in the interconnected lines of the figures: gathering the energy for great works and ascending the sacred mountain to take your place among the ancestors. Carefully consider your place in and relation to this model.

*Hidden Possibilities:* 53:54 > 64:63, the Great Marriages. Prepare and make the crossing.

The Pair exchanges information with 17:18 (Following the Spirit and Renovating the Ancestral Images). It is motivated by 11:12 (Old and New King). The centre and threshold lines relate the process to 7:8 (Armies and the New Group), 15:16 (Activating Liminal Powers to Prepare the Future), 31:32 (Sacred Site and Fixing the Omen) and 47:48 (Oppressed Noble returns to Common Source).

Look at the ages and events these figures suggest for personal connections.

> 11:12 (13:14) 15:16 17:18     31:32     47:48

*Shadow site:* 19:20, Releasing the Spirit and watching the Omens

### Gathering means assembling them.
### Ascending means things don't simply come to you.

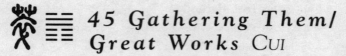 ## 45 Gathering Them/ Great Works CUI

**Gather, assemble, bunch together, collect; crowds; a great effort brings a great reward.**

**Charge to the Oracle:** *When beings meet together and couple, we can assemble them. Accept this and use the energy of Gathering. This means assembling.*

Gathering Them refers to the cycle of ancestral sacrifices keyed to the Four Seasons and the Four Directions or Winds, the Hidden Lands, that precedes any great work. It is a procession, 'going-out-to-meet-them' at the Outskirts Altar. It suggests the sacrifice and feast of the Red Bull that opens the fields and the summer *yue-*sacrifice of first fruits to the gathered spirit tablets in the Ancestral Temple that connects living and dead. These are the great sacrifices and represent a gathering of the people, an inner collection of force in view of great projects, like building the great rammed earth walls of palaces, dikes and dams, or casting the bronze vessels. It is a time of communion with spirit powers and assembly with others through sacrifice and open emotions, concentrating a strong force through connection with Heaven. It frees the feelings in a flow of spirit that unites people, purifying and loosening. The key is the Great, having a firm purpose and ruling idea connected with the Way through which you help and protect others. Through the great sacrifice and the great project the King acts to harmonize Heaven and Earth. He offers the great victims and uses the Great People, ritual specialists and sages, Source Beings who connect the living and the dead and release the power to do great things.

### THE RESPONSE

Gathering Them. Great Works. Make an offering and you will succeed.

The King approaches his Ancestral Temple to ask blessings for all.

Advantageous to see the Great Person to make the sacrifice.

**Advantageous Trial. Harvesting.**

**Use the Great Victims. Wise Words! The Way is open.**

**Advantageous to have a direction to go.**

**Gathering Them**, CUI: gather or call together; groups of people or things; assemble, concentrate, collect; reunite; crowd, multitude, dense vegetation; come to someone's aid. The old character shows two bundles of grass or grain the sign for a soldier or servant who presents them.

CUI (11536/140) shows a jacket or banner (1) with a sign on it (3), the uniform of a soldier or servant, and two bundles of grass (2), assembled or clustered.

Gathering Them describes your situation in terms of collecting and gathering. The way to deal with it is to unite people and things through a common feeling or goal. Concentrate the crowd and turn it into an organized whole. This is pleasing to the spirits. Through it they will give you success, effective power and the capacity to bring the situation to maturity. This is the time for great projects. Be like the King who imagines a temple full of images that unite people and connect them with greater forces. See Great People. Visit those who can help and advise you. Look at your own central idea and how you organize your thoughts. Making a great offering to the spirit of this time generates meaning and good fortune by releasing transformative energy. Put your ideas to the trial. Have a place to go. Impose a direction on things. This brings profit and insight.

## THE SCHOLAR SPEAKS

The hexagram figure shows common labour coming to expression. The mists rise over the Earth. Proceed step by step. First things meet in pairs, then they assemble. Gathering Them means assembling and reuniting. Eliminate the need for fighting and weapons by being alert. Don't be taken by surprise. Gathering

Them implies collecting people together. Labour is its expression. The strong is in the centre and things will correspond to it. This is the source of assembling. Be like the King who imagines having a temple. This involves reverence and presenting things as offerings. See Great People and think about your central idea. This allows you to correct how things come together. Making a great sacrifice generates meaning and good fortune by releasing transformative energy. Having a place to go and imposing a direction on things brings profit and insight. Yield and work with the Heavenly Mandate. By contemplating the place where people come together, you can look at the motives of Heaven, Earth and Myriad Beings.

## THE SHAMAN SPEAKS

**Mists above Earth. Gathering Them.**

**This is a time when Noble One uses eliminating weapons to implement his plans,**

**warning against not taking precautions.**

*Spirit, offered service at the Earth Altar, speaks and spreads joy through the Intermediaries.* Joyous Dancer is working with Field. Rising Mists above stimulate and fertilize through joyous words, while Earth below yields and sustains. This is Metal over Earth: an inner field that sustains outer stimulation and interchange. The ideal Realising Person reflects this by eliminating the impulse to resort to arms through carefully prepared measures, anticipating and dissolving possible conflicts. Work through the receptive and the power of Earth. Release the spirit.

## TRANSFORMING LINES: CHANGE AT WORK

### INITIAL SIX

**Gathering Them. Great Works.**

**This connection to the spirits is not complete,**

**Thus disorder, then Gathering them.**

**Cry out! Announce the oracle! One grasp of the hand brings laughter.**

**Have no cares. Going on is not a mistake.**

*This means your purpose is in disorder*. You are connected to a deep source of energy, but the link with others is unclear. That is why things are so uneven, one moment joyous, the next moment confused. Don't worry. Let people know your real intent. Reach out and touch them and you will find the source of the disarray. The tension will dissolve into laughter and·joy. This is certainly not a mistake. The connection is real.

*Direction*: Follow the stream of events. Proceed step by step. Gather energy for a decisive new move.

### SIX AT SECOND

**Extending the Gathering. Drawn and led out to Great Works.**

**Wise Words! The Way is open.**

**There is a connection to the spirit that will carry you through.**

**Advantageous to make the summer sacrifice.**

*The centre is not changed*. Extend the group and the activity, include more, and draw things out. This will open the Way. Make the sacrifice to the gathered group of ancestors that opens the way to achievement. This is a time for great things, a time of extended good fortune.

*Direction*: Look within to find the way out. Find supportive friends. Gather energy for a decisive new move.

### SIX AT THIRD

**Gathering·Them, then lamenting.**

**No direction is advantageous.**

**Going on is not a mistake. Being Small brings distress.**

*Go on and penetrate the above*. As soon as you begin to gather together with others, a flood of sorrow and painful memories swamps you. There is really nothing you can do here. Release the spirit of the new. It is not a mistake. If you simply try to adapt to the situation, you will be covered in distress and confusion.

*Direction*: Be open to a new influence. It will couple you with a creative force.

### Nine at Fourth

**Gathering Them. Wise Words! The Great Way opens.**

**This is not a mistake.**

*This is not an appropriate situation.* The Great Way opens from this gathering. You can do anything you want now if you act with a full and loving heart. The Great Way is open. Nothing you do would be a mistake. Take action.

*Direction:* Change your group. Strip away old ideas. Be open and provide what is needed.

### Nine at Fifth

**Gathering Them in ranks. Great Works.**

**This is not a mistake. You do not need to offer victims.**

**Trial: an ever-flowing source.**

**The cause of sorrow disappears.**

*The purpose is not yet shining.* You have a position in this gathering, a long-term source of energy and inspiration. You do not need to make a sacrifice. Keep exploring it by asking the oracle. As you do, doubt and sorrow will disappear and all will come clear.

*Direction:* Gather energy in order to act when the call comes. Re-imagine the situation. Gather energy for a decisive new move.

### Six Above

**Gathering Them. Great Works.**

**'Sighs and sobs, tears and moans.'**

**This is not a mistake.**

*This is not yet tranquil above.* Like rites at a funeral, these tears will release the spirit and make a greater connection between people. Expressing emotion is not a mistake. It opens blocked communication.

*Direction:* Communication is obstructed. Proceed step by step. Gather energy for a decisive new move.

# 46 Ascending the Sacred Mountain
## SHENG

**Make the effort, don't worry; climb the mountain step by step; lift yourself, fulfil the potential; advance, rise; intervene at a crucial moment.**

### MYTHS FOR CHANGE: THE STORY OF THE TIME

**Charge to the Oracle**: *Assembling and then rising to what is above is called ascending the Sacred Mountain. Accept this and use the energy of Ascending.*

Ascending shows a procession up the Sacred Mountain, specifically a journey through the old Zhou capital, the 'empty city', up to the Twin-Peaked Mountain that was the ancestral home of the Zhou ancestors. This was the King's Ancestral Temple, where spirit tablets of the Royal Ancestors were housed. A journey up this mountain meant becoming part of the founders, at one with the Great People. It connects with a very old tradition of the *wu* or Intermediaries going up to the Mountain Shrine of the Tiger or Sky Spirit, the temple hidden just below the summit, full of stone phalli sprouted from the Earth. Its meanings include presenting an offering and putting meats into a sacred vessel. It means to rise up, like the sun rising, like ripening grain, to 'climb the steps', and includes the sense of making a timely intervention. In meditation practice, it is the rising of energy from the base of the trunk to the heart centre. Making the connection between above and below involves invading and conquering the demon country of the south. You must put your house in order and free yourself from care, melancholy and compulsive desire. The root of the term means complete, a full cycle, inclusive. It was a small measure, a libation cup full of spirits. It implies that we rise to completion step by step, climbing the Sacred Mountain.

### THE RESPONSE

Ascending. The Intermediaries climb the Sacred Mountain.
Make an offering and you will succeed.

Use this to see the Great People. Have no cares.

Wise Words! Chastising the south opens the Way.

**Ascend,** SHENG: mount, go up, rise; climb step by step, advance through your own efforts; be promoted, rise in office: wages of officials were set at a certain number sheng of rice. The higher their rank, the more sheng they received; accumulate, fulfil the potential; distil liquor; a measure for grain; offer sacrifices to the gods or spirits of the dead, uninterrupted succession of sacrifices in a family. The old character shows a measure for alcohol or grain, brought and poured out in sacrifice.

SHENG[1] (9684/24) shows a measure for grain or alcohol, which is being poured out. 1 and 2 are other versions; 3 shows the character with the meaning to present offerings.

Ascending describes your situation in terms of rising to a higher level and getting something done. The way to deal with it is set a goal and work towards it step by step. Root yourself and push towards the heights. Climb the mountain and connect with the spirits. Bring out and fulfil the hidden potential. This is a very favourable situation. It is pleasing to the spirits. It is the origin of growth, effective power and the capacity to bring things to maturity. See Great People, those who can help and advise you. Look at the great in yourself and how you organize your ideas. Have no cares, fears or anxiety. Set out towards the south, the region of summer, growth, intensity and action. This generates meaning and good fortune by releasing transformative energy. Correct, discipline and put things in order.

## THE SCHOLAR SPEAKS

The hexagram figure shows inner adaptability rising from its roots in the Earth. Earth's centre gives birth to the trees. If you let yourself be led, you can realise your hidden potential. When people assemble and set a higher goal, they call it Ascending. It doesn't simply come to you. Yield to the impulse and work hard to realise the Way. Amass small things to reach what is high and great. Be supple and adaptable and use this time. Penetrate to the core. Adapt and work hard to yield results. What is strong is at the centre and things will correspond to it. This is pleasing to the great spirits. Through it they will give you success, effective power and the capacity to bring the situation to maturity. It will connect you to Great People and to the great in yourself. Have no cares. You will obtain rewards. Set out towards the south. Take action. This generates meaning and good fortune by releasing transformative energy. Make order and set out. Your purpose is indeed on the move.

## THE SHAMAN SPEAKS

**Earth's centre gives birth to the Tree. Ascending the Sacred Mountain.**

**This is a time when Noble One yields to power and virtue,**

**amassing the Small to attain the high and Great.**

*Spirit works through those who lay out the offerings. Offer service at the Earth Altar.* The Lady of Fates is working with the Field. Earth above yields and sustains, while Wind and Wood enter subtly from below, penetrating, pervading and coupling. This is Earth over Wood: inner penetration that ascends the outer field of action. The ideal Realising Person reflects this by gathering in Small things, Ascending to what is Great in the world and in himself. Persist and work through inner inspiration. Watch the manifestation of spirit.

## TRANSFORMING LINES: CHANGE AT WORK

### INITIAL SIX

**Sincere Ascending. Climb the Sacred Mountain.**

**Wise Words! The Great Way opens.**

*This is uniting purposes with the above.* You have been recognized. People have become aware of your value. Now all the doors are open to you. Climb the mountain and find what you desire.
*Direction:* A great and flourishing time begins. If you let yourself be led, you can realise hidden potential. The situation is already changing.

**Ascend the Sacred Mountain.**

**There is a connection to the spirits that will carry you through.**

**Advantageous to make the summer sacrifice. Harvesting.**

**This is not a mistake.**

*There will be rejoicing.* The connection is established. Make the offering and climb the Sacred Mountain. Dedicate yourself to what you believe in and make the great sacrifice to the gathered ancestors. It is all there if you want it to be.
*Direction*: Stay simple and connected to the facts. Release bound energy. The situation is already changing.

Nine at Third

**Ascending through the empty city.**

*This is no place to doubt.* There is no resistance to your efforts. The gates are open. The ceremony is being performed. This is the old capital city that the times have left behind. Don't stop, push on.
*Direction*: Organize your forces. Something significant is returning. Be open and provide what is needed.

Six at Fourth

**Ascending.**

**The King sacrifices and receives blessing on the Twin-Peaked Mountain.**

**Wise Words! The Way is open.**

**This is not a mistake.**

*Yield to this service.* You have found a powerful place in the symbolic life, part of the great sacrifices that connect us to the ancestors. Dedicate your efforts to the common good. The Way is open. This is not a mistake.
*Direction*: Continue in your path. Be resolute. You are connected to a creative force.

## Six at Fifth

**Ascend the Sacred Mountain.**

**Wise Words! Trial: the Way is open.**

**Ascend the steps.**

*This is acquiring a Great purpose.* There are no barriers to your progress. You are welcomed into the temple. Proceed step by step. The Way is open to you.
*Direction*: Connect to common needs and strengths. Be resolute. You are connected to a creative force.

## Six Above

**Ascending in a waning moon. Dim light.**

**'There will be Changes.'**

**Trial: advantageous not to pause. Harvesting.**

*This means affluence is dissolving.* You are climbing the Sacred Mountain in the dark as the moon begins to wane. Don't stop now. Pushing on to emergence will bring both profit and insight in the end.
*Direction*: Renovate a corrupt situation. If you let yourself be led, you can realise hidden potential. The situation is already changing.

ASCENDING

# 47 and 48: The Paradigm

### The Oppressed Noble returns to the Common Source

This Pair involves you in an overall model of thought and action elaborated in the interconnecting lines of the figures: secret connections made in a time of oppression that open to a common source of strength that all can rely on. It embodies a site of radical transformation at the threshold of the human world, a Tiger Transformation and Great Transition where the individual confronts the Ghost River and the shades of the past. Carefully consider your place in and relation to this model.

*Hidden Possibilities*: 37:38 > 64:63, changing discord into creative tension. Prepare and make the crossing.

The Pair echoes and exchanges information with 57:58 (The Intermediaries). It is motivated by 5:6 (Temple and Council: Waiting for Visitors). The centre and threshold lines connect 28 and 29 (the zone of transformation) with 39:40 (Difficulties and Release) and 45:46 (Assembly and Sacred Mountain).

Look at the ages and events these figures suggest for personal connections.

5:6     <u>28 29</u>     39:40     45:46     57:58

*Shadow site*: 17:18, Follow the spirit and Renovate the Ancestoral Images

### Confined means mutual meeting. The Well means interconnecting through the source.

# 47 Confining
## Oppression KUN

**Oppressed, restricted, exhausted, cut off; at the end of your resources; the moment of truth; an oppressed noble; search within to find the way out; site of creative transformation.**

### MYTHS FOR CHANGE: THE STORY OF THE TIME

**Charge to the Oracle**: *Ascending to the end has brought on oppression. The Noble One is oppressed and confined. Accept this and use the energy of Confining.*

Confining shows an old, dilapidated house or a great open mouth in which a tree is confined. It suggests a tight, oppressive, devouring structure and evokes penal codes and punishments, onerous duties, oppression by authority and the inherent emotional distress. It mentions several of the major punishments, which included nose-cutting, foot-cutting, branding, castration, imprisonment, exile and death in various forms, becoming an 'offering to the ancestors'. It also suggests the war duties that were laid upon the feudal lord. This is the oppression of a noble person who is exiled or cut off from others, confined or oppressed by his duties and his precarious position under a tyrannical and exploitative lord. It represents being cut off and isolated as much mentally as physically, alienated from those around you. It implies the threat of poverty, exhaustion, being at the end of available resources, unable to meet the challenges presenting themselves. Communication is blocked, indeed deceptive or deceitful. You do not know who your friends are and words are not to be trusted. Philosophically, however, this oppression is exactly what teaches you about *de*, power and virtue, the power to find what is Great and rely on it. It exhausts the old and awakens you from its collective dream. This oppression also teaches the futility of anger and hatred and shows how the Way opens.

### THE RESPONSE

**Confined and Oppressed. Make an offering and you will succeed.**

**Wise Words! Trial: the Great Person opens the Way. This is not a mistake.**

'If there are words, don't trust them.'

**Confine**, *KUN*: enclosed, restricted, persecuted, surrounded, hard-pressed, stranded; punishment, penal codes, prison; worry, fear, anxiety; fatigue, exhausted, poor, at the end of your resources; disheartened, weary, afflicted, worried. The old character shows a tree inside an enclosure, a big mouth or ramshackle house that threatens to engulf it.

$KUN^4$ shows a tree $MU^4$ (1) in an enclosure $WEI^2$ (2) or old house.

Confined and Oppressed describes your situation in terms of being cut off, oppressed and exhausted. The way to deal with it is to collect the energy to break out of the enclosure and re-establish communication. This is pleasing to the spirits. Through it they will give you success, effective power and the capacity to bring the situation to maturity. Be great and master the situation from within. Find what is truly important to you. Seek those who can help and advise you. This generates meaning and good fortune by releasing transformative energy. The situation is not your fault. Words are not to be trusted. There is a breakdown of communication and you are being isolated by it. You are not believed when you speak. Don't believe what others are telling you to do.

## THE SCHOLAR SPEAKS

The hexagram figure shows outer relations disconnected from the inner flow. The mists are outside the stream. Find supportive people. Ascending without stopping has brought on Confining. Hidden within the situation is the possibility of meeting unexpected help and encouragement. Use Confining to separate your own power to realise the Way from the collective values that are oppressing you. Bring old relationships to an end and move toward new connections. Don't be bound by grudges or bitter feelings. Find the mandate for change hidden in this situation and use it to release a sense of your purpose. What is strong and solid is covered and hidden. It is dangerous to express yourself. Being confined and not letting go of yourself is pleasing to the spirits. Through it they will give you success, effective power and the capacity to bring the situation to maturity. This situation activates your connection to the Way. It can generate meaning and good fortune by releasing transformative energy. Seek those who can help you. Find what is great in yourself, your solid centre. You will not be believed when you speak. Finding value in what your oppressors tell you to do will only exhaust you.

## THE SHAMAN SPEAKS

> Mists outside the Stream. Confined and Oppressed.

> This is a time when Noble One confronts his fate to release its purpose.

*Spirit rewards those who suffer in the Pit, speaking and spreading joy through the Intermediaries.* Joyous Dancer is working with the Ghost River. Mists rise above, while Rushing Water below dissolves direction and shape, flowing on through toil and danger. This is Metal over Water: confined and drawn into the inner stream, the capacity to express the spirit dissolves and flows on. The ideal Realising Person reflects this by yielding to fate, allowing it to release a sense of his real purpose. Hold the heart fast and take the risk. Articulate the new time.

## TRANSFORMING LINES: CHANGE AT WORK

### INITIAL SIX

> Confined and Oppressed. Buttocks punished with a wooden rod.

> If you enter the shadowy gully,

> You will encounter no one for three years.

*This is shady, not brightening.* You have been hurt or punished, but you are your own worst enemy now. Do not retreat into melancholy, darkness and isolation. You will completely cut yourself off.
*Direction:* Express yourself. Find supportive friends. Gather energy for a decisive new move.

**Confined and Oppressed at food and drink.**

**Scarlet sashes are coming on all sides.**

**Advantageous to make presentations to spirits and ancestors. Harvesting.**

**Chastising closes the Way. This is not a mistake.**

*There will be rewards in the centre.* The Noble One in exile. You ostensibly have all you need, but you feel oppressed and confined by lack of recognition. Don't worry, help is on its way. It will change the way you see yourself and your relationships with others. Offer a sacrifice now to the things you believe in. Stay where you are and wait. Don't try to make others take the blame for your situation. This is not a mistake. *Direction:* Gather resources for a great new project. Proceed step by step. Gather energy for a decisive new move.

Six at Third

**Confined and Oppressed by stones, he grasps at thorn-vines.**

**You enter your palace and do not see your consort.**

**Trap! The Way closes.**

*This is riding a strong line, not auspicious.* The exile returns to a melancholy fate. You beat yourself against impossible obstacles and grasp at things that hurt you. You can't even see your friend, who is eager to support you. This kind of behaviour will get you absolutely nowhere. *Direction:* A time of transition. Don't be afraid to act alone. You are connected to a creative force.

Nine at Fourth

**Confined and Oppressed in a bronze war-chariot.**

**It comes slowly, slowly.**

**Distress. There will be completion.**

*The purpose is located in the below. Not an appropriate situation, but allies will come.* The solution to your problems will arrive very slowly. This is partially because you are oppressed and confined by oppressive duties and thoughts. It will take a change of heart to recognize the truth, but all will turn out well in the end.

*Direction*: When the right moment comes, take the risk. Take things in. Be open and provide what is needed.

### NINE AT FIFTH

**Confined and Oppressed. His nose cut, his feet cut,**

**Oppressed by the crimson sashes.**

**Slowly he will be loosened.**

**Advantageous to make offering to spirits and ancestors. Harvesting.**

*The purpose is not acquired yet. Use centring and straightening. Acquiesce in the blessing.* You are punished and oppressed by authority. This is serious, but as the bitter feelings loosen you will be set free. Until this day comes, make offerings to your ideals. What your heart feels deeply will help you through. Make the sacrifice. The spirits will help you.

*Direction*: Release bound energy. The situation is already changing.

### SIX ABOVE

**Confined and Oppressed by trailing creepers, he trips on tree stumps.**

**Say it like this: 'If we stir up the causes of sorrow, then there will be sorrowing.'**

**Wise Words! Chastising opens the Way.**

*Not yet appropriate. Making a move opens the Way.* Stop indulging yourself! This seeming oppression shouldn't even bother you. If you sit around and groan all the time, all you will hear is lamentation. Take yourself in hand. Get yourself in order. That will open the Way. Don't just sit around trying to make everyone feel guilty.

*Direction*: Don't get involved in quarrels or wrangles. Find supportive friends. Gather energy for a decisive new move.

# 48 *The Well* JING

**Communicate, interact; the underlying structure, the network;
source of life-water needed by all, welling up from the depths;
the common people, common needs and strength; site of
creative transformation.**

## MYTHS FOR CHANGE: THE STORY OF THE TIME

**Charge to the Oracle:** *Oppression above will reverse what is below,
welling up from the deep. Accept this and use the energy of the Well.*

Out of oppression comes common good. Well represents the well
field and the common people, an ancient unit of social order con-
sisting of eight fields cultivated by eight families, surrounding a
central well used by all. The root is Two, the Two Protectors that
permit life to exist, the Couple, a local manifestation of Earth and
Heaven. Well is a norm, a model of good order that meets common
needs, an endless and inexhaustible source of the water of life.
The figure that shows the Well and the bucket also means 'us, all
together'. It is a structure that allows access to the Source, a
moment when one finds what supports life without exhaustion
and understands our common origin. Philosophically, this is the
field of power and virtue, shifting and abiding in place. It shows us
what is righteous. It is a tap into the subterranean flow of the Way,
a nipple of the Great Mother.

## THE RESPONSE

> The Well. All of Us. 'You can alter the city, you cannot alter
> the Well.'
>
> Without loss, without gain, they go and they come in their
> order.
>
> The Well is always the Well.
>
> A muddy bottom, a short well-rope or ruining the pitcher:
>
> All are a Trap! They close the Way of the Well.

Well, JING: water, well at the centre of a group of eight fields;
resources held in common, the common people; underlying structure, in good order, well-thought-out; bricklayer's measure; norm,

model; communicate with others, common needs; the water of life, the inner Source. The old character shows the well field system, eight fields grouped around the central well.

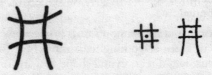

*JING³* (2040/7) represents a well and fields divided among eight families with a well and common field at the centre, the oldest unit of social organization.

The Well describes your situation in terms of an underlying social structure and the natural force that flows through it. The way to deal with it is to clarify and renew your connection to the Source. The water is there for all to draw on. The Well that gives you access to it must be cleaned and maintained. You can change where you live and who you associate with, but you can't change the Well and the needs it represents. Losing and acquiring, coming and going, all are part of the Well and its water. If all you find is mud in the Well, you haven't gone deep enough. Your rope is too short. If you ruin the pitcher used to draw the water, you will be cut off from the spirits and left open to danger.

## THE SCHOLAR SPEAKS
The hexagram figure shows inner penetration flowing out into the world. Above the wood there is the stream. Turn potential conflict into creative tension. When what is above is confined, what is below is reversed. The Well means interpenetrating and free communication. It is the Earth in which the power to realise the Way is grounded. It means staying where you are but shifting your ideas by differentiating what is right. Work for the common good at humble tasks to encourage fortunate meetings. Inner penetrating reaches to the stream and brings it to the surface. The Well nourishes without being exhausted. You can change where you live, but you can't change the Well. It is the solid centre. If you only bring up mud, your rope isn't long enough. You haven't achieved anything yet. If you ruin the pitcher used to hold the water, you will be cut off from the spirits and left open to danger.

Above Wood, the Stream. Well.

This is a time when Noble One toils for the common good to encourage mutualizing.

*Spirit works in those who lay out the offerings to reward those toiling in the Pit.* The Lady of Fates is working with the Ghost River. Rushing Water above dissolves direction and shape, flowing on through toil and danger, while Wind and Wood enter subtly from below, penetrating, pervading and coupling. This is Water over Wood: it reaches the inner ground, where the water wells up from below to support our common life. The ideal Realising Person reflects this by unceasingly toiling for the common good. He inspires people to find ways to share and support each other, carried by the Bright Omens. Dissolve the old self.

## TRANSFORMING LINES: CHANGE AT WORK

### INITIAL SIX

This Well is a bog. They do not drink here.

An old well becomes a pitfall that no creatures come to.

*This is below and the right time is missed.* The sources of life and order are muddy and bogged down. Nothing good will come of doing things this way. It is time to change.
*Direction:* Wait for the right moment to act. Turn conflict into creative tension. You can realise hidden potential. The situation is already changing.

### NINE AT SECOND

This Well is a gully where people shoot fish.

The jug is cracked and leaking.

*This means no associates or friends.* The sources of life and order are not taken care of. Each seeks his own gain. There is no container. His time to change.
*Direction:* Re-imagine the situation

### NINE AT THIRD

**This Well is turbid. They do not drink here.**

**'This makes my heart ache.'**

**If the King made a covenant, we could share this blessing together.**

*Moving and aching. Soon you will accept the blessing.* This is the sorrow of someone who is connected to the source of the common good, but has no one with whom to share it. There is nothing you can do now. Be prepared to move on. In the end you will be recognized and blessings will flow.

*Direction*: Take the risk. Be open and provide what is needed.

### Six at Fourth

**This Well is being lined with tiles.**

*This is adjusting the Well.* A time of inner work and improvement. You may feel cut off from the outer world, but have no fears. This inner preparation is not a mistake.

*Direction*: A time of transition. Don't be afraid to act alone. You are connected to a creative force.

### Nine at Fifth

**This Well has cold, clear springwater to drink.**

*This is centred and correct.* This is a clear, pure source of life-water for everyone to draw on. Use it and give thanks.

*Direction*: Make the effort. If you let yourself be led, you can realise your hidden potential. The situation is already changing.

### Six Above

**This Well receives and gives to all, do not cover it.**

**There is a connection to the spirits that will carry you through.**

**Wise Words! The Way to the Source is open.**

*The Way to the Source located above. This is Great accomplishment.* Receive and give things freely. This is a source of spiritual nourishment for everyone. Don't hide it away. The Way is fundamentally open. You can accomplish great things.

*Direction*: Subtly penetrate to the heart of things. Turn conflict into creative tension. The situation is already changing.

# 49 and 50: The Paradigm

## Revolution and Casting the Vessel

This Pair involves you in an overall model of thought and action elaborated in the interconnected lines of the figures: skinning away the old and grasping or founding the new. It is a key site in the history of the change of the Mandate of Heaven. Carefully consider your place in and relation to this model.

*Hidden Possibilities*: 44:43 > 1, the Lady of Fate emerges. Announce the Omen. Be resolute, you are coupled with a creative force.

The Pair echoes and exchanges information with 31:32 (Sacred Site and Fixing the Omen). It is motivated by 13:14 (Gathering of the People and the Great Being that Emerges). The centre and threshold lines relate the process to 17:18 (Follow the Spirit and Renovate the Ancestral Images), 43:44 (Announce the Omen and the Lady of Fates) and 55:56 (King and Wandering Sage).

Look at the ages and events these figures suggest for personal connections.

13:14 (15:16) 17:18     31:32     43:44     55:56     63:64

*Shadow site*: 15:16, Activate Liminal Powers and Preparing the Future

**Skinning means the old grounds for grief and dissention are departing. The Vessel means grasping renewal.**

# 革 ☰ 49 Skinning/ Revolution GE

**Strip away the old; let the new life emerge; revolt and renew; moulting, melting metals; animal transformation, calling the Bright Spirits; site of creative transformation.**

MYTHS FOR CHANGE: THE STORY OF THE TIME

**Charge to the Oracle**: *The Way welling up from below calls out for revolution. Accept this and use the energy of Skinning.*

Skinning shows a time of Revolution: 'Fire in the Lake: Change Heaven's Mandates.' It includes animal transformations, such as a snake changing its skin or the annual changes of form all animals were thought to undergo, symbolized as the change from bird to fish. It focuses on ritual transformations that occur as the *wu*, the technicians of the sacred, put on the animal mask to call the spirits and change the time. These sorts of dances occurred at Spring's Beginning (New Year), when the *fang xiang* or exorcists, dressed in bearskins and wearing a bear mask with four golden metal eyes, would drive out the old year animals, pushing them over the edge of the world into renewal and change. At this time, the people, too, wore animal masks, men dressed as women, men and woman came together and the things of the old year were destroyed. Everything moves into the liminal state, the fertile chaos called Change. The Queen Mother, Lady of the Beasts, and the moon goddesses are called for the transformations. Perhaps the most dramatic and secret of these rituals are the dances and ceremonies that lead up to melting the metals to cast a new vessel or *ding*, seen in the following figure. The Vessel is a ruling image, a sort of grail that establishes the time and the connection to all the various spirits. It is also the founding sign of a king and a dynasty.

The time of Skinning is great indeed. It is a time when the basic images of our lives go into flux and renewal through that mysterious quality called Change, a time when the world we experience is renewing itself. We co-operate with this by making the time, going through the imaginative preparations. We call on the animal powers and put on the mask, moving into their powerful, creative state. We skin away what is past and done with, challenge our old ideas and experiences. We go into solution, into the liminal zone. When Change occurs, we accept the transformation and welcome the new time.

## THE RESPONSE

**Skinning. Your own day.**

**There is a connection to the spirits that will carry you through.**

**Source of Success: Advantageous Trial.**

**The cause for sorrow disappears.**

Skin/Revolution, GE: Take off or change the skin, moulting; smelting, melt and cast bronze; revolt, overthrow, change, renew; radical change of state; prepare hides; skin, leather and bronze armour, soldiers; eliminate, repeal, cut off, cut away; plumage, feathers used in ritual dances that invoke the Bright Spirits; human skin, change the skin, shaman and masked dances; renewing the generations, a generation during which the Way transforms itself and the law of nature evolves; change Heaven's Mandates, reject the decadent and renew the Way.' The old character shows an animal skin with horns, body and tail stretched on a frame of three branches.

 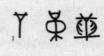

GE (5953/177) represents animal skin, with ram's horns (1) on a frame of tied-together branches.

Skinning/Revolution describes your situation in terms of stripping away the protective cover. The way to deal with it is to radically change and renew the way things are presented. Eliminate what has grown old and useless so that the new can be seen. You must wait for the right moment to act, when the snake is ready to shed its skin and the sun is approaching the zenith. When the right moment arrives, act with confidence. You will be linked to the spirits and they will carry you through. This begins a whole new cycle of time. All your doubts and sorrows will be extinguished.

## THE SCHOLAR SPEAKS

The hexagram figure shows changing awareness coming to expression. In the middle of the mists there is fire. You are coupled with a creative force. The Way of the Well and its deep waters has forced you to skin away the old. Skinning means to reject old motives, sorrows, memories and quarrels. Regulate the way you understand time in order to clarify when the right moment comes. Stream and fire come together for a moment. They are like two women who live together but have different purposes and desires. This is called Skinning. Wait for the right moment. Act and trust what you are doing. Brighten the inner pattern by expressing it. You can promote great growth by correcting the situation. This is pleasing to the spirits. Skin and renew things. Your doubts and sorrows will be extinguished. Heaven and Earth renew themselves and the four seasons accomplish things. Great People change and renew the Mandate of Heaven. Let yielding and serving connect you to Heaven and mutual resonance connect you to the people. The time of Skinning is truly great.

## THE SHAMAN SPEAKS

**Fire in the centre of Mists. Skinning.**

**This is a time when Noble One regulates the measures of time to clarify the new seasons.**

*Spirit reveals itself in the Bright Omens, speaks and spreads joy through the Intermediaries.* Joyous Dancer is working with the Bright Omens. Rising Mists above stimulate and fertilize, joyous words cheer and inspire, while Fire below radiates light and warmth and people experience the Bright Presence of things. This is Metal over Fire: a changing inner awareness that melts away obsolete outer form. The ideal Realising Person reflects this by establishing the rites and rituals that elaborate and clarify the new time. Work through joyous words to bring spirit to expression. Confront the ghosts and shadows.

## TRANSFORMING LINES: CHANGE AT WORK

### INITIAL NINE

**Tightly secured in the yellow bull's skin.**

*Not allowed to act.* Like a shaman in the skin mask, you begin the change of awareness. You can not act yet, but nothing can tear you away from this connection. Be open to the influence when it comes. The metals are melting.

*Direction:* This is an influx of spirit. Don't be afraid to act alone, you are coupled to a creative force.

### SIX AT SECOND

**This is your own day, Skin it!**

**Wise Words! Chastising opens the Way. This is not a mistake.**

*There is excellence in moving now.* This is your time. Move into the dance. You can change the world. Put everything into solution. Don't be shy. Be a hero. Vigorous action opens the Way. This is definitely not a mistake.

*Direction:* Be resolute. You are connected to a creative force.

### NINE AT THIRD

**Skinning. Chastising closes the Way. Trap!**

**Trial: adversity, hungry souls and angry ghosts.**

**When the Skinning words pass round three times,**

**You will be connected to the spirits.**

*This means you will really have it.* Discipline and expeditions won't work now. Danger. The ghosts of the past have arrived. The ritual chant builds the energy to deal with them. Let the call to action go around three times, then act decisively. You can renew the time. The spirits will help you.

*Direction:* Follow the stream of events. Proceed step by step. Gather energy for a decisive new move.

### NINE AT FOURTH

**Skinning. The cause for sorrows disappears.**

**There is a connection to the spirits that will carry you through.**

**'Change Heaven's Mandates.'**

**Wise Words! The Way is open.**

*This is the trustworthy purpose*. The great Change. The metals have melted. Act and have no doubts. All your sorrows will vanish. The spirits are helping you. You are in a position to change the imaginative basis of your world. The Way is open.
*Direction*: The situation is already changing.

NINE AT FIFTH

**Skinning. The Great Person makes a tiger transformation.**

**Even before the omens are cast, he is connected to the spirits.**

*Its pattern is luminous*. When the time comes to change, you must change with it. This is transformation at the core of your being. Take a quantum leap. Let your great creative strength be seen. Pursue what you desire. Even before there is an oracle, people will know you are connected to the spirits. Have no fear. Your inner pattern can brighten events.
*Direction*: A time of great abundance. Don't be afraid to act alone. You are connected to a creative force.

SIX ABOVE

**Skinning. The Noble One makes a leopard transformation.**

**Small People wear a skin mask.**

**Trap! Chastising closes the Way.**

**Stay where you are now. Wise Words! Trial: the Way is open.**

*Its pattern is beautiful*. Change your life with grace and elegance. This is a transformation that can realise things and ground change in the life around you. Don't simply put on another mask. Stay right where you are for now, and the changes will fall into your hands.
*Direction*: Give people a common purpose. This will couple you with a creative force.

# 50 The Vessel/ Transformation DING

Sacred vessel; hold, contain and transform, imagine; meal with
spirits, ancestors and noble people; establish, found, proclaim
the divination.

## MYTHS FOR CHANGE: THE STORY OF THE TIME

**Charge to the Oracle**: *Skinning means nothing other than transforming the Vessel. Accept this and use the energy of the Vessel.*

*Ding* is a ritual vessel that signifies connection with the spirit
world and the ancestors as the foundation of a dynasty or noble
house. It is divination, divinatory incantations and submitting a
question to the oracle, as well as the right moment to act (*shi*). It
is an emblem of power and an alchemical cauldron, suggesting
cooking in a literal and spiritual sense. It offers nourishment to the
warriors and sages and the sage-mind in all of us, brightening the
eye and ear. It suggests a mandate, a fate conferred by Heaven that
is also a duty or responsibility. It means becoming a true and
responsible individual.

The *Ding* has roots in Neolithic worship of the dead. It is the
ultimate symbol of a sacrifice and ritual meal, a symbol for the
oracle itself, the Change. It is also a part of high culture, a skilfully
and magically crafted ritual tool that releases or frees the spirit,
nourishing the sage-mind, beauty, imagination, the world of myth
and the omen animals. It is synonymous with the dragon of creative energy and transformation, with the act of divination
through which the spirits speak and with the rite at the Ancestral
Temple that calls down the spirits. The first bronze *Ding*-vessels
were cast by the Yu the Great, offering communication with the
spirit world as foundation of human culture.

In ancient times Yu the Great received the metals from the
Nine Provinces and the magical animal symbols (*xiang*) from the
Shepherds. He cast the Nine *Ding*-Vessels at the foot of *Jing-shan*,
a sacred mountain, so we could penetrate the forests, valleys and
swamps and none of the river or mountain spirits could harm us.
The vessels showed which were the beneficent spirits and which

were the noxious spirits, what opened the Way and what closed it. They united all the provinces, connected the above and the below. Thus we enjoyed the Mandate of Heaven.

## The Response

> **The Vessel. Transformation. The Way to the Source is open. Wise Words!**
>
> **Make an offering and you will succeed.**
>
> Vessel, *Ding*: A cauldron with three feet and two ears, sacred vessel for cooking offerings, sacrifices and ritual meals; prepare meat in a Ding, sacrifice with a Ding, sacrifice animal and human victims; founding symbol of a family or dynasty, sign of royal blessing; receptacle; hold, contain and transform, transmute; consecrate, connect with the spirits; found, establish, secure; precious, well-grounded; *also*: proclaim the divination, submit to the words of the oracle; a name of Yu the Great who collected the metals of the Nine Provinces, cast the nine tripod vases at the foot of mount Jing and penetrated into the forests, the valleys and the swamps. He united all the provinces and received the blessing of Heaven. The old character shows a sacrificial vessel.

*DING*[3] (10973/206) represents an ancient cooking pot, used for sacrifice to the gods or spirits and a sacred meal.

The Vessel describes your situation in terms of imagination and the transformative capacity of a sacred vessel. The way to deal with it is to contain and transform your problem through an image. You need to see deeply into what your problem means. Security and a new beginning will come from this awareness. It is a time for reflection, for slowly turning and examining things. This is the origin of great good fortune and meaningful events. It releases transformative energy. It is pleasing to the spirits. Through it they will give you success, effective power and the capacity to bring the situation to maturity.

## THE SCHOLAR SPEAKS

The hexagram figure shows inner penetration feeding a spreading radiance and clarity. Above wood there is fire. Be resolute and break through inner obstacles. Once the old has been eliminated, there is nothing that can take the place of the Vessel and its transformative power. Through the Vessel you can grasp renewal. Correct the situation in order to give your fate a solid base. The Vessel means making and using symbols, like fire uses wood. Offer something to the spirits through cooking it. The sage uses this kind of offering to present things to the supreme spirits above and to nourish wise and worthy people. This brightens the understanding of the ear and the eye and lets you see invisible things. What is flexible and adaptable advances and moves to the higher position. Through it you can acquire the centre and connect with what is solid and strong. This is pleasing to the spirits. It is the origin of success, effective power and the capacity to bring the situation to maturity.

## THE SHAMAN SPEAKS

**Above Wood, Fire. The Vessel.**

**This is a time when Noble One corrects his situation to solidify his fate.**

*Spirit works in those who lay out the offerings, revealing itself in the Bright Omens.* The Lady of Fates is working with the Bright Omens. Fire above radiates light and warmth and people experience the Bright Presence of things, while Wind and Wood enter subtly from below, penetrating, pervading and coupling. This is Fire over Wood: an inner penetration that feeds the spreading outer light, cooking and transforming what is held in the vessel. The ideal Realising Person reflects this by correcting his stance and situation through inner work, thus stabilizing the fate given him by Heaven. Work through subtle penetration. This involves fate. Stabilise the dwelling.

INITIAL SIX

**The Vessel. Transform it. The Vessel's overturned foot.**

**Advantageous for clearing the obstruction. Harvesting.**

**Acquire a concubine for the sake of a son.**

**This is not a mistake.**

*This is not rebelling, but adhering to value.* Do something out of the ordinary to establish a connection with the spirit world. Turn things on their head. Get rid of the obstruction. This is not a mistake. It will bring you happiness.

*Direction:* A great and flourishing time is coming. Be resolute. You are connected to a creative force.

NINE AT SECOND

**The Vessel. Transform it. 'There is food in the Vessel.'**

**My companion is afflicted but cannot approach me.**

**Wise Words! The Way is open.**

*Consider the place and complete this without being excessive.* You have something real cooking inside you, a spiritual transformation. Those around you now are afflicted with negative emotions. Stay with the transformation. Don't fear. It is substantial and secure. The Way is open. Proceed on your own.

*Direction:* Search outside the norms. Don't be afraid to act alone. You are connected to a creative force.

NINE AT THIRD

**The Vessel. Transform it.**

**The Vessel's ears are skinned and movement hindered.**

**The pheasant fat not eaten.**

**'We are changing the Mandates of Heaven.'**

**Rain comes on all sides and lessens the cause of sorrow.**

**Wise Words! Completing this change opens the Way.**

*Letting go of your righteousness.* Everything feels clogged up now. Don't worry about it. This is a transformation of the way you experience life in the widest and most fundamental sense. The rain will come and wash away your sorrows. Keep going. The Way is open.

*Direction:* Gather energy for a decisive new move.

### NINE AT FOURTH

**The Vessel's stand is severed.**

**The prince's meal is overthrown and his form soiled.**

**The penalty will be death in chambers.**

**Trap! The Way closes.**

*Is this being trustworthy?* Disaster. Whatever you are contemplating, don't do it. You will betray a trust and soil your higher principles. The Way is closed.

*Direction:* Renovate a corrupt situation. If you let yourself be led, you can realise hidden potential. The situation is already changing.

### SIX AT FIFTH

**The Vessel has golden ears and bronze rings.**

**Advantageous Trial. Harvesting.**

*Centring using a real activation.* A beautiful vision and a loving plan. This is the casting of the precious metals. You have found a way to bring it into the world. This is a great joy. Act on it. It will bring you profit and insight.

*Direction:* This couples you with a creative force.

### NINE ABOVE

**The Vessel has jade rings.**

**Wise Words! The Great Way opens.**

**There is nothing for which this is not advantageous. Harvesting.**

*The strong and the supple are articulated.* This is something truly precious. It can transform your life. The Great Way is open to you now. This can be of benefit to all. It will open a whole new world.

*Direction:* Continue on. Be resolute. You are connected with a creative force.

# 51 and 52: The Paradigm

### The Rouser and the Sacrificer

This Pair involves you in an overall model of thought and action elaborated in the interconnected lines of the two figures: rousing new growth and fixing and articulating the past. These are the Operators, figures who work with the spirit. They represent the threshold between winter and spring, the New King and the Old King, the celebrant and the sacrifice or victim. Carefully consider your place in and relation to this model.

*Hidden Possibilities*: 39:40 > 63 and 64, re-imagine difficulties to release bound energy. Make the crossing and prepare the new.

The Pair exchanges information with 15:16 (Activating Liminal Powers to Prepare the Future). It is motivated by 21:22 (Sacred Meal and Bringing Home the Bride). The centre and threshold lines relate the process to 17:18 (Follow the Spirit and Renovate the Ancestral Images), 23:24 (Stripping the Corpse and The Returning Spirit), 53:54 (The Great Marriages) and 55:56 (King and Wandering Sage).

Look at the ages and events these figures suggest for personal connections.

15:16 17:18 (19:20) 21:22  23:24       53:54 55:56

*Shadow site*: 13:14, The Bright Omens Emerge
from the Gathering of the People

**Shake means rousing it. Bound means stilling it.**

# 51 Shake/Rousing
## ZHEN

**Disturbing and fertilizing shock; sexual energy; wake up, stir up; return of life in early spring; the Rouser and Exorcist.**

**Charge to the Oracle:** *A new lord's implements mean nothing less than a long-living son who extends the line. Use this spirit helper. Accept this and use the energy of Shake. This means stirring things up and rousing them.*

Shake is rain and the spirit that brings the spring rains, violent thunder from beneath that rouses all to new growth after the dead time of winter. It is a dynamic process, the spark of yang born in the breast of yin, the thunder rituals and incantations that inspire both terror and joy. It is the moment when the foetus begins to stir, associated with dawn, the east, the rising sun, green, wood and the announcement of spring's beginning, waking the insects sleeping in the Earth. Shake is the ritual of opening the fields, performed at the Ancestral Temple and the Field Altar, where an offering of dark aromatic millet wine, perfumed with the sensual fragrances of the *orchis* and the River-Mountain festivals, calls the spirits to return. It is also the great exorcism that issues forth from spring's beginning, a burst of violent noise and chaos that frightens away the spirits grown old, those whose time has passed.

As a spirit guide, Shake is the Arouser and Exorcist, driving out the old and rousing and opening the field of the new. He is flamboyant and sexual, luxurious, frightening and inspiring, green and full of juice. He is motion and moves all things. He is an emerging Dragon. In the body Shake operates through the liver, governing the free flow of energy and emotion. It stimulates everything that moves in the body, purifies the blood, links eyes and sexual organs, desire and anger, vision and motivation, giving the capacity to act decisively.

震

Shake. Make an offering and you will succeed.

Shake comes, Frightening, Frightening!

Then laughing words, Shouting, Shouting!

Shake scares us for a hundred miles around.

He does not spill the sacrificial ladle and the aromatic spirits.

Shake, ZHEN: Arouse, inspire; wake up, shake up; shock, frighten, awe, alarm; violent thunder clap [thunder comes from below in Chinese thought], earthquake, put into movement, begin; decisive moment; terrify, trembling; majestic, severe; excite, influence, affect; work, act; break through the shell, come out of the bud; quicken, become pregnant; *also*: appearance of the signs; time, day, occasion, the right time, the constellations and stars which indicate the passage of time, the quality of the moments. The old character shows rain falling from Heaven and the sign for shock, the 'waking of the insects' in early spring and the thunder that opens the fields.

 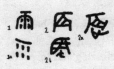

ZHÈN⁴ (620/173) shows rain (1 and 3a) and the sign for shock or cutting through, perhaps a sickle (2a and b).

Shake/Rousing describes your situation in terms of a disturbing and inspiring shock. The way to deal with it is to rouse things to new activity. Re-imagine what you are confronting. Let the shock shake up your old beliefs and begin something new. Don't lose your depth and concentration. What at first seems frightening will soon be a cause to rejoice. This is pleasing to the spirits. Through it they will give you success, effective power and the capacity to bring the situation to maturity. The thunder rolls and everyone is frightened. You can hear them screaming in terror. Then the fright changes to joy and you hear everyone laughing and talking. The sudden shock spreads fear for thirty miles around. Don't lose your concentration. Hold the libation cup calmly so the dark wine arouses and calls the spirits.

## THE SCHOLAR SPEAKS

The hexagram figure shows repeated shocks that stir things up. Reiterating thunder. Re-imagine your situation. Nothing is better for putting a great idea into action than being the first child of thunder. Shake means stirring things up; it means beginning and undertaking things. Anxiously and fearfully inspect and adjust yourself. This is pleasing to the spirits. Through it they will give you success, effective power and the capacity to bring the situation to maturity. The Shake comes and terrifies everyone. The anxiety it causes will ultimately bring blessings. When laughing words ring out, you will have what you need. The Shake startles what is far away and frightens what is near. Don't lose your depth and concentration. When the Shake comes from the Earth, it is time to go out and attend to the Ancestral Temple, the Field Altar and the sacrifice to the gods of the growing crops. Act as master of the ceremonies that bring fertility.

## THE SHAMAN SPEAKS

**Reiterating Thunder. Shake.**

**This is a time when Noble One transforms anxiety and fear through adjusting and inspecting.**

*Spirit manifests in quake and thunder.* This is the Rouser and Exorcist. Thunder rouses and germinates new potential, sprouting energies that thrust up from below, opening the fields so new growth can burst forth. This is the Woody Moment: Shake stirs things up to issue forth. The ideal Realising Person reflects this by focusing his fear and anxiety on correcting his stance and his person. Work through subtle penetration. This involves fate.

## TRANSFORMING LINES: CHANGE AT WORK

### INITIAL NINE

**Shake comes, Frightening! Frightening!**

**Then laughing words, Shouting! Shouting!**

**Wise Words! The Way is open.**

*Anxiety over blessing, it will soon be there.* A profound shock. Everything is turned upside-down. But the anxiety soon turns to joy in a burst of creative energy. Let it move you. The Way is open.

*Direction*: Gather resources in order to act when the call comes. Re-imagine the situation. Gather energy for a decisive new move.

### SIX AT SECOND

**Shake comes bringing adversity, hungry souls and angry ghosts.**

**A hundred thousand cowries lost.**

**Climb the Nine Mounds. Don't pursue what has been lost.**

**On the seventh day you will acquire it.**

*This is riding a strong power*. The fertilizing shock comes. You think you have lost something precious and are plagued by the remorse of the past. Don't grieve. Hide on the frontiers. Climb the mounds of transformation. Everything you lost will soon return of itself.

*Direction*: Let yourself be led, you can realise hidden potential. The situation is already changing.

### SIX AT THIRD

**Shake reviving, Oh! Oh!**

**Shake moves without a mistake.**

*The force does not match the position*. The fertilizing shock rouses your dormant creative energy. Everything is renewed and inspired. Move with it. You will not be making a mistake.

*Direction*: A time of abundance is coming. Don't be afraid to act alone. You are connected to a creative force.

### NINE AT FOURTH

**Shake released from a bog.**

*This is not shining yet*. Everything is bogged down. Release fertile energy from the cloud of confusion. Try to understand where the new impulse comes from and move with it.

*Direction*: Something significant is returning. Be open and provide what is needed.

### Six at Fifth

**Shake comes and goes. Adversity, hungry souls and angry ghosts.**

**Be intent on your desire. Don't lose your purpose.**

**There will be service.**

*Moving in an exposed position without losing the Great.* The fertilizing shock comes and goes. It brings up old memories and quarrels and you must deal with them. Keep your mind on what you want to do and all will be well. You will be involved in the service of greater things.

*Direction:* Follow the stream of events. Proceed step by step. Gather energy for a decisive new move.

### Six Above

**Shake, twisting and turning! Observing, you are terrified, Oh! Oh!**

**Trap! Chastising closes the Way.**

**Shake is not in your body, but in your neighbour's body.**

**Be calm. This is not a mistake.**

**There will be words about a marriage.**

*Not the centre yet. Warning: beware your neighbour!* The fertilizing shock twists and turns, driving people around you into a frenzy. Don't try to put this all in order. Stay aloof. Don't get caught in the trap. This is not the right time to do anything. Be cautious about beginning a relationship now.

*Direction:* Bite through the obstacles. Re-imagine the situation. Gather energy for a decisive new move.

# 52 Bound/Stilling
## GEN

**Calm, still, stabilize; bind, fix, come to the limit or boundary; articulating your experiences; becoming individual; the Sacrificer.**

## MYTHS FOR CHANGE: THE STORY OF THE TIME

**Charge to the Oracle:** *Things cannot be stirred up without finding an end, stilling desire and fixing the limits. Use this spirit helper. Accept this and use the energy of Bound. This means stopping.*

Bound is the active agent that fixes the omens and binds the fates. It is the guard and protector, the spirit of the 'inner work', the mountain temple filled with images of the spirits and the Mountain Men, the sages and diviners who soar like birds beyond the ordinary limits of life. Bound stands at the limit and makes limits, like the mountains that limit the fertile plains roused to life by Shake. It is the limit of Heaven and Earth, the limit of old and new. The power of Earth works through Bound. It acts as the culmination and articulation of things. The old time or the cycle that is ending is bound and opened, offered to the spirits. This is seen in the sacrifice of the Old King, who is sent out to the edge of the world to mark the limits. From this comes renewal, just as Shake follows Bound in the cycle of Eight Helpers.

The term parallels the binding and opening of a sacrificial victim and the stilling of the body, the release of inner awareness through meditative practices. Stilled, the body becomes the source of holy omens, footprints of the spirits. It invokes the image of Tang the Completer and the Duke of Zhou, who offered themselves in sacrifice to Heaven when their people were suffering.

The word with other roots shows a cluster of related images: the buffoons and exorcists who dance at spring beginning, driving out the old; the sacred tree at the Earth Altar, source and root; a deadly poison; a stand or stance; footprints, traces and subtle perceptions; skin, leather and protection. What is sacrificed through Bound stands at the limit of the world and guarantees the birth of new life. Through Bound we read the subtle signs and make the proper offerings within ourselves. Bound opens the subtle body.

As a spirit guide, Bound is the Sacrificer, who leads through perceived limits. He is nemesis. He articulates fate. He is the still point in all turning, the refuge of distant mountains. He is a dog; guarding, watching and finding. In the body, Bound acts through the spleen and stomach, stabilizing and transforming nourishment. It rots and ripens, governs the free flow of ideas, control and protects central energy.

## THE RESPONSE

**Bind its back. Still the personality so it does not catch on things.**

**Move through the chamber to the altar without seeing your people.**

**This is not a mistake.**

**Bound/Stilling**, GEN: Limit, boundary, obstacle; still, quiet, calm, refuse to advance; enclose, mark off, confine; finish, complete; reflect on what has come before; firm, solid, simple, straightforward; the mountain as a limit and a refuge; root, base, cause, beginning; stop, bring to a standstill, stubborn; becoming an individual. The old character shows the eye of the ancestor and a person turning back, focused on the past.

GÈN (6015/138) shows a person (1) turned backwards and the big eye (1 and 3) of the ancestor or spirit.

Bound/Stilling describes your situation in terms of recognizing a limit, or coming to the end of a cycle. The way to deal with it is to calm and stabilize your desire to act in order to understand what has been accomplished. Calm yourself. Don't try to advance. See through your desire. By doing this you stabilize yourself in the world of the spirits and allow them to emerge. Quiet your body. Calm and stabilize your back. This stills your personality so it is not caught up in compulsive actions. Move through your life as if the people you normally recognize were not there. This is not a mistake. It allows you to stabilize and articulate yourself.

## THE SCHOLAR SPEAKS

The hexagram figure shows the limit of things. Joining mountains. Recognizing this limit releases you from compulsive action. You can't stir things up forever. You must also stop them. Bound means stopping. Think over things deeply and don't leave your current situation. Stopping means stabilizing. When the time comes to an end, stop. When the time moves, move. Stir things up or quiet things down without letting go of the right time to move. Then your Way will shine brightly. Bound means stopping yourself. Stopping means staying in your place. What is above and what is below in this situation are connected only through antagonism. They do not meet and associate. Don't get your personality entangled in things. By moving through your life as if people were not there, you will free yourself from error and make no further mistakes.

## THE SHAMAN SPEAKS

> Joining Mountains. Bound.
>
> This is a time when Noble One ponders and does not issue forth from his hidden place.

*Spirit words bind us and accomplish fate.* This is the Sacrificer. Mountain limits and articulates what is complete to suggest what is beginning, closing the cycle of seasons. This is the Earth Moment: Bound fixes the final form. The ideal Realising Person reflects this by staying within and pondering his own nature and the nature of fate and spirit. Work through joyous words to bring spirit to expression.

## TRANSFORMING LINES: CHANGE AT WORK

### INITIAL SIX

> Stilling. Bind and open his feet. Offering it.
>
> This is not a mistake
>
> An ever-flowing and advantageous Trial. Harvesting.

369

*Not letting go of what is correct.* When an impulse to action comes, try to hold back before it leads you into compulsive entanglements. This is not a mistake. It can change your whole life for the better. *Direction:* Beautify things. Release tensions. The situation is already changing.

### SIX AT SECOND

**Stilling. Bind and open his calves. Offering it.**

**Cannot rescue his following.**

**'My heart is not glad.'**

*You can still listen and respond.* Though you can take this opportunity to stop running after impossible desires, you cannot help others who are on the same course. Though this makes your heart ache, still yourself. Do not fail to heed this call. *Direction:* Renovate a corrupt situation. If you let yourself be led, you can realise hidden potential. The situation is already changing.

### NINE AT THIRD

**Stilling. Binding the loins, separating the spine.**

**Adversity, hungry souls and angry ghosts.**

**Acrid smoke smothers the heart.**

*Exposed to danger, the heart smothered.* You are cutting yourself in two, separating yourself from real and legitimate desires. The acrid smoke from this repression smothers your heart. You don't have to make this sacrifice. It won't help anyone, least of all you. *Direction:* Strip away old ideas. Be open and provide what is needed.

### SIX AT FOURTH

**Stilling. Binding and opening his trunk. Offering it.**

**This is not a mistake.**

*This means stopping the body's drives.* Still your compulsive actions, emotions and desires. This frees you from mistakes and lets you see where your real motivations lie. It calms and stabilizes the heart. *Direction:* Search outside the norms. Don't be afraid to act alone. You are connected to a creative force.

## SIX AT FIFTH

**Stilling. Binding his jaws. Offering it.**

**His words have order.**

**The cause for sorrow disappears.**

*This is centred and correct.* If you reflect and restrain your speech, what you say will have order and elegance. When you can communicate like this, your sorrows will vanish.

*Direction:* Proceed step by step. Gather energy for a decisive new move.

## NINE ABOVE

**Stilling. Generous at the Boundary. Offering it.**

**Wise Words! The Way is open.**

*This is munificent completion.* Meet people with generosity, honesty and care and you will receive it in return. This is the end of your isolation. You have learned what you need to face your new life. The Way is open.

*Direction:* Release bound energy. The situation is already changing.

# 53 and 54: The Paradigm

### The Great Marriages

This Pair involves you in an overall model of thought and action elaborated in the interconnected lines of the figures: the way of marriage as an image of the soul's journey to realization. It contrasts a marriage that proceeds in a recognized manner with one that involves a radical change of state, a quantum change. Carefully consider your place in and relation to this model.

*Hidden Possibilities*: 64:63, make the crossing and prepare the new.

The Pair exchanges information with 37:38 (Dwelling and the Ghosts that Haunt it). It is motivated by 39:40 (Difficulties and Release). The centre and threshold lines relate the process to 19:20 (Releasing the Spirit and Watching the Omens), 33:34 (Retreat and Advance), and 51:52 (Rouser and Sacrificer) and 57:58 (The Intermediaries).

Look at the ages and events these figures suggest for personal connections.

19:20     33:34 (35:36) 37:38 39:40     51:52     57:58

*Shadow site*: 11:12, New King and Old King

**Gradual Advance means the marrying woman awaits the man's move. Marrying the Maiden means a woman's completion.**

# 53 Gradual Advance/Marrying Woman JIAN

Smooth, adaptable progress; infiltrate, penetrate like water; ceremonies leading to a formal marriage; a seed figure.

## MYTHS FOR CHANGE: THE STORY OF THE TIME

**Charge to the Oracle**: *Things cannot be stopped without end. Accept this and use the energy of Gradual Advance through the Marrying Woman. This means advancing.*

Gradual Advance is a model of a particular kind of change, imaged in the marriage of the Older Sister. It is a formal ritual progression that leads to union and establishment in the symbolic world, imaged by the infiltrating power of wind, wood and water. This change occurs step by step, through a subtle, gradual and sure advance. It is regular development that proceeds in stages, crossing thresholds in the advance to union and its celebration in dance and festival, its perfection in the symbolic order. The root is water and the term suggests leading water in channels, the course of a river, the watercourse way.

Marriage was one of the major mythic events. Spouses worship the ancestors together and form an inseparable unit in death. A noble married only once. Family alliances, ancestors, politics and religion were all involved. A man married a sororal group, and the 'junior sisters' who went with the First Bride or Consort formed a close-knit group. The love between man and woman that marriage engendered and the emotions and jealousies it provoked was considered a potent and dangerous emotion that doubled the creative force of the cosmos, the connection between Heaven and Earth. It was channelled and articulated in the marriage rites and the River-Mountain festivals and was seen as an image of the fundamental process of Change.

This figure portrays an advance to a goal such as the union of marriage and the sacred dances that connect the couple to the spirit or symbolic world. The Wild Goose, which was presented at the marriage ceremony, is a symbol of this journey that includes the melancholy of separation, the risks that surround love and the vow or bond that founds an enduring union. The migrations of the wild geese were seen as the great movements of the soul, connected with the spring and autumn festivals. They suggest the *wu* dancing with feathers in front of the Ancestral Temple and the men taken away to war, those who followed King Wu into the Mu wilderness and wilds of Shang. This image invokes bird omens and bird dances, the transformation dances that connect to spirit energies, and the Hidden Temple where unions are made, symbolized as red threads that bind a man and woman in a fated relation. We see souls transformed to birds, life as a flight, a migratory journey made in pairs. The name of this figure describes their flight, crossing the water, skimming, gliding and settling at each stage in their journey.

## THE RESPONSE

**Gradual Advance. Marrying Woman.**

**Wise Words! The Way is open.**

**Advantageous Trial. Harvesting.**

**Gradual Advance,** JIAN: Advance by degrees, gracefully; penetrate slowly and surely like water; adapt, infiltrate; flexible, supple, submissive; permeate, influence, affect; formal marriage and festivities of the eldest daughter; channels in which water flows; the skimming, gliding flight of wild geese. The old character shows the sign for river, a central axis or wheel and a trench or channel. It also suggests a high mountain in central China where kings made sacrifice.

JIAN[4] (1544/85) shows a river, a wheel (1) and a trench or groove, a channel for the water. The old character (2 and 3) suggests a waterwheel. Without the wheel, the character means cut through, chop off (4 and 5).

Gradual Advance describes your situation in terms of gradually achieving a goal with the image of the elder daughter's wedding procession. The way to deal with it is to advance slowly and steadily through subtle penetration. Move through the woman and the yin. Through infiltrating, you find the place where you belong. Proceed step by step, and don't try to dominate the situation. This generates meaning and good fortune by releasing transformative energy. You will ultimately achieve mastery and find a new field of activity. Put your ideas to the trial. This brings profit and insight.

## THE SCHOLAR SPEAKS

The hexagram figure shows an inner limit that stabilizes outer growth. Above the mountain there is a tree. Gather energy for a decisive new move. You can't just stay in one place. Infiltrating means advancing. Be like a woman given in marriage who gives priority to the man's initiative. Depend on your moral and intellectual strength and your power to realise the Way to improve the everyday situation. This will certainly advance you. By moving through yin and the woman you achieve mastery and a new field of activity. You acquire the place you desire. Pushing on brings real achievement. Correct yourself in order to advance. This lets you correct the way power and responsibility are assigned. You will acquire a solid place in the centre. Stabilize your desire and be adaptable. Gently penetrate to the core of the situation. Thus the new energy that is stirring will not be exhausted.

## THE SHAMAN SPEAKS

**Tree above Mountain. Gradual Advance.**

**This is a time when Noble One resides in eminence, power and virtue to improve the vulgar.**

*Spirit words bind us and accomplish fate, working in those who lay out the offerings.* These are the Operators, the Sacrificer and the Lady of Fates. Wind and Wood above enter subtly, penetrating, pervading and coupling, while Mountain below limits and articulates what is complete to suggest what is beginning. This is Wood over Earth: on the inner field that supports outer penetration and coupling. The ideal Realising Person reflects this by firmly residing in his innate power to actualize the Way, transforming what is meanspirited and grasping. Work through joyous words to bring the spirit to expression. Renovate the Ancestral Images.

### INITIAL SIX

**Gradual Advance. The Marrying Woman.**

**Wild geese settle on the riverbank.**

**Small son encounters adversity, hungry souls and angry ghosts.**

**There are words. Nothing is lacking.**

*This is righteous, not a mistake.* First steps of the path to union. You encounter danger from the past, but the creative energy is still there. This is not a mistake. Have no fear. Speak out. You lack nothing. *Direction:* Gather energy for a decisive new move.

### SIX AT SECOND

**Gradual Advance. The Marrying Woman.**

**Wild geese settle on the stone.**

**Eating and drinking, Feasting! Feasting!**

**Wise Words! The Way is open.**

*This is not simply gratification.* The sacred meal. On the path to union, you find a secure place and a warm connection. Enjoy yourself now. The Way is open. The journey will soon resume. This is the paradise time of the River-Mountain festival.
*Direction:* Subtly penetrate to the heart of things. Turn conflict into creative tension. The situation is already changing.

### NINE AT THIRD

**Gradual Advance. The Marrying Woman.**

**Wild geese glide over the high plateau and the ancient forest.**

**The husband goes on campaign and does not return.**

**The wife is pregnant and does not nurture a child.**

**Trap! The Way closes for them.**

**Advantageous to resist becoming an outlaw. Harvesting.**

*A bunch of flocking demons, the wife lets go of the Way. Yield to and mutually protect each other.* Separated on the path to union. You have taken a wrong turn. Things are falling apart in mutual recrimination. The Way is closing and creative energy dispersed. Firmly resist the temptation to become violent or withholding. Find what you can do to help each other.

*Direction*: Let everything come into view. Strip away old ideas. Be open and provide what is needed.

### SIX AT FOURTH

**Gradual Advance. The Marrying Woman.**

**Wild geese settle on the trees.**

**'Someone' acquires a branch to rest on, the rafters of the house.**

**This is not a mistake.**

*This is yielding and using subtle penetration.* This is a resting place after a great transition and a great portent of future happiness. Have no fear, this is not a mistake.

*Direction*: Through retiring you will be coupled with a creative force.

### NINE AT FIFTH

**Gradual Advance. The Marrying Woman.**

**Wild geese settle on the grave mounds.**

**The wife is not pregnant for three years.**

**When this is complete, absolutely nothing can stop you.**

**Wise Words! The Way is open.**

*This is acquiring the place you desire.* This is the penultimate step on the path to union. Your creative energy makes contact with the ancestors and the guardian spirits. This takes time, but when it is finished nothing will stop you. Have no fears. The Way is open.

*Direction*: Stabilize your desires. Release bound energy. The situation is already changing.

### NINE ABOVE

**Gradual Advance. The Marrying Woman.**

**Wild geese glide over the high plateau and the ancient forest.**

**Their feathers can be used in the great spirit dances.**

**Wise Words! The Way is open.**

*This does not allow disorder.* The journey ends in the world of the spirit. Your love becomes a symbol that can activate fundamental energies in the world we live in. Because you understand what symbols can do, the Way will always be open to you.

*Direction*: Re-imagine your situation. Gather energy for a decisive new move.

# ·54 *Marrying the Maiden* GUI MEI

**The marriage of the younger daughter; change over which you have no control; realise your destiny or hidden potential; radical change of state; passionate, irregular relationship, desire, compulsion; a seed figure.**

MYTHS FOR CHANGE: THE STORY OF THE TIME

**Charge to the Oracle**: *When you advance you must find a place to marry and change, returning to the place you belong. Accept this and use the energy of Marrying the Maiden.*

Marrying the Maiden is a model of a kind of change imaged by the marriage of the Younger Sister and a particular historic incident. It is a sudden change of state, a transformation that occurs outside of your control and leads to fulfilling your innate destiny or virtue. The root of the word suggests both calming or tranquillizing and arriving at the fulfilment.

Marrying the Maiden is based on an historical incident in the story of the Change in the Mandate of Heaven. Di Yi, the 'Great Ancestor' and Shang Ruler, gave one of his daughters in marriage to King Wen, spiritual father of the Zhou Dynasty, when the Zhou were just emerging as major vassals to the Shang. She went to the marriage as principal wife, followed by her younger sisters. When the marriage to the Leading Wife produced no offspring, however, one of the sororal brides, the Lady of Shu, was raised to be principal wife. She is the 'marrying maiden' who became mother of King Wu and the Duke of Zhou, the great heroes who obtained the Mandate of Heaven, established the Zhou as a ruling dynasty and renewed the time, creating a new Golden Age.

The name of this figure combines the image of a girl sent to her husband's house to marry with the idea of returning to your own country, returning to yourself or your home, the spontaneous movement of a being who, by yielding to its innate nature, fulfils its destiny. The term also suggested a goal, intention or destination. It was used to describe the Three Refuges (*Buddha*, *Dharma* and *Sangha*) and the return to the Source in death. It was further used to

379

denote relations outside the mainstream, illicit or irregular unions outside the norms and based on passion that lead to major changes.

## The Response

**Marrying the Maiden. Chastising closes the Way and leaves no advantageous direction.**

**Marry/convert**, GUI: give a young woman in marriage; transform, reveal hidden potential; return to where you belong; restore, revert; loyal. The old character shows a marriage procession with pennants with tassels at the top and the signs for the great and a broom held in the hand.

**Maiden**, MEI: young girl who is not yet nubile; younger sister; daughter of a secondary wife; person in a servile position. The old character shows a maiden with blossoming breasts.

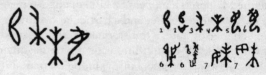

GUI: (6369/77) is composed of (1) a rolling, waving movement, with a variant (2) meaning pursue vigorously, and a broom held in the hand (3) as a banner or standard. 6 below shows variants. MEI (7660/38) shows a luxuriant tree (4) meaning abundant, late summer and a kneeling woman (5) with her head filled with spirit (6 above). 7 shows two variants with the knife of sacrifice.

Marrying the Maiden describes your situation in terms of a change you must go through which is beyond your control. You are not the one who has chosen. The force involved is larger than you are. The way to deal with it is to accept it and let yourself be led. You cannot escape the situation. It reflects a deep and unacknowledged need. It is moving you towards a new field of activity, the place where you belong. Don't try to discipline people or take control of the situation. That will cut you off from the spirits and leave you open to danger. Don't impose your will, have a plan or a place to go. Being free of such plans will bring you profit and insight. This is a very special situation that, in the long run, can lead to great success.

## THE SCHOLAR SPEAKS

The hexagram figure shows self-expression cheerfully following rousing new energy. Above the mists there is thunder. The situation is already changing. In order to advance you must have a way to convert your hidden potential. Bring this potential to completion through the woman and the yin. Don't try to dominate the situation. Adapt and provide what is needed. By bringing everything to completion you will understand what is unfit to be used. Converting the Maiden is the great righteousness of Heaven and Earth. If Heaven and Earth did not mingle like this, the Myriad Beings would never emerge. For the Maiden, this is both an end and a beginning. Stir up expression and pleasure. This is the way to Convert the Maiden. Punishing people or imposing your will cuts you off from the spirits and leaves you open to danger. It is not the right situation to do that. Don't make plans or impose directions. Be supple and adaptable and ride on the strong, solid force.

## THE SHAMAN SPEAKS

**Thunder above Mists. Marrying the Maiden.**

**This is a time when Noble One uses what is enduring and complete in order to determine what is flawed.**

*Spirit speaks and spreads joy through the Intermediaries, manifesting in quake and thunder.* These are the Operators, the Rouser and the Joyous Dancer. Thunder rouses above and germinates new potential, while Rising Mists from below stimulate and fertilize, joyous words cheer and inspire. This is Wood over Metal: rousing outer energy that converts the Maiden's potential to stimulate, inspire and call the spirit. The ideal Realising Person reflects this by meditating on what is whole and enduring, thus understanding the flaws in himself and others. Work through subtle penetration. This involves fate. Follow the spirit.

## TRANSFORMING LINES: CHANGE AT WORK

### INITIAL NINE

**The Marrying Maiden with her sister-brides.**

**She marries as a junior sister.**

A halting gait lets you tread.

**Wise Words! Chastising opens the Way.**

*Fix the omen. You receive gifts and mutual support.* You are in the position of the junior wife and have no overt power. That does not mean you can't influence things and achieve your desire. This situation suggests Yu the Great and his ceaseless work from the shadows. Put yourself in order and do what you have to do.

*Direction:* Release bound energy. The situation is already changing.

### NINE AT SECOND

**The Marrying Maiden.**

**Those who squint can see.**

**Trial: the Way is open for the Mountain People, hidden in the shadow.**

**Harvesting.**

*The rules have not changed yet.* The place of the hidden spirit-workers. The junior wife keeps a low profile. Stay out of sight for now. Don't get involved in struggles for power. Look at things from an independent perspective. You will learn a lot this way, and be able to unfold your plans.

*Direction:* A fertile shock is coming. Re-imagine the situation. Gather energy for a decisive new move.

### SIX AT THIRD

**The Marrying Maiden as a servant, given with her elder sister.**

**'Watching her hair grow.'**

**She reverses this and marries as a companion bride.**

*This is not appropriate yet.* The junior wife is in the subservient position of a serving maid. Have patience, ease and courage. In the end you will reverse things and gain a strategic position. Be ready. You will sabotage everything if you simply become a sycophant.

*Direction:* Contain your great strength. Be resolute. You are connected to a creative force.

NINE AT FOURTH

**The Marrying Maiden draws out the time.**

**Delaying the marriage lets her find the right time.**

*There is both waiting and moving.* The junior wife must know how to wait and when to act. Let things go. Forget about deadlines. This will increase your worth. You will know when it is the right time to act.
*Direction:* A significant connection is approaching. Something important returns. Be open and provide what is needed.

SIX AT FIFTH

**Great Ancestor Di Yi gives the Maidens in Marriage.**

**The leading wife's sleeves were not as fine as her junior sister's sleeves.**

**'Changes are coming': the Moon Almost Full.**

**Wise Words! The Way opens.**

*Your situation is at the centre. This is using value to move.* An omen of great future happiness, fertility and power. The moon is almost full. There will be changes. Accept the secondary position willingly for now. It carries great power. The junior wife will be queen. Your success is assured.
*Direction:* Express yourself. Find supportive friends. Gather energy for an important new move.

SIX ABOVE

**The Marrying Maiden.**

**This woman carried a basket with nothing in it.**

**This noble sacrificed a goat with no blood.**

**There is no advantageous direction.**

*At the top with nothing in it. This is receiving an empty basket.* This is the barren womb of the senior wife. No substance, no blood and no passion. An empty and fraudulent sacrifice. Nothing you can do will help. The time has passed it by. Don't make any more plans. Just leave.
*Direction:* Turn conflict into creative tension. The situation is already changing.

MARRYING THE MAIDEN

# 55 and 56: The Paradigm

## The New King Receives the Mandate and the Wandering Sage Begins his Journey

This Pair involves you in an overall model of thought and action elaborated in the interconnected lines of the figures: the king who receives Heaven's Mandate and his dark partner who Sojourns in the shadows to make new connections. It embodies a site of radical transformation, the emergence of Heaven's Bright Omens and their passage across the threshold of life and death as the Flying Bird. Carefully consider your place in and relation to this model.

*Hidden Possibilities:* 28 > 1, a transition that breaks old boundaries, connecting you to creative force.

The Pair exchanges with and is motivated by 62 and 30, Bright Omens and the Flying Bird. The centre and threshold lines connect the zone of transformation with 33:34 (Retreat and Advance), 35:36 (Rising and Setting Sun), 49:50 (Revolution and the new Vessel) and 51:52 (Rouser and Sacrificer).

Look at the ages and events these figures suggest for personal connections.

<u>30</u> (31:32) 33:34 35:36       49:50 51:52       <u>62</u>

*Shadow site:* 9:10, Gathering the Ghosts and Mating with the Spirit

**Abounding means there were many previous grounds for sorrow. Sojourning means connecting the scattered few.**

# 55 Abounding/ Receiving the Mandate FENG

Plenty, copious, rich, generous, profusion; culminating point, overflowing; activate inner creative energy; the King receives the Mandate of Heaven, a sign of great change; site of creative transformation.

## MYTHS FOR CHANGE: THE STORY OF THE TIME

**Charge to the Oracle**: *Finding the place to marry necessarily means becoming Great. Accept this and use the energy of Abounding. Receiving the Mandate. This means being Great.*

Abounding suggests a *heng* or image-fixing ritual. This particular version of the *heng*-ritual was celebrated at the height of summer, when the year changes at the solstice and the dark influx begins. The King would withdraw into seclusion in the Mourning Hut to magically fix the forms of coming abundance by sacrificing to the dark forces that will bring the harvest. The character also suggests playing the war tambours for the armies that would become active in autumn after the harvest ritual. It represents offerings that bring happiness, wine-drinking feasts and the wine vessel used at the Outskirts Altar, a great vessel full of blessings. Its root is pig, combining hidden riches and facing danger.

The term *feng* is also the name of King Wu's military capital on the Feng River, just before the events of the conquest of Shang. At this time, King Wu was in mourning for his father King Wen, beginning the three years of isolation in the Mourning Hut prescribed for a Royal Ancestor. A solar eclipse occurred on or about 20 June 1070 BCE, at the solstice. King Wu took this as a direct omen from Heaven that Shang was about to fall and that he had finally received the Mandate for Change. When the sky became darker, the inhabitants of the capital saw the Dipper appear in the heavens, the palace of *Shang Di* and a powerful omen of military victory. King Wu made a turtle divination to see whether he should remain in mourning or take arms immediately. The turtle oracle works in matched pairs of positive/negative statements. Here we have the answer to the charge 'perhaps stay in mourning'. It says: 'Trap! The Way closes!' King Wu then made the *yi*-sacrifice at noon. His War Leader announced the results at the Earth Altar, and smeared the drums with blood and set his armies marching into the wilderness of Mu to fight the battle that ended the rule of the Shang. In a radical and shocking action he not only broke the prescribed mourning, but carried his father's corpse, which had not been enshrined in a spirit-tablet, with him into battle to ensure the support of Heaven. This act of obedience to the Mandate that broke all the rules was to bring great abundance to all.

## THE RESPONSE

**Abounding. He receives the Mandate. Make an offering and you will succeed.**

**The King sacrifices at the Earth Altar: 'No mourning!'**

**He makes the sacrifice at noon and sets the armies marching.**

**Abound,** FENG: abundant harvest; fertile, plentiful, copious, numerous; prolific, exuberant, overflowing; full, culminating, ripe, sumptuous, luxurious; have many talents, friends, riches; eclipse, omen or sign of a great change; name of King Wu's military capital at Feng and his war leader, the Duke of Zhou; victory, renewal of the time. The old character shows a ritual cooking vessel or big war drum, ears of grain and a threshing floor.

FENG[1] (3541/151) is both a cooking pot and a big drum with decorations (4). Other forms show ears of grain (1), a threshing floor (2) and a ritual vessel (3) like a cornucopia.

Abounding describes your situation in terms of abundance and fertile profusion to come. There is a fundamental change preparing. The way to deal with it is to be exuberant and expansive. Overflow with good feeling, support and generosity. Give with both hands. This is pleasing to the spirits. Through it they will give you success, effective power and the capacity to bring the situation to maturity. Imagine yourself as the King whose power bestows wealth and happiness on all. Rid yourself of sorrow, melancholy and care. Be like the sun at midday. Shed light on all and eliminate the shadows.

## THE SCHOLAR SPEAKS

The hexagram figure shows brightness and warmth permeating the world and stirring up growth. Thunder and lightning bring everything to culmination. Assemble all your force. Don't be afraid to act alone. Acquiring a field of activity means having a great idea. Abounding refers to your great idea. Many things have brought you to this point, among them quarrels and sorrows. Cut through legal arguments and let punishment take place. Brightness and awareness stir everything up. This is the source of abounding. Imagine yourself as a king whose power confers benefits on everyone. Honour what is great. Rid yourself of all sorrow and melancholy. Shed your light on everything below Heaven. When the sun reaches the centre, it begins to set. When the moon becomes full, it begins to wane. Heaven and Earth fill and empty all things. There is a time to associate with others and build things up, and a time to let structures dissolve so the new can emerge. This is even truer of people and of the souls and spirits that govern the world.

## THE SHAMAN SPEAKS

> **Thunder and Lightning culminate. Abounding. Receiving a Mandate.**

> **This is a time when Noble One uses severe litigation that involves serious punishment.**

*The spirit that manifests in quake and thunder reveals itself in the Bright Omens.* The Rouser is working with the Bright Omens. Thunder above rouses and germinates new potential, while Fire and brightness below radiate light and warmth and people experience the Bright Presence of things. This is Wood over Fire: an inner brightness that permeates and rouses the outer world, opening to a new spring. The ideal Realising Person reflects this by clearly demarcating what is and what is not responsible behaviour. A cycle is beginning. Bite through the obstacles.

### INITIAL NINE

**Abounding. Meeting his Lord as an equal.**

**The ten-day week. This is not a mistake.**

**There is honour and reward in going.**

*More than a full ceremonial week would be a disaster.* In the Mourning Hut, you encounter someone or something that will change the course of your life. It is a deep mutual recognition. Stay with this for a complete ritual period. Go through all the stages. It is not a mistake. If you hold on to the connection, it will bring you honour and reward.

*Direction*: A transition. Be very Small. Don't be afraid to act alone. You are connected to a creative force.

### SIX AT SECOND

**Abounding screens him. The great cycle is full.**

**Feng is so dark at noon we see the Dipper, constellation of fates.**

**Charge: 'If he goes forward, we will know doubts and affliction.'**

**Response: 'You have a far-reaching connection to the spirit that will carry you through.'**

**Wise Words! The Way is open.**

*Trustworthy purpose is shooting forth.* The time is full, the Mandate for Change draws near. This is the omen. Although you still feel isolated and unsure, you have a profound connection to the spirits that is working at a great distance to create connections. Fear not. The Way is opening.

*Direction*: Rouse your sense of strength and purpose. Be resolute. You are connected to a creative force.

### NINE AT THIRD

**Abounding veils him.**

**Feng is so dark at noon we see only dimly.**

**'He breaks his right arm.' This is not a mistake.**

*This does not yet allow completing Great affairs.* In the Mourning Hut, unable to move at the moment. Do not worry, the time is coming. Look at the omens rising in the sky. You see such extraordinary sights that you lose the capacity to respond. Don't worry. This is not a mistake. A new spirit is being born.

*Direction:* A fertile shock is coming. Re-imagine your situation. Gather energy for a decisive new move.

### NINE AT FOURTH

**Abounding screens him. The great cycle is full.**

**Feng is so dark at noon we see the Dipper, constellation of fates.**

**He meets the Hidden Lord.**

**Wise Words! The Way is open.**

*Not an appropriate situation. This is shadow not brightening. Moving opens the Way.* An omen and a contact with the spirit of Change. You see the Hidden Lord who is moving events and acquire the capacity to move with them. These are extraordinary things that most people can't understand. In this solitude and obscurity, you meet something that makes it all clear. The recognition is immediate. Hold on to the connection. The Way is open.

*Direction:* Accept the difficult task. Release bound energy. The situation is already changing.

### SIX AT FIFTH

**Abounding. He receives the Mandate.**

**The jade talisman. 'Held in this containing beauty.'**

**There will be reward and praise.**

**Wise Words! The Way opens.**

*There will be rewards.* You receive the Mandate from Heaven and acquire the ability to usher in the coming abundance. The next chapter in the book of life is full of beauty, joy and love. Rewards and praise will be showered on you. The Way is opening.

*Direction:* Revolution and renewal. You are coupled with a creative force.

**Abounding. He has the Mandate.**

**The roof screens the Mourning Hut.**

**'Will he peep through the door, alone without people,**

**Not admitted to audience for three years?'**

**Trap! The Way closes.**

*Hovering at the border of Heaven, isolation will come of concealing its birth.* The time is passing you by! Do not stay in mourning for the past. Your melancholy and pain are in danger of isolating you. Break out of this trap! Don't shut yourself in. Grasp the changing time and act. If you don't, the Way will close.

*Direction:* Become aware of your situation and join with others. Don't be afraid to act on your own. You are connected to a creative force.

# 56 Sojourning at the Borders/Quest LU

Journeys, voyages outside the norm; wandering, exile; soldiers on a mission; quest, searcher, wandering sage or minister of the King, relations with the shadow lands; site of creative transformation.

## MYTHS FOR CHANGE: THE STORY OF THE TIME

*Bringing something to an end means letting go of the old residence. Accept this and use the energy of Sojourning.*

The root of Sojourning is *fang*, direction, the Four Sides, thus wandering in all directions to the four Hidden Lands. It is travelling in both literal and spiritual realms. The word connects with *Lu*, Treading, and the dance of the *wu*-Intermediaries, for the *wu* are the spiritual wanderers who travel in the Hidden Lands. It means an army unit (500–1000 men) on campaign, a banner or standard, and a ritual vessel for offering food and wine, a *lu-ting*. It is also a rest house or an inn, making a halt on a journey or a breathing space.

Sojourning suggests wanderers, herdsmen, hermits, knights errant and wandering diviner/magicians, the *fang-shi* – all those who 'travel on the roads', sojourning in the All-Under-Heaven. It is the King's dark brother, the wandering sage, on the ritual tour of the borders that was held immediately after the *heng*-ritual of fixing abundance at high summer. The good sojourner is King Wu himself, inspecting the boundaries of the new kingdom and 'connecting the few' after the victory over the Shang and the execution of the Shang tyrant. The careless sojourner is the nomad war god Wang Hai, Shang ancestor and son of the moon goddess. A herdsman, metal-worker and warrior-magician, he danced for the King of Yi and so inflamed his wife that she succumbed to passion. He 'lost his flocks in Yi' and was sacrificed by her husband the King.

## The Response

**Sojourning. The Small. Make an offering and you will succeed.**

**Sojourning. Advantageous Trial. Harvesting.**

Sojourn/Quest, Lu: travel, journey, voyage; stay in places other than your home; visitor, lodger, temporary guest; way, passage, seeking support; wild plants, uncultivated; lower officials, barbarians, outside the frontiers; live in exile, search for your own way; small group with a common goal; soldiers on a mission, army group of 500–1000 men; sacrifice on a mountain or to the spirits of a mountain; spine, force in the back, stilling desire. The old character shows two soldiers following a banner.

LÜ³ (7489/70) shows two men (2) under a flag (1). 3–5 are variants.

Sojourning/Quest describes your situation in terms of wandering, journeys and living apart. The way to deal with it is to mingle with others as a stranger whose identity and mission come from a distant centre. You are outside the normal network, on a quest of your own. Be small and flexible. Adapt to whatever crosses your path. This is pleasing to the spirits. Through it they will give you success, effective power and the capacity to bring the situation to maturity. Be willing to travel and search alone. Put your ideas to the trial. This generates meaning and good fortune by releasing transformative energy.

## The Scholar Speaks

The hexagram figure shows an inner limit that stabilizes changing awareness. Above the mountain, there is fire. Don't be afraid to act alone. If your ruling idea is exhausted, you must let go of where you live. Use your travels to connect solitary individuals. Brighten and consider things. Don't be held up by complications. Make clear decisions even if they are painful. Being small and adapting to what crosses your path is pleasing to the spirits. What is supple and flexible is moving to the centre in the outer world. By yielding and working with it, you connect with what is solid and strong. Limit and stabilize your desire when you join with others. This makes you aware of things. It is why being small is pleasing to the spirits. Be willing to travel and search alone. Put your ideas to the trial. The time of sojourning is truly and righteously great.

## THE SHAMAN SPEAKS

Fire above Mountain. Sojourning.

This is a time when Noble One uses brightness and consideration in punishing but does not relax the rules.

*Spirit words bind us and accomplish fate, revealing the Bright Omens.* The Sacrificer is working with the Bright Omens. Fire and brightness above radiate light and warmth and people experience the Bright Presence of things, while Mountain below limits and articulates what is complete to suggest what is beginning. This is Fire over Earth: the inner field supports a continually changing awareness of the outer world. The ideal Realising Person reflects this by supporting what is correct through consideration and clarity. A cycle is ending. Bring home the bride.

## TRANSFORMING LINES: CHANGE AT WORK

### INITIAL SIX

Sojourning. The journey in fragments, Cling! Clang!

He is split off from his place and grasps disaster.

*The purpose is exhausted, a disaster.* The journey is falling apart before it has begun. You grasp at fragments. People can't understand you. You are in imminent danger. Stop! Do you really want to act like this?

*Direction*: Become aware of yourself! Don't be afraid to act on your own. You can be connected to a creative force.

### SIX AT SECOND

Sojourning. Approaching a rest house.

Take care of your goods.

You acquire a young vassal.

Advantageous Trial. Harvesting.

*Complete this without being excessive.* On the journey, you come together with others, though you must still take care. You have also made a friend who is willing to help you.
*Direction:* You can establish something significant. Be resolute. You are connected to a creative force.

NINE AT THIRD

**Sojourning. Burning down the rest house.**

**You lose your young vassal.**

**Trial: adversity, hungry souls and angry ghosts.**

*This truly uses injuring. His righteousness is lost.* On the journey, at the rest house. You destroy what you have found through violent passions and you frighten your friend away. Try to understand where this comes from. You are confronting danger that has its roots in the past. If you understand its inner meaning, this seeming disaster could mark a profound change to a new state of being.
*Direction:* You will emerge and be recognized. Re-imagine the situation. Gather energy for a decisive new move.

NINE AT FOURTH

**Sojourning. He finds a place to abide.**

**Acquiring goods and an emblem axe:**

**'My heart is not glad.'**

*Not acquiring the right situation, his heart is not yet gladdened.* A stop on the journey. You have found a place, with responsibility and power to go with it. But these things bring sorrow, not happiness, for deep in your heart you know that you have forsaken what you really set out for.
*Direction:* Stabilize your desires. Release bound energy. The situation is already changing.

SIX AT FIFTH

**The Sojourner shoots a pheasant, with one arrow it disappears.**

**Bringing this to completion brings praise and a mandate.**

*This reaches up to what is above.* You can complete your connection, the purpose of the journey, with one try. Your friends will support you. You will receive a mandate from above. This will bring you praise and much increased responsibility.

*Direction*: Retire from old involvement. You are coupled with a creative force.

### NINE ABOVE

**Sojourning. The bird burns down its nest.**

**The Sojourner first laughs, then cries out and sobs.**

**'He loses his cattle in Yi.'**

**Trap! The Way closes.**

*Righteousness burns it down. If he could hear he would do absolutely nothing.* You think you can take things lightly, but you may soon have cause to lament. Everything you care about will vanish. You will soon be crying, not laughing. Consider your attitudes and change your heart or the Way will close to you.

*Direction*: Be Small and be careful. Don't be afraid to act on your own. You are connected to a creative force.

# 57 and 58: The Paradigm

## The Intermediaries: the Lady of Fates and the Joyous Dancer

This Pair involves you in an overall model of thought and action elaborated in the interconnected lines of the figures: the activities of the two Intermediaries who lay out the offerings and call the spirits, giving them a voice in the human community. Carefully consider your place in and relation to this model.

*Hidden Possibilities*: 38:37 > 63:64, change discord into creative connection. Make the crossing and prepare the new.

The Pair exchanges information with 9:10 (Gathering the Ghosts and Mating with the Spirit). It is motivated by 47:48 (Oppressed Noble returns to Common Source). The centre and threshold lines relate the process to 17:18 (Follow the Spirit and Renovate the Ancestral Images), 43:44 (Announce the Omen and the Lady of Fates), 53:54 (The Great Marriages) and 59:60 (Dissolution and Articulation).

Look at the ages and events these figures suggest for personal connections.

9:10    17:18    43:44 (45:46) 47:48    53:54    59:60

*Shadow site*: 7:8, Launching the Armies and the New Group that Results

**Subtle Penetration working with concealed influence. Open means seeing and letting it be seen.**

# 57 Subtle Penetration/ Spreading the Fates SUN

Gently penetrate to the heart; supple, flexible, subtle, determined; enter from below; support, nourish, the base or ground; an Intermediary, the Lady of Fates who lays out the offerings; a seed figure.

## MYTHS FOR CHANGE: THE STORY OF THE TIME

**Charge to the Oracle**: *The Sojourner finds no place to be accepted and rest. Accept this and use the energy of Subtle Penetration. This means entering.*

Subtle Penetration, the Elegant Dancer who also manifests as the Royal Bride, lays out the offerings on the low altar and carries the fates to the beings. She presents things in offering, crosses thresholds and transmits orders from Heaven. Her wrapped food offerings are an image of the Myriad Creatures toiling and labouring on the field of Earth, for life is brought and carried by her winds. She is connected to the Central Palace where fates are consigned and represents a profound penetration of the above into the below which can lead to the awakening of wisdom. She prepares the food and drink for the great meal shared by humans and spirits and nourishes the people on ancient virtue. She is a spirit-caller and healer, offering the virtue or *de* that actualizes an individual being. Subtle Penetration works through hidden influences. She is the silent power of wind and wood in the Earth. She regulates power and virtue, controls the omens, works and plans from hiding and knows the right moment.

As a spirit guide, Subtle Penetration is the Lady of Fates, the one who lays out the offerings and penetrates to hidden influences. She penetrates to the core, elegant and powerful, moving like wind and wood in the earth. She is a healer, a matchmaker, brings each thing to its fate. She is a bright strutting cock, strong-scented. In the body, Subtle Penetration operates through the liver, governing the free flow of energy and emotion. It stimulates everything that moves in the body, purifies the blood, links eyes and sexual organs, desire and anger, vision and motivation, giving the capacity to act decisively.

## THE RESPONSE

> **Subtle Penetration through the Small.**

> **Make an offering and you will succeed.**

> **Advantageous to have a direction to go.**

> **Advantageous to see the Great Person. Harvesting.**

> **Subtle Penetration,** SUN: enter into, put into, permeate, infiltrate; mild, subtle, docile; submit freely, be shaped by; penetrate to the core; dispose, arrange; food, lay out food offerings; confer an honour; choose or be chosen support, the ground from which things grow; approach the Earth Altar; foundation, base, nourish from below; wind, weather; wood, trees; the Lady of Fates who lays out the offerings and penetrates to hidden influences. The old character shows wrapped offerings laid out on an altar.

 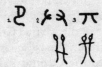

> XÙN (4767/49, see also 4730) represents an altar stand (3) with wrapped meat offerings or seals on it (1) and a pair of hands presenting the offering (2).

Subtle Penetration describes your situation in terms of the penetrating influence of the one who carries out the fates. The way to deal with it is to penetrate to the core of the problem by being supple and adaptable. Enter from below. Let the situation shape you. Be humble and compliant; adapt to whatever crosses your path. Take the pervasive action of the wind, or growing plants extending their roots and branches as your model. This is pleasing to the spirits. Through it they will give you success, effective power and the capacity to bring the situation to maturity. Hold on to your purpose. Have a place to go. Impose a direction on things. See great people. Seek out those who can help and advise you. Think about the great in yourself and how you organize your thoughts. All these things bring profit and insight.

## THE SCHOLAR SPEAKS

The hexagram figure shows Subtle Penetration over time. Following winds. Turn potential conflict into creative tension. If you are travelling and don't have a place of your own, this means Subtly Penetrating from outside. It means being humble and hiding your virtues. Subtle Penetration pares away in order to realise the Way. Evaluate things in private. Balance and equalize opposing forces. Carry out what you have been told to do. What is solid and strong has reached the centre. It is correcting things and its purpose is moving. Be supple and adaptable in order to yield and work with the strong. That is why adapting to what crosses your path is pleasing to the spirits. Plan things by thinking of what is truly great. That is what will help you.

## THE SHAMAN SPEAKS

**Following Winds. Subtle Penetration.**

**This is a time when Noble One spreads the mandates to move us to service.**

*Spirit works through those who lay out the offerings.* This is the Lady of Fates. Wind and Wood enter subtly, penetrating, pervading and coupling. This is the Woody Moment: Subtle Penetration spreads the fates and awakens the inner seed of a new generation. The ideal Realising Person reflects this by involving the directives of Heaven in all that he does. Work through rousing and inspiring. A cycle is beginning.

## TRANSFORMING LINES: CHANGE AT WORK

### INITIAL SIX

**Subtle Penetration. Advancing and withdrawing, act like a warrior.**

**Advantageous Trial. Harvesting.**

*Doubting your purpose, then regulating it.* Subtle Penetration is not vacillating or timidity. Make decisions firmly and aggressively. Change directions as many times as you need to. Be decisive. If you hesitate you will undermine your real purpose. This is not a time to be timid. Be like King Wu when he set the armies marching into Shang. *Direction*: Accumulate the Small to achieve the Great. Turn conflict into creative tension. The situation is already changing.

### NINE AT SECOND

**Subtle Penetration beneath the bed. Offerings on the altar.**

**Use diviners and Intermediaries in great number.**

**Wise Words! The Way opens.**

**This is not a mistake.**

*This means acquiring the centre.* Subtle Penetration is also a healing ritual. You must penetrate to the core of this old story, full of sexual intrigue and dark ancestors. Use intermediaries, who can see and call the spirits, and diviners, who know the past. Get to the bottom of it and free yourself from its grasp. This is not a mistake.
*Direction*: Proceed step by step. Gather energy for a decisive new move.

### NINE AT THIRD

**Repeating Penetration, urgent and pressing.**

**Distress.**

*This exhausts your purpose.* Here Penetration is forcing the issue. You are pushing too hard. This only produces confusion. You won't accomplish your desires like this.
*Direction*: Dispel obstacles to understanding. Take things in. Be open and provide what is needed.

### SIX AT FOURTH

**Subtle Penetration. Lay out the offerings.**

**The cause for sorrow disappears.**

**In the fields the King catches three kinds of game.**

*This means there is achievement.* Through Subtle Penetration you have arrived at a position to influence things. You have the information and recognition you need. This is the royal hunt. Act through Subtle Penetration and you will achieve everything you desire.
*Direction*: You are coupled with a creative force.

## NINE AT FIFTH

**Subtle Penetration. Trial: Wise Words! The Way is open.**

**Lay out the offerings. The cause for sorrow disappears.**

**There is nothing that is not advantageous.**

**'If you initiate something, it will not be completed.'**

**Ancestors and descendants. Threshing the grain.**

**Your work will be reworked.**

*The situation is centred and correct.* Act now. Everything will benefit. Go through with what you have been planning. Act through Subtle Penetration. Watch the process carefully before it is unveiled, and after it has begun. This is a very favourable time. Set the stage for action, like King Wu waiting at the Fords.

*Direction:* Renovate a corrupt situation. If you let yourself be led, you can realise hidden potential. The situation is already changing.

## NINE ABOVE

**Subtle Penetration beneath the bed.**

**He loses his goods and emblem axe.**

**Trial: Trap! the Way closes.**

*The above is exhausted. Correcting things is a trap.* This is not the time to penetrate the past. You will lose your possessions and your position. Leave it alone and be happy with what you have. If you start digging all over again, the Way will close.

*Direction:* Connect with commons needs and strengths. Turn conflict into creative tension.

# 58 Open/Expression
## DUI

**Communication, self-expression; opportunity; pleasure, joy, excitement; persuade, exchange; the marketplace; calling the spirits; a seed figure.**

MYTHS FOR CHANGE: THE STORY OF THE TIME

**Charge to the Oracle**: *It enters then it stimulates you. Accept this and use the energy of the Open. This means stimulating.*

Open is the Joyous Dancer, the *wu* or spirit-medium who calls down, mates with and speaks for the *shen* or spirits. She is instrumental in opening the fields in spring, going up to the Mountain Shrine to meet the Tiger Spirit and bringing back the fates of beings who are rejoining the human community. She is the Young Ancestress who conceives by stepping in a footprint of Di, the High Lord, or becomes pregnant after swallowing the egg of the Dark Bird. In all things, she is the mediator, the one whose inspiring words bring joy. We see her in the luminous vapours rising from open waters, fertile marshes and sunlit lakes and in the words from people's mouths that connect and inspire us. Her character is also read as joy, delight and pleasure (*yue*). She is words that connect people, and she presides over the market-place where people come together and news passes from mouth to mouth. She inspires sexuality and satisfaction, expressed as the moment when the harvest is home and the winter secure. She is the stimulating and loosening one, persuasive speech, delight and freedom from constraint, the Joyous Dancer whose words make the spirit present here among us.

As a spirit guide Open leads through joy and cheering words, magic and pleasure. She dances with the *shen* and feels the spirit in her body and gives it words. She is rising mists and open water. She gladdens all things that welcome her. She is a dancing goat and a sheep. In the body, Open acts through the lungs, skin and nervous system, regulating the rhythm of life, making energy descend and disperse. It connects the surface with the central nervous system, and is involved in sexual stimulation and the power of inner images.

# THE RESPONSE

**Open. Express it. Make an offering and you will succeed.**

**Advantageous Trial. Harvesting.**

**Open/Expression**, DUI: interact, interpenetrate, an open surface, open a passage or way; opportunity; express yourself, persuade, cheer, urge on; delight, pleasure, joy, excitement; responsive, free; gather, exchange, barter, trade; speech and words; the mists that rise from water. The old character shows a person, an open mouth, and the joyous words that emerge. It is the root of the word 'to speak' and suggests the old spirit-mediums.

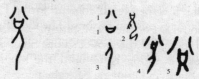

DUI (11757/10) shows a person (3) with an upturned face and opened mouth (1) and the words of the spirit (2) that rise from it. 4 and 5 are variants.

Open/Expression describes your situation in terms of opening communication, pleasure and exchange. The way to deal with it is express yourself openly and interact with others. Cheer people up and urge them on. Talk, bargain, barter, exchange information. Enjoy yourself and free others from constraint. This is pleasing to the spirits. Through it they will give you success, effective power and the capacity to bring the situation to maturity.

## THE SCHOLAR SPEAKS

The hexagram figure shows expression and interaction between people. The mists come together. Find a supportive group. Stay inside it. When you penetrate something, you must rouse it to action. Open means stimulating things through expression. It means being visible and visiting people. Join with friends to discuss and practise things. What is strong and solid is in the centre. What is supple and adaptable is outside. Put your ideas to the trial through expressing them and urging people on. That way you both yield and serve Heaven and connect with others for mutual benefit. If you explain things to people before they set to work, they will forget how hard the labour is. If you explain why something is difficult and oppressive, they will even face death willingly. By explaining the central idea, you encourage people at their tasks.

## The Shaman Speaks

**Mists coming together. Open.**

**This is a time when Noble One talks with partners and friends, explaining through repeating.**

*Spirit speaks and spreads joy through the Intermediaries.* This is the Joyous Dancer. Rising Mists stimulate and fertilize, joyous words cheer and inspire. It is the Metal Moment: Joyous Dancer calls the spirits, inspires and reveals innate form. The ideal Realising Person reflects this by repeatedly engaging in spreading the words and the works of the spirit. Work through subtle penetration. This involves fate.

## Transforming Lines: Change at Work

### Initial Nine

**Harmonious Opening. Express it.**

**Wise Words! The Way is open.**

*Do not doubt this movement.* Open yourself to this influence. Expect real harmony to develop. The Way is open. Don't hold back.
*Direction:* Look within to find the way out. Find supportive friends. Gather energy for a decisive new move.

### Nine at Second

**Opening. A connection to the spirit will carry you through. Express it.**

**Wise Words! The Way is open.**

**The cause for sorrow disappears.**

*This is a trustworthy purpose.* Open yourself to this influence. It will open a whole new world. Reach out. The Way is open. Old sorrows and frustrations will simply vanish.
*Direction:* Follow the stream of events. Proceed step by step. Gather energy for a decisive new move.

### SIX AT THIRD

**Coming Opening. Trap! The Way closes.**

*This is not an appropriate situation.* This may look like an interesting opportunity, but there is nothing in it. Do not open yourself to this. Turn away or be trapped. The Way is closing.

*Direction:* Be resolute. You are connected to a creative force.

### NINE AT FOURTH

**Opening, bargaining words. No peace yet. Express it.**

**Enclose the contention and there will be rejoicing.**

*There will be a reward.* You are discussing this opportunity and everyone's temperature is rising. Put a clear limit on negative emotions. If you actively seek harmony, the situation will soon be filled with joy.

*Direction:* Articulate your ideas. Take things in. Be open and provide what is needed.

### NINE AT FIFTH

**Opening. A connection to the spirits will carry you through.**

**Strip away the outmoded! Express it.**

**There will be adversity, hungry souls and angry ghosts.**

*Correcting this situation is appropriate.* This opening is an opportunity for connection, dangerous and exciting. It is filled with spirit, but you will be forced to confront past memories and negative experiences. Strip away your old ideas and face up to the challenge. It is time to put the situation straight.

*Direction:* If you let yourself be led, you can realise hidden potential. The situation is already changing.

### SIX ABOVE

**Prolonging the Opening. Draw out the words.**

**Express it. Extend the joy and pleasure.**

*This is not shining yet.* Extend the opening and possibility for connection. Don't let go of this opportunity. Draw it out as far as possible. Express yourself. Keep the possibilities open. You will be very sorry if you simply let go. This could be a lasting source of joy and pleasure.

*Direction:* Find supportive friends. Gather energy for an important new move.

# 59 and 60: The Paradigm

### Dissolution of the old Self and Articulating the new Times

This Pair involves you in an overall model of thought and action elaborated in the interconnected lines of the figures: a self-sacrifice that dissolves obstacles between the spirit and the human world, revealing the key moments where you can articulate and act on the river of time. It embodies a site of radical transformation where the Ghost River, the river of the past, flows through the Opened Heart and is articulated. Carefully consider your place in and relation to this model.

*Hidden Possibilities*: 27 > 2, nourishing the spirits and accepting the ordeal connects you with the primal power of realization.

The Pair exchanges with and is motivated by 29 and 61, the Ghost River and the Opened Heart. The centre and threshold lines connect the zone of transformation with 3:4 (Sprouting and Nurturing the New), 5:6 (Temple and Council), 19:20 (Releasing the Spirit and Watching the Omens) and 57:58 (The Intermediaries).

Look at the ages and events these figures suggest for personal connections.

3:4 5:6      19:20   <u>29</u>      57:58  <u>61</u>

*Shadow site*: 5:6, In the Temple and the Council: Waiting for 'Visitors'

**Dispersing means the Bright Presence breaks through.
Articulating means stilling it.**

# 59 Dispersing/ Gushing HUAN

Dissolve, clear up, scatter; dispel illusions, break up obstacles,
eliminate resistance; melt the rigid; blood of sacrifice;
dispersing the self, end of normal life;
site of creative transformation.

## MYTHS FOR CHANGE: THE STORY OF THE TIME

**Charge to the Oracle:** *Stimulate it then scatter it abroad. The blood of sacrifice. Accept this and use the energy of Dispersing. This means radiance and the bright omens.*

Dispersing means to radiate and disperse energy, to distribute, expand, spread and scatter. It is something brilliant or striking that dissolves, cleanses and frees. As an oracular response it indicates: 'The omen is good. Sacrifice is accepted. A time to act. Disperse the obstacles.' In its oldest meanings it is a symbolic death, the blood of sacrifice gushing or spurting from the victim and the celebrant who lays out the offerings at the Earth Altar. As this blood flows over things, both literal and metaphorical, it clears away obstacles and activates spirit in accord with Heaven. Like the tributaries that flow into a great river, its transformative quality opens the way to blessing.

## THE RESPONSE

Dispersing. Blood flows from the sacrifice.

Make an offering and you will succeed.

The King approaches the Ancestral Temple to receive blessings for all.

Advantageous to step into the Great Stream.

Advantageous Trial. Harvesting.

Disperse, HUAN: scatter clouds, clear away obstacles, dispel illusions, fear and suspicion; clear things up, dissolve resistance; untie, separate, change; mobilize the rigid, melt ice; fog lifting, mists clearing; blood gushing from a sacrifice, ample flow; *also*: long, deep, far away; fix one's gaze on; high antiquity. The old character shows the Ghost River and a man at the entrance to a cave with a knife in his hands.

*HUÀN* (4962/85) shows water or river, *SHUI*[3] and *XIONG*[4], made up of a person (1) at the entrance of a cave or abyss (2-3), looking all around with a knife or stick (4) in his hand (5). The later character shown on the right suggests looking at something beautiful while passing it from hand to hand.

Dispersing describes your situation in terms of the possibility of eliminating misunderstandings, illusions and obstacles. The way to deal with it is to clear away what is blocking clarity and understanding. Make an offering and you will succeed. Scatter the clouds, melt the ice, dispel fear and illusions, clear up misunderstandings, and eliminate suspicions. Let the fog lift and the sun shine through. This is pleasing to the spirits. Through it they will give you success, effective power and the capacity to bring the situation to maturity. Be like the King who imagines a temple full of images that unite people and connect them with greater forces. This is the right time to embark on a significant enterprise or to enter the Stream of Life with a purpose. Put your ideas to the trial. That brings profit and insight.

### THE SCHOLAR SPEAKS

The hexagram figure shows fluid movement gently penetrating the world. The wind moves above the stream. Take things in and provide what is needed. When something is expressed it scatters and spreads clarity. This is Dispersing. Dispersing means that the light shines through. The early Kings used this time to make offerings to the highest powers and establish temples. Dispersing pleases the spirits; through it they will give you success, effective power and the capacity to bring the situation to maturity. What is solid and strong keeps coming without being exhausted. What is supple and flexible acquires the outer situation and connects with the strong above. Be like the King who imagines a temple full of images that connect with greater forces. Step into the Stream of Life. Make ready your vehicle, the boat that will carry you, and go on to achieve something solid.

Wind moves above Stream. Dispersing.

This is a time when Early Kings made sacrifice to the High Lord and established the altars.

*Spirit rewards those toiling in the Pit, working through those who lay out the offerings.* The Lady of Fates is working with the Ghost River. Wind and Wood above enter subtly, penetrating, pervading and coupling, while Rushing Water below dissolves direction and shape, flowing on through toil and danger. This is Wood over Water: an inner stream that permeates the outer world, dissolving and dispersing obstacles. The ideal Realising Person reflects this by emulating the ancient rulers who established the connection with the High Lord by creating symbols through which we can share their blessing. Work through subtle penetration. This involves fate. Find the common source.

## TRANSFORMING LINES: CHANGE AT WORK

### INITIAL SIX

**Dispersing. The blood of sacrifice.**

**Use the strength of a horse to rescue this.**

**Wise Words! Invigorating strength opens the Way.**

*This means yielding to the impulse.* This affair is in trouble, and you must come to the rescue. Be willing to make a sacrifice. If you really rouse yourself, you can open the Way for the spirit to flow. *Direction*: A deep and sincere connection. Take things in. Be open and provide what is needed.

### NINE AT SECOND

**Dispersing the obstacles. Blood flows over the altar table.**

**Fleeing your support.**

**The cause for sorrow disappears.**

*You acquire what you desire.* Let go of what you habitually depend on and activate your creative spirit. Open yourself to the new. This will bring clarity and disperse the obstacles you are confronting. Your frustration will disappear and you will obtain what you desire.

DISPERSING

*Direction*: Let everything come into view. Strip away old ideas. Be open and provide what is needed.

### Six at Third

**Dispersing the obstacles. Blood flows over his body.**

**The cause for sorrow disappears.**

*Locate your purpose outside*. Disperse the obstacles to the spirit. Don't identify with your need to express yourself or your craving for personal power. Focus entirely on the needs of the work. That way there will be no cause for sorrow and the blessing can flow.

*Direction*: If you let yourself be led, you can realise hidden potential. The situation is already changing.

### Six at Fourth

**Dispersing the obstacles. Blood flows over the flock.**

**Wise Words! The Way to the Source is open.**

**Disperse them and go to the hilltop shrine.**

**You are not in hiding, this is a place to ponder.**

**'It is not what one would ordinarily think.'**

*This is the Great Shining*. Disperse the obstacles to the spirit. Let go of the flock of thoughts that usually surround you. You have a great opportunity now and you need to see it clearly. Go where you can talk to the spirits. This is not simply going into hiding. You need a place to ponder things deeply. The moment you do this, the new will come shining through.

*Direction*: Stay out of quarrels and wrangles. Find supportive friends. Gather energy for an important new move.

NINE AT FIFTH

**Dispersing sweat, a King's command.**

**Blood flows over the King's residence.**

**This is not a mistake.**

*This is correcting the situation.* You are involved in a great project. Work hard to disperse the obstacles to achievement. Don't think about anything else now. This is not a mistake. In the end this will correct your entire situation. The centre is changing. Be part of it. *Direction:* There is something immature in the situation that needs to be nourished. Take things in. Be open and provide what is needed.

NINE ABOVE

**Disperse the bad blood.**

**Leave it, send it away, then come forth.**

**This is not a mistake.**

*This is putting harm at a distance.* Disperse the obstacles to connection. Remove the cause for conflict. Exorcize it. Send it far away. Then you can emerge into the light and have the place you deserve. You make no mistake in doing this.
*Direction:* Take the risk. Take things in. Be open and provide what is needed.

# 60 *Articulating the Crossings* JIE

**Sense the right time; measure, limit; articulate speech
and thought; chapters, intervals, music and
ceremonies; loyal and true.**

## MYTHS FOR CHANGE: THE STORY OF THE TIME

**Charge to the Oracle**: *You cannot continually scatter the radiance.
Articulate the Crossings. Accept this and use the energy of Articulating.*

Articulating refers primarily to a joint or juncture in time, a crossing point of Heaven and Earth, of the horizontal and the vertical. It is used to indicate acupuncture points that give access to the meridians and the flow of energies in the body. It represents the critical moments in time through which things can be affected and movement harmonized with the Way. The root is bamboo: nodes or joints on the plant, the strips of bamboo used for books, a bamboo flute and its natural measures or intervals. It is a chapter, a paragraph, an interval, a key or significant detail, a tablet attesting a mandate, the annual or seasonal feasts and rituals that articulate sacred time. Through these 'crossings' or 'joints', the energy that animates the Myriad Beings condenses and displays itself as symbols (*xiang*), symbols of transformation that in turn give access to primal energy or Way, joyous words from the other shore. The roots of the pair Dispersing and Articulating are water and bamboo. Together they signify the sprouts of virtue and the second birth, the spirit that grows in the heart.

## THE RESPONSE

**Articulating the Crossings. Make an offering and you will succeed.**

**Bitter articulation will not allow Trial.**

**Articulate**, *JIE*: Distinguish and join things; express ideas in speech; section, chapter, interval, unit of time; rhythm; months of the year, signs of the zodiac; limits, regulations, ceremonies, feasts, rituals, holidays; token of authority; measure, economise, moderate, temper; firm, loyal, true; degrees, classes, levels; the 24 periods of the solar calendar, marking the changes of the four seasons. The old character shows two bamboo sprouts and a person kneeling in front of a vessel of cooked food.

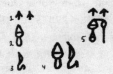

JIE (1450/118) shows a person (3) kneeling before a pot of food (2) and two bamboo segments or nodes (1). 4 and 5 are variant forms.

Articulating describes your situation in terms of the relations between things. The way to deal with it is to articulate and make the connections clear. Express your thoughts. Separate and distinguish things. Make chapters, sections and units of time. Create a whole in which each thing has its place. This is pleasing to the spirits. Through it they will give you success, effective power and the capacity to bring the situation to maturity. But don't harm yourself or others. Limitations that are bitter and harsh will prevent you from putting your ideas to the trial.

### THE SCHOLAR SPEAKS
The hexagram figure shows expression Articulating the stream of events. Above the mists is the stream. Take the situation in and provide what is needed. Things can't simply spread out. They must be articulated. Articulating means holding things in. Cut things to size and calculate the measures. Think about what realising the Way means before taking action. Articulating is pleasing to the spirits. Through it they will give you success, effective power and the capacity to bring the situation to maturity. Apportion the supple and the solid. Keep the strong at the centre. Harsh limits will prevent you from putting your ideas to the trial. Your Way will be exhausted. Express things, take action and take risks. This is the right time to articulate your situation. Correct excess, stay in the centre and communicate with others. Heaven and Earth articulate and the four seasons accomplish their aims. By using Articulating to shape the measures and the times, property will not be injured and the people will not be harmed.

## THE SHAMAN SPEAKS

**Above Stream, the Mists. Articulating the Crossings.**

**This is a time when Noble One uses measure, number and rules, deliberating power and virtue to move.**

*Spirit rewards those toiling in the Pit, speaking through the Intermediaries.* Joyous Dancer is working with the Ghost River. Rushing Water above dissolves direction and shape, flowing on through toil and danger, while Mists rising from below stimulate and fertilize, joyous words cheer and inspire. This is Water over Metal: inspiring words from within that articulate the stream of events. The ideal Realising Person reflects this by creating measures and models of action that engender the ability to realise the Way. Work through joyous words to bring the spirit to expression. Eliminate oppressive structures.

## TRANSFORMING LINES: CHANGE AT WORK

### INITIAL NINE

**Articulating the Crossings.**

**Don't come out of the inner door and chamber.**

**This is not a mistake.**

*This means knowing when to interpenetrate and when it is blocked.* This is not a time to act. Stay in your place within. Contemplate what is important to you. This is not a mistake.
*Direction:* You are facing a dangerous situation. Take things in. Be open and provide what is needed.

### NINE AT SECOND

**Articulating the Crossings.**

**Not coming out of the outer gate and chamber,**

**Trap! The Way closes.**

*This is letting go of the right time's ending.* This is a time to act. Leave your habitual ways of thought and enter the new time. If you don't, you will surely regret it. The Way will close and you will be on the outside looking in.
*Direction:* A new time is beginning. Give everything a place to grow. Strip away old ideas. Be open and provide what is needed.

### SIX AT THIRD

**Articulating the Crossings.**

**If it is not like Articulating, it will be like lamenting!**

**This is not a mistake.**

*Lamenting. Whose fault is this?* This is the time to set limits and create order. If you don't, you will always end up being sorry. Everything will dissolve in a flood of tears. If you articulate things now, you will make no mistake.
*Direction*: Wait for the right moment to act. Turn conflict into creative tension. The situation is already changing.

### SIX AT FOURTH

**Articulating the Crossings.**

**Quiet articulating, peaceful and secure.**

**Make an offering and you will succeed.**

*This is receiving the Way above.* Articulate your ideas and feelings quietly and peacefully and you meet a warm response. This creates success and inspires friends to join you.
*Direction*: Express yourself and inspire others. Find supportive friends. Gather energy for a decisive new move.

### NINE AT FIFTH

**Articulating the Crossings.**

**Sweet Articulating. Wise Words! The Way is open.**

**Going on like this brings honour and reward.**

*Stay in the centre of the situation.* Articulate your thoughts and feelings with sweetness, grace and delight. The Way is open. You meet with honour and esteem. This is a significant time for all.
*Direction*: A significant connection is approaching. Something important returns. Be open and provide what is needed.

### SIX ABOVE

**Bitter Articulating.**

**Trial: Trap! The Way closes.**

**Repent this and sorrow disappears.**

*Its Way is exhausted.* You want to impose harsh measures through bitter speech. Don't do it. You will do nothing but harm. If you will only give up your bitterness, the cause for sorrow will disappear. *Direction*: Connect your inner and outer lives. Take things in. Be open and provide what is needed.

# 61 and 62: The Paradigm

### The Opened Heart and the Flying Bird

This Pair involves you in an overall model of thought and action elaborated in the interconnected lines of the figures: the connection of inner and outer in the thought of the heart that spreads the word across the threshold of life and death. It is a major site of radical transformation at all levels and a transition to the great festival times. Carefully consider your place in and relation to this model.

*Hidden Possibilities:* 27:28 > 2:1, accepting the ordeal and nourishing the ability to stand alone connects you to the primal powers.

The Pair connects with sites of creative transformation at 9:10 (Outskirts Altar), 15:16 (Activating Liminal Powers to Prepare the Future), 31:32 (Sacred Site and Fixing the Omen) and 41:42 (The Offering and the Blessing). The zone of radical change between the figures incorporates 55:56 (The New King and the Wandering Sage) and 59:60 (Dissolving the Self and Articulating the Times).

Look at the ages and events these figures suggest for personal connections.

9:10    15:16       31:32    41:42     55:56 (57:58) 59:60

*Shadow site:* 3:4, Sprouting and Nurturing the New

**Centring and Connecting means it becomes trustworthy. Small Traverses means it moves through being excessively Small.**

# 61 Centring and Connecting to the Spirits ZHONG FU

Sincere, truthful; connect your inner and outer lives; a heart emptied and at peace; connection to the spirit; capture, spoils, captives offered in sacrifice; major site of initiation and creative transformation, the Opened Heart.

MYTHS FOR CHANGE: THE STORY OF THE TIME

**Charge to the Oracle:** *Articulate the Mandate then trust in it. Connect the heart with the spirit. Accept this and use the energy of Centring and Connecting.*

This figure connects two very important terms in the world of Change. *Fu* 'connection to the spirits' is part of a phonetic family that includes a variety of interrelated meanings. It is a return to and of the spirit, establishing the myriad blessings that flow from the ancestors and Heaven through the act of sacrifice: benediction, celestial favour and great prosperity. It also means capture, spoils, booty; to take prisoners as victims for sacrifice; to drive out evil spirits. It is a Founding Father, an offering to the ancestors and a contract to recognize partners, a jade talisman and a bronze sacrificial vessel. Through all these meanings it points at connection to the spirit world and the carrying wave of blessing and energy that pours forth through that connection.

*Zhong*, centring, is another term that permeates the ancient ritual world. It means moving to or being at the centre, an equal or still point between opposites. It is an arrow that hits the centre of the target, the equinoxes, the pivotal points of the year. It is the 'coming in and going out' of the souls from the centre, the heart and its inner animation, the activity of the *shen* or spirits in the heart and their harmonizing influence. It refers to the inner world: meditation and the inner Way, putting something to the trial through divination. The root is a banner placed at the centre point of the Four Sides, a hole or link to the world of the dead and the ancestors.

Centring and Connecting to the Spirits represents an access to the thought of the heart. It opens a centre where the vital forces are rooted in the self, the inner riches of 'pigs and fishes' hidden in the Stream of Life. It is the space between Heaven and Earth where the Myriad Beings live, a mediating space that connects the inner and outer lives of all things. Thus it signifies divination and a symbol given by the spirits that is realised, proved and manifested in life. It is trust in the images that flow from the heart and the spirit that makes them true.

## THE RESPONSE

Centring and Connecting to the Spirits. 'Little pigs and fishes.'

Wise Words! The Way is open.

Advantageous to step into the Great Stream.

Advantageous Trial. Harvesting.

**Centre**, ZHONG: inner, central, calm, stable; balanced, correct; put in the centre, mediate, between; the inner life, the heart; a stable point that lets you face the vicissitudes of life. The old character shows an arrow or banner at the centre of a target.

**Connect**, FU: accord between inner and outer; sincere, truthful, reliable, verified; have confidence; linked to and carried by the spirits; capture prisoners, take spoils; be successful; incubate, hatch. The old character shows the claws of the bird spirit or ancestor and its prey.

ZHONG (2719/2) shows a flag or arrow in the middle of a target, a 'centre'. FU² (3582/39) shows a bird's claws grasping a child, its young or captives taken by the armies.

Centring and Connecting to the Spirits describes your situation in terms of the need to bring your life into accord with the spirits. The way to deal with it is to make connecting the inner and the outer parts of your life your central concern. Be sincere, truthful and reliable. Make your inner vision and your outer circumstances coincide. Empty your heart so you can hear the inner voices. Act through these voices with sincerity and honesty in connecting with others. This will link you to the spirits and they will carry you through. Swim in the stream of the Way and gather the pigs and fishes. This generates meaning and good fortune by releasing transformative energy. This is the right time to enter the Stream of Life with a purpose, or to embark on a significant enterprise. Put your ideas to the trial. That brings profit and insight.

## THE SCHOLAR SPEAKS

The hexagram figure shows inner expression permeating the outer world. Above the mists is the wind. Take the situation in and provide what is needed. Articulate and trust yourself. Centring and Connecting to the Spirits means being trustworthy. Think about legal actions before getting involved and put off serious judgements. Be flexible and adaptable within so the strong can acquire the centre. Expression and penetration will link you to the spirits and let you change the way power and responsibility is assigned. Swim in the stream of the Way and gather the pigs and fishes. This is the right time to embark on significant enterprises. Ride in an empty wooden boat. Put your ideas to the trial. That brings profit and insight and connects you with Heaven above.

## THE SHAMAN SPEAKS

**Above Wind there are the Mists. Centring and Connecting to the Spirits.**

**This is a time when Noble One deliberates the rites that release the people from death.**

*Spirit works through those who lay out the offerings, speaks and spreads joy through the Intermediaries*. These are the Intermediaries. Wind and Wood above enter subtly, penetrating, pervading and coupling, while Mists rising from below stimulate and fertilize, joyous words cheer and inspire. This is Wood over Metal: an open centre that allows inspiration to pervade and influence the world. The ideal Realising Person reflects this by deliberating the Great symbols that that can release us from the fear of death. Persist and work through inner inspiration. This is the Great Transition.

### INITIAL NINE

**Centring and Connecting to the Spirits.**

**Make the sacrifice for the repose of the dead. Let the mourners go home.**

**Wise Words! The Way opens.**

**If strangers come do not feast them.**

*The purpose has not changed.* Stay alone and quiet and think about what you want to do. That will make the connection and open the Way. If you are always worrying about other people, you will have no peace. Don't take on their problems now.

*Direction*: Dispel illusions. Take things in. Be open and provide what is needed.

### NINE AT SECOND

**Centring and Connecting to the Spirits.**

**A calling crane hidden in the shade. Its offspring respond in harmony.**

**'I have a winged wine vessel.**

**Come to me and I will simply pour it out.'**

*This is the centre of the heart's desire.* This is the profound call of one soul to another and the call of the inner self. Respond to it. It can change your life. Don't hesitate to answer.

*Direction*: A flourishing time is coming. Increase your efforts. Strip away old ideas. Be open and provide what is needed.

### SIX AT THIRD

**Centring and Connecting to the Spirits.**

**'We have taken the enemy.'**

**Sometimes we drum, sometimes we stop.**

**Sometimes we weep, sometimes we sing.**

*This is not an appropriate situation.* You find an equal and a rival. Back and forth, again and again, you have something to love and fight with. This is the paradox of victory, the inner identity between winner and loser.

*Direction*: Accumulate the Small to achieve the Great. Turn conflict into creative tension. The situation is already changing.

### SIX AT FOURTH

**Centring and Connecting to the Spirits.**

**'Changes are coming': the Moon Almost Full.**

**The horse's yoke-mate disappears.**

**This is not a mistake.**

*This is breaking away and grouping with the above.* You are on your own now. This is a special moment in which your usual connections disappear. Things are almost ripe. The Change is coming. Don't be afraid to act alone. Preserve your integrity. This is not a mistake. It connects you with what is above.

*Direction*: Make your way step by step. Turn conflict into creative tension. Gather energy for a decisive new move.

### NINE AT FIFTH

**Centring and Connecting to the Spirits.**

**A connection that binds us together.**

**This is not a mistake.**

*It is appropriate to correct the situation.* This connects you to others on a deep spiritual level. You can truly help people now. Put things right. Act energetically. This is not a mistake.

*Direction*: Diminish your passionate involvement. Make the sacrifice. Something significant is returning. Be open and provide what is needed.

### NINE ABOVE

**Centring and Connecting to the Spirits.**

**A soaring sound, wings mounting to Heaven.**

**Trial: Trap! The Way closes.**

*Why let this last?* This is enthusiasm that flies above itself and carries you away. There is no real substance here. Ask yourself why you are doing this. The Way is closing. Danger. If you go on, you will fall into the hunter's net.

*Direction*: Set limits and articulate desires. Take things in. Be open and provide what is needed.

# 62 *Small Traverses/ The Flying Bird*
## XIAO GUO

**A transition; adapt to each thing; very careful, very Small; spread the word, stay in the process; major site of initiation and creative transformation.**

## MYTHS FOR CHANGE: THE STORY OF THE TIME

**Charge to the Oracle:** *Possessing it and traversing necessarily means you are making a crossing. Accept this and use the energy of Already Crossing.*

This is a transition or passage to a new time, a passage that must be realised through the Small and the power of the yin. It suggests enlisting the aid of the Small People, nobles without patrimony who acted as scribes, diviners, ministers, attendants, soldiers and cooks, dependent on the changing whims of a ruler who employed or dismissed them. It presents the image of a bird in danger of being caught by hunters, a bird who must fly low, moving towards autumn and the festivals of harvest and realization, and the Flying Bird, the words that will cross the river of life and death. It is concerned with making actions and the words of omen coincide through very scrupulous attention, a ritual in which every detail counts and every step is carefully measured. It is a bird of omen, a dance that calls the spirit and houses it in an image or tablet.

This time of transition is a journey through liminal space where rules dissolve and borders are crossed, imaged as the hunter and the prey, the bird taken or not taken in the net. It is a quality of the Way, the 'littlest possible thing (*ji*)', something hardly visible that is the precise place where things turn and change. It is a time for great care with an expectation of great results, the penultimate step. Remember, in this time you are the bird, not the hunter. Motto: 'Keep a Small heart.'

## THE RESPONSE

**Small Traverses. Make an offering and you will succeed.**

**Advantageous Trial. Harvesting.**

This allows Small affairs, it does not allow Great affairs.

The flying bird brings the omen as it leaves. Spread the word.

'Above is not the proper place, below is the proper place.'

The Great Way is open.

**Small**, XIAO: little, flexible, adaptable; humility, what is common to all; adapt to whatever happens; make things smaller, lessen, yin energy. The old character shows a river dividing two banks, the undifferentiated flow of life connecting the Small things.

**Traverse/Exceed**, GUO: go across, go beyond, surpass, overtake, overgo; get clear of, get over; cross the threshold, surmount difficulties; transgress the norm, outside the limits; anomaly, unique, different. The old character shows three footprints, the sign for stop and a dwelling with a mouth inside. Outside it, a hand makes an offering to the spirit.

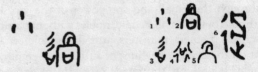

XIAO³ shows three grains of rice or sand or a river between two banks. GUO⁴ (6574/162) is a mountain pass and the completion of an action: steps (2), a foot (3) and the crossing (4). It suggests a skeleton and a mountain-ridge (5), a crossroads (6) with a foot (3).

Small Traverses describes your situation in terms of a seemingly overwhelming variety of details. The way to deal with it is to carefully adapt to each thing in turn. Be very careful and meticulous. Adapt conscientiously to whatever comes. This is pleasing to the spirits. Through it they will give you success, effective power and the capacity to bring the situation to maturity. Put your ideas to the trial. That brings profit and insight. The time allows you to do Small things. It does not allow you to do Great things. The flying bird leaves this message behind: the above is not suitable, the below is suitable. Don't go up, go down. This generates great good fortune and meaningful events by releasing transformative energy. Keep your sense of purpose. Don't look to others to solve your problems.

## THE SCHOLAR SPEAKS

The hexagram figure shows an inner limit restricting new energy. Above the mountain there is thunder. Don't be afraid to act alone. If you have found something to trust you must move it. Through being very small you can move beyond. When you are active, be excessively polite. When you are mourning, be excessively compassionate. When you are paying, be excessively frugal. Being small is pleasing to the spirits. Through it they will give you success, effective power and the capacity to bring the situation to maturity. Putting your ideas to the trial brings profit and insight. The flexible and adaptable acquires the centre. Small matters generate meaning and good fortune by releasing transformative energy. What is strong and solid has lost its central position. Great matters are not allowed. This is truly the symbol of a flying bird who leaves a message behind: the above is not suitable, the below is suitable. Above you will be thwarted. Staying below will yield results.

## THE SHAMAN SPEAKS

Above Mountain there is Thunder. Small Traverses.

This is a time when Noble One uses excessive courtesy in moving,

Excessive mourning in loss,

Excessive frugality in availing of things.

*Spirit words bind us and accomplish fate, manifesting through quake and thunder.* These are the Operators. Thunder above rouses and germinates new potential, while Mountain below limits and articulates what is complete to suggest what is beginning. It is Wood over Earth: an inner field that restrains and protects new growth through an excessive concern with being Small. The ideal Realising Person reflects this transition through his concern with the fitting and the sincere. He is carried by the Bright Omens through the Tiger's Mouth.

## TRANSFORMING LINES: CHANGE AT WORK

### INITIAL SIX

Small Traverses. He acts like a flying bird.

Trap! The Way closes.

*This is why it is not allowed.* Stay low, stay humble and stay grounded. Don't try to impress people. Don't fly away. If you do you will surely regret it.

*Direction:* A time of abundance is coming. Continue on. You are connected to a creative force.

### Six at Second

**Small Traverses. He passes by his grandfather spirit,**

**Meets his grandmother spirit.**

**He does not extend to the Leader, he meets the servant.**

**This is not a mistake.**

*The servant is not allowed to exceed and pass by.* Identify with people in secondary roles. Don't push yourself forward. Gladly accept the supporting position. Don't try to dominate. Embrace the yin. You will see all your wishes fulfilled. The connections will have deep, enduring value.

*Direction:* This has enduring value. Be resolute. It connects you to a creative force.

### Nine at Third

**Small Traverses. You can not exceed defending yourself against this.**

**If you carry on, you may be killed.**

**Trap! The Way closes.**

*Carry on and be killed. This is why the Way closes.* You over-extend yourself in an impossible situation. If you are lucky, you can fend off harm. You are in real danger. You must stop acting like this. You are over-reaching when you should be Small.

*Direction:* Gather resources so you can respond when the real call comes. Re-imagine the situation. Gather energy for a decisive new move.

SMALL TRANSVERSES

NINE AT FOURTH

**Small Transverses. This is not a mistake.**

**He does not pass it by, he meets it.**

**Let the adversity that is going be a necessary warning.**

**Don't use this in a long-term Trial.**

*This is not an appropriate situation. If you complete it, it will not last long.* The transition is made. The Small has found the connection. This is not a mistake. Take a look at the dangers you have just passed through, the memories and ghosts. Let them be a warning. Don't go back!
*Direction:* Stay humble and connected to the facts. Release bound energy. The situation is already changing.

SIX AT FIFTH

**Small Traverses. Shrouding clouds bring no rain yet.**

**'It comes from our western outskirts.'**

**A prince with a string-arrow grasps another in a cave.**

*This is the climax above.* The culmination is coming, the autumn rains and the harvest. You make an enduring connection with someone who is in retreat. This will open up a whole new life.
*Direction:* A stimulating influence. It connects you with a creative force.

SIX ABOVE

**Small Traverses. You don't meet it, you pass it by.**

**The flying birds scatter and are trapped. The Way closes.**

**This is called a disaster and a blunder.**

*This is overbearing at the climax.* Danger and arrogance. You over-reach yourself, flying higher and higher. This won't accomplish anything. A disaster from within and without. Change now!
*Direction:* Step outside of the situation. Don't be afraid to act on your own. This will connect you to a creative force.

# 63 and 64: The Paradigm

### The Crossings: 'Burning Water'

This Pair involves you in an overall model of thought and action elaborated in the interconnected lines of the figures: making the crossing and preparing the new, an image of the voyage of the soul preparing for and entering the great Stream of Life. It represents the reconnection of the two qualities of the way, light and water, after it has passed through the primal gates. Carefully consider your place in and relation to this model.

*Hidden Possibilities*: 64:63 > 63:64, preparing for and making the crossing.

The Pair exchanges information with 39:40 (Comings and Goings and Release). It is motivated by 37:38 (Dwelling and the Ghosts that Haunt it). The centre and threshold lines relate the process to 3:4 (Sprouting and Nurturing the New), 5:6 (Temple and Council), 35:36 (Rising and Setting Sun) and 49:50 (Revolution and the new Vessel).

Look at the ages and events these figures suggest for personal connections.

3:4 5:6       35:36 37:38 39:40      49:50

*Shadow site*: 1:2, Dragon and Dark Animal Goddess

**Already Crossing means setting things right. Not Yet Crossing means exhausting the masculine will.**

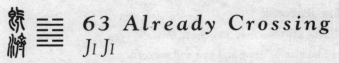

# 63 Already Crossing
## Ji Ji

Begun, already underway, in progress; everything in place;
proceed actively; crossing to the River-Mountain festival;
prima materia, the burning water; a primal seed figure.

## MYTHS FOR CHANGE: THE STORY OF THE TIME

**Charge to the Oracle:** *Possessing it and traversing must mean we are
making a Crossing. Accept this and use the energy of Already Crossing.*

Already Crossing is part of a pair that forms the 'gates' of Change.
'Crossing', which literally means to cross a river in a boat or at a
ford, suggests the souls and spirits entering the Great Stream, a
metaphor for experiencing the voyage of life. *Ji* or 'crossing' is also
the name of one of the four Great Rivers and 'crossing the *Ji*' is a
metaphor for going to the River-Mountain festival and for a bride
being taken to her husband's ancestral home. The Small Fox, a
crafty shape-changing animal at home in the dream world as well
as symbol of a potential suitor, is common to both figures, as is a
campaign into the Demon country. Crossing further suggests realising or achieving something, helping, aiding or rescuing. It adds
what is lacking and represents an understanding in depth of what
is useful and profitable. The Pair is made up of fire and water, the
vertical elements, and suggests all the metaphors of cooking, transforming and being in a continual creative relation to the process of
Change.

Already Crossing means that things are in their place, in process.
We are on the voyage, crossing the stream, cooking the food. There
is a correct alignment of force, a stable vessel. We are in the world of
manifestation now, autumn and harvest, surrounded by danger but
secure within. The situation requires care and attention, co-operating
with something already underway. In terms of the martial arts, this
shows an optimum arrangement of inner energies.

> Already Crossing. The Small Fox.
>
> Make an offering and you will succeed.
>
> Advantageous Trial. Harvesting.
>
> Wise Words! Initiating things opens the Way,
>
> Completing them brings disorder.

**Already,** JI: in progress, going on; completed, finished, mark of the past tense; thus, that being so. The old character means finishing a meal. It shows a person turning away from food cooked in a vessel.

**Crossing,** JI: cross a river, overcome an obstacle, begin an action; bring help; succeed, bring to a conclusion; benefit, elegant and dignified. The old character shows the flowing river and a field of grain, or a boat with three people in it.

JI² (768/26) shows a pot of cooked food and a man turning away from it (1). JI⁴ (841/85) shows water or a river (2) and a field of grain; a shallow, uniform place or ford (3 and 3a).

Already Crossing describes your situation in terms of a crossing that is already underway. The way to deal with it is to actively go on with what you are doing. You are in the middle of fording the stream of events. Things are already in their proper places. Adapt to whatever crosses your path. Give aid and encouragement. This is pleasing to the spirits. Through it they will give you success, effective power and the capacity to bring the situation to maturity. Put your ideas to the trial. That brings profit and insight. Stay with the process. That generates meaning and good fortune by releasing transformative energy. Trying to bring things to completion creates disorder. Remain underway.

### THE SCHOLAR SPEAKS

The hexagram figure shows clarity in action. The stream is above the fire. Things are cooking. Keep gathering your energy and put it at the service of the action underway. Having gone past the midpoint, you are now fording the stream. This means setting things right. Think deeply about problems and sorrows. Prepare to defend against them. Adapt to whatever crosses your path. This is pleasing to the spirits. Through it they will give you success, effective power and the capacity to bring the situation to maturity. Put your ideas to the trial. That brings profit and insight. You are in the right place. Correct the balance between what is supple and adaptable and what is strong and solid. Stay in the process. That generates meaning and good fortune by releasing transformative energy. Through being adaptable you acquire the central position. Completing things, and thus stopping the action, creates disorder. Your Way will be exhausted if you do that.

## The Shaman Speaks

Stream above Fire. Already Crossing.

This is a time when Noble One ponders distress to provide a defence against it.

*Spirit reveals itself in the Bright Omens, rewarding those toiling in the Pit.* This is the Ghost River and the Bright Omens. Rushing Water above dissolves direction and shape, flowing on through toil and danger, while Fire below radiates light and warmth and people experience the Bright Presence of things. This is Water over Fire: inner brightness joined with outer danger represents crossing to the other shore. The ideal Realising Person reflects this by seeing into all causes that might disturb the process and providing a defence against them. He is carried by the Bright Omens.

## Transforming Lines: Change at Work

### Initial Nine

Already Crossing.

Braking his wheels. Trailing her cord in the water.

The Small Fox soaks its tail.

This is not a mistake.

*This is righteous and not a mistake.* You have a great connection, but you are starting too quickly. Hold back. Start slowly. Let yourself be lured on. This is not a mistake.

*Direction*: Re-imagine the situation. Gather your energy for a decisive new move.

### SIX AT SECOND

**Already Crossing.**

**A lady loses her jade hairpin. Do not pursue her.**

**On the seventh day she will return.**

*This is using the Way of the centre.* The bride crossing to the River-Mountain festival. In the midst of the crossing, it seems like what you hope and care for is lost. Don't worry. Don't chase it. When the time comes, it will find you without trying. Have no cares. You will soon have what you desire.
*Direction*: Wait for the right moment to act. Turn conflict into creative tension. The situation is already changing.

### NINE AT THIRD

**Already Crossing.**

**The High Ancestor subjugates the Demon Country.**

**Three years go by and he controls it.**

**Small People should not use this.**

*Three years – this is weariness.* The Shang King Wu Ding makes the crossing to subdue the Demon Country. You are embarked on a great enterprise. It will take time to complete. Keep a firm purpose. Don't listen to what others try to tell you. You will win in the end and realise your heart's desire.
*Direction*: This is a new beginning. Strip away your old ideas. Be open and provide what is needed.

### SIX AT FOURTH

**Already Crossing.**

**Clothes in tatters. The wadded silk is soaked.**

**'Be careful till day is done.'**

*This means there is a place to doubt.* Things look good, but they could change in a minute. Be careful. You are in the middle of an important passage. Don't relax yet. Be vigilant.

*Direction*: Revolution and renewal. This couples you with a creative force.

### NINE AT FIFTH

**Already Crossing.**

**The eastern neighbours slaughtered many cattle.**

**The summer sacrifice of the western neighbour was not like this**

**When we received the great blessing.**

*The western neighbour's season is not like this. The Way is open and the Great is coming.* When you think of the Shang tyrant who has fallen you can see how real hidden worth is blessed and recognized. Don't try to impress people. The sincerity of your feeling and your dedication to it are what count most. Be yourself. Accept your blessings. Heaven holds out its mandate.

*Direction*: Accept the difficult task. Release bound energy. The situation is already changing.

### SIX ABOVE

**Already Crossing. He soaks his head.**

**Adversity, hungry souls and angry ghosts.**

*Why let this last?* You fail in the crossing. You have got yourself in too deep. You are faced with dangers you don't have the means to confront. Why go on like this?

*Direction*: Find supportive friends. Gather energy for a decisive new move.

# 64 Not Yet Crossing WEI JI

**On the edge of a change; gather your energy, everything is possible; wait for the right moment; prima materia, the burning water; a primal seed figure.**

MYTHS FOR CHANGE: THE STORY OF THE TIME

**Charge to the Oracle:** *The great enterprise can never be truly exhausted. In truth each end is a new beginning. Accept this and use the energy of Not Yet Crossing.*

Not Yet Crossing is part of a pair that forms the 'gates' of Change. 'Crossing', which literally means to cross a river in a boat or at a ford, suggests the souls and spirits entering the Great Stream, a metaphor for experiencing the voyage of life. *Ji* or crossing is also the name of one of the four Great Rivers and 'crossing the *Ji*' is a metaphor for going to the River-Mountain festival and for a bride being taken to her husband's ancestral home. The Small Fox, a crafty shape-changing animal at home in the dream world as well as symbol of a potential suitor, is common to both figures, as is a campaign into the Demon Country. Crossing further suggests realising or achieving something, helping, aiding or rescuing. It adds what is lacking and represents an understanding in depth of what is useful and profitable. The Pair is made up of fire and water, the vertical elements, and suggests all the metaphors of cooking, transforming and being in a continual creative relation to the process of Change.

Not Yet Crossing means that we are preparing to make a major move or transition. We are on the riverbank, gathering the force to cross. We are preparing the food. We are in the world of potential, the season when the fruits ripen. The term suggests the tree on the Earth Altar, the necessity to offer preparatory sacrifices and making ritual announcements. We are poised at the entrance, preparing for transition, readying ourselves to embark on the journey.

Not Yet Crossing.

Make an offering and you will succeed.

The Small Fox on the muddy bank.

If she soaks her tail,

There is no advantageous direction.

**Not Yet,** WEI: has not yet occurred (but will occur in the course of time); incomplete, doesn't exist yet. The old character shows a tree grown and flowered but not yet fruiting.

**Crossing,** JI: cross a river, overcome an obstacle, begin an action; bring help; succeed, bring to a conclusion; benefit, elegant and dignified. The old character shows the flowing river and a field of grain, or a boat with three people in it.

WEI[4] (12149/75) shows a luxuriant tree, meaning abundant. It is the eighth Earthly Branch, late summer, when everything is at its maximum development but fruit is not yet ripe. JI[4] (841/85) shows water or a river (2) and a field of grain; a shallow, uniform place or ford (3 and 3a).

Not Yet Crossing describes your situation in terms of being on the verge of an important change. The way to deal with it is to gather your energy to make this decisive new move. You are about to launch a plan, cross the river or overcome an obstacle. The possibilities are great. Be sure your plans are in order and that you have accumulated enough energy to make the crossing without getting stuck. This is pleasing to the spirits. Through it they will give you success, effective power and the capacity to bring the situation to maturity. Don't be like the Small Fox that gets almost across the river and then soaks her tail in the mud of the opposite shore. That would leave you with nowhere to go and nothing to do that would help you.

## The Scholar Speaks

The hexagram figure shows the potential for order. Fire is located above the stream. Things aren't cooking yet. But they are moving towards their proper place. Life cannot be exhausted. The potential is always there. That is the meaning of not yet fording. It implies diminishing masculine drive. Carefully consider and distinguish all the beings that surround you. Gathering your energy for a decisive new move is pleasing to the spirits. Through it they will give you success, effective power and the capacity to bring the situation to maturity. By being supple and adaptable you can acquire the central position. The Small Fox who crosses a river to the muddy shores beyond never lets go of her centre. If you start out, then soak your tail, there is no plan or direction that can help you. Don't end the movement, continue it. You aren't in the right place yet. But what is supple and what is strong and solid are acting in harmony to move you towards where you belong.

## The Shaman Speaks

**Fire above Stream. Not Yet Crossing.**

**This is a time when Noble One uses consideration to mark off the beings residing on the Four Sides.**

*Spirit rewards those toiling in the Pit, revealing itself in the Bright Omens.* This is the Bright Omens and the Ghost River. Fire above radiates light and warmth and people experience the Bright Presence of things, while Rushing Water below dissolves direction and shape, flowing on through toil and danger. This is Fire over Water: an inner change that restrains the spread of outer awareness, in preparation for crossing the Stream of Life. The ideal Realising Person reflects this by considering and demarcating a place for all of the Myriad Beings. Hold the heart fast and take the risk.

## Transforming Lines: Change at Work

### Initial Six

**Not Yet Crossing. Soaking her tail.**

**Distress.**

*This is truly not knowing the end.* You start too soon and fall into the water. You don't understand yet, so hold back.

*Direction*: Turn conflict into creative tension. The situation is already changing.

### NINE AT SECOND

**Not Yet Crossing.**

**Braking his wheels. Trailing her cord in the water.**

**Wise Words! Trial: The Way opens.**

*This is using the centre to move correctly.* Everything is loaded, but don't start yet. By restraining your eager desires, you can truly open the Way. Think about what you want in this matter. You are not quite ready yet. Let yourself be lured into action.
*Direction*: You will emerge and be recognized. Release bound energy. Gather energy for a decisive new move.

### SIX AT THIRD

**Not Yet Crossing. Chastising closes the Way.**

**Advantageous to step into the Great Stream. Harvesting.**

*This is not an appropriate situation.* On the edge of the great move. Don't try to discipline people or set out on an expedition. Step into the river with a clear will and purpose. What you are beginning now will bring all you want.
*Direction*: Ground yourself in the world of the spirit. Be resolute. You are connected to a creative force.

### NINE AT FOURTH

**Not Yet Crossing. Wise Words! Trial: The Way is open.**

**The cause of sorrow disappears.**

**The power of Shake subjugates the demon country.**

**In three years there will be celebrations in the Great City.**

*The purpose is moving.* The Duke of Zhou subdues the barbarians. This is the time to make the crossing. The Way is open. Your misgivings will simply disappear. Arouse your energy. Get rid of the past. In the end there will be great achievements. Your entire world will be transformed.
*Direction*: You don't really understand the situation yet. Something significant is returning. Be open and provide what is needed.

SIX AT FIFTH

**Not Yet Crossing. Trial: The Way is open.**

**Without a cause for sorrow.**

**This is Noble One's shining.**

**There is a connection to the spirits that will carry you through.**

**Wise Words! The Way is open.**

*His brilliance opens the Way.* Act on your plans. Make the crossing. The Way is open, no sorrow in sight. Your sincere spirit will shine through. Sense what is important. The spirits will help you. The Way is open.

*Direction:* Stay out of quarrels and wrangles. Find supportive friends. Gather energy for a decisive new move.

NINE ABOVE

**Not Yet Crossing.**

**There is a connection to the spirits through drinking liquor.**

**This is not a mistake. Soak your head.**

**There is a connection to the spirits in letting go of what is past.**

*This is truly not remembering the juncture.* The voyage is over. Celebrate your accomplishments. The spirits will be there with you. This is not a mistake. It is time to let go of the past. The joyous spirit will carry you through.

*Direction:* Release bound energy. The situation is already changing.

# Key to the Hexagrams

Find the lower trigram of your figure on the left side of the page, and the upper trigram of your figure on the top of the page. Trace down the columns. Where they meet you will find the number of the hexagram you are considering. Turn to that number in the book to find the Name and related texts.

| | | FORCE | FIELD | SHAKE | PIT |
|---|---|---|---|---|---|
| **FORCE** | | 1 | 11 | 34 | 5 |
| **FIELD** | | 12 | 2 | 16 | 8 |
| **SHAKE** | | 25 | 24 | 51 | 3 |
| **PIT** | | 6 | 7 | 40 | 29 |
| **BOUND** | | 33 | 15 | 62 | 39 |
| **PENETRATING** | | 44 | 46 | 32 | 48 |
| **RADIANCE** | | 13 | 36 | 55 | 63 |
| **OPEN** | | 10 | 19 | 54 | 60 |

LOWER TRIGRAMS

Key to the Hexagrams

**UPPER TRIGRAMS**

| BOUND | PENETRATING | RADIANCE | OPEN | LOWER TRIGRAMS |
|---|---|---|---|---|
| 26 | 9 | 14 | 43 | FORCE |
| 23 | 20 | 35 | 45 | FIELD |
| 27 | 42 | 21 | 17 | SHAKE |
| 4 | 59 | 64 | 47 | PIT |
| 52 | 53 | 56 | 31 | BOUND |
| 18 | 57 | 50 | 28 | PENETRATING |
| 22 | 37 | 30 | 49 | RADIANCE |
| 41 | 61 | 38 | 58 | OPEN |

Key to the Hexagrams

# Times of Change

- <u>Neolithic communities</u> (to c. 2200 BCE): origins of the oral tradition; moon cults and jade cults, temples of the Goddesses, first tombs and rituals of the dead and the passage to 'paradise'. The first agricultural communities, basis of the peasant layers of the culture, a period seen by later Daoist thinkers as an image of the original purity before the evolution of culture heroes and their virtue and ambitions.
- <u>Xia</u> (c. 2200–1766 BCE, undocumented): The first of the Three Dynasties; emergence of Bronze Age culture and the line of Kings, beginning with Tang the Completer.
- <u>Shang or Yin</u> (c. 1766–1170 BCE): first fully documented great Bronze Age culture; royal palaces of pounded earth and monumental tombs; the Bronze Vessels; elaborate ancestor worship, oracle bone divination (the Numinous Turtle) and human sacrifice. Root of much of the later mythology and sacred cosmos.
- <u>Zhou</u> (c 1170–221 BCE): battle of Muye and the overthrow of the Shang; history of the Mandate of Heaven involving Kings Wen, Wu and the Duke of Zhou; yarrow stalk divination emerges as a royal practice. Origins of the texts of Zhouyi, one of three early 'yi-books'.

   <u>Western Zhou</u> (1170–771 BCE): Height of Zhou power, feudal authority and ritual practice; a period seen by later Confucian thinkers as a version of paradise or a golden age in which all is in balance under a virtuous ruler in accord with Heaven.
   <u>Eastern Zhou</u>
   <u>Spring and autumn</u> (722–481 BCE): disintegration of the power of the Zhou kings; revision of the Zhouyi texts about 800 BCE at the court of King Yuan.

<u>Warring States</u> (403–221 BCE): collapse of the Zhou culture into a period of individual lords and constant internecine conflict; the 'flowering of a hundred schools', and the 'disputers of the Way': Confucius, Laozi, Zhuangzi, the Legalists, Mozi; major revisioning of the use of the *Zhouyi*, the roots of *Dazhuan* and *Shuogua*.

- <u>Qin</u> (221–207 BCE): brief 'universal empire'; Qin Shi Huang Di conquers the warring states; *Zhouyi*, as a divination manual, escapes his burning of the books; beginning of codification of written language.

- <u>Han</u> (202 BCE–220 CE): the first enduring imperial state; codification of culture and emergence of an official bureaucracy; emergence of Confucianism as official Imperial philosophy; codification of the classics or *jing*, the books of ancient culture and the golden age, first among them *Yijing* or Classic of Change.

- <u>Tang</u> (618–907): height of the poetic and artistic side of Chinese culture, sponsored by influence of Buddhist and Daoist thinkers; symbols of Change reflect deep structures of the poetry and visual art.

- <u>Song</u> (960–1279): emergence of Neo-Confucianism, gathering foreign influences into a new moral ethic; Zhuxi's version of *Yijing* that comes to dominate later thinking.

- <u>Qing or 'Manchu'</u> (1644–1911): last dynasty before the emergence of the republic in 1912; Jesuit scholars at the Imperial court; Kangxi Palace Edition of *Yijing*, standard for the received text; evolution of printing techniques makes *Yijing* available to all; foreign (Western) powers gain entrance to China; fall of the traditional culture; foreign translation of the classics begins.

- <u>Republic of China</u> (1912–1949): modern diaspora begins; Richard Wilhelm in China; contacts with C.G. Jung; the 'journey to the west'; Wilhelm's translation first published in 1927; Wilhelm/Baynes version in 1950.

- <u>People's Republic</u> (1949): systematic destruction of classical culture; after a period of extreme repression, study of *Yijing* begins again: 'revision of antiquity'; reconstruction of Early Old Chinese and major archaeological studies (many by Western scholars) begin a complete revision of the tradition. Globalization of *Yijing*; translation into most Western languages.

444

# Bibliography and Further Reading

## Other works of interest by the author

*I Ching Plain and Simple*, Harper/Element, 2004.

*The Classic Chinese Oracle of Change* (revised edition), London: Chrysalis/Vega, 2002.

*The Illustrated Encyclopedia of Divination*, Harper/Element, 2002.

*The Oracle of Kuan Yin, Goddess of Compassion*, Little, Brown, London, 2001.

*Symbols of Love*, Little, Brown, London, 2002.

*Ta Chuan: The Great Treatise*, St Martins Press, New York, 2000.

*The Way of I Ching*, Harper/Element, 2002.

## Early Old Chinese, the *Zhouyi* and the *Mawangdui* manuscripts

Bernard Karlgren, *Grammata Serica Recensa*, Museum of Far Eastern Antiquities, Bulletin 29, Stockholm, 1957.

Bernard Karlgren, 'Word Families in Chinese', *Bulletin of the Museum of Far Eastern Antiquities* 5 (1933), 1–120.

Richard Alan Kunst, *The Original Yijing: A Text, Phonetic Transcription and Index with Sample Glosses*, University Microfilms, Ann Arbor, 1985. See Kunst's bibliography for an extensive survey of the literature in Western languages and Chinese.

David N. Keightly (ed.), *The Origins of Chinese Culture*, University of California Press, Berkeley, 1983.

David N. Keightly, *Sources of Shang History*, University of California Press, Berkeley, 1978.

Michael Loewe, *Ways to Paradise*, George Allen & Unwin, London, 1979.

S.J. Marshall, *The Mandate of Heaven: Hidden History in the Book of Changes*, Curzon Press, Richmond, Surrey, 2001.

Richard Rutt, *Zhouyi: The Book of Changes*, Curzon Press, Richmond, Surrey, 1996.

Edward Louis Shaughnessy, *The Composition of the Zhouyi*, University Microfilms, Ann Arbor, 1983.

Edward L. Shaughnessy, *I Ching: The Classic of Changes, The First English Translation of the Newly Discovered Second-century* BCE *Mawangdui Texts*, Ballantine Books, New York, 1996.

Edward L. Shaughnessy, *Before Confucius*, SUNY, 1997.

Iulian K. Shchutskii, *Researches on the I Ching*, Princeton University Press, Princeton, 1979.

Roderick Whitfield, ed., *The Problem of Meaning in Early Chinese Ritual Bronzes*, SOAS, University of London, 1990.

Wu Jing-Nuan, *Yi Jing*, The Taoist Center; University of Hawaii Press, 1991.

## Journals with new scholarship

*Early China*, journal published by the Institute of East Asian Studies, University of California, Berkeley.

Steve Moore, ed., *The Oracle: The Journal of Yijing Studies* has been publishing a wide variety of new scholarship and speculation for several years.

## For readers of Chinese

Two very useful Chinese dictionaries have been published recently:

Lin Xinglong, ed., *Xin bian jiagu wen zidan*, International Culture Publishing Company, Beijing, 1993.

We Hua, ed., *Zhouyi da cidian*, Zhong-shan University Press, Canton, 1993.

One of the most significant accomplishments of twentieth-century sinology has also just been published, the *Ricci* Dictionary, fruit of over forty years of research.

*Dictionaire Ricci de caractères chinois*, Descleè de Brouwer, Insituts Ricci, Paris-Taipei, 1999.

## For a bibliography of works in English on Yijing

Edward Hacker, Steve Moore, Lorraine Patsco, *I Ching: An Annotated Bibliography*, Routledge, New York, 2002. See also the *I Ching Bookmarks* website at: http://www.zhouyi.com.

## The two major secondary texts

David Hawkes, trans., *Ch'u Tz'u – the Songs of the South*, Oxford University Press, Oxford, 1959.

Arthur Waley, trans., *The Book of Songs*, Allen & Unwin, London, 1937/1969.


## A sample of early Chinese literature

Burton Watson, trans. and ed., *Columbia Book of Chinese Poetry*, Columbia University Press, New York, 1984.

Burton Watson, *Early Chinese Literature*, Columbia University Press, New York, 1962.

Burton Watson, *The Tso Chuan: Selections from China's Oldest Narrative History*, Routledge and Kegan Paul, London, 1968.


## Other Sources of Interest

Derk Bodde, *Festivals in Classical China*, Princeton University Press and the Chinese University of Hong Kong, 1975.

Walter Burkert, *Homo Necans, The Anthropology of Ancient Greek Sacrificial Ritual and Myth*, trans. Peter Bing, University of California Press, Berkeley, 1983.

Roderick Cave, *Chinese Paper Offerings*, Oxford University Press, Hong Kong, 1998.

Scott Davis, *Jiegou yu lishi: luetan Zhongguo jujing de zucheng wenli: Structure and History: remarks on problems of ancient Chinese classical texts*, Taibei, Wenshize Chubanshe, 1995.

Scott Davis, 'Originating Instrumentality and the *Chen* Family', in *East Asian History* 10; December 1995, 19–52.

Scott Davis, *Yuedu Yijing: gudai yuzhouguan de lantu (Reading the Yijing: a blueprint of ancient Chinese cosmology)*, Taibei: Jianhong Chubanshe, 1996.

Scott Davis, 'A Study of Two Compositional devices in King Wen's Design of the Zhouyi', unpublished manuscript.

Wolfram Eberhard, *The Local Cultures of South and East China*, E.J. Brill, Leiden, 1968.

François Jullien, *The Propensity of Things: Towards a History of Efficacy in China*, trans. Janet Lloyd, Zone Books, New York, 1995.

Claude Levi-Strauss, *From Honey to Ashes*, Harper, New York, 1973.

Claude Levi-Strauss, *Structural Anthropology*, Harper, New York, 1963.

Donald S. Lopez Jr., ed., *Religions of China in Practice*, Princeton University Press, Princeton, 1996.

Stephen Owen, *Traditional Chinese Poetry and Poetics: Omen of the World*, University of Wisconsin Press, Madison, 1985.

Mary Renault, *The Bull from the Sea*, Penguin, Harmondsworth, 1962.

Pu Songling, *Strange Tales from Make-do Studio*, Foreign Languages Presses, Beijing, 1996.


# Histories of Ancient China

Patricia Buckley, ed., *The Cambridge Illustrated History of China*, Cambridge University Press, Cambridge, 1996.

Michael Loewe and Edward L. Shaughnessy, eds., *The Cambridge History of Ancient China*, Cambridge University Press, Cambridge, 1998.

Endymion Wilkinson, *Chinese History: A Manual*, Harvard University Asia Center, Cambridge, 1998.


# A look at early Chinese art and archaeological artefacts

Jessica Rawson, ed., *Mysteries of Ancient China*, British Museum Press, London, 1996.

Xiaoneng Yang, ed., *The Golden Age of Chinese Archeology*, National Gallery of Art, Washington, Yale University Press, New Haven, 1999.

*Historical Relics Unearthed in New China*, Foreign Languages Press, Beijing, 1972.


# Correlative Systems and their development

Stephan D.R. Feuchtwang, *An Anthropological Analysis of Chinese Geomancy*, Editions Vithagna, Vientiane, Laos, 1974.

Joseph Needham, *Science and Civilization in China*, vol. 2, Cambridge University Press, Cambridge, 1956.

Manfred Porkert, *The Theoretical Foundations of Chinese Medicine: Systems of Correspondence*, MIT Press, Cambridge, MA, 1974.

Tjan Tjoe Som, *Po Hu T'ung: The Comprehensive Discussions in the White Tiger Hall*, 2 vol., E.J. Brill, Leiden, 1952.

Helmut Wilhelm, *Heaven, Earth and Man in the Book of Changes*, Seven Eranos Lectures, University of Washington Press, Seattle and London, 1977.


# The Great Treatise or Commentary on the Attached Words

Stephen Karcher, *Ta Chuan: The Great Treatise*, St Martins Press, New

York, 2000.

Willard J. Peterson, 'Making Connections, "Commentary on the Attached Verbalizations" of the Book of Change', Harvard Journal of Asiatic Studies, 42/1m June 1982, 67–112 and 'Some Connective Concepts in China', in *Eranos* 57/1988.

Gerald Swanson, *The Great Treatise: Commentary Tradition to the Book of Changes*, University Microfilms, Ann Arbor, 1974.

Wu Jing-Nuan, *Yi Jing*, The Taoist Center; University of Hawaii Press, 1991.

## On Divination and its traditions

Stephen Karcher, *The Illustrated Encyclopedia of Divination*, Harper/Element, 2001.

Michael Loewe and Carmen Blacker, eds., *Oracles and Divination*, Shambala, Boulder, 1981.

George Kerlin Park, 'Divination', Encyclopedia Britannica, 15th ed., Macropedia, v.5, 916-20.

Phillip Peek, ed., *African Divination Systems: Ways of Knowing*, Indiana University Press, Bloomington, 1991.

Jean-Paul Vernant, ed., *Divination et rationalité*, Editions du Seuil, Paris, 1974.

Ngo Van Xuyet, *Divination, magie et politique dans la Chine ancienne*, Presses Universitaires de France, Paris, 1976.

## On the depth psychological approach

Robert Aziz, C.G. *Jung's Psychology of Religion and Synchronicity*, SUNY, 1990.

Jolande Jacobi, *Complex/Archetype/Symbol*, Princeton University Press, Princeton, 1974.

C.G. Jung, CW11, *Psychology and Religion: West and East*.

Stephen Karcher, 'Jung, the Tao and the Classic of Change', *Journal of Religion and Health*, 38/4 and *Harvest*, Winter 1999.

Stephen Karcher, 'Divination, Synchronicity and Fate', *Journal of Religion and Health*. 37/3, Fall 1998, originally Guild of Pastoral Psychology, Lecture no. 263.

Stephen Karcher, '*Which Way I Fly is Hell*, Divination and the Shadow of the West', *Spring* 55/1994.

Stephen Karcher, 'Oracle's Contexts: Gods, Dreams, Shadow, Language', *Spring* 53/1992.

Stephen Karcher, 'Making Spirits Bright: Divination and the Demonic

449

Image', *Eranos* 61/1992.

Roderick Main, ed., *Jung on Synchronicity and the Paranormal*, Routledge, London and Princeton University Press, Princeton, 1997.

Mary Watkins, *Invisible Guests: The Development of Imaginal Dialogues*, Sigo Press, New York, 1990.

## Myths and Rituals of Ancient China

Sarah Allan, *The Way of Water and Sprouts of Virtue*, SUNY, 1997.

Sarah Allan, *The Shape of the Turtle*, SUNY, 1991.

Anne Birrell, *Chinese Myths*, British Museum Press, London, 2000.

Anne Birrell, trans., *The Classic of Mountains and Seas*, Penguin Classics, London, 1999.

Anne Birrell, *Chinese Mythology*, Johns Hopkins University Press, Baltimore and London, 1993.

K.C. Chang, *Art, Myth, and Ritual, The Path to Political Authority in Ancient China*, Harvard University Press, Cambridge, MA, 1983.

Anthony Christie, *Chinese Mythology*, Paul Hamlyn, London, 1968.

Constance A. Cook and John S. Major, *Defining Chu: Image and Reality in Ancient China*, University of Hawaii Press, Honolulu, 1999.

Marcel Granet, *Danses et legendes de la Chine ancienne*, Annals du Musée Guimet, Presses Universitaires de la France, Paris, 1959.

Marcel Granet, *La pensée chinoise*, Paris, 1934.

Marcel Granet, *Festivals and Songs of Ancient China*, trans. E.D. Edwards, Routledge and Sons, London, 1932.

Marcel Granet, *Chinese Civilization*, Routledge and Kegan Paul, London, 1930.

Marcel Granet, *Etudes sociologiques sur la Chine*, Presses universitaire de la France, Paris, 1953.

Marcel Granet, *The Religion of the Chinese People*, trans. Maurice Freedman, Harper, New York, 1975.

Henri Maspero, *China in Antiquity*, trans. Frank A. Keirman, University of Massachusetts Press, 1978.

## Warring States: China in Transition and Later Commentators of Interest

Chu-yun Hsu, *Ancient China in Transition: An Analysis of Social Mobility 722–222 BCE*, Stanford University Press, 1965.

Kenneth J. De Woskin, ed. and trans., *Doctors, Diviners and Magicians of Ancient China, Biographies of Fang-shih*, Columbia University Press, New York, 1983.

A.C. Graham, *Disputers of the Tao*, Open Court, Lasalle, IL, 1985.

Jaques Gernet, *Ancient China from beginnings to the Empire*, trans. Raymond Rurdorff, Faber and Faber, London, 1968.

Richard John Lynn, trans., *The Classic of Changes: A New Translation of the I Ching as interpreted by Wang Bi*, Columbia University Press, New York, 1994.

David Roy and Tsuen-Hsuin Tsien, eds., *Ancient China: Studies in Early Civilization*, Chinese University Press, Hong Kong, 1978.

Larry Schultz, *Lai Chih-te (1525–1604) and the Phenomenology of the Classic of Change*, University Microfilms, Ann Arbor, 1982.

Kidder Smith Jr., Peter K. Bol, Joseph Adler and Don Wyatt, *Sung Dynasty Uses of the I Ching*, Princeton University Press, Princeton, 1990.

Aihe Wang, *Cosmology and Political Culture in Early China*, Cambridge University Press, Cambridge, 2000.

## The Development and Practice of Original Tao

Chow Tse-tung, 'The Childbirth Myth and Ancient Chinese Medicine: A Study of Aspects of the Wu Tradition', in David T. Roy and Tsuen-Hsuin Tsien, eds., *Ancient China*, Chinese University Press, Hong Kong, 1978.

Kenneth Dean, *Taoist Ritual and Popular Cults of Southeast China*, Princeton University Press, Princeton, 1993.

Deng Ming-Dao, *Chronicles of Tao: The Secret Life of a Taoist Master*, HarperSanFrancisco, 1993.

N.G. Girardot, *Myth and Meaning in Early Taoism*, University of California Press, Berkeley, 1983.

Livia Kohn, ed., *The Taoist Experience: An Anthology*, SUNY, 1993.

Livia Kohn, *Early Chinese Mysticism*, Princeton University Press, Princeton, 1992.

D.C. Lau and Roger T. Ames, *Yuan Dao: Tracing Dao to its Source*, Ballantine, New York, 1998.

Charles Le Blanc, *Huai Nan Tzu: Philosophical Synthesis in Early Han Thought*, Hong Kong University Press, Hong Kong, 1985.

Harold D. Roth, *Original Tao: The Inward Training (Nei-yeh) and the Foundations of Taoist Mysticism*, Columbia University Press, New York, 1999.

Kristofer Schipper, *The Taoist Body*, trans. Karen C. Duval, University of California Press, Berkeley, 1993.

Arthur Waley, *The Way and its Power: A Study of the tao te ching and its Place in Chinese Thought*, Allen & Unwin, London, 1936.

Holmes Welch and Anna Seidel, eds., *Facets of Taoism: Essays in Chinese Religion*, Yale University Press, New Haven, 1979.